BI 3026203 8

D1589858

LLPA

CONTEMPORARY ISSUES IN CRIMINOLOGY

y date tamped belo
ghts

BIRMINGHAM CITY
UNIVERSITY
DISCARDED

CONTEMPORARY ISSUES IN CRIMINOLOGY

Edited by

LESLEY NOAKS, MIKE MAGUIRE
AND MICHAEL LEVI

CARDIFF

UNIVERSITY OF WALES PRESS

1995

© The contributors, 1995. Crown copyright for chapters 15 and 16.

All rights reserved. No part of this book may be reproduced, stored in a retrieval system, or transmitted, in any form or by any means, electronic, mechanical, photocopying, recording or otherwise, without clearance from the University of Wales Press, 6 Gwennyth Street, Cardiff CF2 4YD.

British Library Cataloguing in Publication Data

A catalogue record for this book is available from the British Library.

ISBN 0-7083-1297-7

**Published with the financial assistance of the
British Society of Criminology**

UNIVERSITY OF
CENTRAL ENGLAND

Book no.   30262038

Subject no   364 | N oa

INFORMATION SERVICES

Cover design by Pentan Design Practice

Typeset at the University of Wales Press
Printed in Wales by Dinefwr Press, Llandybïe

Contents

CRIMINAL JUSTICE ISSUES

Acknowledgements

The editors would like to thank all of the contributors to this volume and all those who participated in the 1993 British Criminology Conference at Cardiff. We would also extend our thanks to the British Society of Criminology for their support both for the conference and the publication of this book.

Thanks are due also to the School of Social and Administrative Studies, University of Wales, Cardiff and the team of helpers at the 1993 conference, too numerous to mention individually but without whom neither the conference nor this publication would have been possible.

Editors and Contributors

Mike Brogden is Professor of Criminal Justice and Director of the Institute of Criminology and Criminal Justice at the Queen's University of Belfast.

Maureen Cain is a Research Fellow in the Institute of Judicial Administration, University of Birmingham.

Ian Clegg is a Lecturer in the Centre for Development Studies, University of Wales, Swansea.

Garry Coventry is Senior Lecturer in the National Centre for Socio-legal Studies, at La Trobe University, Australia.

David Dixon is a Lecturer in Policing and Criminal Law at the University of New South Wales, Australia.

Simon Gardiner is Senior Lecturer at the Anglia Law School, Anglia Polytechnic University.

Brian Gormally is Deputy Director of the Northern Ireland Association for the Care and Resettlement of Offenders.

Maggy Lee is a Researcher at the Institute for the Study of Drug Dependence, London, and lectures in criminology at Birkbeck College, University of London.

Roger Leng is Reader in Law in the School of Law at the University of Warwick.

Michael Levi is Professor of Criminology in the School of Social and Administrative Studies, University of Wales, Cardiff.

Mike McConville is Professor of Law in the School of Law at the University of Warwick.

Kieran McEvoy is now Assistant Director of the Institute of Criminology and Criminal Justice at the Queen's University of Belfast.

Eugene McLaughlin is a Lecturer in the Faculty of Social Science at the Open University.

Mike Maguire is Reader in Criminology and Criminal Justice in the School of Social and Administrative Studies, University of Wales, Cardiff.

George Mair is shortly to take up a post as Professor of Criminal Justice at Liverpool John Moores University.

Rod Morgan is Professor of Criminal Justice in the Faculty of Law, University of Bristol.

John Muncie is Senior Lecturer in Criminology and Social Policy at the Open University.

Karim Murji is a Lecturer in the Department of Sociology and Social Policy, Roehampton Institute, London.

Lesley Noaks is a Lecturer in the School of Social and Administrative Studies, University of Wales, Cardiff.

Fiona Paterson is Principal Research Officer in the Central Research Unit at the Scottish Office.

Robert Reiner is Professor of Criminology in the Department of Law, London School of Economics.

Andrew Sanders is Deputy Director of the Centre for Criminological Research at the University of Oxford.

Ian Taylor is Professor of Sociology at the University of Salford, Greater Manchester.

Christopher Trotter was, at the time of writing, a Lecturer at Monash University, Australia.

Reece Walters is a Lecturer in Criminology in the Institute of Criminology, University of Wellington, New Zealand.

Jim Whetton is a Lecturer in the Centre for Development Studies, University of Wales, Swansea.

Claire Whittaker is Senior Research Officer at the Home Office, London.

Lucia Zedner is Fellow and Tutor in Law, Corpus Christi College, Oxford.

1

Introduction

Emerging from the 1994 American Society of Criminology Conference in Miami, one of us (Michael Levi) was struck by the fact that although there were many interesting and methodologically sophisticated papers on a broader range of topics by US authors than one would find in a British conference, 'theory' seemed to be much more alive and well among British (or, in the case of Stan Cohen, former British) criminologists than among their American counterparts. The articles in this collection, selected from what we viewed as the best among those presented at the British Criminology Conference 1993 in Cardiff, bear testimony to that theoretical embeddedness. We have organized the papers in four sections: international perspectives on criminology and criminal justice; policing and prosecution; criminal justice issues; and crime, justice and the underclass. All of the papers display some theoretical as well as empirical qualities which go beyond the particular data or direct subject matter that they cover. Because of this, we hope that readers will not simply skim them in terms of whether or not their labels connect with their own specialist subject areas. Such specialization by criminologists risks losing that very interconnectedness of the particular with the general which is a vice of the technicist society. Emphasizing both the salience and problematic character of analysing crime and sanctions in different countries, we have decided to commence our selection with articles by Zedner, Clegg and Whetton, Brogden, and Cain. However, quite apart from the broad 'country coverage' that shows the rich diversity and dispersal of conceptualization and research methodologies, we would stress that all of the articles raise questions and, on occasion, propose solutions to theoretical and policy questions that we believe to be important to criminologists everywhere.

Zedner issues a siren call warning us about the dangers of glossing over local variations and making glib cross-cultural comparisons, either at a theoretical or policy implementation level. The problems that she identifies affect not only the substance of doing research and developing theory, but also the way in which we write about them, since the tension between the safe route – merely describing what happens in one country and what happens in another – and the risky route – trying to generalize without losing cultural grounding – has to be managed. (Though the article does not say so, this is a major difficulty with intra-national studies also, since the boundaries of the nation state artificially elide local traditions). Perhaps, as she implies, what we need are good role models or examples to emulate. Clegg and Whetton embark on an even more complex project, reflecting on the mutual disconnection of criminology and development studies; pointing up (in a fashion similar to Zedner) the difficulties of applying western models to Third World settings; and finally focusing on the importance of maintaining pluralism and on the role of informal justice mechanisms and their interaction with state controls in sustaining social regulation in Third World countries. Brogden's 'Policing Apartheid' examines in a grounded, detailed way the continuities and changes in the modes of discourse used in policing the old and new South Africa, concluding that the South African police 'are faced with a particular historical legacy that requires organizational and legal, as well as cultural, change if that particular police force is to have a new, consensual future'. Cain's essay is also a theorization of policing (taken in an even broader sense than Brogden): in this instance, the policing of culture in Trinidad and Tobago. Cain juxtaposes structure and culture and examines their points of articulation and disjunction, thereby presenting an ontology which, she claims, 'makes it possible to explain in the same way the policing of labour, the policing of politics and resistance, the policing of women, and the policing of culture'. All of these accounts in the first section aim to be grounded in the sense that they avoid using all-embracing explanatory terms such as 'colonialism' which, though relevant, are far too general to be able to account for variations in crime and crime control.

Policing and prosecution research has been one of the growth areas of research in the 1980s and 1990s, fuelled by the 'need' to evaluate the impact of the Police and Criminal Evidence Act 1984 and the Prosecution of Offences Act 1985, and by the Royal Commission on

Criminal Justice 1993, as well as by general changes arising from the need to manage policing (and its costs) 'efficiently and effectively'. The articles in this section examine at least four facets of these changes. McLaughlin and Murji examine 'the new managerialism' in the police and the development of 'quasi-markets' for a variety of police functions, and the consequences of these trends for what the police do. Dixon questions whether rules can ever truly regulate police, analysing 'police accountability' through close analysis of empirical data as well as conceptual critique. Levi draws on his work for the Royal Commission (Levi 1993) to point up some similarities and differences in the prosecution of serious fraud compared to other crimes. He discusses the particular dilemmas for political independence generated by the fact that some targets of investigators are major companies and/or those involved in the shadowy world of the arms trade, and notes that despite perceptions that élites are prosecuted only with great caution and care, the framing of culpability in a complex organizational and even global setting gives rise to risks of misattribution and therefore miscarriages of justice. However, the principal component of this section of the book is an extended 'authors meet critics' symposium – the first time that this has been done by the British Criminology Conference – around *The Case for the Prosecution* (McConville, Sanders and Leng 1991), in which Dixon, Morgan and Reiner present cogent cost-benefit analyses of that text and the authors variously refine their thinking in the light of those criticisms (and their own after-thoughts) and/or defend their original analysis.

The criminal justice issues section reflects the variety of research and thinking on dealing with crime in different countries. Trotter's work is part of the slowly growing counters to the conventional wisdom that 'nothing works', arguing on the basis of a study of supervision in the community in Victoria, Australia, that rates of reoffending can be significantly reduced by such techniques. Mair examines the historical development of specialized activities in probation, noting that their idiosyncratic nature and lack of accompanying evaluation mean that few generalizable initiatives have been developed in this area. Paterson and Whittaker use what to some people south of the border may superficially seem to be a parochial study of bail practice in Scotland (including practitioner accounts) to develop insights into the interaction between criminal justice cultures and their implications for bail and remands in custody, of the kind commended by Zedner in her opening essay. Gormally and McEvoy argue that because of the particularly acute nature of the relationship between politics and prison in Northern Ireland, a uniquely clear light is shone upon that relationship which illuminates the dynamics which always occur in the management of prisons and prisoners. As they emphasize, prisons are there to manage the consequences of social conflict, not to end it, and they note the importance of a well-informed policy community: the contrast with what one might term 'penal populism' as practised in the USA is clear. The section ends with an article on youth justice by Lee, based on multi-agency research (including interviews with young people and their parents), and suggests that cautioning by the police may not necessarily be in the best interests of youth. It also questions how different, at a symbolic level, cautioning actually is compared with supposedly 'alternative' formal justice mechanisms.

Our selection concludes with three papers that raise even broader considerations of the relationship between politics and both social and penal policy. Muncie, Coventry, and Walters discuss the politics of youth crime prevention in Australia and in England and Wales, reconceptualizing the issues in terms of disaffection and structural disadvantage of youth, and suggest that we subordinate the dominant policy questions of controlling youth to a wider social justice agenda which emphasizes reintegration rather than punishment. Gardiner takes up similar 'inclusionary' themes in his analysis of the role of the Criminal Justice Act 1991 – now repealed in part – in managing the underclass. He argues that although the spreading of control within the community has its dangers, greater democratic accountability in that process would make control more social. Finally, Taylor reassesses some themes in *The New Criminology* (Taylor, Walton and Young 1973) and examines within the context of free-market ideology the connection between critical criminology and diverse conceptions of 'the public interest'.

Both Braithwaite (1993) and Nelken (1994) have criticized acerbically some current modes of criminological discourse (or *dialogues des sourds*). However, we hope that the selection of articles in this volume and in its companion volume *Gender and Crime* helps to illuminate the interrelationship between the economy, culture and the state, and its manifestations in both crime and crime control. Despite research funding pressures towards narrow empiricist and policy issues, the reader will find in this book a broad range of contemporary theoretical approaches to the analysis of crime and justice issues.

References

Braithwaite, J. (1993). 'Beyond positivism: learning from contextual integrated strategies', *Journal of Research on Crime and Delinquency*, 30(4), 383–99.

Levi, M. (1993). *The Investigation, Prosecution and Trial of Serious Fraud*, Royal Commission on Criminal Justice Research Study No. 14 (London, HMSO).

McConville, M., Sanders, A. and Leng, R. (1991). *The Case for the Prosecution* (London, Routledge).

Nelken, D. (ed.) (1994). *The Futures of Criminology* (London, Sage).

Taylor, I., Walton, P. and Young, J. (1973). *The New Criminology* (London, Routledge).

International perspectives on criminology and criminal justice

2

Comparative research in criminal justice

LUCIA ZEDNER

Introduction

Given the huge body of research on crime, criminal law, and criminal justice systems in specific countries and the growing interest of criminologists and criminal lawyers in the systems of countries other than their own, it is perhaps surprising that truly comparative studies of criminal justice remain in their infancy. For the most part, existing studies have focused on procedural differences with little attempt to set these in any broader context. At best, existing comparative studies address one area of the criminal law or the criminal justice system (for example policing, prosecution policy, adjudication, or penal sanctions). Explanations of difference tend to be confined solely to the component part under scrutiny or, at best, to the structural imperatives of the system under observation. Reference is rarely made to the broader political or socio-economic structure or to the cultural context in which these differences evolved.

This chapter will examine the attractions, benefits and possible pitfalls of doing comparative research and offer some observations on various theoretical models available to the comparativist. Borrowing from the work of legal anthropology, it will suggest approaches which seem to mirror the actual working patterns of the comparativist and to offer resolutions to some of the methodological and theoretical problems singular to comparative work.

Comparative research as a basis for policy-making

It is instructive to begin by exploring briefly the political history of comparative research and, in particular, the imperatives behind it.

Indeed, the recent impetus appears to derive less from the desire for better academic understanding *per se* than from pragmatic, policy-oriented imperatives. Comparativists have been called upon to examine the laws, systems and practices of criminal justice in other jurisdictions in a bid to illuminate the failings of the domestic system, to identify areas for improvement, and to proffer solutions drawn from their researches.

This impetus dates back at least to the 1970s, a time when the American criminal justice system seemed to have run out of 'self-reformative power' and academics were dispatched to Europe to seek out new solutions to domestic problems (Weigend 1980: 383). American legal journals soon bubbled over with articles exploring the lessons to be learned from the 'continental' model of criminal justice. (See, for example Langbein 1977; Langbein 1974: 439; Langbein and Weinreb 1977: 1549.) (The very fact that it appeared unproblematic to speak of the 'continental' model as if it were an undifferentiated whole should immediately raise a note of caution.[1]) Impressed by the relative efficiency and fairness of what they saw, writers like Langbein and Weinreb were quick to recommend the adoption (wholesale or in part) of the 'inquisitorial model'. The model proposed was just that: a model or ideal type avowedly bearing little relation to the detail or practical working of any one system but ostensibly capturing the 'spirit' of continental criminal procedure.

Almost at once, critics countered with searching questions about the actual functioning of these 'model' systems.[2] They demonstrated that many of the attributes so lauded by would-be comparativist policy-makers were in practice little different from those which already existed in America. Most devastatingly, the idealized portrait of the *juge d'instruction* presiding over police investigations to ensure adherence to due process and fair play turned out to be little more than a chimera. Statistical evidence showed that, in the mid-1970s, only 14 per cent of criminal cases were referred to the *juge d'instruction* and that in the vast majority of cases the police completed their investigations unhindered by judicial supervision (Weigend 1980: 390). Even in those cases which were referred, the role of the *juge* appeared generally passive. An unhappy consequence was that constraints on police powers remained underdeveloped on the false premise that the *juge* would protect the rights of the accused, whereas in practice he or she rarely had sight of the case until the investigation was completed.

Given that 'the myth of judicial supervision' had been so roundly exploded in the American journal literature, it is perhaps curious that many reformers in Britain remained wedded to the idea that importing the inquisitorial model would miraculously solve problems of an increasingly beleaguered adversarial system in Britain a decade later. It is more surprising still that the Royal Commission on Criminal Justice should have heeded these calls and itself looked to the 'continental' model for solutions. None the less, in 1991, shortly after Viscount Runciman's appointment as chairman of the Commission, Professor Leonard Leigh and I were asked to undertake a comparative study of the pre-trial criminal administration in France and Germany on behalf of the Royal Commission (Leigh and Zedner 1992). Despite the general discrediting of 'borrowing' tactics in the academic literature, we were specifically asked 'to advise upon the suitability of the French or German models of procedure for adoption or adaptation in England and Wales' (Leigh and Zedner 1992: 67).

Explanation of this request lies, at least in part, with the media. Journalists who had played such an important role in securing the reopening of the cases of the Guildford Four, the Maguire Seven and so on, were equally forward in identifying the factors which they deemed responsible and the solutions which might prevent any reoccurrence. Many column inches were given over to the supposed advantages of the 'continental system' and, in particular, to the role of the examining magistrate. A piece in *The Guardian* from February 1991 is typical, questioning 'whether justice is served by the adversarial system in England and Wales, where prosecution and defence lawyers do battle in front of the judges'. It went on, 'reformers prefer the French inquisitorial system, where judges take a more active role in managing police investigations and leading questioning at the trial'.

It is far from clear how much those who called for the introduction of an examining magistrate in England really understood of the workings of the French system. None the less, the idea of importing a new, untainted, independent figure to preside over the police investigation seemed, like cherry pie, to be a good idea. The examining magistrate was presented as a *deus ex machina* who could be relied upon to intervene from on high every time an investigation was in trouble. This enthusiasm for things French is perhaps uncharacteristic, certainly unprecedented, and no doubt requires explanation. One should remember that these calls for reform took place against a climate of crisis: confidence in English criminal justice was extremely low, and political pressure was mounting for a profound reappraisal of the workings of the system. The generalized desire for something effective to be done, and fast, may provide at least a partial explanation for the turn to foreign jurisdictions for solutions.

Not only did those who called for movement toward an inquisitorial system fail to appreciate that the *juge d'instruction* actually plays an effective role in only a very limited number of cases, they failed also to consider the damage that might be done by a *juge* who is less than even handed. As we argued in our report to the Royal Commission 'a biased examining magistrate can do untold harm to the defence' (Leigh and Zedner 1992: 23). If he refuses to credit and hence to pursue an exculpatory account, the defence case will be damaged beyond repair since the trial court will tend to presume that what is said in the dossier is correct. We were consequently sceptical of the claim that judicial oversight would necessarily provide protection against the miscarriages of justice under scrutiny nor could it always guarantee attainment of the truth. We argued that:

> the public clamour for the introduction of an examining magistrate represents an attempt to solve, by means of a magic wand, problems which can only be resolved by the restructuring of the existing system and by the expenditure of time and money in the administration of criminal justice

and we concluded that:

> we do not believe that adoption, certainly in the crude form which is sometimes suggested in respect of the examining magistrate, is either feasible or desirable. (Leigh and Zedner 1992: 67–8)

Ultimately, then, we were unable to make the sorts of recommendations which many media and legal campaigners might have wished. Struck by the profound differences between the systems we observed and our own, our recommendations were generally cautious. Our reticence was not born out of a new breed of legal xenophobia, and our preference for seeking to bolster the adversarial system was not simply a misplaced manifestation of rampant patriotism. Rather we were impressed by the serious limitations of policy-oriented comparative research, not least for those who go abroad like some modern peripatetic surgeon in search of new medicine or organs with which to remedy domestic ills. Without proper regard for the social body in which apparently attractive procedures or institutions operate, the attempt to transplant may prove fatal. Just as those who engage in interdisciplinary study caution against the haphazard borrowing of conceptual tools and categorizations from other disciplines, so the comparativist must be wary of borrowing from abroad.

Recognition of the limitations of comparative research as a basis for domestic policy-making is unlikely to impede the growth of cross-national debate about crime and criminal justice. The increasing internationalization of the world economy and the growth in human mobility mean that crime is no longer regarded as a domestic problem. As a consequence, the value of understanding what goes on 'abroad' inevitably grows.[3] The European Community too has had a catalytic effect: the lowering of internal border controls, to say nothing of the incentives provided by EC subsidies, has generated new types of criminals and new forms of crime.[4] To a considerable extent political concern has shifted away from traditional preoccupations with public order and street crime and towards cross-border crimes such as terrorism, drug-trafficking and fraud. The decreasing effectiveness of conventional methods of crime control forces policy-makers to think imaginatively about cross-national collaboration.[5] Such efforts rely on co-operation, compatibility of laws, or perhaps even harmonization, and these in turn require better understanding. In addition, one might argue that as our perceptions of 'home' and 'abroad' shift and melt, that which would formerly have been deemed comparative becomes instead domestic. While many English people still have problems about identifying themselves as Europeans and speak and write as if Europe were another place, the longer-term consequences of the Single European Act may ultimately be that within the member states the very term comparison will lose much of its present resonance.

Even if one remains sceptical about comparative research as a basis for policy-making, the imperatives towards understanding the criminal justice systems of other countries seem likely to continue to grow. As Downes points out in the foreword to his own excellent comparative study *Contrasts in Tolerance*, the ease of air travel and the proliferation of conference circuits contribute also to the 'import–export' model of criminological enquiry (Downes 1988: 2). It is timely, therefore, to reflect upon the nature and value of comparative research and, in particular, to consider the methodological and theoretical issues it occasions.

Some methodological issues

Before going on to explore possible theoretical models for comparative research, it is perhaps prudent to say something about the methodological hazards involved. Most obviously, 'criminological tourism', to borrow a disparaging but often all too apt tag, may make one vulnerable to the dangers faced by real tourists. One may misread or oversimplify local customs. One may even be subject to the duplicity of the bazaar where the unwary can be all too readily inveigled into buying versions of truths which any streetwise local would recognize instantly as sham. The danger is all the greater if one travels abroad with the same misty-eyed vision of the traveller who sees only the picturesque and the good. Comparative scholars are not immune from the temptations of the holiday romance and are inclined to write in breathless praise of the liberalism of Scandinavian penal policy or the efficiency and fairness of German investigations. True one cannot help but be impressed 'by the harmonious working relationships in Germany between prosecutors and police' and by the 'humane and liberal spirit' in which they operate (Leigh and Zedner 1992: 71) but other systems are not flawless. Suspects in Germany are often held in custody awaiting trial for periods which we would regard as intolerably long, and there are no absolute legal time limits on their detention. If comparative criminology is to rise above the level of the travelogue, we must be as critical and inquiring abroad as we would be at home.

Linguistic difficulties, too, are a major inhibition to effective comparison. Anything less than complete fluency leaves one vulnerable to misinterpretation. In turn, one is liable to miss subtleties of intonation, nuances of speech, or most problematic of all, that which is left unsaid (Gadamer 1966: 59–68). The dangers are perhaps greatest where linguistic labels promise apparent similarity. Where criminal justice agencies or processes have the same name, it seems all too reasonable to assume that they connote like bodies. Institutions which appear to be identical may, in fact, operate very differently in different settings. Official descriptions of the work of similar agencies may mask substantial differences in their actual form, culture, and purpose.

The very notion of 'crime' itself is too easily taken as a unitary phenomenon constant across nations or, worse still, a useful catch-all term, as Burnham (1993: 73) points out. Individual crimes, too, often appear to translate easily into recognizable categories but may denote quite different activities, values, or levels of seriousness. At best, such categories offer imprecise bases for comparison and, at worst, they may become so gross as to be meaningless. At another extreme, awareness of local difference may become so acute that finding counterparts proves impossible. The differentiated meanings of crime derive from legal categorization, political agendas, media discourse, or rather from some combination of all three. The fuzziness of crime categories and their malleability under local conditions are such that it may make very little sense to talk of comparing levels or trends in 'crime' across countries.

Tables which purport to compare phenomena like 'domestic violence' or 'public order offences' may simply be offering up quite different fruit for comparison. We can say very little of use by measuring oranges against pears (or even Coxs against Granny Smiths), and the scientific pretensions of amassed statistical tables should not blind us to the hollowness of their contents. Unless we can develop some satisfactory mechanism for allowing for variance in meaning then cross-national statistical surveys may tell us very little of worth. At very least, some account needs to be made of the social and cultural context within which laws are formulated, crimes recorded, convictions dealt out, and sentences passed.

A balance between lumbering insensitivity and too precious a regard for the difficulties must be struck. These problems should not be regarded as wholly insuperable, however, but rather as the very key to developing a satisfactory methodology. Sensitivity to the context of the criminal law (Nelken 1987), the relationship between law and criminal justice and, perhaps more importantly still, between criminal law and political and social culture may provide one route out of this methodological abyss. By allowing us to appreciate the importance of the local environment in generating law and legal practices, we may be less likely to fall into the trap of treating facts and figures as if they had been propagated in identical sterile laboratories.

Employed with care, cross-national comparison allows for a greater sensitivity to the normative context and may make us less ready to talk of the 'crime problem' as a natural phenomenon, much like earthquakes and floods, or of 'punishment' as a God-given inevitability. As Downes's comparative study of post-war penal policy in England and Wales and the Netherlands has shown, penal systems are shaped and moulded by differing 'cultures of tolerance' (Downes

1988). The lesson is similarly illustrated by the example of recent German criminal justice history which reveals that rising crime rates do not automatically dictate a parallel growth in the prison population. At a time when such a view was axiomatic in Britain, the West German prison population was reduced despite rising crime and, contrary to popular expectation, with no deleterious effect on crime levels (Feest 1980; Graham 1990). Our response should not be to raise our hands in delight and empty our prisons forthwith, but to examine with care the local socio-economic and political conditions which made such a policy possible.

Theoretical models for comparison

While comparative research clearly raises an array of methodological difficulties, it is the larger theoretical issues which must most engage: not least because they demand an immediate response to the question 'Comparison, what for?' The import of this enquiry may seem less pressing when sunning oneself at some pavement bistro between interviews. But, if this is not to be criminological tourism, then some hard questions must be asked about 'why' and 'where' one undertakes comparative study. The question of 'where' is addressed least consciously: convenience or inclination appear often to be more determinative factors in selecting a country for study than any coherent reasoning. Until relatively recently, for example, the vast majority of comparisons were made with North America. No doubt the relative lack of linguistic difficulties (though even these may have been underestimated) was a primary inducement. It is arguable that more fruitful comparisons may often be made with other European countries whose history, culture, and economic development are so much closer to our own. This is not to deny that lessons may be learned from observation of far and different countries but rather to suggest that they are liable to be more attenuated (or to use a more concrete image, more battered and travel-worn) than those derived from near and like nations.[6] A separate issue arises in respect of units for comparison. Whilst it may often make sense to conduct comparisons between one country and another, the fluid nature of national boundaries and the unnerving tendency of nations to fragment and re-form must make us wary of assuming homogeneity of culture or identity.[7]

The 'why' of comparative research is more troubling still and it may be helpful to look at contrasting theoretical approaches as possible models for research.

The positivist approach

A model, much favoured by scholars of comparative criminal procedure, is one which we might label positivist or 'scientific'. Comparativists in this tradition focus on identifying similarity and difference of form and substance in the systems under scrutiny. Many start with the working assumption that criminal justice systems across countries are of the same *genus*, differing only in varieties of form. The comparison of apparently differing systems serves, therefore, a dual purpose: revealing that set of core principles, structures, and procedures which are shared by most systems of criminal justice, whilst distinguishing those traits which are mere externalities. To borrow from Barton L. Ingraham (1987: x), an analogy may be drawn from zoology wherein comparative study allows one to describe 'the skeleton common to all modern procedural systems' whilst revealing 'significant differences in their muscles, viscera, and organs'. A less rigid variant on the same approach is the view that there are core attributes of a criminal justice system which one can expect to find irrespective of the form and culture of any given system.[8]

The 'same animal, different fur' assumption made most often by many of those concerned primarily with comparisons in criminal procedure suggest that, whatever the system, there are identical functions to be performed and common problems to be resolved. Hence, whether the model adopted is adversarial or inquisitorial, the basic aims (of inhibiting crime, punishing the guilty, incapacitating the dangerous and so on) are the same. What lies at issue is merely the means to their attainment. Those who have had the benefit of prolonged exposure to different legal systems tend to find such conclusions harder to stomach. Let me quote from a letter from Professor David Nelken, who having moved to Italy from England concluded that:

> the contrasts between the English and Italian legal systems are extreme and inexhaustible. Living here has given me a jaundiced view of comparative research which sets out to show that all societies face similar problems even if they solve them somewhat differently. What is more striking is the power

of culture to produce relatively circular definitions of what is worth fighting for and against, and the way institutions and practices express genuinely different histories and distinct priorities. (Nelken 1992: 6)

Nelken's observations are shared by those (and I number myself among them) who are more impressed by the dissimilarities of different criminal justice systems than their underlying commonality.[9] The sense of contrast is most clearly accentuated when one opens one's gaze to reflect upon wider questions about the relationship between definitions of crime, the determination of crime-seriousness, and the use and range of penal sanctions in different jurisdictions. Questions about the relationship between crime control and political culture or socio-economic structure broaden the canvas further still. In so doing they make visible underlying differences in attitudes and responses to crime perhaps not immediately apparent to those whom, without naming names, we might disparagingly label 'biological positivists' and whose work focuses more on the mechanics of criminal processes than their meaning.

An anthropological approach

A second and possibly more fruitful possibility is that suggested by the work of anthropology.[10] The anthropologist's concern with history, culture and social structure combines to illuminate dissimilarities and to sharpen contrasts. The result is to heighten the sense of distance which is lost in so much of the procedural work described above. Immersion in one's own legal system tends, inevitably, to solidify assumptions and blunt critical faculties. Laws appear 'natural', modes of implementation 'inevitable' and relationships between criminal justice agencies 'necessary'. Legal historians attach great value to the distance of time in providing the perspective to recognize that apparently immutable laws were the product of historical accident or that formidable legal institutions were once fiercely contested (Hay 1975; Ignatieff 1978; Zedner 1991). Perspective may be provided in much the same way for the comparativist by distance – both geographical and cultural.

Observing other possibilities not merely excites the scholar out of the torpor of parochialism but demands that one regards anew the domestic topography of legal norms, institutions, and their interaction. The gain is not only in coming to understand another legal system but in the fresh perspective offered by seeing one's own legal system with the eyes of an outsider.[11] The position of 'outsider' offers further advantages in that it allows the researcher to ask questions of extraordinary *naïveté* (false or otherwise). Moreover, as a 'nobody' one may be allowed access to information or be made party to disclosures which prudence might withhold from a fellow national. The very loss of status which is so disturbing when one first ventures abroad may thus be turned to one's advantage.

The question quickly arises, however, how much one can understand as an outsider. The 'insider' versus 'outsider' dilemma is one with which anthropologists have grappled for many years and we can usefully learn from their experiences (Geertz 1983: 222) According to Geertz, the credibility of anthropology traditionally rested on the myth of the anthropologist as 'chameleon fieldworker, perfectly self-tuned to his exotic surroundings' (Geertz 1983: 222). This fiction was brutally blown apart by the posthumous publication of the diaries of Bronislaw Malinowski (1967), which revealed another, less romantic truth. The 'great man' of anthropology 'had rude things to say about the natives he was living with, and rude words to say it in. He spent a great deal of time wishing he were elsewhere'. This, in Geertz's view, raised the disturbing question: 'if it isn't, as we had been led to believe, through some sort of extraordinary sensibility, an almost preternatural capacity to think, feel, and perceive like a native . . . how is anthropological knowledge possible?' The question applies, surely, with equal force to comparative criminology.

The reassessment and recasting of the anthropological endeavour prompted by the publication of Malinowski's diaries centred around whether comparative research is best advanced by maintaining the perspective of distance or by seeking the self-identification of fellow feeling. A middle way exploits the differential merits of each approach according to the subject under scrutiny. The perspective of distance allows one to understand the global structure of, for example, a body of laws, the rules of evidence, or the sentencing framework. The immediacy of immersion is perhaps more appropriate to the empathetic understanding of concepts such as fear of crime, canteen culture, racial tension, sense of community, and so on. The advantage of mixing both approaches is that one risks neither the worst excesses of abstraction and generality nor the smothering entanglement of intimacy (which is, after all, the very thing that most comparativists are seeking to escape). To return to Geertz, by varying one's pitch in this way it may be possible 'to produce an interpretation (of the way a people lives) which is neither imprisoned within their mental horizons, an ethnography of witchcraft as written by a witch, nor systematically deaf to the distinctive tonalities of their existence, an ethnography of witchcraft as written by a geometer (Geertz 1983: 223).

Part of the attraction of this approach is that it mirrors very well the common practice of the comparative researcher. Doing comparative work rarely entails selling one's home and tearing up one's passport, forever to live among the drug dealers of Delhi or the detectives of Düsseldorf. Neither can one, with credibility at any rate, write about continental criminal procedure without stepping outside the ivy-clad walls of an Oxford College. Rather the research process entails developing a general theoretical (but distant) understanding at home-base, punctuated by a series of forays (often of increasing duration) into the terrain of study. This itinerary is matched by an intellectual journey which takes one from the perspective of global structures to the minutiae of local detail and back and forth over the course of the research in 'a sort of intellectual perpetual motion' (Geertz 1983: 235). While periods of fieldwork provide for immersion in local culture (of the court, the prison, the police station), the journeys between make possible an intellectual distancing. Once more library-bound, the researcher can engage in the detached reflections and distanced evaluation which are the very stuff of comparison.

Conclusion: comparison and criminological knowledge

Until now most comparative work has focused on substantive areas of crime or the varieties of criminal procedure and justice systems. Relatively little attention has been given to comparing how different countries think about crime: how local value systems provide differing normative frameworks for defining what is and what is not 'criminal', for scaling relative crime-seriousness, or determining appropriate sanctions. Nor has there been much by way of 'comparative criminology' in the sense of comparing the criminologies of different countries. One need spend very little time abroad to be struck by the stark variations in academic culture, and these differences in outlook necessarily impact upon approaches to and understanding of crime and crime control. In turn, the local preoccupations of academics tend to reflect wider political concerns and can be highly informative of how a country thinks about crime.

As international journals, the conference circuit, and the overseas sabbatical combine to shrink the academic world, we might expect criminological knowledge to tend towards ever greater homogeneity. Certainly there is evidence already of what Heidensohn terms the 'diffusion of new discovery' (Heidensohn 1991: 8), so that new concerns or new knowledge enter our national consciousness with a rapidity second only to the latest Hollywood blockbuster. A good example here is the entry of the victim into the criminological scene. Universally the 'forgotten actor' of criminal justice a few decades ago, the victim sprang to the front of the criminological agenda thanks largely to the collaborative efforts of an international network of academics who hosted conferences, set up journals, and carried out cross-national victim surveys.[12] So it is that one can talk of the common outlook and shared intellectual and political agenda of the international 'victims' movement'.

Paradoxically, however, as Shapland has pointed out, one is hard-pressed to identify present equivalents to the sweeping influence on criminological thought of the great criminological minds of Ferri, Durkheim, Garafalo, or Mannheim.[13] Is it, as Shapland suggests, that 'our mental barriers have become stronger, our inner prejudices more exclusionary'? Or is it, rather, that in this post-modern era we are more sensitized to the fragmentary and kaleidoscopic qualities of social life and less prepared to accept the grand visions of modernism. If we recognize that criminality is contingent on local political, social, and economic structure (Lacey 1994), then we must expect criminology (or rather criminologies) also to be local and hetero-geneous. Relativism has its critics and it serves us little to know that 'Africans marry the dead and in Australia they eat worms' (Geertz 1986: 181). But we should not, in our bid to transcend national boundaries, underestimate the value of 'local knowledge'. It would be counterproductive indeed if the pursuit of the comparative flourished at the expense of the rich diversity of current criminology.

Notes

[1] As Weigend (1980: 386) pointed out 'there is no such thing as "European criminal procedure"; rather, on that small continent, a multitude of

procedural systems have grown and prospered independently of each other'.

2 Goldstein and Marcus were highly critical of the practice of '"borrowing" from the institutions of another country', Goldstein and Marcus 1978: 1570; Goldstein and Marcus 1977: 240.

3 This is reflected in the proliferation of international organizations, projects and colloquia, both academic and professional, devoted to promoting international understanding in crime and criminal justice; to take just a few random examples: the Society for Criminal Law Reform; the International Penal and Penitentiary Foundation; Association Internationale de Droit Pénal; International Comparisons in Criminal Justice; and Penal Reform International.

4 The founding of the Association of Lawyers for the Protection of the Financial Interests of the European Community (a grouping of national 'associations') in 1990 recognized the need to improve understanding and co-operation between member states in the effort to combat 'Eurocrime'. In addition to hosting twenty-four seminars, conferences and training sessions in the period 1990–3, the Associations now produce *AGON*, an information bulletin 'for the exchange of information and ideas' (*AGON* 1993: 9). See also Heidensohn and Farrell 1991 for more general discussion of the implications of European integration on crime and crime control.

5 The setting up of the consultative body TREVI in 1976 to combat terrorism in Europe and the broadening of its brief to encompass international crime such as narcotics and weapons trading in 1985, the implementation of the Schengen Accord in respect of border controls, and the co-operation of police within Benelux are a few of the more important developments in the 'internationalization' of policing. (See Fijnaut 1991: 103–20.)

6 A criticism made by some of the otherwise warm reviews of Braithwaite (1989) was that his heavy reliance on practices of 'reintegrative shaming' in Japan provided a questionable basis for their possible success in less collective societies such as our own.

7 As the anthropologist E. E. Evans-Pritchard (1963) queried, 'are the Australian Aboriginals to be regarded as one group or as many? are the Chinese or the English to count as a single unit and equivalent, as such, to, shall we say, a Penan horde?'

8 As Weigend (1980: 418) has argued 'some structural components of the criminal process seem to be universal and independent of procedural ideology'.

9 The stance is hardly new. In a lecture in 1963 Evans-Pritchard called for greater emphasis on 'the importance for social anthropology, as a comparative discipline, of differences . . . in the past the tendency has often been to place the stress on similarities' (Evans-Pritchard 1963: 17).

10 And in particular, the work of Clifford Geertz, see references.

11 David Downes (1988: 2) discusses the advantages and pitfalls of the 'stranger' in comparative research.

[12] For example, the repeated International Symposia on Victimology, the *International Review of Victimology*, and works like Joutsen 1987; Van Dijk, Mayhew, and Killias 1990; Kaiser, Kury, and Albrecht 1991.

[13] See Shapland (1990), Heidensohn and Farrell (1991: 15). Sir Leon Radzinowicz is perhaps the last remaining of these 'universal men' of criminology.

References

Adler, F. (1983). *Nations Not Obsessed with Crime* (Colorado, F. B. Rothman).

Association Internationale De Droit Pénale, *The Criminal Justice System of the Federal Republic of Germany* (Toulouse, Èrès, 1981).

Associations of lawyers for the protection of the financial interests of the European Community *AGON* (launched 1993).

Barak-Glantz, I. L. and Johnson, E. H. (1981). *Comparative Criminology* (Beverly Hills, Sage).

Beirne, P. (1983). 'Cultural relativism and comparative criminology', *Contemporary Crises*.

Beirne, P. (1991). *Comparative Criminology: An Annotated Bibliography* (New York, Greenwood Press).

Braithwaite, J. (1989). *Crime, Shame and Reintegration* (Cambridge, Cambridge University Press).

Burnham, R. W. (1993). 'The promise and the perils of comparative criminology', *Howard Journal of Criminal Justice*, 23, 67–72.

Capelletti, M. (1989). *The Judicial Process in Comparative Perspective* (Oxford, Oxford University Press).

Clinard, M. B. (1978). *Cities with Little Crime: the Case of Switzerland* (Cambridge, Cambridge University Press).

Chambon, P. (1972). *Le Juge D'Instruction* (Paris, Dalloz).

Cole, G. F. *et al.* (eds.) (1987). *Major Criminal Justice Systems: A Comparative Survey* (Beverly Hills, Sage).

Damaska, M. (1973). 'Evidentiary barriers to conviction and two models of criminal procedure: a comparative study', *University of Pennsylvania Law Review*, 121, 506.

Damaska, M. (1981). 'The reality of prosecutorial discretion: comments on a German monograph', *American Journal of Comparative Law*, 29, 119.

Damaska, M. (1986). *The Faces of Justice and State Authority* (Yale University Press).

Devlin, P. (Lord) (1981). 'The judge in an adversary system', *The Judge* (Oxford, Oxford University Press).

Downes, D. (1988). *Contrasts in Tolerance: Post-War Penal Policy in the Netherlands and England and Wales* (Oxford, Oxford University Press).

Eser, A., and Huber, B. (1985, 1987, 1990). *Strafrechtsentwicklung in Europa*, vols. 1, 2 and 3 (Freiburg, Max Planck).

Eser, A., 'A century of penal legislation in Germany', in Eser, A. and Thormundsson, J. (eds.) (1989). *Old Ways and New Needs in Criminal Legislation* (Freiburg, Max Planck).

Evans-Pritchard, E. E. (1963). *The Comparative Method in Social Anthropology* (London, Athlone Press).

Feest, J. (1988). *Reducing the West German Prison Population: Lessons from the West German Experience* (NACRO Occasional Paper).

Fijnaut, C. (1991). 'Police co-operation within western Europe', in Heidensohn and Farrell (eds.), *Crime in Europe*, 103–20.

Frase, R. S. (1990). 'Comparative criminal justice as a guide to American Law Reform', *California Law Review*, 79, 539.

Gadamer, H-G. (1966). 'Man and language' in *Philosophical Hermeneutics* (Berkeley, University of California Press), 59–68.

Geertz. C. (1975). ' Thick description: toward an interpretive theory of culture' in Geertz *The Interpretation of Cultures* (London, Hutchinson), 3–30.

Geertz, C. (1983). 'From the native's point of view: on the nature of anthropological understanding' in *Local Knowledge: Further Essays in Interpretive Anthropology* (New York, Basic Books).

Geertz, C. (1983). 'Local knowledge: fact and law in comparative perspective' in *Local Knowledge: Further Essays in Interpretive Anthropology* (New York, Basic Books).

Geertz, C. (1988). *Works and Lives: The Anthropologist as Author* (Oxford, Polity Press).

Goldstein, A. (1974). 'Reflections on two models: inquisitorial themes in American criminal procedure', *Stanford Law Review*, 26, 1009.

Goldstein, A. S. and Marcus, M. (1977). 'The myth of judicial supervision in three "inquisitorial" systems: France, Italy and Germany', *Yale Law Journal*, 87, 240.

Goldstein, A. and Marcus, M. (1978). 'Comment on continental criminal procedure', *Yale Law Journal*, 88, 1570.

Graham, J. (1990). 'Decarceration in the Federal Republic of Germany', *British Journal of Criminology*, 30, 150–70.

Gurr, T. R., Grabosky, P. N. and Hula, R. C. (eds.) (1977). *The Politics of Crime and Conflict: A Comparative History of Four Cities* (Beverly Hills, Sage).

Hay, D. (1975). 'Property, authority and the criminal law' in D. Hay *et al.*, *Albion's Fatal Tree* (London, Penguin).

Heidensohn, F. (1991). 'Introduction: convergence, diversity and change', in Heidensohn and Farrell (eds.), *Crime in Europe*, 3–13.

Heidensohn, F. and Farrell, M. (eds.) (1991). *Crime in Europe* (London, Routledge).

Heiland, H-G, Shelley, L. I., and Katoh, H. (eds.) (1991). *Crime and Control in Comparative Perspective* (De Gruyter, Berlin).

Herrmann, J. (1974). 'The rule of compulsory prosecution and the scope of prosecutorial discretion in Germany', *University of Chicago Law Review*, 41, 468.

Herrmann, J. (1978). 'Development and reform of criminal procedure in the Federal Republic of Germany', *Comparative and International Law Journal of South Africa*, 11, 183.

Herrmann, J. (1983). 'Federal Republic of Germany: diversion and mediation', *Review International de Droit Pénal*, 54, 1043.

Herrmann, J. (1987). 'The Federal Republic of Germany', in Cole *et al.* (eds.) (1987) *Major Criminal Justice Systems* (Beverly Hills, Sage).

Ignatieff, M. (1978). *A Just Measure of Pain: the Penitentiary in the Industrial Revolution* (London, Macmillan).

Ingraham, B. L. (1987). *The Structure of Criminal Procedure* (New York, Greenwood Press).

Jescheck, H.-H. (1970). 'Principles of German criminal procedure in comparison with American Law', *Vancouver Law Review*, 56, 239.

Joutsen, M. (1987). *The Role of the Victim in European Criminal Justice Systems: A Crossnational Study* (Helsinki, HEUNI).

Kaiser, G. and Albrecht, H-J. (eds.) (1990). *Crime and Criminal Policy in Europe* (Freiburg, Eigenverlag Max-Planck-Institut).

Kaiser, G., Kury, H. and Albrecht, H.-J. (eds.) (1991). *Victims and Criminal Justice* (Freiburg, Eigenverlag Max-Planck-Institut).

Klein, M. W. (ed.) (1989). *Cross-national Research in Self-reported Crime and Delinquency* (Dordrecht).

Kube, E. and Störzer, H. U. (eds.) (1991). *Police Research in the Federal Republic of Germany* (Berlin, Springer-Verlag).

Lacey, N. (1995 forthcoming). 'Contingency and criminalisation', in Loveland, I. (ed.), *The Frontiers of Criminality* (London, Sweet and Maxwell).

Langbein, J. (1974). 'Controlling prosecutorial discretion in Germany;', *University of Chicago Law Review*, 41, 439.

Langbein, J. (1977). *Comparative Criminal Procedure: Germany* (West).

Langbein, J. and Weinreb, L. (1977). 'Continental criminal procedure: myth and reality', *Yale Law Journal*, 87, 1549.

Leigh, L. H. and Zedner, L. (1992). *The Royal Commission on Criminal Justice Research Study No. 1: The Administration of Criminal Justice in the Pre-Trial Phase in France and Germany* (London, HMSO).

Linnan, D. K. (1984). 'Police discretion in a continental European administrative state: the police of Baden-Württemberg in the Federal Republic of Germany', *Law and Contemporary Problems*, 47, 185.

Malinowski, B. (1967). *A Diary in the Strict Sense of the Term* (reprint 1989, London, Athlone Press).

Mannheim, H. (1965). *Comparative Criminology* (London, Routledge).

McKillop, B. (1990). 'Behind the faces of justice', *Bulletin of the Australian Society of Legal Philosophy*, 15, 55–77.

Mendelson, W. (1983). 'Self-incrimination in American and French Law', *Criminal Law Bulletin*, 19, 34.

Merryman, J. H. (1988). 'How others do it: the French and German judiciaries', *South California Law Review*, 61, 1865.

Miyazawa, K. and Ohya, M. (eds.) (1986). *Victimology in Comparative Perspective* (Tokyo, Seibundo).

Nelken, D. (1987). 'Criminal law and criminal justice: some notes on their irrelation', in Dennis, I. *Criminal Law and Criminal Justice* (London, Sweet and Maxwell).

Nelken, D. (1992). 'Law and disorder: a letter from Italy', *Socio-Legal Newsletter*, 8, 6.

Ploscowe, M. (1935). 'The investigating magistrate (juge d'instruction) in European criminal procedure', *Michigan Law Review*, 33, 1010.

Robert, P. (1986). 'Un mal nécessaire? La détention provisoire en France', *Déviance et Société*, X(1), 57–64.

Schlesinger, R. B. (1976). 'Comparative criminal procedure: a plea for utilizing foreign experience', *Buffalo Law Review*, 26, 361.

Schmidhauser, J. R. (ed.) (1987). *Comparative Judicial Systems: Challenging Frontiers in Conceptual and Empirical Analysis* (London, Butterworth).

Schmidhauser, J. R. (1987). 'Alternative conceptual frameworks in comparative cross-national legal and judicial research', in Schmidhauser, *Comparative Judicial Systems*.

Schram, G. (1969). 'The obligation to prosecute in West Germany', *American Journal of Comparative Law*, 17, 627.

Shapland, J. (1991). 'Criminology in Europe', in Heidensohn and Farrell (eds.), *Crime in Europe*, 14–23.

Tomasson, R. F. (ed.) (1986). *Comparative Social Research, Volume 8: Deviance*.

Van Dijk, J. *et al.* (eds.) (1986). *Criminal Law in Action: An Overview of Current Issues in Western Societies* (Arnhem, Gouda Quint).

Van Dijk, J., Mayhew, P. and Killias, M. (1990). *Experiences of Crime across the World: Key Findings of the 1989 International Crime Survey* (Holland, Kluwer).

Volkmann-Schluck, T. (1981). 'Continental European criminal procedures: true or illusive model', *American Journal of Criminal Law*, 9.

Weigend, T. (1980). 'Continental cures for American ailments: European criminal procedure as a model for law reform', in Morris, N. and Tonry, M. (eds.) *Crime and Justice*, vol. 2 (Chicago, University of Chicago Press).

Weigend, T. (1983). 'Criminal justice: 2, comparative aspects', *Encyclopedia of Crime and Justice*, 2, 537–46.

Zedner, L. (1991). *Women, Crime and Custody in Victorian England* (Oxford, Oxford University Press).

3

In search of a Third World criminology

IAN CLEGG AND JIM WHETTON

Introduction

The initial intention of this paper was to assess the actual and potential implications of the current emphasis on economic, administrative and political reform in developing countries for the administration of criminal justice. Within this general context, particularly in relation to the high profile given to decentralization, participation and an increased role for non-governmental organizations (NGOs), a particular concern was to examine the extent to which this would lead to a renewed advocacy of various forms of informal or non-state justice. However, in reading and rereading the relevant development studies and criminology literature we were reminded of the puzzling reciprocal neglect of these two fields of study and of the inadequacy or irrelevance of much of the existing Third World crime literature. As a result, we felt that it would be more appropriate to focus on some fundamental questions concerning the nature and task of criminology in developing societies.

To this end, firstly, we reflect on some of the reasons why criminology and development studies have failed to connect. Secondly, we examine some of the problems involved in transferring theories and models from criminology in the developed world and ask whether previous attempts to develop a criminology of the Third World have been theoretically flawed. Thirdly, taking the example of sub-Saharan Africa, we attempt to show, through a discussion of the literature on the state and civil society, that a recognition of the specificity of these societies means that a different criminological agenda may need to be constructed. In this we stress the importance of focusing on pluralism and the significant role played by informal justice.

Development studies and criminology: a failure to connect?

It is some twenty years since Clinard and Abbott wrote *Crime in Developing Countries* (1973). In it they noted that standard criminology texts made almost no reference to 'less developed countries' and that, similarly, there was little or no mention of crime in texts on development. A decade later, Colin Sumner (1982) noted that little had changed in this respect and, after criticizing the orthodoxy of Clinard and Abbott, he sketched out an agenda for an analysis of crime and justice in underdeveloped countries. Although adopting a somewhat different theoretical standpoint from Sumner, Stan Cohen (1982) reached similar conclusions on the irrelevance of much of the criminological discourse to the Third World. Another decade later, the situation remains largely unchanged. Criminological writing in developed countries still seems silent on the Third World. Although the production of work on crime in Third World countries has increased, much of it has failed to escape from the dead-end of modernization theory, and there are few signs of the emergence of a specifically Third World theoretical criminology. The development studies literature continues to devote little attention to any serious study of crime or social control.

Before turning to Colin Sumner's influential critique of Clinard and Abbott and his attempt to outline an alternative, Marxist, approach to crime in colonial and post-colonial society, it may be useful to refer to some of the changes within development studies in the last decade. These have a bearing on the way in which development studies has largely ignored the traditional subject matter of criminology.

The effect of the changed political and economic climate of the 1980s on criminology has been usefully summarized and debated in the contributions to Young and Matthews (1992), and we do not propose to elaborate on this here. The trend towards 'administrativization' noted by Ruggiero (1992) in this volume and earlier criticized by Cohen in *Visions of Social Control* (1985) has also been a characteristic of development studies, especially over the last decade. As in criminology, the emphasis in development studies has shifted to a concern with cost-effective interventions, measurement of inputs and outputs, and exploration of forms of decentralization and privatization. Staff of development studies institutions are increasingly involved in contract work, especially the design, monitoring and evaluation of programmes and the managerial training that accompanies this. To some extent this is a matter of the financial survival of institutions whose main income comes from training and consultancy contracts with donor governments or from multilateral agencies such as the World Bank or the World Health Organisation. Our own experience is that this climate and the constraints imposed by funding agencies have made it difficult to follow up the sort of radical agenda suggested by Sumner, even when funds for work on criminal justice (which, apart from policing, has a low priority) are made available.

It is, of course possible to discern a tendency in development studies which is not unlike that of left realism in criminology in terms of its attempt to find a middle ground between the wearily angry cynicism of post-1960s radicalism and contemporary managerialism. This approach, whilst less theoretically rigorous than left realism, has largely abandoned the macro-perspective of various forms of Marxist analysis of the causes and nature of 'underdevelopment' within the context of the world economic system for more detailed and local analyses of the nature of poverty and inequality and the design of more effective development programmes. In this, a prime concern has been 'targeting' those social groups (the poor, the landless, women and children) perceived to suffer most acutely from the negative aspects of development. Rather like left realism, the approach entails an ambiguous attitude to the state. On the one hand, much emphasis is given to promoting community or beneficiary participation, decentralization and grass-roots organization as alternatives to the incompetent, corrupt, malign state. On the other hand, there is a nostalgia for the Keynesian, interventionist state and a strong critique of the privatization or marketization of the state sector that has been a common feature of the structural adjustment programmes imposed on Third World states by the World Bank and 'donor' governments. This ambiguity has lead to confused thinking about the nature of community and the state which parallels attitudes to informal justice within criminology.

Very often it seems as if development studies which, unlike criminology, has not overtly confronted post-modernism, has gone through a process of deconstruction. This is particularly noticeable at the hard end where the range of consultancy and training can range from forestry or rain-fed farming to health care delivery, from infrastructure programmes like rural feeder roads, dams or rural electrification to the place of prostitution in the urban informal economy and its contribution to the spread of HIV infection. All of this involves 'experts' from many base disciplines, conflicts between technologists, economists and sociologists over priorities, as well as debates about whether and how to ensure that 'marginal' groups are included in the process of development, or at least shielded from its most negative aspects.

Although much of this work implicitly touches on topics that are of relevance to criminology, apart from underlying assumptions that 'traditional' indigenous systems of social control are breaking down and that this engenders crime (by the poor and by the rich), there is rarely an explicit focus on crime. The fact that these assumptions are frequently unexamined is largely due to the way in which the two classic base paradigms in development studies (modernization theory and varieties of Marxist analysis), whilst identifying different causes of change, tend to assume similar types of impact on culture and social structure.

It is also relevant to note the work of the main UN agencies concerned with crime and development such as the five-yearly UN Congresses on the Prevention of Crime and the Treatment of Offenders, the UN Interregional Crime and Justice Research Unit (UNICRI) in Rome and the various regional agencies. The UNICRI publication – *Essays on Crime and Development* (Zvekic 1990) – shows the onset of deep pessimism about the value of much of the theory and methodology used in these institutions over the last three decades. On a theoretical level this appears to be partly due to a curiously belated recognition by the international criminology network that the modernization paradigm is flawed. Not only has economic growth failed to materialize in many areas of the Third World but poverty and inequality are increasing. The implications of this are that the underlying premises on replications of patterns of development and, hence, the transferability of theories of the causes of crime and solutions, are inadequate. On a methodological level, the search for global patterns of crime and their correlation with indices of development has proved to be a miserable failure, partly because of the inadequacies of the initial hypotheses rooted in modernization theory and partly as a result of the unreliability of official data and the technical and financial difficulties in processing it. This has lead some (for example Burnham 1990) to advocate abandoning attempts to link social development and crime and to argue for the disaggregation of data in order to examine national or subnational patterns. There is also a growing emphasis on the value of finding indigenous solutions based on 'traditional' forms of social control and dispute resolution, linking with the current ideological stress on community participation and indigenization in development discourse.

'Crime, justice and underdevelopment'

With this background in mind, we turn to Sumner's chapter – 'Crime, justice and underdevelopment: beyond modernisation theory' (1982) – as a first step in posing the question of whether a criminology of the Third World as a whole is a realistic enterprise.

Sumner's explanation of why there had been so little criminological work of any value in or on the Third World drew attention to the dominance of the modernization paradigm. He spent much of his chapter demolishing the contributions of orthodox criminologists such as Clinard and Abbott which he saw, correctly, as being based on a conjunction of modernization theory and classic Chicago criminology. In essence, his critique was that together these theories rested in a false conception of the nature, case and direction of change in the Third World and led to a narrow focus on urban, working-class crime, ignoring, for example, the power structure which was responsible for criminalizing the poor as well as the crimes of the post-colonial state or foreign capital in the guise of multinational companies. Stan Cohen, in his paper 'Western crime control models in the Third World: benign or malignant' (1982), produced a somewhat similar critique of the ideological and material transfer of the orthodox criminological model. Rather like Sumner, Cohen was less concerned with criticizing the theory itself than stressing that the different history – colonialism and dependent development – of most Third World societies meant that theory and practice grounded in the developed world were frequently irrelevant.

If it was not surprising that such orthodox criminology contained little of value, Sumner found it more odd that radical criminology, especially in its less abolitionist, more Marxist variants, had 'rarely attended to the significant role of crime and criminal law in social development' (1982: 3). He did not provide an answer to this, nor to the equally puzzling neglect of crime by development studies despite the, then, popularity of forms of Marxist discourse on development or 'underdevelopment'.

Sumner set out his own basic position as follows:

Economic systems do not work automatically, they need to be created, protected and legitimated. Certain political and ideological forms are so necessary to an economic system that they can be considered organic to it. These forms interpenetrate with the purely economic. In this sense, certain criminal (as well as civil) laws, and the violation of those laws, can be seen as components of the motor force of economic development: the relations and struggles between classes constituted by the mode of production. Crime, whether as law or law violation, has historically been integral to the establishment of new economic formations. (1982: 4)

He went on to argue that a study of (criminal) law and its violations during the colonial period would aid in understanding *inter alia* the process of the creation of wage labour and the incorporation of peasant societies into a capitalist mode of production, as well as providing important comparative material on 'practices of moral-political control which develop in response to conflicts spawned by class relationships of exploitation and domination constituting the capitalist mode of production' (1982: 10).

Although studies of colonial labour regimes and land policy and, indeed, the whole debate about the incorporation of pre-capitalist modes of production were not new, Sumner's book and especially the contributions by Shivji (1982) and Sweet (1982) on Tanganyika, Snyder (1982) on Senegal and Fitzpatrick (1982) on Papua New Guinea provided clear illustrations of the value that an analysis of colonial legal systems could play in understanding these processes.

Sumner's rejection of the evolutionist modernization model and adoption of the underdevelopment approach led him to emphasize the difference in the patterns and forms of social control between nineteenth-century Europe and Third World societies. Indeed, like Cohen, it was on this basis that he questioned the relevance of orthodox, developed-country criminology which assumed that such societies would experience the same set of transformations and social problems as the already developed societies and, hence, that similar solutions could be applied. Whilst there can be little argument with this proposition, the adequacy of the underdevelopment perspective as a theoretical basis for the analysis of contemporary Third World societies has been increasingly questioned within development studies.

This stress on the 'unique' characteristics of colonial and post-colonial societies also led Sumner to argue that recognizing the specific nature of the colonial and post-colonial state provided a basis for what he felt should be a major item on the criminological agenda: crimes by the state such as torture, genocide, illegal executions, corruption. His analysis of the colonial and post-colonial state was rather summary. He noted the inheritance of an autocratic colonial state that did not separate law from political administration and the 'exceptional distance between an over-centralised state and a mass of poor people' (1982: 28). He argued that, typically, such a state is 'sitting on a powder keg of class tensions', 'can rarely command respect' and because of divisions among ruling élites is unlikely to 'rely on an integrated, dominant class hegemony' but rather on coercion and terrorism.

The Marxist tenor of this analysis, perhaps, gives us a clue as to why Sumner's agenda for a criminology of the Third World has not been followed up to any great extent. The tide of Marxist analysis ebbed considerably in the 1980s, and the appropriateness and value of the application of variants of Marxist theory on state and class formation to the Third World have been questioned. This, coupled with the move of development studies and criminology away from macro-theory, has created a situation in which much of the theoretical underpinning of Sumner's approach has been eroded or disregarded. Ironically, many of the criticisms of modernization theory can also be levelled at the type of approach adopted by Sumner. Thus, for example, it shares the same form of determinism and assumes that the experience of colonialism and 'underdevelopment' is largely similar everywhere, failing to explain marked differences in rates and patterns of growth between contemporary Third World countries. Although the shift in the criminological agenda towards the 'crimes' of the state, the rich and multinational companies has given rise to some important work (for example Braithwaite 1984; Jones 1988; Baxi 1990), presenting an inverse image of the orthodox emphasis on 'crimes' of the poor, it equally risks the charge of ignoring important aspects of the daily reality of crime and victimization in these countries.

In a situation in which criminology appears to have made few gains in developing adequate 'descriptions' of crime in most Third World countries, let alone in producing usable theory, and in which development studies has largely continued to ignore crime, we are led to ask whether it is realistic or useful to attempt to develop a specifically Third World criminology.

Recognizing specificity and diversity

Birkbeck (1985), in response to Sumner (1982), Cohen (1982) and Huggins (1985), identified a problem in the way in which there was a tendency to use geographic terms and divisions as a surrogate for social diversity. He noted that the use of regional terms in criminology has meant: criminological studies undertaken in a specific area with no explicit attention to theoretical relevance; studies which recognize regional distinctiveness but do not apply a distinctive theory (for example Clinard and Abbott) on the grounds that causal factors are universal; and studies which claim that regional distinctiveness requires a distinct criminological theory (for example Sumner, Cohen, and Huggins).

As we have seen, the grounds for this last position are that 'societal conditions' are so different in the Third World from those in western Europe and North America – the home of criminology – that new theory is needed to take account of these conditions. In his critique, Birkbeck stressed the imprecision of terms such as the Third World, asking whether there is sufficient internal homogeneity and difference from the rest of the world to make the category analytically useful for criminology. Indeed he went further and accused Sumner *et al.* of gross stereotyping which belied the diversity of contemporary Third World societies and which was due, in part, to their theoretical emphasis on the unifying and determining nature of the colonial phase. He also raised the issue of their 'marked inability to handle post-colonial developments' (1985: 219) and questioned the relevance of the colonial material to an understanding of present problems. Finally he noted that whilst Sumner *et al.* had stressed the importance of analysing the creation and imposition of (criminal) law in the context of processes of economic change, state and class formation, they had not gone on to formulate a systematic criminological theory specific to the Third World.

Many of the problems identified by Birkbeck are shared by development studies, where there is a constant debate over the object of study and the theoretical integrity or analytical value of the systems of classification, and their associated indicators, which have been used to discriminate between different countries or societies. The relative decline of macro-theory and the increasing differences between regions and countries in terms of standard quantitative indices such as rates of economic growth, levels of per capita income, infant mortality rates, as well as less easily quantifiable criteria like human rights, have led to a situation in which the generalizations of the 1950s to the 1970s seem questionable. The outcome, as noted earlier, appears to have been an acceleration of the deconstruction of development studies into a range of more or less technical specialisms and intervention techniques together with a recognition that, as 'cultures' vary, interventions must be locally appropriate and that, if they are to be sustainable, there must be 'community participation'. Much of the emphasis is on local solutions to local problems.

Birkbeck's largely pragmatic conclusion was that rather than discussing all criminological theory in terms of whether it is regionally or societally specific, it is more realistic to accept that some theory is and some is not specific and that, instead of developing new and distinctive theories, the existing ones should be carefully tested in different Third World settings.

Our position is that it is important to begin by recognizing the specificity and diversity of Third World societies. By this we mean acknowledging that regions, nations and, as nations are often artificial territorial constructs of colonialism, social groups in the Third World, all display wide variations in culture as well as in economic, social and political institutions. It also involves recognizing, as we discuss in more detail below, that, despite the generally shared experience of colonialism (which itself is not a unified category) and insertion into the world economic system, societies in the Third World have a pre-colonial history. This means that continuities between this past and the present (the *longue durée*) are at least as significant for developing an understanding of these societies as the relatively epiphenomenal colonial period.

A major problem lies in knowing where to pitch the level of specificity. It is perfectly possible to undertake criminological work at a national level, or, following Young and Matthews (1992), to disaggregate to a lower geographical and social level. This has been done in many Third World countries. However, we would argue that this work has frequently lacked a more general and diachronic analysis of the context of crime, criminalization and social control, such as the nature of the state, processes of class formation, and the existence of and relationships between civil and political society. In the following sections of the paper we seek to demonstrate, through the example of sub-Saharan Africa, both the problems involved in applying explanatory approaches derived from developed country experience and the need for any criminology to be rooted in an analysis of the specificity of these societies. (We realize that by taking the societies of a sub-region as our object we also expose ourselves to the charge of overgeneralization.)

Models of transformation: the problem of exogeny

We start by referring to Stan Cohen's (1985) discussion of the transformations of the master patterns for controlling deviance. Cohen's outline of the first major transformation noted a number of key characteristics: the increasing involvement of the state in deviancy control with a centralizing, bureaucratic, rationalized apparatus for control, punishment, care, cure: the differentiation and classification of deviant groups together with the emergence of monopoly-seeking experts; the segregation of deviants into prisons and asylums; and a shift in focus from body to mind. In his 1982 article Cohen assumed that elements of this pattern were imposed as part of the colonial criminal justice system and retained after independence.

However, a number of the key characteristics of this transformation were missing or assumed different dimensions. Whilst the colonial state did become heavily involved in deviancy control, this was, as the contributors to Sumner's volume indicated, mostly restricted to the criminalizing of behaviours of the indigenous population which were perceived as antithetical to the creation and maintenance of capitalist economic and social relations, and to the subsequent processing of such criminalized offenders. In the British African colonies not only were the bulk of court appearances of this kind, but most of them were dealt with in so-called 'native' courts or tribunals presided over by members of local indigenous élites (Clegg and Harding 1985). It would be difficult to describe these as either bureaucratic or rational. In addition, there is good evidence (for example Hailey 1950) that a considerable proportion of the indigenous population continued to use alternative means of dispute resolution outside the formalized system implemented by the colonial state. There were few signs of differentiation and classification (except between colonizers and colonized) or of the emergence of experts. Prisons, which were part of the colonial inheritance, were not for behaviour change but punishment and, indeed, the colonial authorities tended to favour the use of extra-mural penal labour as a cost-effective alternative. Finally, it would be hard to find evidence of any evidence of a shift from body to mind as the object of penal repression, unless one adopts Fanon's (1961) interpretation of colonialism as cultural imperialism.

It is important to note the exogenous origin and the colonial context, as the thrust of Cohen's (and to some extent Foucault's) argument was that these changes in patterns of deviancy control were intimately, if not determinately, related to other secular changes in European society during the eighteenth and early nineteenth centuries. These changes had not occurred in sub-Saharan Africa at the time of colonialism and, as outlined below, many still have not occurred. Thus, without adopting Sumner's position in its entirety, it would be more accurate to identify a colonial criminal justice model which had local variations but which did not accord in nature or context with transformations in Europe.

There are similar difficulties in respect of the destructuring movement identified by Cohen, summarized as 'away from' the state, the expert, the institution, the mind. Despite the fact that indigenous dispute settlement in Africa (and elsewhere in the Third World) appears to have been a major source of inspiration for early proponents of community justice in developed countries and, in adapted forms, continues to deal with a large range of conflicts and disputes, there is little evidence of the destructuring movement having been adopted by the formal state system in sub-Saharan Africa. This is puzzling given the extent to which decentralization and participation are currently popular in other fields. Certainly, there are many advocates of an increased use of indigenous forms of dispute settlement (for example Adeyemi 1990), including Cohen (1982) himself. However, given the nature of the transformations under colonialism, this seems not so much advocacy of a move 'away from the state' as of a move 'back to' forms of indigenous processes and institutions which, as we discuss below, display aspects, such as patriarchy and control by élites, which would have been disapproved of by community justice advocates.

Cohen had clear doubts about the reality of the destructuring movement and tended to see, instead, the continued voracious absorption of deviancy control into the centralized apparatus of the state. Using Foucault's concept of disciplinary power, he also noted the way 'the system penetrates the space of the family, the school and the neighbourhood' (1985: 83). Once again, it is not easy to find any evidence of this, or of the extension of the carceral archipelago or the development of Donzelot's (1979) tutelary complex in our region and, as Fitzpatrick (1988) indicates, this may be the case in other Third World societies. As we outline briefly below, the nature of the state, of civil society, the place of family and kinship, all appear to be sufficiently different and specific to doubt the applicability of these approaches.

Modernization, post-colonialism or the longue durée

At this point we are left with some major questions. Are we dealing with a situation of time-lagged and partial transfer of patterns or systems of social control – a position very similar to the generalizations of varieties of modernization theory? Is the colonial experience so determining that the nature of the post-colonial state, social formations and, possibly, of systems of social control are predicated on this and require a different history and discourse of the kind advocated by Sumner? Or, taking into account the *longue durée* of African societies, do we need to write a history of quite specific, and different, transformations in patterns of social control?

One of the key sets of issues which needs to be addressed in the context of these questions centres around the nature of the state and civil society in the region under discussion. We would argue that the way in which these are conceptualized is likely to have profound implications for the development of a criminology that responds to the specificity of societies in the region. Unfortunately, lack of space allows us to do no more than sketch an outline here. This outline is drawn from some recent work in development studies which has begun to address questions of the state, politics and administration in the context of the economic reform programmes associated with structural adjustment. In this literature a major question, given the current concerns with poor economic performance and authoritarian government, is the extent to which political liberalization, if achievable, is likely to provide conditions for more effective economic management. We do not propose to address this, but a useful summary can be found in Healey and Robinson (1992).

The interventionist state: modernization and Marxist models

Concern with the nature of the post-colonial state has, in fact, been a persistent feature of development studies discourse since the early 1960s. Initially, this was partly due to the dominant consensus that the state should play a major role in the promotion of national unity and economic and social development. Modernization theorists were also concerned with identifying the social and economic conditions which would allow new states to develop stable and democratic political structures. On the basis of their largely evolutionist and structural functionalist perspective, the history of already developed European and North American societies was used to identify various functional prerequisites such as high levels of mobility, urbanization, industrialization, literacy and the development of civic culture. The rapid demise of multipartyism and the emergence of varieties of single-party and military regimes in sub-Saharan Africa (and elsewhere) was not, at the time, seen as necessarily a hindrance to development. There were claims (for example Apter 1965) that the heterogeneity of the societies and uneven internal development might mean that single-party, authoritarian rule was more likely to be conducive to modernization, stability and growth and that it was essential for the state to have autonomy to initiate and implement effective economic and social policies. Others (for example Geertz 1963) were, from the start, more pessimistic, pointing to the way in which 'primordial loyalties' could undermine attempts to build a modern political and administrative system. However, the general tenor of the period was one of commitment, both by outside commentators and much of the African élite, to 'statism', in which the interventionist state was seen as continuing to play the central economic role that had been a characteristic of the late colonial period. Lack of democracy tended to be explained or justified by reference to the specificity of African political traditions or the need to promote national unity.

From a Marxist perspective (shared, as we have seen, by Sumner), the rapid rise of various forms of authoritarian regime, the persistence and deepening of inequality could be explained largely in terms of continuities between the colonial and post-colonial state, processes of indigenous class formation set in train during the colonial period and the peripheral nature of such societies. This gave rise to an extensive literature which attempted to grapple with the problem of applying Marxist concepts of class and class formation in a situation where the classic signposts increasingly appeared to be absent. Apart from difficulties in characterizing the nature of the mode of production or, rather, the articulation between different (for example subsistence or peasant and capitalist) modes of production and, thus, the nature of and relationships between social formations, the state presented a particular problem. Given the low level of development of an indigenous private industrial and commercial sector and the major economic role played by the state, the question of who controlled the state assumed particular pertinence.

Whilst there is no space here to analyse the debate in any detail, it can be noted that, with the recognition of the weakness of an indigenous capitalist class, it proved difficult not only to maintain the use of terms such as 'national' bourgeoisie, but also to see this class as politically or economically dominant. Instead, there was a growing tendency to identify, as the core of a dominant class, the occupants of the state, sometimes known as a 'bureaucratic' bourgeoisie or even 'state class'. The argument here was that as the state controlled access to key economic resources it became the major avenue for access to capital as well as political power. Indeed it has been argued that the state itself became a key factor in the process of class formation (Young 1988). The links between this class and the nascent entre-preneurial bourgeoisie were also extensively debated (for example Leys 1976; Mamdami 1976; Saul 1976; Swainson 1980). Sandbrook (1982: 80) noted that there appeared to be 'an inversion of the usual relationship between economic and political power; those who control, or have influence upon, the state apparatus have often sought to translate their political power into economic power, thereby joining the indigenous bourgeoisie'. Thus, much of the Marxist discourse came to focus on the 'over-determined' (namely Alavi 1972; Leys 1976) nature of the post-colonial state as a key problematic. In this, the emphasis was on the way in which the 'autocratic and hegemonic imperatives of the colonial state endured beyond independence and provided the organisational framework for its post-colonial successor' (Healey and Robinson 1992: 22). This was a similar perspective to that used by Sumner.

The weak state: patrimonialism and the longue durée

However, by the 1980s, particularly in response to the difficulties of applying Marxist class analysis, commentators were beginning to argue that class was of limited value in understanding African society and politics. As Sandbrook summarized:

> What emerged from colonial rule were overwhelmingly peasant, not capitalist societies. Peasants are notoriously difficult to mobilise on a national class basis . . . social stratification has not yet crystallised sharp rural class divisions. There is a small sector of capitalist production,

mainly in cities. However, the modern capitalist classes, the bourgeoisie and proletariat, are still embryonic. Class alone fails to explain African political life. (1985: 63)

This theme is repeated, with variations, in the literature of the last decade. The recognition of the absence of the formation of a hegemonic bourgeoisie, of an apparent disjunction between state and civil society, of the only partial incorporation of significant sectors of the population – the 'uncaptured peasantry' (Hyden 1980) – all led to a search for alternative forms of explanation that better matched the specificity of sub-Saharan African societies. Allied to this was the mounting evidence of low or negative economic growth, infra-structural collapse, increasing external indebtedness, persistent fiscal crises (in part due to unsustainable levels of public expenditure), growing poverty and inequality, which shifted attention in the 1980s to the theme of the decay of the post-colonial state. The terms 'weak' or 'soft' came to be used to describe a state which, despite having a relatively powerful armoury of control mechanisms, lacked legitimacy and was unable to prevent political secession and the rampant development of a parallel economy (namely MacGaffey *et al.* 1991; Maliyamkono and Bagachwa 1990).

A major focus has been on the anatomy of 'personal rule' and patrimonialism. Although there have been various formulations, the tenor of such explanations has been the way in which patron–client relationships 'founded on an intricate and informal network of personal alliances which link communities in a pyramidal manner' provide 'the main form of social articulation and the primary form of linkage between state and society' (Healey and Robinson 1992: 28, 29). The state, as the major avenue of access to resources and the main source of rewards, is central to this process. Politics is largely about competition for access to and control of rewards and the ability to use these both for personal advancement and to maintain the networks.

In a recent book, Bayart (1993) has placed this in a wider historical perspective. Influenced by the Annales school and Braudel, he has emphasized the way in which the continuity of African formations over the *longue durée* has been hidden in comparison with the highlighting of episodes of European penetration. The thrust of his argument is that much of the writing on Africa ignores the indigenous roots of the African state and fails to grasp the continuity of social formations and social processes through the colonial period. Thus, the process of élite formation, although accelerated during the colonial period, generally predates colonialism and independence represents a decisive point only in that it enabled access to and control of the greatly increased resources of the post-colonial state.

Bayart goes on to argue that the distinction between a 'bureaucratic' and a 'business' bourgeoisie is overdrawn. Indeed, like Hyden (1983), he doubts the value of using the term bourgeoisie in sub-Saharan Africa, given the absence of a significant private, modern, productive sector and the lack of a classic bourgeois ethos. Instead, he argues that it is more fruitful to look at the long-term process of dominant class formation through what he terms 'the reciprocal assimilation of élites'. He also argues that the peasantry is not sufficiently homogeneous to be seen in class terms.

Whilst Bayart shares the view that African politics can be seen in the terms of patron–client networks, he warns that these should not be seen only in terms of family, kin or ethnicity. Networks are, in practice, extremely heterogeneous, providing vertical and horizontal links which transcend but do not nullify divisions of income, power and status. Networks also have to be maintained through the distribution of rewards. In this sense, 'the social struggles which make up the quest for hegemony and the production of the state bear the hallmarks of the rush for spoils in which all actors – rich and poor – participate in the world of networks' (1993: 37). Interestingly this leads Bayart to a rather classic explanation of 'delinquency' in which the poor are just copying the criminal tendencies of the rich.

An important aspect of Bayart's approach is his stress that the post-colonial state in Africa cannot, any longer, be taken as an exogenous structure as characterized by modernization and dependency theory. 'It functions as a rhizome of personal networks and assures the centralisation of power through the agencies of family, alliance and friendship in the manner of ancient kingdoms . . .' (1993: 261). As such, he emphasizes that there is no clear distinction between civil and political society and that 'the private order is not separate from that of the state' (1993: 160).

The purpose of this, very partial, outline of some of the literature on the African state is to indicate the growing recognition that many of the classic perspectives used both in development studies and, by extension, African criminology have not sufficiently grasped the specificity of African societies. In the search for parallels, Callaghy

(1988) has mentioned the early mercantilist state in Europe and Bayart has pointed to Greek city states, the Hellenic monarchies and the Roman empire, thus stressing that Africa is not 'pathological'. Whilst too much value should not be placed on these parallels, they do indicate that extreme caution needs to be exercised in using criminological theory produced in the context of developed societies or based on ideas that African society has been sufficiently transformed to make such theory relevant.

Prospects for change

We do not propose to debate here the prospects for the installation of more democratic forms of government in Africa. One of the problems with the present emphasis on 'good government', and the tying of aid to this, is that it still presents the western model as one to emulate, both as a value in itself and because it tends to correlate liberal democracy with efficient economic management (ODI 1992). If we accept the view that the most useful parallels are with, for example, the early European mercantilist state, or post-independence nineteenth-century Latin America, then it may take a considerable time for the patrimonial state to decline and for the sort of robust capitalist class that Hyden (1983) saw as necessary for democracy and efficient economic management to emerge.

Within such a perspective it seems unlikely that we can expect the reform of the existing African 'state' justice systems into something that would accord with the concept of professionalized justice that Maureen Cain (1988) saw as being able to offer a degree of protection to subordinate classes. As Ghai (1986), in a wider review of law and governance in Africa, has noted, few post-colonial governments have valued the rule of law or legality other than as rhetoric and have consistently relied on intimidation and coercion. Even if the more flagrant violations of human rights are eventually diminished by a mixture of internal and external pressures, it may be optimistic to expect the patrimonial state to introduce changes that would curb the 'corruption' and factional conflict which Bayart and others have seen as intrinsic to African political and economic life.

This pessimism was shared by Sumner, who felt that the 'limiting framework and demands of the international capitalist economy' were 'too strong to allow such measures as the full democratisation of the legal process, the reconstruction of criminal codes to penalise more serious crimes (such as ministerial corruption) and the revival of mediation and restitution' (1982: 38). However, two points need to be made here. Firstly, it is more relevant, in Africa, to look for endogenous limitations to criminal justice reform than exogenous ones. Secondly, it is not so much a question of reviving mediation and restitution – which are already widely used – but of examining the context in which they are used and for whose benefit.

Some elements of an African criminology

Given the widespread abuse of human rights both by the state and armed opposition groups and, indeed the wholesale breakdown of 'law and order' in many parts of Africa, as well as the pervasive oppression of women and children and the normality of 'corruption' and the parallel economy, it is difficult to construct a conventional agenda for criminology. In such a situation, leaving aside the more classic problem of the conflict between imported and indigenous 'law', constructing definitions of 'crime' or 'deviance' is itself far more problematic than Sumner envisaged. In this concluding section we do not intend to develop a full agenda but, instead, to draw attention to the importance of researching the wide range of mechanisms for handling disputes and imposing social control which lie outside the formal state system. Much important work on crimes of the state, corruption, illegal economic activity, oppression of women, children and ethnic minorities will continue to be carried out by journalists and researchers who are not explicitly relating their work to criminology.

The 'state' system

Our experience is that conventional, quantitative studies of the state criminal justice system in Africa are likely to pay only minor dividends at present. There are a number of reasons for this. Firstly, the official figures on reported crime (when available) are of even less value for a descriptive understanding of the nature, frequency and distribution of criminalized behaviour than elsewhere. This is largely because the majority of such behaviours go unreported, are not necessarily perceived as crime, and are dealt with through the wide range of non-state institutions and processes which we discuss below. Secondly, detection rates are extremely low and this, combined with the widespread use of police 'discretion', means that cases and persons taken to court are unrepresentative, biased towards those who do not have the benefit of protection or 'discretion'. Thirdly, the small range of alternative sentences open to the courts, tends to make sentencing a relatively mechanical process.

In our study of decision-making in urban magistrates courts in Kenya and Zambia (Clegg *et al.* 1988; Clegg and Harding 1990), we adopted a more qualitative approach which allowed us to focus on process and discourse in the court. This provided significant evidence of the extent to which, in Zambia at least, the inherited colonial procedural code is undergoing a process of indigenization. A key part of this appears to be the extent to which the prosecution is ready to encourage and magistrates are prepared to allow cases in which there is *de facto* evidence of a felony to be withdrawn on the application of the victim, on the basis of restitution and reconciliation. We feel that this type of study (see also, for example, Cole 1990) is likely to throw more light on the operation of the formal, state system, how offenders are processed and how 'law' is being reconstructed in practice than those which rely solely on administratively generated data.

Pluralism and informal justice

Whilst significant numbers of offenders are processed by the state system in Africa, it is our contention that criminology in Africa must begin with a recognition of the extensive and pervasive role played by a whole range of non-state institutions and processes of dispute handling and social control as well as a concern with the nature of their articulation with the state. A first step in this would be to produce an adequately theorized account of what has often been termed legal pluralism, in the countries of the region. There is also the question of whether, rather than using the concept of legal pluralism, which makes distinctions between legal orders, a more sociological approach should adopted. Following Gundersen's (1992) concern with relating the 'law' which emerges in dispute settlement arenas to the power relations and norms within the community, it may, in the end, be more useful to conceptualize the object of study as a plurality of normative orders and systems of social control.

One of the immediate problems in getting to grips with pluralism is the absence of an adequate typology. The early dichotomy drawn between colonial law and indigenous law is clearly inadequate in the contemporary period and was over-simple even in the colonial period (Clegg and Harding 1985). As Santos (1992), in a more general overview, has noted, the dividing line between state and non-state has become increasingly difficult to draw with the contemporary pro- liferation of infra- and supra-state institutions. Merry (1992) has drawn a distinction between state law, popular justice and indigenous or local law. She identifies popular justice as a legal institution located on a boundary between the two others. Popular justice is linked to the state because it is often supervised and financed by the state, with powers to impose recognized penalties such as fines or imprisonment. The links with local law 'develop out of the myriad mechanisms of social control and conflict management existing within the family, village, neighbourhood and organisation' (1992: 163). Her illustra- tions of popular justice in post-colonial societies refer to the large range of 'courts' and 'tribunals', mainly established since indepen- dence, which have aimed to revive elements of indigenous law and procedure and have been ideologically justified in terms of a critique of colonialism and the imposition of a foreign legal order. Her definition could, however, also apply to the so-called native courts and tribunals which were a characteristic element of the colonial justice system in much of sub-Saharan Africa.

Merry's conclusion is that popular justice in post-colonial societies seems more clearly an extension of state law than elsewhere and has served to reinforce the power of existing élites rather than empower- ing local people. This should not be surprising. Apart from the small number of 'socialist' regimes, such as Mozambique (Sachs and Welch 1990) which did genuinely aim to create popular justice, the ideological content of the critique of western legal systems was often deeply conservative, stressing the values of a social order based on hierarchies of gender, age and wealth. This reactionary indigenous response, which is more concerned with maintaining and reproducing hierarchy than empowerment, needs to be differentiated from the concept of popular justice. Neither does Merry examine indigenous or local law, appearing to be content to leave it as a residual non-state category. In reality it is necessary to approach this concept of local law with some care. As Le Roy (1985) has pointed out, much contemporary 'local law' reflects new forms of state penetration into local communities and, as such, differs from the ideal type of 'folk laws' (namely Popisil 1971). Snyder (1981) and Chanock (1985) have also stressed that much of the so-called customary law of the colonial period in Africa was itself constructed in the interaction between imposed European law and indigenous processes of dispute settlement. Moore (1986), in an account of legal and political ideas and practices among the Chagga people of Kilimanjaro, has attempted to document this process of interaction and trans-formation over a longer period.

This recognition of the diachronic nature of forms of indigenous law and settlement processes is important in two ways. Firstly, much of the original advocacy of alternative or informal justice drew its ideological support from a romantic vision of largely mythical simple, natural, consensual communities. However, as many commentators (for example Fitzpatrick 1992) have noted, the communities which provided the material base for this manufactured Utopia had already begun to be penetrated by capitalist social relations and, as Merry (1982) stressed, dispute settlement was often coercive and controlled by local élites. This should alert us to the danger of a facile antithesis between imported state law and indigenous community-based law and of compounding this with the equally facile antithesis between the 'bad' state and the 'good' community. Secondly, it indicates that it is necessary to focus on the forms of articulation between state and non-state on the grounds that forms of community-based justice may be 'deeply embedded in the historical process of state construction and state transformation and tend to represent a transitional moment in such a process' (Santos 1992: 140).

State penetration or the construction of élite power?

The main thrust of much of the criticism of informal justice has been that, in one way or another, in practice it represents an extension of the state, reflecting wider processes of decentering, penetration and absorption. In the context of sub-Saharan Africa this perspective is likely to be too simplistic. As we have attempted to outline, there are quite specific features of the state and of political and civil society which make it inappropriate to adopt varieties of liberal democratic or Marxist models. In this situation it is difficult to see the wide range of non-state institutions and processes of conflict management and social control simply as means by which the state reproduces itself.

In a recent account of popular tribunals in Mozambique, Gundersen (1992) has stressed the importance of looking at power relationships (class, gender, seniority) as the context for the substance of the 'law' produced in these tribunals and other non-state forms. The analysis of court discourse and decisions indicated fairly clearly the dominance of the lay male judges intent on upholding conservative values, often at odds with the official party ideology. Gundersen's underlying argument appears to be that the egalitarian, consensual community is a myth, and that more powerful members of the community will use non-state forms of justice institution to maintain or reinforce hierarchy and the associated sets of values. The work of Martin Chanock (1978; 1985) on the development of customary law in Malawi and Zambia during the colonial period provides clear evidence of a similar process of the reinforcement of patriarchy and seniority – a theme also stressed by Bayart.

Thus, rather than adopting the extension of the state perspective, we would argue that it is more useful to see non-state judicial and conflict management institutions as sites of power which play a significant role in the long drawn out process of élite formation described by Bayart. In this perspective, control of such institutions is likely to confer significant local economic and political advantages. Similar conclusions have been drawn by Fitzpatrick (1980; 1982) and Paliwala (1982) in their study of village courts in Papua New Guinea.

However, as one of us has indicated in a study of dispute settlement in the Solomon Islands (Clegg and Naitoro 1992), this is not just restricted to institutions sponsored by the state. Where the state is 'weak', and the boundaries between the state and the private order are blurred, as in much of sub-Saharan Africa, élites are likely to use the whole range of non-state institutions and processes to defend and enhance their power. A study of these could, thus, provide significant evidence of ways in which factional power is constructed and contested, social control exerted and disputed and definitions of normality and deviance negotiated or enforced. Given the exogenous nature of much of the state justice system and its definitions of crime as well as the general 'weakness' of the state, this seems a useful point to begin a criminology which links to some of the contemporary concerns of development studies.

In taking this position we are suggesting that Fitzpatrick was, perhaps, over-optimistic when he suggested the possibility of counter-power emerging or surviving in 'places where the viability of alternative traditions and the relative absence of disciplinary power have restricted the ability of state law to present an adequate synopsis of power and society' (1988: 196).

References

Abel, Richard L. (ed.) (1982). *The Politics of Informal Justice: Volume 1: The American Experience, Volume 2: Comparative Perspectives* (New York, Academic Press).

Adeyemi, Adedokun A. (1990). 'Crime and development in Africa: a case study of Nigeria' in Zvekic (ed.), *Essays on Crime and Development*.

Alavi, H. (1972). 'The state in the post-colonial societies of Pakistan and Bangladesh', *New Left Review*, 74.

Apter, D. E. (1965). *The Politics of Modernisation* (Chicago, Chicago University Press).

Baxi, Upendra (1990). 'Social change, criminality and social control in India: trends, achievements and perspectives' in Zvekic (ed.), *Essays on Crime and Development*.

Bayart, Jean-François (1993). *The State in Africa: the Politics of the Belly* (Harlow, Longman).

Birkbeck, Chris (1985). 'Understanding crime and social control elsewhere: a geographical perspective on theory in criminology', *Research in Law, Deviance and Social Control*, 7, 215–46.

Braithwaite, J. (1984). *Corporate Crime in the Pharmaceutical Industry* (London, Routledge Kegan Paul).

Burnham, Robin W. (1990). 'Crime, development and contemporary criminology' in Zvekic (ed.), *Essays on Crime and Development*.

Cain, Maureen (1988). 'Beyond informal justice' in Matthews (ed.), *Informal Justice?*

Callaghy, T. M. (1988). 'The state and the development of capitalism in Africa: theoretical, historical and comparative reflections' in Rothchild, D. and Chazan, N. (eds.), *The Precarious Balance: State and Society in Africa* (London, Westview).

Chanock, Martin (1978) 'Neo-traditionalism and the customary law in Malawi', *African Law Studies*, 16, 80–91.

Chanock, Martin (1985). *Law, Custom and Social Order: the Colonial Experience in Malawi and Zambia* (Cambridge, Cambridge University Press).

Clegg, Ian and Harding, Phil (1985). 'Criminal justice and the colonial state in East and Central Africa'. Paper presented to the Development Studies Association Conference, Bath University.

Clegg, Ian, Harding, Phil and Whetton, Jim (1988). *A Comparative Study of Magistrates' Courts in Kenya and Zambia*. Report presented to the governments of Kenya and Zambia and the ODA Swansea: Centre for Development Studies.

Clegg, Ian and Harding, Phil (1990). *Researching Courts: A Study of Urban Magistrates' Courts in Kenya and Zambia*. Papers in International Development, No. 2 Swansea: Centre for Development Studies.

Clegg, Ian and Naitoro, John (1992). 'Customary and informal dispute settlement in the Solomon Islands' in Bottomley, Keith, Fowles, T. and

Reiner, R. (eds.), *Criminal Justice: Theory and Practice Vol. 2* (London, British Society of Criminology).

Clinard, M. B. and Abbott, D. J. (1973). *Crime in Developing Countries* (New York, Wiley).

Cohen, Stanley (1982). 'Western crime control models in the Third World: benign or malignant?' in Spitzer, S. and Simon, R. (eds.), *Research in Law, Deviance and Social Control*, 4, 185–99.

Cohen, Stanley (1985). *Visions of Social Control* (Cambridge, Polity Press).

Cole, Bankole A. (1990). 'Rough justice: criminal proceedings in Nigerian Magistrates' Courts', *International Journal of the Sociology of Law*, 18, 299–316.

Donzelot, Jacques (1979). *The Policing of Families* (New York, Pantheon).

Fanon, Frantz (1961). *Les Damnes de la Terre* (Paris, Maspero).

Fitzpatrick, Peter (1980). *Law and State in Papua New Guinea* (London, Academic Press).

Fitzpatrick, Peter (1982). 'The political economy of dispute settlement in Papua New Guinea' in Sumner (ed.), *Crime, Justice and Underdevelopment*.

Fitzpatrick, Peter (1988). 'The rise and rise of informalism' in Matthews (ed.), *Informal Justice?*

Fitzpatrick, Peter (1992). 'The impossibility of popular justice', *Social and Legal Studies*, 1, 199–215.

Geertz, Clifford (1963). 'The integrative revolution: primordial sentiments and civil politics in the new states' in Geertz, C. (ed.), *Old Societies and New States: The Quest for Modernity in Asia and Africa* (New York, Doubleday).

Ghai, Yash (1986). 'The rule of law, legitimacy and governance', *International Journal of the Sociology of Law*, 14, 179–204.

Gundersen, Aase (1992). 'Popular justice in Mozambique: between state law and folk law', *Social and Legal Studies*, 1.

Hailey, Lord (1950). *Native Administration in the British Territories, Vols I and II* (London, HMSO).

Healey, John and Robinson, Mark (1992). *Democracy, Governance and Economic Policy: Sub-Saharan Africa in Comparative Perspective* (London, Overseas Development Institute).

Huggins, M. (1985). 'Approaches to crime and development' *Comparative Social Research*, 8, 17–36.

Hyden, Goran (1980), *Beyond Ujamaa in Tanzania: Underdevelopment and the Uncaptured Peasantry* (London, Heinemann).

Hyden, Goran (1983). *No Short Cuts to Progress* (Los Angeles, University of California Press).

Jones, T. (1988). *Corporate Killing: Bhopals Will Happen* (London, Free Association Books).

Le Roy, E. (1985). 'Local law in black Africa: contemporary experiences of folk law facing state and capital in Senegal and some other countries' in

Allott, A. and Woodman, G.R. (eds.), *People's Law and State Law, The Bellagio Papers* (Dordrecht, Foris Publications).

Leys, Colin (1976). 'The "overdeveloped" post-colonial state: a re-evaluation', *Review of African Political Economy*, January–April, 39–48.

MacGaffey, Janet *et al.* (1991). *The Real Economy of Zaire: the contribution of smuggling and other unofficial activities to national wealth* (Philadelphia, University of Pennsylvania).

Maliyamkono, T. L. and Bagachwa, M. S. D. (1990). *The Second Economy in Tanzania* (London, James Currey).

Mamdami, M. (1976). *Politics and Class Formation in Uganda* (London, Heinemann).

Matthews, Roger (ed.) (1988). *Informal Justice?* (London, Sage).

Merry, Sally (1982). 'The social organisation of mediation in non-industrial societies: implications for informal community justice in America', in Abel (ed.), *The Politics of Informal Justice*.

Merry, Sally (1992). 'Popular justice and the ideology of social transformation', *Social and Legal Studies*, 1.

Moore, Sally (1986). *Social Facts and Fabrications: Customary Law on Kilimanjaro 1880–1980* (Cambridge, Cambridge University Press).

ODI (1992). *Aid and Political Reform* ODI Briefing Paper London Overseas Development Institute, January.

Paliwala, Abdul (1982). 'Law and order in the village: Papua New Guinea's village courts' in Sumner (ed.), *Crime, Justice and Underdevelopment*.

Popisil, L. (1971). *Anthropology of Law: A Comparative Perspective* (New York, Harper and Row).

Ruggiero, Vincenzo (1992). 'Realist criminology; a critique' in Young and Matthews (eds.), *Rethinking Criminology: the Realist Debate*.

Sachs, Albie and Welch, Gita Honwana (1990). *Liberating the Law: Creating Popular Justice in Mozambique* (London, Zed Books).

Sandbrook, Richard (1982). *The Politics of Basic Needs: Urban Aspects of Assaulting Poverty in Africa* (London, Heinemann).

Sandbrook, Richard (1985). *The Politics of Africa's Economic Stagnation* (Cambridge, Cambridge University Press).

Santos, Boaventura de Sousa (1992). 'State, law and community in the world system: an introduction', *Social and Legal Studies*, 1, 131–42.

Saul, John (1976). *The State and Revolution in East Africa* (New York, Monthly Review Press).

Shivji, Issa (1982). 'Semi-proletarian labour and the use of penal sanctions in the labour law of colonial Tanganyika' in Sumner (ed.), *Crime, Justice and Underdevelopment*.

Snyder, Frank (1981). *Capitalism and Legal Change: an African Transformation* (London, Academic Press).

Snyder, Frank (1982). 'Colonialism and legal form: the creation of 'customary' law in Senegal' in Sumner (ed.), *Crime, Justice and Underdevelopment*.

Sumner, Colin (ed.) (1982). *Crime, Justice and Underdevelopment* (London, Heinemann).

Swainson, Nicola (1980). *The Development of Corporate Capitalism in Kenya 1918–1977* (London, Heinemann).

Sweet, C. (1982). 'Inventing crime: British colonial land policy in Tanganyika' in Sumner (ed.), *Crime, Justice and Underdevelopment.*

Young, C. (1988). 'The African state and its political legacy' in Rothchild, D. and Chazan, N. (eds.), *The Precarious Balance: State and Society in Africa* (London, Westview).

Young, Jock and Matthews, Roger (eds.) (1992). *Rethinking Criminology: the Realist Debate* (London, Sage).

Zvekic, Ugljesa (ed.) (1990). *Essays on Crime and Development* (Rome, United Nations Interregional Crime and Justice Research Institute).

4

Policing apartheid – the discourses of the South African Police*

MIKE BROGDEN

Introduction

> Our culture . . . our dispositions, skills, methods and techniques had much in common with those of a close-knit gang of thugs. We differed from other thugs in that we form part of the broader police community appointed to bring such thuggery to justice. We also differed from other thugs in that our dispositions and skills were employed 'constructively', in terms of the government's aims and policies that were being furthered by our operations. (Captain Dirk Coetzee in sworn testimony of his experiences in the Security Branch of the South African Police)[1]

In South Africa, the practices of a police force that has regularly maimed, tortured and assassinated those whom it is conventionally bound to protect have ceased to shock. The record of deaths of unarmed people from Sharpeville to Boipatong is unique for a force which claims a genesis in the Peelian tradition (Van Heerden 1982). In its unashamed use of torture, it has a barbaric record (Foster, Davis and Sandler 1987; Fernandez 1991). With continuing revelations of rampant deaths in custody, until the election of President Mandela,

---

*This chapter was written before the election of the new, non-racist South African government and the subsequent transformation of the South African Police (SAP) into the South African Police Service (SAPS). Necessarily much of the culture illustrated above is now under sustained critique, internally by South African police officers, as well as by external commentators. That culture, however, reflects a particular moment in police history. Despite the fact that many welcome changes are being slowly introduced into the SAPS, the new government is faced with a particular historical legacy that requires organizational and legal, as well as cultural, change if that particular police force is to have a new, consensual, future.

there was little concrete evidence of change in institutional and individual practices.

There is one sense in which the South African Police (SAP) remains exceptionally peculiar. Many institutional discourses seek to provide for the credibility or legitimacy of the organization to a potentially critical client group. As the novelist Rian Malan has recently pointed out, one abnormality of the late apartheid state was its relative honesty. In its myopic commitment to the norm of white supremacy, the state and its police institution rarely saw the need to regret actions which most other police forces would seek to conceal or excuse. The discourse of the South African state in relation to policing is notable for its relative bluntness in describing the morally indefensible. Police discourse in South Africa is not a language of legitimation – if by legitimation we mean justification. Pretoria's police generals – as in the attempt to disparage Dr Gluckman's revelations over custodial deaths[2] – have not recognized that an occasional act of contrition or explanation might be desirable if the police of South Africa are to be purged. Despite certain justificatory attempts by the white South African state in the face of the 'total onslaught' (Posel 1984) of the mid-1980s, little recognition of guilt has appeared. The brutal character of South African policing has been reduced to a simple problem. The state has never evidentially sought to indulge in the apologetics that a legitimatory discourse implies.

Conventionally, there are at least three quite different levels of police discourse. In western societies, there is the formal state portrayal of the police institution and of its accountability relation, the vocabulary of accountability and of consent. Secondly, there is what Reuss-Ianni (1983) once described as the management culture, the language of organization, of efficiency, and of crime control. Then there is the lexicon of the rank-and-file culture – seeking to depict the pragmatic realism of those at the rough end of policing. In South Africa, these three languages share such common resonances that in effect they often appear as monothetical. It may be that the immediate task facing the minister of law and order in Pretoria is different from that of the white sergeant in the Platteland of the Cape. But their discourses contain similar symbols, common conceptions of the priorities of policing, and of an indistinguishable destiny.

One qualification, however, is important. Despite the efforts of some South African academics, we know little of the specific behavioural motives of the rank-and-file police. In South Africa, even in these post-apartheid times, much remains secret. Although the researcher is no longer threatened with penal sanction for publishing material deemed offensive by the police authorities, practices of obsessive secrecy remain. Our knowledge of the police culture and police discourses in South Africa inevitably draws for the most part on secondary sources and on the public pronouncements of in-house publications – such as the police journal, *Servamus*.

There is a further qualification. Police discourse has a multiple character. Within that wide rubric, there are subordinate systems of meaning and justification that sometimes diverge as well as converge. For example, the political commitment of the SAP as an institution, the maintenance of a society of institutional racial, class, and gender inequalities, may contrast with the occupational ambition of police officers. But more commonly they intersect. As Steytler (1990) has noted in relation to the career of the former security police captain, Dirk Coetzee, the security police's political commitment to assassinate black and white activists often overlapped with Coetzee's own perception of furthering a police career. Occupational discourse may supplement or act as a substitute for political discourse. It is not necessary for the latter to infiltrate the whole force. Where political theory fails to motivate members, the organizational structure and rewards may replace it and produce the same result – for example, in Coetzee's account, the Askaris (ANC guerillas 'turned' SAP) imbibed an occupational discourse which included the 'termination' of their former colleagues, while apparently denying the political imprimatur. The language of the apartheid police institution and that of occupational ambition combine to further policing practice. Multiple discourses therefore rarely reflect direct material relations but enjoy, through those complex intertwined relationships, a relative autonomy of practice. Recognizing the existence of different discourses within the same institution allows for a relative autonomy between discourse and practice, and explains some of the contradictions. In this chapter, we explore and account for three of those key South African police discourses, the political, the religious, and the occupational.

The functions of the discourses

The discourses of the SAP serve several functions. Like discourses in other police forces, they furnish a common set of symbols, shared meanings which bind the members of the force within one body. As such, they provide the cement of rank-and-file police culture. In this sense, the language of state policing in South Africa defines not just the police themselves but also the opposition, the symbolic *Swart Gevaar* (black danger). The major political, occupational and religious discourses converge so that the state police are defined in terms of their opposites. Whereas other police forces forge their identity through their allegorical opposites (Young 1983) – the roughs, the bucks, the toe-rags and so on – South African discourse uniquely constructs its own social unity through a disparagement of the majority population. As Fernandez notes of the SAP rank-and-file: 'Many are still besieged by a "skop, skiet, and donder" mentality which brooks no cheekiness from Blacks' (Fernandez 1991: 48).

Secondly (Brogden and Shearing 1993), the discourses connect the rank-and-file culture to police management culture and to the culture of the apartheid state. Discourse is the major device by which state interests – the exigencies of white domination – are linked to the practical occupational problems of rank-and-file policing. Police discourse links state problematic with the occupational problematic. The discourse of the SAP serves as an easing device that lubricates the relationship between rank-and-file and state.

> This protection that enabled us to operate above the laws of the country and above the regulations of the police, . . . was vested in a culture belonging to a clique that is more like a close-knit family. The culture is a syndrome of arrogant exclusiveness – of being above the law – of secrecy, necessity, loyalty to one another, mutual trust and mutual understanding, and of a very special relationship between superiors and subordinates. Aspects of this culture, such as the exclusiveness, secrecy, and necessity are explicitly and implicitly respected by the rest of the police force and by the subservient community at large . . . (Coetzee 1991: 1)

This culture is reinforced in the intimacy of the police canteen, the work-group, and the patrolling Casspir. It is most evident in the policing of the rural areas where the structures of apartheid have been most resistant to change. In South Africa, occupational discourse, reflective in part of the cop culture, rarely diverges from the imperatives of the larger state.

Socialization into police discourse – the case of the Patrys Junior Detective Club

The common discourse of the SAP is not simply a product acquired through the course of the police career. It certainly expresses the cultural attributes of policing as a masculine – white – occupation. However, it draws primarily upon the normal education of the white South African male. Many current South African police officers underwent a unique anticipatory socialization in the culture and language of policing. One hitherto unexplored feature of this socialization lies in the youthful experience of many present-day senior officers within the Junior Detective Club. Until the 1970s, for security reasons, the SAP relied mainly on white recruits. But that policy had obvious limitations – policing through a predominantly whites-only strategy could never provide adequate manpower. One resort was to recruit juveniles, guaranteeing amongst other things a reservoir of labour. As Minister Le Grand said, 'we're undermanned and using the schoolboys for help seemed like a good plan. It also gave them some idea of what a policeman is about . . . we really need them'.[3]

Early in the 1960s, South Africa's English-language press carried stories of an Afrikaner children's club (organized by the magazine *Patrys*) whose members were encouraged to report their parents to the authorities if they suspected them of being un-South African. *Patrys* was a monthly children's magazine published in Johannesburg by the Voortrekker Press, a publishing group of the Afrikaner Nationalist Party, whose most senior members were to be found on its board of directors. The magazine was for white children only, and published only in Afrikaans. The club's patron was the head of Johannesburg CID and the membership regulations made it clear that members were to report to the commandants at police stations and accompany the police on raids – invariably against black Africans. The club accepted members aged twelve to eighteen years, who were issued with Junior Detective membership cards and requested to affiliate themselves to their nearest police stations. The club membership card carried the words 'Would you like to be a detective? Are you twelve years old?' and carried the imprimatur 'Authorised to cooperate with the South African Police'. It was signed with the signature stamp of the chief commissioner of the SAP.

'I have again helped to arrest two Bantu' boasted the Afrikaner child in the pages of *Patrys*, adding 'I very much enjoy going along on these raids'. Another child asked if he could be paid for arresting black South Africans and was told that this could be arranged. Yet another Afrikaner boy's letter read :

I have gone along a couple of times with the police detective who handles the bloodhound to look for tracks and to help search for fingerprints. To which an editorial footnote commented 'Well done, young fellow!! You are indeed a true member of our Patrys Detective Club!' (quoted in Clarke 1969).

In his novel, *The Caterpillar Cop*, the crime writer James McClure quotes several similar letters from *Patrys*. A youth from the Orange Free State writes:

I spent nearly my whole holiday working as a member of the Detective Club. The station commandant said I was very useful to him as I arrested nine Bantu and one Coloured female. I also went on raids in the van. It was very nice.

Similarly, a thirteen year old from the Transvaal:

In our English-language oral exam, I had to pretend that I was a member of the Special Branch finding out if a man was a liberal. Because I belonged to the Detective Club, I knew the proper way to ask questions . . .

The junior edition of the magazine, circulated widely in Afrikaner junior schools, was little more than an indoctrination process in the 'Black Danger' and in the historical threat to the Volk from English-speaking South Africans – they are told how:

the English later punished our women and children, burned their houses down, and set their pastures alight. These concentration camps caused the deaths of 26,000 women and children through hunger and sickness.

The same age-group is told of the heroic young 'Sapie Greyling, a *volk* hero. The English never thought the children of the *Afrikaner volk* could be so valiant'.

South Africa's black people received more mention than non-Afrikaner whites, nearly all of it derogatory. A photo-strip series mirrored for juniors the adult account of the Great Trek on the frieze that adorns the 'Voodoo temple' of Afrikanerdom, the Voortrekker Monument in Pretoria. 'The building in the woods' had as its villain a savage, loin-clothed, African who is preoccupied with plunging his spear into whites to add to his collection of skulls. Read by the majority of Afrikaner children because of its wide and official circulation, *Patrys* boasted of the Boers' slaughter of black South African tribes in the early days and described the Afrikaner people as 'brought into being by God himself'. A story in the April 1973 edition entitled 'Brotherly Love', featured three South African policemen roaming illegally hundreds of miles inside Ian Smith's UDI Rhodesia, killing armed black Rhodesians who objected to illegal white minority rule in their country. Another story, in the same location, 'When the Cat's Away', encouraged the idea of the 'right' of white South Africans to roam southern Africa, shooting black people. One 'amusing' item is entitled 'How to scare the living daylights out of blacks' ('Jump out at them, dressed outlandishly!'). In the mean time, photographs were appearing in the pages of *Patrys* encouraging a kind of 'bounty-hunter' attitude by showing Detective Club members being paid for arresting black adults. One example is of fifteen-year-old members of the Patrys Detective Corps receiving ten Rand each from a police brigadier at the Police Wachthuis in Pretoria for apprehending a black man. The article notes that this child police force operated also in the then Rhodesia and south-west Africa.

Members were encouraged to form themselves into gangs with dramatic names and badges (one of the latter showed a black man caught in the sights of a rifle). In McClure's thriller, the dead 'Hennie . . . had formed a hunting pack of junior detectives, called the "Midnight Leopards"'.On the ground, these 'junior detectives' formed themselves into what were little more than teenage wolf packs which, on some occasions, conducted marauding sorties into black townships. The *Sunday Express* (30 January 1966) quotes one such example:

> Armed with blank-firing pistols and handcuffs, the four youth – all aged 16 – spent their school holidays arresting an average of 15 Africans a day – mainly for offences under the Pass and Tax legislation. They bought their own equipment and were planning to equip themselves with walkie-talkie sets.

The club disappeared from external scrutiny in 1975, after revelations of its quasi-Nazi nature appeared in the English-language press. That was the year in which draconian additions to South Africa's Official Secrets Act hid all police activities under a curtain of censorship. So it is not known if the club was disbanded or went underground. What is certain is that its membership totalled more than 25,000 and that its structure, its close official relationship with the SAP and the regular appearance of police recruitment advertisements in the columns of *Patrys* established it as the main recruiting source for the adult police force over a period of at least sixteen years.[4] Learning the norms and values of the SAP started early in South Africa.

The Afrikaner culture of the SAP

Recruits snared by the web of *Patrys* were one reason that the culture of the SAP became predominantly an Afrikaner culture. But that source fitted within a larger mosaic. In the years of South African English hegemony, vertical stratification divided the two white groups. English South Africans dominated the private professional areas. Afrikaners, and especially rural Afrikaners, occupied the lower ranks of state occupations. Post-1948, in the succeeding years of Afrikaner supremacy, state employment became the 'normal' vehicle for Afrikaner advancement. Policework, in particular, became an Afrikaner preserve. In addition to the state bias towards recruiting Afrikaners, the low-paid and humble status of the occupation ensured that – together with the state railways – it became almost the only job-reserved occupation into which ill-educated (and, before the war, illiterate) rural Afrikaners could enter. This process of *verafrikanisering* ensured that cultural forms of struggle entered into the institutional politics of the police force – the major site of that struggle being over the use of Afrikaans as the administrative language of the force (Van der Spuy 1990).

In the 1990s, the SAP has a more varied recruitment basis than twenty years ago. The late apartheid state largely overcame its fear of placing the defence of apartheid in the hands of black officers. Less than half of new recruits are white and there are increasing proportions of so-called 'coloureds', Indian and black officers. However, at the general staff level of some forty generals there are only three non-white generals, two Indian and one black. As the pyramid narrows, the proportion of whites greatly increases. Of those whites, the vast majority are of Afrikaner stock. Consequently, while the recruitment base might have changed over the years, the higher echelons of the SAP were dominated by the type of white male who had been socialized through the Patrys Detective Club. It is probable that until recently the majority of senior members of the SAP entered via that recruitment channel.

Secondly, despite the different racial composition of the 1990s, police culture remains Afrikaner culture (Brogden and Shearing 1993). At the general level, Indian, black, and 'coloured' police officers, like white officers, are subject to many of the same experiences of social ostracism from the majority community in South Africa. Officers from the 'non-white' races are especially liable to be placed in the front-line of confrontational policing in the townships. The state has perfected the policy – especially with regard to the reserve units of Municipal Police and of Kitzconstabels – of recruiting new officers from remote locations. This 'stranger-policing-stranger' policy, a remnant of imperial practice (Brogden 1987), has ensured that many black police officers are obliged to treat the SAP as a substitute community for the ones from which they have been excluded. As a result, black members of the SAP share many of the key attributes of police culture.

In earlier years, several commentaries had noted the tendency of black officers to assault their civilian peers (South African Institute of Race Relations 1947) and their tendency to act as black *SAP* rather than as *black* police. A more recent perception is articulated in a Capetown study:

> There is a racist Police culture that even black policemen take on. A black policeman tells jokes like an Afrikaner and speaks like an Afrikaner. He speaks and writes like them. There is a culture within which these people are trapped. We need a deep understanding of what these people are ensnared into. They tell jokes about Boesak and Tutu. These things overlap with religion. The police go for Conservative religion. It is a conservative culture. (quoted in Shearing and Mzamane 1992: 7)

The emblems and culture of the SAP have developed a surrogate affinity for them. Many black police officers appear to have internalized crucial parts of the Afrikaner discourse of the SAP.

Thirdly, as a key bastion of the white state, probably more than in any other country colonized by Europeans, police culture came to reflect in large part the imperatives of the state. Socialized at home into the Boer Herrenvolk, at school into the youth Voortrekker movements and the Patrys Detective Corps, through state and the Dutch Reformed Church into the defence of the Volk, and finally in the SAP itself, through the Afrikaanse Kultuurvereeniging van die Suid-Afrikaanse (AKPOL), the career SAP member had imbibed a culture in which the discourse of policing and of the state had both similar contents and similar imperatives.

AKPOL, established in 1955, was especially significant until recent years: 'because policemen felt a general need to express their Christian-National sentiments more fully within their own ranks and so foster a feeling of solidarity' (quoted in Van der Spuy 1990). The Association, with a membership of some 12,000 police officers, has as its symbol the Voortrekker Monument. While comprising only about 10 per cent of the total complement of the SAP, the Association's members operate as 'culture-holders' who work at cultural maintenance and reproduction both within and outside the force. Working with white youth groups, the Association promotes a cultural synthesis between state and church that has the police as its centre. Its commitment to the Afrikaner search for ethnic autonomy, is expressed in its motto, 'The trek continues' – an emotionally powerful reference to the history of Afrikaner struggle for survival and independence.

Institutions such as AKPOL serve to reinforce through the police career, the predispositions acquired through Afrikaner childhood socialization. The result is a style of policing in which occupational imperative combines with the political and religious dogmas that underpin the white state.

The discourses of South African Police

South African policework is sustained and legitimated by a circular ideology, a constellation of values rooted in the Christian-Nationalist conception of the 'Volk'. That belief system provides the discursive framework that justifies police violence and the criminalization of black people. It bridges the gap between state and the rank-and-file member of the SAP. It operates as a host culture that sustains the police culture. This wider culture has its roots in the key folk values of 'Afrikanerdom' that spawned apartheid. It is this culture of ethnic self-preservation which pervades and informs South African police culture. It is a culture which has created strategies of survival that have charted the Afrikaner triumph over the English, despite their Anglo-Boer war defeat, and has guided them for generations in their struggles with the native peoples of South Africa.

At the heart of the narrative of Afrikaner culture are several related discourses. First, a political discourse historically produces police officers as the defenders of an endangered 'civilization'. Secondly, a religious discourse represents state policing as part of a 'mission' bedrocked on the family unit. These twin themes are backed by a further, occupational, discourse which seeks to define South African police practices as essentially no different from police routines elsewhere. Police duties involve tough, pragmatic decisions and personal sacrifice the world over. South African policework is only

different in degree from that experienced by police officers universally.
Supporting these intertwined discourses are subsidiary vocabularies –
for example, of organization and of a technical professionalism.

These meanings connect and unify the functionaries at all levels of
the state from president all the way down to the rank-and-file police
member. As one of the chroniclers of Afrikanerdom, the policeman
and police historian Dippenaar, clearly understands it, it 'fortunately'
permits 'men of vision like Vorster' (a minister of law and order and
later prime minister) to 'connect with the police sub-culture'.[5] In this
history 'written from the belly of the beast itself' (Van der Spuy 1990:
86), the meanings that define the Volk and its mission are identified as
constituting a united crusade to maintain white supremacy. Political,
religious and occupational discourses lubricate the relations between
police and the larger state.

Political discourse – delegitimating opposition

SAP accounting is informed by a narrow ethnocentric view of history.
It is a selective chronicle that highlights the treachery of the British
and the blacks in the face of an heroic Afrikaner determination to free
the Volk from the yoke of repression. 'The history of South Africans .
. . mirrored the history of the South African Police. The two have
been, and are still, inextricably linked' (quoted in Steytler 1990).
These themes of sabotage by the blacks and British on the long
historical march are symbolized by the frieze of the 'great trek' from
British rule that decorates the 'Voodoo temple' of the Voortrekker
Monument, the Anglo-Boer, and the righteous wars against black
barbarism and treachery (Worrall 1972). The historical interpretation
that informs SAP political discourse weaves together several themes –
a social Darwinian explanation of political conflict, a demonology of
the communist enemy, a rigid equation of law with morality, the
assumption that policing priorities inevitably involve coercive
confrontations with the black subject mass, a denial of the value of
political accountability, and ethnic authority (or what Van der Spuy
(1990: 102) following Van den Berg calls a 'Herrenvolk Democracy').

In his South African version of a Reithian police history, Dippenaar
(1988) dismisses the entire history of black politics as a product of the
machinations of international communism and imperialism. This
'academic' rhetoric, reinforced by Pretoria scholarship, has sought to
drain political legitimacy from black struggle at the same time as it
has articulated the SAP's paranoid search for the enemies of the Volk.

That history contains an implicit explanation of deviance and of social disorder. As a University of South Africa criminology course text explains it:

> In every society there is constant polarization of forces which tend to violate the fundamental relations and those which tend to maintain them. Crime will tend to decline to the extent to which philosophies and values which seek to preserve the fundamental relations predominate. Should less conservative philosophies prevail, crime will tend to increase. (UNISA 1983: 95)

Van der Spuy has argued that this historical interpretation contains a critical subtext. It operates with a social Darwinian perspective of modernization and development (and one which draws sustenance, in part, from UNISA's criminology). In that thesis, the function of policing is simply to deal with the evolutionary less-civilized, and more primitive, peoples while they 'catch-up' with the civilized law-abiding. Former academic and Prime Minister Vorster summarizes traditional Afrikaner social science's view of crime and policing.

> Had our country been inhabited by a homogeneous population subscribing to a uniform political philosophy with a traditional appreciation of the norms of civilised society, and a thorough knowledge of and strict adherence to the laws of the country, the task of the Police would have been far more pleasant. However, as we do not live in such a country, the task of the Police is more difficult. The multi-racial composition of our population should be borne in mind. This results in the Police having to persuade people who fundamentally differ from each other and who respect their own distinct norms, to obey laws they do not understand and maintain a kind of order which is foreign to their nature. (quoted in Dippenaar 1988)

This historical discourse allows the Afrikaner culture to criminalize black resistance and to represent the 'ordinary' crime of the black townships as due not to the pressure cooker of communities artificially constructed and legally and socially debased by apartheid, but as innate to black tradition. As the tutor of such groups, the SAP necessarily has occasion to teach severe lessons to the backward pupils.

Secondly, in a long historical tradition, the SAP discourse operates with a conspiracy theory of politics. Confrontations and protesting crowds are mobs inspired by communist agitators. Where the police

have a bad reputation in the townships, it is because communist-
infiltrated agencies such as Radio Freedom incite the black population
to violence. Criticism is a communist-inspired 'smear' tactic to
discredit the police. 'Troublemakers', 'agitators', 'ringleaders' (*SAP
Annual Report* 1980: 7), 'terrorists' and 'radicals' conspire to
undermine law and order (De Witt 1988) by intimidating those
'ordinary persons who do not want to submit themselves to their
authority' (ibid: 33). 'Unrest' at school is due to the presence of
'trained guerillas' (*Annual Report* 1980) while the police killings at
places like Sebokeng and Viljoenskroon are seen as activities 'forced
on [the police] by mischievous, radical, agitators' (*Annual Report*
1988). Political action is thus deprived of any rational meaning. Black
and white resistants are not sane, but simple puppets manipulated
from Moscow. To these interpretations, there has been added a
discourse of black-on-black violence – the claim that black people are
ethnically predisposed to settle conflicts by force. The police role is to
do whatever it can to keep these primitive inclinations and the
activities which they promote within bounds.

> Faction fights have always been a part of the Zulu life-style. The reasons
> for the feuds are lost in antiquity, but it is considered an honourable
> tradition to carry on a vendetta from one generation to the next. Faction
> fights have no political connotations. They start without warning as a
> result of some provocative action or remark. (*SAP Yearbook* 1991: 83)

As Rauch (1991) points out, no one refers to the Second World War as
'white-on-white' tribal violence. Nor is the violence taking place in
Europe between Croats, Serbians, and Bosnian Muslims defined as
either tribal or white-on-white violence. The black-on-black theme
serves to blame blacks, rather than apartheid and its white authors,
for the depredatory experience of township life at the same time as it
elevates the SAP to the position of neutral referee arbitrating between
uncivilized peoples before a world audience. Latterly, black militancy
and resistance have been reconstructed through the political
vocabulary of *total onslaught* and later that of *revolutionary war*. In
the words of the former spy, Captain Craig Williamson:

> Law enforcement officers, such as members of the SAP . . . understand that
> the RSA is faced with a revolutionary onslaught which, if it is ever allowed
> to succeed, will plunge the southern tip of Africa into chaos. (*Servamus*
> 1981)

In the post-war years, the spectre of communism has been melded with the historical themes to mobilize the police to stand firm against resistance to apartheid (Van der Spuy 1990). Black opposition was a communist-inspired plot (deduced from the alignment of the South African Communist Party with the ANC), and it was the duty of the police, as champions of Christian-Nationalism, to resist it. This conception of communism and its implications for policing is outlined in the UNISA's 1983 criminology course guide.

> Communism today is a Marx inspired, Moscow directed, international criminal conspiracy against civilization, based on a God-denying philosophy of life, sustained by faith in the dialectic, backed by the devotion of its fanatical believers and to no uncertain extent by the armed might of the Red Armies. The RSA is today experiencing an armed and an ideological onslaught from the communist ranks. South Africans who have been indoctrinated with this ideology have adopted the fundamental relations as interpreted by communism and justify the violation of accepted South African fundamental relations on these grounds. (UNISA 1983: 97)

In this interpretive framework in which protest is individualized and pathologized (Van der Spuy 1990), law, order, and democracy are juxtaposed against the godless, communist forces of anarchy, or more simply, any point of view that is not conservative.

Thirdly, legal tradition has law as an all-determining imperative (Turk 1981). Law is viewed instrumentally and unproblematically. Thus the several Terrorism and Emergency Acts are a simple necessity. The role of the police under such legislation is directly an extension of their normal duties. Infringement of that legislation is only an extreme form of normal criminality. Police officers themselves enforce law which, remarkably, involves no discretion (Coetzee 1993). As the former head of police science at UNISA enunciated it, 'Law and order are not separate concepts. Law is order' (Van Heerden 1982: 12).

Political discourse contains a fourth element – the assumption that policing inevitably involves confrontation with black subjects, whether they be assemblies of industrial strikers, faction disputes at the mines, tribal groups at war, 'fanatical' crowds of black uprisers, demonstrators, and protestors. In this account of the policing of social problems, it is assumed that *normal* policing is *public order* policing – crimework in the discourse of the SAP is often an afterthought. While it is true that in practice most policework in western countries has a public order function as dominant practice (Brogden 1991), only in South African police discourse is that public order function given authoritative primacy over crimework. Secondly, such public order work necessarily involves the threat and often the use of state violence. It is assumed that the primary police skill is the ability to use force to terminate disputes. This perception of policework is reinforced by a discourse of weaponry and threat – from the yellow police patrol bakkie (resembling a mobile dog-catcher) to that emblematic submarine-on-wheels, the CASSPIR personnel carrier, to a range of personal armoury. Policing in South Africa is portrayed as maintaining law through armed force.

Fifthly, political accountability is regarded as anathema. Historical experience – specifically the Second World War conflicts over police loyalty to the imperial mandate of the South African state – had taught the SAP that political obeisance entailed schism and intra-police conflict. Discourse opposed the development of an accountability culture – being responsive to formal political accountability meant the resurrection of the Anglo-Afrikaner factions that divided the force in the 1940s. That schism had only been healed with the development of a disciplined force formally independent of government. In this historical account of the ethnic split in the force, in which the division between the dominant white groups is highlighted, the majority population – black people – are dummy players irrelevant to the serious *internal* problems of the SAP. Accountability to white society, in SAP discourse, has only increased the tensions within the organization. Accountability to black communities is literally beyond the pale.

Sixthly, in myriad pronouncements the SAP upholds its political mission by reference to claimed origins within the original London Metropolitan police (Coetzee 1993) and (in what elsewhere might be regarded as Orwellian double-talk) to democratic policing. For example, the police as the upholders of democratic principles had to bear the cost of international vilification during the emergency.

> The Government of the Republic, which had been democratically elected by the inhabitants of the country, decided to stand by its decision, despite the fact that this would inevitably lead to international isolation . . . The S.A. Police understood and supported the government. (Dippenaar 1988: 734)

By the 1970s, according to Dippenaar, South Africa was besieged by a multidimensional onslaught, orchestrated by communist imperialist powers and enacted by terrorist organization. The aim of this onslaught was the violent overthrow of the South African democratic state, and the destruction of its Christian values (Van der Spuy 1990). Inevitably the enemies of this democratic social order used 'tried and tested Communist techniques' to denigrate and subvert legitimate police actions under the rule of law.

> The Police swiftly identified the methods used by the subversive elements . . . (resisting) the attempted undermining of the democratic state by denigrating it and assailing its power bases and presenting them as corrupt – a tried revolutionary method in which the foreign media, in particular, participate. They placed the S.A.P. in the forefront of international criticism, and accusations of police brutality were spread in an unscrupulous manner. (*Annual Report* 1985)

Complaints against the police are a communist plot to subvert democratic South Africa. Those who aid the complainants – lawyers and the liberal press – are similarly castigated as agents of sedition.

Finally, these themes are interwoven with a remarkable presentation of the SAP – in an extraordinary reconstruction of the Reithian imagery – as an institution that is and always has been directly at the *service* of the *community*.

> Traditionally [the SAP] have been regarded as an organisation which renders service. This 'service' is regarded as a very important prerequisite for successful policing, as it not only promotes good attitudes and close co-operation, but also projects the image of the Force as a body of the authority of the State. (White Paper 1990: 7)

Similarly, state and police rhetoric have promoted a remarkable conception of police service:

> . . . policing in the Republic has indeed developed into a community service which at present forms the corner stone of an orderly society . . . Its activities are aimed at the lessening of conflicts and latent threats . . . to the orderly community: the informal pacifying of conflict by mutual relationships and the rendering of a variety of community services. . . . the community determines the roles and continually evaluates it in order to bring it in harmony with the changed structure. From the point of view of the Police, the person who accepts the role of maintaining law and order, that is the police officials, must in the executing of that role adapt his behaviour and the structure to the expectations of the community. (Minister of Law and Order Adrian Vlok, White Paper 1990)

Community, police social service, together with the notion of South Africa as a democratic defence against a defiling communism, are the key concepts in a political discourse that links the manifesto of the white state with the succeeding conception of the police as a Christian bulwark against evil. Criticisms are delegitimated by pathologizing their source. The political discourses of the SAP provide an interpreted history of social development which portrays the police not just as the thin blue line of civilization but rather as the active spearhead of Christian standards and social order.

Religious discourse – the police officer as worker-dominee

Many police forces incorporate elements of religion into their formal codes and practices. At a superficial level, the SAP is little different from some western police organizations in its adherence to religious totems. In the SAP, however, religion plays a central rather than a peripheral role as symbolized by the 'eternal symbols of the Force' namely the 'flag, banner and creed' (*Annual Report* 1985: 35). In the discourse of Afrikanerdom, the Calvinist creed of the Dutch Reformed Church is crucial to linking the state to its functionaries. Institutional religion plays a secular function in defining the functions of the SAP:

> it can only justly be claimed that the Force has, in the principles on which its duty has been performed, always maintained Christian norms and civilised standards. The Force has ensured the acknowledgement and maintenance of the individual freedom of faith and worship has ensured the inviolability of freedom in our country. The Force has at all times ensured the independence of the judiciary and equality in the eyes of the law as well as maintaining law and order and promoted the spiritual and material prosperity of its people. (Vlok, quoted in Van der Spuy 1990)

Religious discourse intertwines with political discourse. Law derived from God gives meaning to the role of the police as the bulwark of civilized order, resisting those who are unable to comprehend that state of Grace. Critically, state religion blesses the chasm between the police and the policed. For example, in police training, the ethics course sanctifies social divisions:

> race can be described as that above-personal historically determined grouping of people that came into being under the presiding hand of God,

and is associated with each other through spiritual-physical hereditary qualities that enable us to distinguish one group from another. (*Police Ethics Training Manual* 1991: 64).

The police mission is to guard over the lesser peoples of South Africa whose resistance to what God has proclaimed must be broken.

The creed that sustains Afrikanerdom and apartheid appears in a variety of mini-ceremonies through the police career. The South African Police Code of Honour illustrates the way that racial policing derives from the religious mandate given to the SAP through the medium of the Christian National Foundation – the theological justification of white superiority in guiding black people up the evolutionary path:

> As a member of the SAP that serves a nation with a Christian National Foundation, a nation that in its meetings at the highest level, acknowledges the honour and sovereignty of God above all else and therefore believes in an upright and honest way of life. I educate myself in the service of God and my country.

In the police creed, in the Code of Honour, in *Servamus*, and especially at the daily parade ceremonies, state religion confers blessings on these worker-priests. Policing, recruits are taught, is not simply an occupation but a sacred mission, a religious calling, in the life and survival of the Volk.

> It is so that the all-knowing God thought fit to exercise His authority on earth using the service of people, parents, officials of the Government. Therefore the wearers of the fine uniforms of the police are also the mandate-holders of God . . . (Minister Kruger quoted in *Argus* 1977).

In this occupational practice, the police officers serve as a kind of worker-priest (or dominee). As the SAP chaplain blessing a group of riot police, phrases it, the officers are 'children of God'.[6] The chaplains, conferring religious largesse at the daily parade, are central to the mediation of the police role through institutional religion. Police are Christian soldiers. Within this frame of meaning, police are defined as persons chosen by God to fulfil a sacred mission. 'Police work is a calling, like the work of a minister or a teacher' (Commissioner Van der Merwe[7]). Police are secular ministers. This calling requires police to promote the order of racial segregation – a divine order that is right and good even though only the chosen few have the intelligence to understand this. This lack of comprehension leads to resistance that makes policing difficult and regrettably coercive.

In the midst of the repression of the state of emergency of the 1980s, the Police Yearbook of the period reminded those officers who were suffering the hardships of the violent policing, that they did so on behalf of 'the King of Law and Order – Jesus Christ' (1985 Yearbook). For the South African Police, the 'thin blue line' is a line drawn by God in Deuteronomy and defended by God's workers. *Servamus* identifies police as:

> ministers of God . . . the front line of defence against the total breakdown of law and order. Police the world over must uphold their stance against this encroaching, patient evil.[8]

The fact that in this fight the police are often forced to use violence is a tribulation that they must face with courage. Strength is to be found in God, and it is for this reason that religious ceremonies such as the church service that accompanies police parades are so important. The discourse draws on the justifications central to the Afrikaner culture of which it is part to make police violence a sacred mission. .Far from being a source of humiliation and degradation, violence and the willingness to face violence is a source of pride and an act of sacrifice. Police officers have been chosen by God to perform the difficult task of maintaining God's order. They are an elected people within an elected people – an élite within an élite.

This conception is developed and given 'academic' legitimacy in courses offered by UNISA. In one of its texts, students, among whom are members of the SAP, are encouraged to see themselves as part of a struggle in which many institutions work together to 'counteract criminalism'. Central among these is 'the church', 'the prime bastion against criminalism' which works to harness 'man's innate religious elements in the struggle against disorderliness and criminalism' (UNISA 1983: 98). God and country are united because the laws of the state are, by definition, the laws of God. To obey the state is to obey God. To resist the state is to resist God and those who work to overcome this resistance must, as children and ministers of God, use the means at their disposal to uphold God's sovereignty.

> Evil and permissive force are almost unstoppably at work in the process of destroying authority in nearly every sphere (but) timeous and responsible action has, fortunately, always controlled this degeneration of life. (Minister of Law and Order Kruger, quoted in Van der Spuy 1990).

The religious discourse reinforces the denial of democratic, political accountability. According to a course document from the SAP College for Advanced Training, the police mandate is from God not from secular authority.

> The state has received its authority from God and has, in turn, given authority to the police. (quoted in Rauch 1991)

The Calvinist theory of the state is theocratic in that it sees law and state as finding their origin and legitimacy in the will of God. Therefore the state functionaries are required to enforce certain moral religious precepts. The effect of this is to remove secular claims for accountability. The relationship between the police and civil society is mediated through God and the state, removing the policed as an immediate point of reference for accountability – subversion tends to obviate the need for democratic accountability (Rauch 1991: 6).

The family as the pivotal social unit of Calvinist theology is moulded into service with religion in the constitution of this directive relationship between God and the SAP. Police-wives are exhorted to sustain their men. The critical role of the latter is outlined in *Servamus*:

> Do you realise just how important you, as the wife of a member of the SAP, really are? . . . Through the ages, the cornerstone of the inner strength of the family as the unit on which the nation has been built has been the mother. Behind every successful man you will most certainly find, not merely a woman, but a woman with strength of character and determination of purpose. It is true that your husband may be in the front line of our ordered society, in the heat of the battle, but you must be that quiet, unseen source of his strength for that battle, from you must flow the strength that he needs to come out of that battle unscathed and victorious . . . If she is a sour and disgruntled wife, it will not be long before her husband will also find his work a burden and a bore . . . If she is constantly grumbling about the way in which the policeman is providing for his family, she will make him disgruntled and dissatisfied with his job . . . The policeman has a high and sacred calling – but so has the wife of a policeman. He may be the wheel that has to turn to keep our slightly mad society from falling apart – but then she ought to be the 'nut' which keeps that wheel functional and in its place. . . . fulfil that high calling to which you, as the wife of a policeman, have been called. (August 1990)

Family and church combine as the fundamental institutions on which the South African police officer can rely when in need. The 'wife' is fundamentally important to comfort her husband and to relieve him from the toils and pressures of his calling. She furnishes the unity and bedrock of the family. In turn, the family represents the core unit of society and police organization.

Religious discourse also plays an important role in demonizing opposition. Resistance to SAP practices is not just evil but also transformed into Satanic practice in the work of one eccentric officer (who is however treated with some authority by *Servamus*).

> As Christian policemen we have a double authority to educate the public. We can show them the methods by which Satan slowly entraps our children ... I have the blood of Jesus over me ... without this nobody can hope to wage war for Christ against the enemy (May 1991).

As clerics in uniform, police officers undergo the trials of danger and vilification of a diabolic opposition, with the fortitude of the calling. More secular forms of organization are irrelevant to such a priesthood. The white state has a theocratic base which incorporates its servants within one creed. The fundamentalism of the Dutch Reformed Church is not so much a civil religion as an Afrikaner ideology justifying apartheid (Ngcokvane 1989). Church and state are tightly intertwined in personnel through the National Party and through a divine ideology that sanctifies the separation of races. The religious discourse that connects state with the police culture (Van Zyl Smit 1990) is of central importance to the SAP – not merely because it provides for solace in times of danger but also because it connects the key concerns and practices of the police culture with the larger imperatives of the white state.

Occupational discourse – 'So we had to shoot him. Car theft is a serious crime'

The occupational ideology of the SAP serves to obfuscate the overt partisan effects of the religious and political discourses. In an apparently pragmatic decision-making process, SAP officers construct as occupational necessities the wider exigencies of apartheid. Decisions are made not because of the dictates of the wider structures of apartheid. Rather, they are the immediate result of necessary, practical, requirements. This occupational discourse contains its own complex sub-set of vocabularies, each operating within its own paradigmatic cloisters. Occupational discourse feeds on ideologies of organization, of professionalism, and of scienticism or technicism.

Occupational discourse in its very accounting of the 'normal' work problems encountered by rank-and-file officers elsewhere elicits sympathy. Manpower shortages, low pay, and adverse working conditions dominate police 'talk'. These cogs in apartheid's machine are trapped, like police officers universally, in the remorseless – and uncaring – grinding wheels of authority. For example, the problem of maintaining a white life style, in an occupation that was relatively underpaid, came to a head in the late 1980s. The predicament was expressed by one policeman, complaining about overwork (due to the surge of black resistance):

> We are expected to work day and night, and on our days off and we are sick and tired of it. Improved perks are nice but you cannot use them to feed your family. (*Pretoria News* 25 April 1990)

Claims of underpayment were exacerbated by the effects on morale of the emergency operations in the unwinnable 'battleground' of the townships. Social life was strained and the military structure of the SAP appeared impervious to career ambitions. One such officer summed up his reasons for resigning in the following terms:

> Being a cop in the field and working long hours I had to sacrifice time I normally would have spent with my family to study and improve myself. After four years, I obtained a BA Police Science through UNISA so as to be able to climb the promotional ladder. But my colleagues who did not study were promoted with me as there was a policy change for free promotion . . . While doing duty on the detective unit, instead of a 40 hour week, I gave you a 76 hour week without grumbling or moaning as it was 'part of being a detective'. And when finances were tight and a shortage of new police vehicles occurred, I and others did our bit to look after resources at our disposal. On weekends, public holidays and days off, we did not hesitate to report for special duties when ordered to do so at the very last minute as this was also part of the job. Earlier this year I attended an officers' training course in Pretoria and after three months of intensive management training I was transferred to Kempton Park even though there were three vacancies for a detective lieutenant in my area, George. Over 300 of us stood at the end of the training course and listened while we were transferred throughout the country without regard to our personal circumstances, family or financial commitments. I went through all the channels as we are required to do and requested the Commissioner to reconsider the transfer as it would cause me financial as well as other hardships, due to family commitments but was informed by letter to report to Kempton Park. It is obvious that no one cared . . . all I can say is

yesterday I was an officer in the SAP and today I sit without a career and without employment. (*Argus* 3 February 1990)

Nor did the organization's demands meet the state's formal commitment to upholding the family and family values. The police officer is taken for granted – a manifestation of the universal police culture – by the dictates of authority. The following account of family life by the wife of a riot squad policeman provides a sense of the frustrations and strains of police family life occasioned by the state's crackdown on black resistance:

> . . . now he leaves at odd times, and is constantly on stand-by. Once he came in late and a little more than an hour afterwards – we had just got into bed – he was called out and did not return until the next morning. The children who used to sit at the breakfast table with him, sometimes only see him as they prepare for school early in the morning . . . I don't keep food warm for him any more, because he is too tired to eat a proper meal when he comes home in the early hours of the morning. My biggest concern is his safety . . . he could be knifed or overpowered by the crowds at any time and never come home at all. My personal relationship with him is under stress. I hear myself saying things to him that I do not mean . . . . I have been thinking of giving up work but we cannot afford it. (*Cape Times* 16 October l985).

These occupational accounts are contextualized within a picture of the police organization as developing and operating according to the inevitable logic of technological development rather than of being constructed to serve the dictates of apartheid. In Dippenaar's history, for example, the police institution is depicted as evolving over time into a technologically advanced, internally complex, bureaucratic and impartial machine geared towards the demands of policing a modern conflict-ridden world. Dippenaar furnishes a technicist history which contrives an apolitical rendering, failing to reflect the socio-political processes that have influenced the organizational development of the force. As Posel (1984: 2) has argued:

> Large areas of state control are depoliticised by being depicted in technical terms which disclaim their political contestability. The legitimation of such policies then devolves upon 'proving' their effectiveness, rather than demonstrating their 'democratic' basis.

Similarly, Dippenaar's historical recounting of changes in the police organization takes for granted that policework in South Africa should prioritize public order policing as opposed to crimework. Public order policing is perceived as unproblematic normal policing. High policing, the policing of the security of the state is presumed to be the standard police priority, not low policing, the control of crime on the street.

What increasingly characterizes the occupational discourses of the SAP in the 1990s is an attempt to validate conduct by reference to a variety of scientific and technical devices. By assembling an array of technical equipment, operating a technical service division, and utilizing a variety of technical 'testing' devices, the SAP is attempting to define crucial areas of its decision-making as governed by neutral science. For example, arguments over the access which black people have to careers in the police institution – for instance the debates surrounding affirmative action – are reconstructed as technical matters to be solved by a variety of scientific testing devices (Shearing 1992). Similarly the discourse of scientific problem-solving is a recurrent theme in the contemporary SAP literature. This discourse constructs the police as experts and professionals rather than as actors advancing political agendas.

Where problems occur between white police officers and black people, resolution is sought through scientific devices. Criticism of police handling of 'riots' is responded to by having members of riot squads psychometrically evaluated by clinical and industrial psychologists at the Institute of Behavioural Sciences (*Annual Report* 1990: 52). Similarly problems of recruit entry are dealt with through the 'scientifically screening' of all applicants (*Annual Report* 1980). Through this 'scientification of police work' (Ericson and Shearing 1986) policing becomes just another 'expert system' requiring 'expert knowledge' (Ericson 1992) rather than a realm of political values and conflicts. Political conflict is denied and reduced to scientific questions of 'personality' or 'crowd psychology'. Scientism or technicism, as occupational discourses, have primary functions for the SAP. They provide the police with an aura of professionalism that carries with it notions of service, self-sacrifice and specialized knowledge to be placed at the disposal of the 'community'. This also lends legitimacy to the police culture by defining it as a 'professional' sub-culture that sets police personnel apart from the lack of expertise of their lay critics who know nothing of the practical realities of policework.

Secondly, scientism legitimates SAP activities that might otherwise be considered controversial. SAP documentation waxes lyrical about 'scientific' innovations – for example, the first use of a 'sneeze' machine to control 'riots' in Soweto (*Yearbook* 1976). 'Fingerprint science' is exalted as an apolitical technical exercise. A police register of fingerprints of all black persons over sixteen years of age was justified

> . . . because so many blacks, unlike Whites, Coloureds and Indians, cannot be identified by name alone and, furthermore, do not reside at permanent addresses for long continuous periods, with the result that identification by means of fingerprints is the only infallible method that can be used. (quoted in Prior 1988)

Fingerprint science appears to reduce to a simple technical matter, the mass fingerprinting of black people and subsequent record-keeping across the country.

Thirdly, as scientists are considered to be objective and value-free, SAP members are portrayed as para-scientists whose judgements are based on objective scientific criteria. A recent example of the use of the rhetoric of social science to legitimate the carrying of weapons in demonstrations has been the defence offered for the carrying of weapons' symbols by Inkatha supporters. When the government accepted a definition of spears, sticks and shields as 'cultural weapons', rather than simply as weapons, they joined Inkatha in mobilizing a 'scientific' anthropological reference to justify this practice.

Fourthly, there has been an attempt to pathologize blacks as violent beings through the 'black-on-black' violence theme. The internecine conflicts in the black townships, often provoked and promoted by the SAP and the South African Defence Force, has been used by the SAP to promote an image of itself as a vital buffer between warring, primitive, black tribes. This 'black-on-black' theme has been used to promote the thin-blue-line thesis of the SAP as the bulwark of those civilized values that will prevent South Africa collapsing under the chaos which majority rule will introduce.

> . . . to date the police have managed to save the lives of thousands of people in many unrest situations through their fearless and sensitive conduct, and therefore fulfil their task with distinction. (Vlok quoted in *Daily Dispatch* 27 January 1990)

In Dippenaar, the innate secrecy of the subculture is constructed as a virtue when reinforced by state legislation concealing police practices from public scrutiny. When the force becomes a target of *terrorist* attacks, this onslaught provides a powerful justificatory device for whatever powers the police might accrue (Van der Spuy 1990).

Horrific practices are reconstructed as occupational problems which can be dealt with by appropriate foresight. Dirk Coetzee, as a security police officer, had a periodic mandate to assassinate ANC activists and sympathizers. He always came prepared for the exigencies of this craft! Thus, in one case, he describes in a relatively casual manner the problem of transporting one victim:

> He and Spyker came running out of the bush, dragging the corpse behind them. We bundled the body into a thick white plastic bag used by the mortuary to transport bodies. I kept a supply of these in the boot of my car. (Coetzee 1991: 107)

Another SAP officer explains, with appropriate professional objectivity, the necessity of murdering escaping suspects:

> He drove faster and faster. We drove after him. Put on the blue light. He wouldn't stop – just driving faster and faster. So we had to shoot him. Car theft is a serious crime – 26,000 Rand out of somebody's pocket (BBC *Cutting Edge* February 1993).

On the same programme a colleague was shown to be operating with an even broader remit. 'When someone has done wrong, you have to shoot him for that.' Coetzee's account contains many such pragmatic scenes that police officers elsewhere might understand if not sympathize with. Precipitating violent deaths is an occupational hazard and one to which one can become relatively accustomed.

> The body was put on a huge pyre of dense bushveld wood and tyres, and cremated. The hands feet, and face are destroyed quickly but it takes about seven to nine hours before nothing but ashes remain. All the while, we were carrying on with talking and drinking around a braai [barbecue]. (Coetzee 1991: 63)

Occasionally, even hardened police officers had a certain squeamishness about some of the tasks they were required to perform. Coetzee (1991: 63) recounts a bungled poisoning episode in which the dosages received from a senior SAP officer, Lieutenant-General Neethling, had been miscalculated: '. . . the reason why the

victims were thus doped . . . that nobody had the courage to shoot a
helpless and fully conscious man at point blank range' (1991: 63).

Coetzee's biography contains many scenes that reflect the
occupational cynical discourse of a career police officer faced with
problems and duties not of his making, but which he is expected to
resolve successfully and without complaint. Like other police
organizations, many operations are mismanaged because of factors
outside the control of the individuals entrusted with the task. Poison
does not work despite multiple dosages, assassinations are bungled
because of unforeseen circumstances, and agents on whom the police
are forced to rely, are often corrupt, using the SAP for their own
criminal purposes. 'Hippies' whose lifestyle annoys the security
police, experience an unsuccessful attempt to burn them out.
However, proper police planning can normally avoid foreseeable
hazards.

> My instructions were that they were not allowed to shoot and that it must
> look like a robbery. They were therefore to take some of his personal
> possessions like his wallet, watch and robbery, and his car as well. I
> cautioned them to wear old clothes and old shoes that I could destroy if
> necessary. They were also to see that their pockets were empty so that
> nothing could be lost at the site of the crime – no cigarettes, no ID books,
> no watches with names or serial numbers etc. (Coetzee 1991)

Similarly, a continuing feature of the functionaries of the South
African state, has been their relative honesty – or *naiveté* – in
defending routine violence that is formally abhorrent to other
national police forces. Two reactions to the common use of torture
illustrate the historical continuity of both practice and language. The
first in reply to a question to an SAP detective constable about
recovering stolen stock:

> There are three ways. The first is that we hit them. The second is the
> electric shocks. And the third is the gas mask. The shock usually works as
> they are terrified of electricity. But the gasmask always works. That way
> you put the gasmask over his head. Then you tell him that if he won't talk
> you'll stop the air going in so he can't breathe. Then you stop the air. When
> he faints, you let the air go in again and bring him round. Then you tell
> him that this time you were merciful. You brought him back from the other
> side. The next time, if he doesn't talk, you're going to let him stay there.
> When this happens, they always talk. (Duncan 1964: 31)

The constancy of these rationales for the use of torture appears throughout South African police history. In his study of the abuse of non-political detainees, Fernandez (1991) notes a Capetown case in which a suspected gangleader had died through a faulty electric shock machine. One of the detectives in the case commented that he saw nothing wrong with placing a bag over the suspect's head while the shock treatment occurred.

To understand these non-problematic accounts of the use of violence – often as the Gluckman case has most recently documented, ending in death – is to recognize two elements. In the first place, policework in South Africa deals with non-humans – kaffirs, Munts – the lesser races as inculcated in police recruits from the days of the Patrys Speurklub. In the words of Brigadier Jan du Preez, 'All I have against a kaffir is his colour' (quoted in Coetzee 1991: 12). In the same way that the white farmer may use an electric prod on an unwilling bullock, so does the police officer deal routinely with 'uncooperative black people'. The dehumanization of the symbolic and real police property provides for one aspect of the routinization of torture practice.

Secondly, South African policework depends primarily for evidence in criminal cases on confessions. For a variety of reasons – technical incompetence, shortage of resources, and absence of appropriate language skills (Afrikaans is the primary medium of the force, although for most black people it may constitute a third language) – detective work hinges around the pivot of obtaining a confession. Reliance on confession evidence – governed only by the ancient and non-enforceable British inheritance of the Judges' Rules – is, in effect, normal policework. Routines around the extraction of confessions become the normal practice of South African policing. Detective work in South Africa is reduced to finding appropriate suspects – and then applying sufficient pressure, physical or mental, to ensure that they admit the offence. The courts normally find such evidence sufficient. Reliance on confessions reduces the need to gather evidence, to construct the evidence for a case, and to find witnesses. It reduces the police task to a bare minimum.

Consequently, when South African police officers recount the violence of the police station experience, it is constructed in the context of a normal, routine, and necessary occupational practice. Together with the dehumanizing of the human subjects of policing, deaths in custody (210 in 1992) and lesser police crimes require no legitimation, no justification but simply occasional accounting to a social audience which is interfering in the orthodox practices of professional policing. (Coetzee's account contains many other ingredients, which reflect an occupational cultural discourse which would be recognizable to the police occupation universally – blue movies are smuggled over the border from Swaziland and circulated around the Pretoria headquarters. Car radios from vehicles stolen from ANC activists are given a new life in the cars of senior officers.)

Steytler (1991) has argued that it is in the convergence of the political and occupational discourses of the SAP that the conditions ripe for the death squads emerged. In euphemisms similar to those of the CIA in Vietnam, higher command determined the broad requirements for persons to be 'removed'. Occupational discourses reduced the permissive syntax to a practical, neutral, problem of policework. The partisanship of the political and religious vocabularies of the SAP is rendered relatively innocuous when sieved through the occupational mesh.

Conclusion

South African policework is presently subject to enormous pressure for change with the coming of the 'new South Africa'. While the abolition of apartheid has left many of its major structures – the fault lines of socio-economic class are often contiguous with those of colour – the SAP, prompted by National Party politicians, is showing certain signs of recognizing the dire necessity for change. A third of the General Staff have scuttled into retirement. International advisers and monitors have been received with relative openness. Changes in training and in codes of conduct are being discussed with a remarkable *naïveté*.

But structures of discourse are deeply embedded. The childhood socialization through institutions like the Patrys Speurklub ensured that the cultural embodiment of a racist and violent police force has become part of the soul of many older Afrikaner police. Sundering the material bases of particular discourses – for example, through the political renaissance of the New South Africa – does not destroy a language which is incapable of surmounting the history of the white state, and which reflects an ideology buried deep in the souls of many white South Africans.

One recalls fragments of a counter-discourse which perhaps has more substance. At a meeting between an international group of police officers and academics and SAP generals at the headquarters in Pretoria, the former were treated to a harangue about the lies of the liberal press by one, General DelaRosa. The latter given the task of 'selling' the SAP to the international contingent could find little reason for regret or remorse. His own career had reached a high point at Ventersdorp in 1991 when the SAP guardians at a President De Klerk election meeting had killed two members of the far-right AWB demonstration. On leaving the meeting, Chief Jim Harding, commissioner of the Halton Regional Police in Ontario, is alleged to have commented on DelaRosa – 'he's no racist – he'd kill anyone, black or white!'

Notes

1 The latter part of this article draws on Chapter Three of M. Brogden and C. D. Shearing, *Policing the New South Africa* (London, Routledge, 1993). I acknowledge Clifford Shearing's contribution to this work.
2 See General J. Coetzee's paper to the SAP Committee on Police Training and Codes of Conduct (Graaf Reinet, 1993).
3 1981. Cited in *Work in Progress* 1981.
4 A curious footnote on police origins is the background of the SAP general who allegedly supplied poison to the hit squads. Lieutenant-General Lothar Neethling was born in Nazi Germany and, in 1945, adopted by foster parents in South Africa through the medium of an extreme white supremacist group on the basis of his Aryan background and features.
5 Quoted in Van der Spuy 1990.
6 BBC documentary, *Children of God*, March 1991.
7 Quoted in the South African *Daily Mail*, 29 June 1991.
8 Article by M. Botha, *Communism and the Police*, May 1991.

References

Brogden, M. E. (1987). 'An act to govern the internal land of the island', *International Journal of the Sociology of Law*, 15(2).

Brogden, M. E. (1991). *On the Mersey Beat* (Oxford, Oxford University Press).

Brogden, M. E. and Shearing, C. D. (1993). *Policing the New South Africa* (London, Routledge).

Clarke, L. (1969). 'South African childhood', *Bedside Guardian* (Manchester).

Coetzee, D. (1991). *Testimony Prepared for the Harms Committee*, mimeo, unpublished.

Coetzee, J. (1993). 'Legal training in the South African Police', *Memorandum to Committee on Police Training and Codes of Conduct* (Graaf Reinet).

DeWitt, General H. G. (1988). 'Policing the changing society' in *SAP – Quo Vadis?*, International Symposium on Policing (Pretoria, UNISA).

Dippenaar, M. (1988). *The History of the South African Police, 1913–1988* (Silverton, Promedia).

Duncan, P. (1964). *South Africa's Rule of Violence* (London, Methuen).

Ericson, R. V. (1992). *The Division of Expert Knowledge in Policing and Society*, mimeo, Toronto, University of Toronto, Centre of Criminology.

Ericson, R. V. and Shearing, C. D. (1986). 'The scientification of police work', in Bohme, G. and Stehr, N. (eds.), *The Knowledge Society, Sociology of Science Yearbook*, 10 (Dordrecht, Reidel).

Fernandez, L. (1991). *Police Abuses of Non-Political Criminal Suspects: A Survey of Practices in the Cape Peninsula Area* (Capetown, University of Cape Town, Institute of Criminology).

Foster, D., Davis, D. and Sandler, D. (1987). *Detention and Torture in South Africa* (Cape Town, David Phillip).

Goodhew, D. (1991). 'Between the devil and the deep blue sea: crime and policing in the western areas of Johannesburg *c.*1930–1962', paper given at History Workshop *Structure and Experience in the Making of Apartheid*, University of Witwatersrand.

McClure, J. (1972). *The Caterpillar Cop* (London, Gollancz).

Ngcokvane, C. (1989). *Demons of Apartheid* (Braamfontein, Skotaville Publishers).

Posel, D. (1984). 'Language, legitimation, and control: the South African state after 1978', *Social Dynamics*, 10(1), 1–16.

Prior, A. (1988). *The South African Police and the National Security System*, mimeo, Capetown, University of Cape Town, Institute of Criminology.

Rauch, J. (1991). 'Deconstructing the SAP', paper presented at the Conference of the Association of Sociologists of Southern Africa, University of Cape Town.

Reuss-Ianni, E. (1983). *Street Cops and Management Cops* (New Brunswick, Transaction Books).

Shearing, C. D. (1992). 'Affirmative action: the case of the South African Police' *Proceedings of the Conference in a New South Africa* (Port Elizabeth).

Shearing, C. D. and Mzamane, M. (1992). *Community Voices on Policing in Transition* (Belleville, Community Law Centre, University of the Western Cape).

Smit, B. F. (1988). 'National police: pipedream or reality?' International Symposium on Police (Pretoria, UNISA).

Steytler, N. (1990). 'Policing political opponents: death squads and cop culture', in Van Zyl Smit, D. and Hansson, D. (eds.), *Towards Justice* (Cape Town, Oxford University Press).

Turk, A. (1981). 'The meaning of criminality in South Africa', *International Journal of the Sociology of Law*, 9, 123–55.

UNISA, Criminology (1983). *Only Guide for KRM 100–5* (Pretoria, University of South Africa).

Van Heerden, T. (1982). *Introduction to Police Science* (Pretoria, UNISA).

Van der Spuy, E. (1990). 'Political discourse and the history of the South African Police', in Van Zyl Smit, D. and Hansson, D. (eds.), *Towards Justice* (Cape Town, Oxford University Press).

Van Zyl Smit, D. (1990). 'Contextualising criminology in contemporary South Africa', in Van Zyl Smit, D. and Hansson, D. (eds.), *Towards Justice* (Cape Town, Oxford University Press).

Worrall, D. J. C. (1972). 'Afrikaner nationalism: a contemporary analysis' in Pothol, C. P. and Dale, R. (eds.), *South Africa: Abuse in Perspective* (New York, Free Press).

5

Labouring, loving and living: on the policing of culture in Trinidad and Tobago

MAUREEN CAIN

Introduction

This chapter arises from two current projects: one is my continuing work on realist and feminist methods and the other is a text on criminology for students in the Caribbean and the Third World. The two projects are connected, for the argument at the end of this chapter is that only a contemporary realist ontology and epistemology can adequately explain the policing of culture as well as the policing of labour, politics and women in the colonial context (and, I therefore presume, anywhere else).

The form of this chapter, depending as it does primarily on secondary sources, arises from its intended use (when expanded) as lectures and chapters in a textbook. I first present examples (rather than sustained accounts) of the policing of labour, politics, women, and culture in Trinidad and Tobago and the Caribbean. In the final section I argue that neither instrumentalist accounts nor postmodernisms are adequate to the task of explaining both the policing of labour *and* the policing of culture. Instead I argue that only a realist approach can account for both patterns of relational power and for the autonomous power of forms of cultural expression.

Before presenting my first set of examples, I must clarify the concept of policing. I use the term in the sense of Donzelot (1979) and Cain (1989) to imply both surveillance and the persuasion of the surveilled to internalize an altered set of standards. Policing is thus less unquestionably benign in intentions or successful in its outcomes than socialization, and is broader than Foucault's disciplines, which are an historically specific form of policing. Policing is a constructive change-oriented form of control. A metaphor of pushing and cajoling along is more apposite than one of beating down. Yet this form of constructive power is seen as integrated with a negative power which is always potentially available, not as an historical alternative to it.

The policing of labour

Until 1838 the control of labour in Trinidad was the direct responsibility of the planter class. The whip was the main device, since it did not keep workers too long from the fields (Dodd 1979). Indeed, the acquisition of labour seems to have vexed the planters more than controlling the work-force. After emancipation the need to secure a labour force, now from the reluctant ex-slaves, remained the main preoccupation, although through the nineteenth century control of those in work also became problematic. In this period following emancipation the ex-slaves, now free workers, tested their freedom. They fought for control over their own time (Trotman 1986: 46). The ex-slave population of Trinidad like the indigenous population of Kenya (Willis 1991) refused all long-term contracts and would work only when they needed cash for a specific purpose. Meanwhile small-scale trade, which had begun under slavery, provided an alternative livelihood, an economy of the Afro-Caribbean population which completely by-passed the planter population and their export-oriented mono-cropping.

The planters' response was a successful call for taxes on and licensing of small-scale traders, initiating a strategy used later to good effect in the new African colonies (Anderson and Killingray 1991), with the inevitable result that an indigenous economy was never allowed to flourish (Trotman 1986). The Vagrancy Acts of 1838 enhanced the effects of this strategy by rendering all those who were not plantation workers at risk of arrest. The definition of a vagrant included fortune tellers, mendicants, obeah practitioners, gamblers, persons acting suspiciously on the street, on a wharf, or in a public place and, to make quite sure of the effect, 'every person wandering abroad'.

In the same year as the emancipation process was completed (1838) twenty-one labour ordinances were passed by the legislative council. Eight of these were subsequently disallowed by the Colonial Office as admitting slavery by the back door. Thus one battery of laws attempted to drive citizens to become plantation labourers, while another set attempted to determine how they should perform this work.

Unsurprisingly, also in 1838, a police force was established, officered by ex-patrial English and manned in the middle ranks by Scots and Irish ex-policemen and in the lower ranks by ex-slaves from Barbados. Magistrates in the local districts were given summary powers in relation to both labour and vagrancy infringements. Although these magistrates were state officials and not lay people, their local situation at a time when transport through the wet and sometimes densely forested island was extremely difficult, ensured that they would be vulnerable to pressure from their only middle-class neighbours, the planters.

From 1845 on a new labour strategy was devised, and increasing numbers of workers on ten-year indentureships were imported from the Indian sub-continent. The legislative response to this new work-force was the Master and Servants Ordinance of 1846 (Trotman 1986: 196). Thereafter the criminal sanctions of fines and imprisonment could be imposed for such delicts as illness or misconduct at work! None the less there was constant conflict over the interpretation of the indentured workers' contracts and evidence of increasing organization among the East Indian work-force, leading to a number of plantation strikes in the 1870s (Singh 1988).

There was also conflict about lands, to which East Indians were entitled on the expiry of their indentureships, as well as squatted lands. Here, according to Trotman (1986), there was planter ambivalence: resistance to the settlement of East Indians since this reduced their dependence, coupled with the planters' need for a seasonal labour force adjacent to the estates. As the estates expanded, the East Indian landowners found themselves vulnerable to title frauds, in the face of a planter-oriented judiciary.

As late as 1918 attempts were still being made to coerce casual African labour to regular estate work. The Habitual Idlers Ordinance of that year left the definition of habitual idling to the discretion of the magistrates. Ultimate legal authority was thus ceded to the planter class and its agents, although the isolation of the magistrates from the central state had been reduced during the 1870s by the development of a railway system.

The colonial power's interest in all this was evidenced by the presence of both the navy and troops in the 1870s and 1880s and enhanced by the expansion of the Trinidad oil industry. The first shaft was sunk in 1864, although the real development happened after the First World War. By the time of the labour struggles of the late 1930s the island was supplying two thirds of UK demand (Craig 1988). Thus in 1937 the British government sent marines in support of the efforts of the local state to control a wave of strikes and 'riots' led by Uriah Butler and censured and eventually recalled the governor of the island for not being tough enough. In so far as the labour 'unrest' throughout the region led to the Moyne Commission and the eventual development of social welfare policies in the islands, the strikers can be regarded as having successfully forced a wedge between the interest of the Metropole in stabilizing the flow of oil and the interest of the indigenous planter and capitalist class in avoiding taxation. The development of the oil industry in any event involved a shift of power from the planter-based legislative council to international suppliers of capital. In the contemporary period, labour is policed through an Industrial Relations Act which, where possible, individualizes disputes, presenting them for resolution to an Industrial Court.

The policing of politics and resistance

The best regional sources on this topic are from Jamaica and for the colonial period, perhaps, Venezuela. None the less, I will confine my discussion to Trinidad and Tobago. Here the Black Power Revolution of 1970 and the Black Muslim coup attempt in 1990 yield rich sources for analysis (Deosaran 1993; Mahabir 1980; 1988; and Ryan 1991).

Trinidad (but not Tobago) has an urban black lumpen proletariat. According to Mahabir the violent confrontations between steel bands in the 1950s were an assertion of an authentic black identity by the young males of this group. Violence, she argues, was integral to the music. These urban disorders were eventually contained by the ruling People's National Movement (PNM), which encouraged the sponsorship of bands by capitalist enterprises, as well as more direct political patronage of 'Desperadoes', one of the most popular steel bands in Trinidad (now sponsored by the West Indian Tobacco Company). The violence stopped, the music was co-opted in part only by the mixed race middle class, and the price or the profit was the continued development of black identity through pan (steel drums made from disused steel oil barrels).

This black identity was crucial in providing support for a student-led Black Power revolt in 1970. Those participating saw the colonial imbalance in wealth persisting, saw the white and middle-class alliance as excluding them, saw the model of legality provided by the colonists still in place (Mahabir 1980). The response of the PNM government to the increasing scale of demonstrations and strikes and the eventual mutiny in the army was the Emergency Powers Act of 1970. Marches and public gatherings were prohibited, a curfew imposed, and eighty-seven soldiers and fifty-four civilians were arrested, convicted and imprisoned. A guerilla movement persisted for five years after this, and conditions in the prisons were placed on the political agenda, not least after an outbreak of fire in the Port of Spain prison in 1974. Two reports on the prisons were published (Seemungal 1974; Abdullah 1980).

The prison reports demonstrate the move from repressive to constructive policing: the Abdullah Report in particular expresses unprecedented concern for the plight of prisoners (Hagley 1993b). But more importantly, as Mahabir (1980) argues, not only was the political resistance criminalized, but it was also ultimately denied. The government of the day insisted that class-based society had ended with independence and that the Black Power Revolution itself was a 'sociological' and not a political phenomenon. The event was reinterpreted as a Black Opportunities Revolution not a Black Power Revolution.

In the same way exclusion from the political process is not seen as an 'appropriate' explanation of the attempted coup in 1990, although political power was even more obviously what was sought on this occasion. Instead, the lack of employment for black youth (some 43 per cent of males between fifteen and nineteen were unemployed in 1990) is offered as an explanation, with the Muslim religion and its charismatic leader Abu Bakr offering an alternative (and in the establishment view less satisfactory) basis for self-respect. Yet it is also clear that the gap between rich and poor was widening at this time, as the median income fell while the mean stayed constant (Cain and Birju 1992). Moreover, from 1988 to 1990 the number of remands in custody leapt from 2,843 to 'almost 34,000' (Hagley 1993a; 1993b), and the proportion of offenders sentenced to imprisonment also increased (Cain and Birju 1992). It is reasonable to assume that the young black male 'lumpen proletarians' were the primary victims of this apparent change in judicial policing.

Apart from a change of government from the cross-ethnic bourgeois alliance of the National Alliance for Reconstruction to the

Afro-Caribbean PNM, the results of the 1990 coup attempt are not clear.

The policing of women

At this point I have to move beyond the confines of Trinidad since data of this kind are only now becoming available. As well as Trotman (1984) and Craig (n.d), I include the analyses of Mair (1986) and Dadzie (1990) on Jamaica, since these strongly support the theoretical insights of Craig in particular.

Mair documents how women under slavery laboured in the fields in even higher proportions than the men, both because they were strong and also because they were blocked from many of the skilled artisanal jobs around the estate which, apart from skilled domestic work, were reserved for men. Dadzie claims that women were 'the lowest and most exploited'. They ran the same risk of flogging and other punishments as men did, but were also exposed to sexual assaults. Moreover, for most women there were no lasting benefits or special concessions arising from sexual encounters with white men or other plantation owners. They were always at risk of being sent back to the fields or of losing their children, and they were also for obvious reasons vulnerable to the vindictiveness of white women. Their sexuality, argues Dadzie, posed an extra hardship for slave women. Yet the historiography of the day, which has been accepted, is that the slave women were all competing and conniving for the attentions of the white 'massa' and the upward social mobility which might follow from his 'favours'.

The first lesson from this tale is that slave women have been policed also by posterity. And the creation of such a myth, which mystifies the past, serves to justify the present. Note instead that the myth was male created, and that such fragile 'upward mobility' applied only to a very few, primarily in the first two centuries of slavery and that the women themselves were always vulnerable despite the freedom which they might (or might not) secure for their children.

I do not know what the forms of resistance were here. We do know that slave women fiercely resisted their other peculiarly female function, that of childbirth. Throughout the slavery period the low fertility of women was a constant cause of planter concern. Dadzie and Mair argue that this low reproduction rate was itself a form of resistance. The women used the techniques of induced abortion, prolonged lactation, and infanticide. (Remember here Toni

Morrison's *Beloved* 1987). There is some evidence for the latter in court cases, and certainly in official reports to the Colonial Office. Planters and contemporary observers expressed the view that black women were not 'co-operating'. There were constant inducements to procreate, such as direct payments or better working conditions for mothers, but to no avail.

Further evidence that the low birth rate was a form of resistance can be derived from the fact that after emancipation the birth rate rose. Yet in this case too there was a refusal by the authorities to see the women's refusal as a political statement; rather, in the most benign interpretations, their poor health was blamed.

In the post-emancipation period, women's direct control of the labour supply caused an acute labour shortage. The birth rate went up, indeed, but both in Tobago (Craig n.d) and in Jamaica (Mair 1986) women would not let their children return to work on estates as apprentices or for any inducement. Women would not, if they could help it, produce slave children or near slave children. Their individual abhorrence, and doubtless also their word-of-mouth control of and dependence on each other, were extremely effective.

What is particularly interesting about the post-emancipation situation in Trinidad is that different institutions appear to have been used to police the urban African women and the rural Indian women (Trotman 1984). At emancipation, Port of Spain was a city of 6,781 women and 4,912 men. The women worked as domestics, hucksters, washer women, and sempstresses. As Trotman says: 'more often than not the price women paid for independence from the plantation was economic marginality in the city' (1984: 61).

In Port of Spain poor black women were policed by the newly created state police. Thirty years later, in 1869, prostitutes were required to register and to submit themselves for periodic checks for venereal disease. The police used this regulation to harass all working-class women, who were also frequently charged with indecent behaviour, riotous and disorderly conduct, using obscene and profane language, and other public order offences in which police evidence alone was enough to convict (Trotman 1984). Women, says Trotman, were 'chief victims of cultural conflict' and 'main carriers of a code antagonistic to the plantations'. It seems that it was to these women's way of *being* that the police of the day and their employers took exception. Their ways caused consternation among the moral entrepreneurs and arbiters.

There were, however, divisions in the social order along class, political and ethnic lines which dramatically affected the way Trini women were policed. For example, in 1888, the Colonial Office exercised pressure to secure the passage of a Bastardy Ordinance requiring fathers to support their illegitimate children. The planter class, however, wanted to maintain their illegitimate children by largesse rather than obligation. The legal argument that only those women could apply for support who were 'not common or reputed prostitutes' circumvented the difficulty. A woman now ran the risk of having her moral character put on trial as part of a man's courtroom defence. Applications dropped and the former system of father's discretionary 'bounty' was *de facto* reinstated (Trotman 1986).

The Bastardy Ordinance also reflected a peculiar, virtually a deliberate, failure to understand the situation of East Indian women. In 1890, 62 per cent of children born were illegitimate according to the authorities (Trotman 1986: ch. 8) who refused to validate Hindu marriages. Official recognition of their cultural practice would have helped these women more.

The state, however, left the policing of East Indian women in the private hands of East Indian men. By the 1880s, 60 per cent of murder victims were East Indian, and through the second half of the nineteenth century the proportion of these victims who were women ranged from 60 per cent to 100 per cent. (Trotman 1986: 170). Rapes also increased dramatically from 1870–99. Trotman attributes this to 'female deficient communities' on the plantations. One judge of the period attributed the attacks to the 'loose character of coolie women' (Trotman 1984: 62). For both, perhaps, the greater independence of the East Indian woman, with independent rights to property or a return passage at the end of indentureship, compounded the 'shortage' (which also bothered the planters for whom the violence was a nuisance). Trotman's examination of the court records revealed that perpetrators were very often refused lovers or jealous husbands.

However, rather than seeing women as a scarce resource over which men were in a state of natural and inevitable competition, I prefer a different analysis. In the first place, if men were indeed competing with each other, the violence should have been inter-male. But the violence was against the desired object – and this oddity needs to be explained. Indeed, it can only be explained as an attempt by men to control women – an attempt at the policing of women.

The forms that resistance took are unknown to me. Recent work on the 'creolization' of East Indian women[1] suggests that resistance there was, as well as accommodation between the sexes and between the ethnic groups. Male human nature is not really a strong enough concept to make sense of all that.

The policing of culture

Finally, in this skate across some of the secondary sources, I want to consider the policing of culture. I shall subdivide this topic into the policing of leisure, the policing of religion, and the policing of the incomprehensible.

Ottley discusses an 1849 Act in which the Trinidad police were given powers to 'seize and carry away any drum, gong, tambour, bangee, or chac chac in use at any dance or assembly at any time on a Sunday or after ten o'clock in the evening of any weekday' (1964: 38). According to Trotman (1986: ch. 8) this ruling was reaffirmed in 1883, although the playing of European instruments after 10.00 pm was allowed. He argues that the European and Mulatto population feared that drumming, by either Africans or East Indians, would provide an occasion for meeting. And meetings, one might assume, could be politically dangerous. This is an instrumental explanation for the banning of late-night drums. That there was resistance is apparent from the riot in Arouca in 1891 following 'a Bamboula or drum dance contrary to law all Monday in the village. The rowdies had been feasting the public holiday and drinking heavily' (Ottley 1964). The local police were beaten when they tried to intervene, as were eight other officers armed with sticks who were sent as reinforcements. Apparently the Irish policemen were particularly upset at being beaten by 'the drunken scum of the population'. Ottley, however, gives no follow-up information, and neither, one must assume, do the police records which were his source. But it is easy to see why, as he tells us, it was still 'a disgrace' to be a policeman at the turn of the century.

The best-known example of the policing of leisure in Trinidad is the 'Canboulay riots' of the late 1880s. This period saw the beginning of a long fall in the price of sugar (partly if temporarily compensated for by a buoyant cocoa price). In Port of Spain, armed gangs for 'drinking, gambling, and fighting' (Brereton 1979), and wearing distinctive dress roamed the streets. The British chief of police (Captain Baker) was determined to stop this, and his move against the

Canboulay revellers, Brereton says was part of that. The bands came from the barrack yards and there were both male and 'jamet' bands, claiming territorial bases. The bands took to the road at Canboulay singing kalinda songs which the press of the day regarded as 'lewd.'

The two concerns that the authorities had were: firstly, the fact that the crowds carried torches and the houses were wooden; and, secondly, the explicitly lewd or sexual masques. There was transvestite *mas'* (men in long nightdresses), there was *pis en lit mas'*, there were women with exposed breasts, and there was sexual horseplay. Cutting across these practices in an attempt to both police and participate was an array of class, ethnic, and gender forces. Ottley says that the middle-class Mulatto population also took to the streets to ape and mock both the white Colonists and the 'bush negroes'. The French planters had originally supported the Mardi Gras celebrations which were unknown to the British. Others argue that it was the black and mulatto middle class which was most concerned about the 'lewdness' of the black participants, as race increasingly took precedence over class in the island's stratification system in the post-emancipation period (Brereton 1979: 94). What is clear is that black men and women and English males were on opposite sides in this matter. After attempts to control the festival in 1868, 1878 and 1879 had failed, in 1881 the torches were collected up and a massive fight with the police ensued. Thirty-eight of 150 police were injured, and the outcome at the end of the Sunday night was inconclusive. The Port of Spain Council asked the governor for a conciliatory gesture. He addressed the masqueraders and agreed to withdraw the police until Ash Wednesday morning. Later the press condemned the chief of police for agreeing to this.

The year of 1882 was quiet, 1883 was 'disorderly again'. In 1884 the government took power to prohibit 'torch processions' and any disorderly assembly or assembly of ten or more with sticks. Effectively the government took power to abolish carnival. It continued, however, quietly and with increasing middle-class participation. In 1895 the transvestite *mas'* was abolished. Business people began to see the potential of the festival and to organize costume bands. More recently competition between the bands has given middle-class judges greater influence, while the tourist industry has led once again to attempts to control the festival.

In recent years there have been successful campaigns to police a popular form of dance called 'wining' which has now disappeared from television coverage, but not from popular practice. When I crossed the stage in 1989 policemen were standing there to supervise the dance, although this has now stopped. These attempts were parodied in a 1992 calypso ('Doh Wine . . .').

In 1993 the organizers attempted to turn the independently progressing bands into a parade for spectators. One route only was approved for bands wishing to cross the stage. Resistance continues successful, in the form of refusals to cross (which means the band can select its own route within the limits of the one-way system) and 'Monday night *mas*", which began around 1988. Participants continue to refuse to parade in their costumed 'sections' except when being judged.

Whose fun is it anyway? It seems that the sexually explicit activities of the women are particularly offensive to those who draw their model of womanhood from European ideals of passivity and 'attractiveness'. Thus, these attempts at control could be explained in either economic or gender terms. However, I believe that any attempt to explain the policing of Canboulay/carnival in these terms alone would be missing a crucial ingredient. I shall develop this theme further in the next section, but first I wish to present examples of the policing of religion and the policing of obeah.

Earl Lovelace's play *The Wine of Astonishment* (1982) has well advertised the fact that the Spiritual Baptist religion was illegal in Trinidad and Tobago until as late as 1953. Not only was it illegal, it was maligned as both primitive and devilish – a fearful set of customs from darkest Africa! Maybe the central place of the 'mother' of the church in both organization and liturgy put the Baptists beyond the pale, or perhaps it was the 'centre pole', or the ringing of bells, or the white turbans.

The full story remains to be explored academically. What is more thoroughly documented in the literature is the Mohurrum Massacre of 1884, and the policing of Islam (Norman 1885; Singh 1988). This is of particular importance in the present context because of Singh's attempt at an instrumental political-economic explanation.

Mohurrum (Mohurram, Hosay etc.) is the re-enactment of the historical events which led to the death of the prophet Mohammed's grandsons. There used to be a procession on the tenth day of this festival – a 'mixture of piety and profanity'. Hindus and Africans were involved too, for Hinduism can embrace many gods and the Africans, being bigger often helped to carry the Tazias (Tadjah).

Within a decade of the first East Indians arriving, Mohurrum was becoming popular as a national working-class festival (Singh 1988).

As indicated earlier, by the 1870s the East Indian workers were testing their strength on the estates as an organized work-force. The image of 'manageable' Indians as opposed to 'unmanageable' Africans was waning, and the 'coolies' were now seen as reckless and their co-ordinated action as a danger to society. There was a wave of plantation strikes in 1872, and during a strike at the Cedar Hill plantation in 1882 the estate manager was allegedly attacked. The sugar planters met to consider concerted action. Meanwhile British naval vessels anchored offshore (Singh 1988).

Later in the year an Ordinance was passed to control Indian festivals, rendering participants liable to arrest and sentences of imprisonment or fines. Thus when, in 1884, workers from a number of plantations joined up on the final day of the festival to carry the Tazia to the sea at the southern town of San Fernando, police gathered to bar the way to the town, having been brought by special train from Port of Spain. Ottley (1964) says soldiers were held in reserve. The Riot Act was read. There is no record of what the tassa-beating, largely non-English-speaking crowd made of this (Norman 1885). The police then fired on them. According to the local police report, fourteen were killed and four or five were 'likely to die'. Singh says sixteen were killed and over a hundred wounded, basing his estimates on reports in contemporary newspapers.

Singh argues that in addition to a generalized concern at the growing strength of the 'coolies', who had got the idea that they were 'powerful and could do what they liked' (Ottley 1964), there was a growing concern about the multiracial character of the event. This is borne out by the clause in the Ordinance which reads: 'No other than an immigrant or the descendants of immigrants shall take part in any such procession' (Norman 1885). In Singh's view the social and political construction of Afro-Indian racism in Trinidad can be dated from this moment, which must be seen as a clear attempt to inhibit the unity of the poor and the plantation workers. Viewed in this light the Mohurrum Massacre is a critical episode of class warfare.

Certainly the political, spiritual, social and economic segregation of these two groups has continued, although the splendid but localized Mohurrum (Hosay) festival still attracts large crowds of Africans as spectators. The mixture of the sacred – prayers and the dance and kiss of the two moons on their way to battle, the three or four magnificent 'tombs', the kerbside fires of woodshavings and the beat of the tassa – and the profane – the thronging crowd of neighbourhood and other local spectators eating sweetmeats, perhaps, and later drinking beer – persists. Ironically, these days it is African Muslims who patrol the streets in sober robes while Hosay is being celebrated, chanting (in 1992) 'Hoosay not a bacchanal'.

But beyond Singh's instrumental account lies an additional and not incompatible possibility, that the 'foreignness of the festival was *in itself* an affront to the British. 'They came on waving their sticks and yelling' says Captain Baker's report. 'Those in front were dancing and leaping in a most diabolical manner' (Norman 1885: 11). Enough indeed to make the police fire on them at thirty yards . . . The 'Policing of Otherness' is part of the policing of culture, and I believe that it lies below and legitimates the more obviously instrumental policing practices. The best-developed example in the Caribbean literature concerns obeah.

In Picton's code of 1800 (just after the British took over the island from the Spanish) Article II prohibited obeah. In 1801 there were suspected poisonings on the estates, and an *ad hoc* 'committee' with powers to adjudicate was set up (de Verteuil 1992). Among its powers this committee had the authority to mutilate and to burn alive. Most punishments, however, were designed to get the victim back to work as soon as possible. The purpose, says de Verteuil, was 'to brutalize the whole slave population into subjection' (1992: 35). Four years later twenty-three 'negroes and negresses', one overseer, twenty-three mules and four oxen were poisoned in a single case. The planters became fearful. The planters also feared that the slaves would kill themselves as well as each other. There were a great many suicides, and the sometimes lethal practice of 'eating dirt' was common in Trinidad.

Certainly poisonings and obeah were mixed up in the minds of the planters, although it is recorded that in the famous Jacquet case of 1803 on the de Verteuil estate the poisoning was done with arsenic powder bought from the local store by a slave who, as captain of the mill, could be presumed to be buying it for his owner. That Jacquet ended up killing those close to him and a child of the de Verteuil family, because his 'enemies' in the hot-house situation of personal dependence would not touch his arsenic-laced brew, simply compounded one tragedy within the overall obscenity of personal slavery.

And, of course, apart from the poisoning of themselves or their property, the planters attributed the frequency of abortions amongst the slave women to obeah. At first sight then it seems that obeah was criminalized on instrumental grounds. Yet on a second look, as we have seen in the recorded case just discussed, it was not obeah at all that caused the poisoning deaths, and as Mair (1986) and Dadzie (1990) argued, the abortions were almost certainly intended. There is, and was, no need to attribute either the deaths or the abortions to a religious or magical practice. I suggest that belief in the potency of obeah stemmed from its strangeness, its otherness, its total unknowability within the Britishers' discursive frame. The unknowable, the other, is powerful and, because it is other, also dangerous.

Jamaican data clarify the situation a little more. After one of the many slave uprisings, in 1760, it was enacted that it was illegal to use blood, feathers, parrots' beaks, broken bottles, grave dirt, rum, or eggshells in the administering of an oath. An oath bound by obeah was considered, by all sides it seems, unbreakable (Edwards 1976). From 1833 all obeah 'dealers' could be characterized as rogues and vagabonds under the Vagrancy Acts. (That one came in 1838 in Trinidad.) This act was replaced in 1839 by one which included 'myalism' as well as obeah. In 1855 another Obeah Act was passed: but the drafters had problems with the definition. Yet another Obeah Act was passed in the following year, increasing the penalty but also showing confusion in the definition (Edwards 1976). There must have been confusion in the administration too, by this time, since all three Acts were in force together. To compound the situation an amendment in 1892 increased the penalty yet again. Not before time in 1898 a consolidating statute was passed and the final Jamaican Obeah Act, changing the penalties yet again, was passed in 1903.

This legal history conceals as it constitutes a range of fears and cultural understandings which Edwards (1976) has exposed. In 1760 and the early years there was clearly a genuine fear of secret societies and rebellion and of poisoning. Whether or not the second fear was reality-based in relation to obeah, the laws were passed for instrumental reasons. In the middle years of the nineteenth century, however, after emancipation, this instrumental justification for the obeah laws no longer existed. What was being policed now was 'black magic' and blasphemy, something devilish perhaps, but the draftspeople were not quite sure what they wanted to illegalize, except that it was something that other people do, something that was feared as an alternative source of power, although the harms that this power might do could no longer be specified. *The difference was the danger.*

By 1898 the situation was clear again. By now obeah could clearly be defined as a fraudulent practice. No possibility of the truth of obeah was allowed. Flogging was deemed the appropriate punishment for the fraudsters. It was, of course, and to some extent still is in the Caribbean, deemed the appropriate punishment for many things. By 1903 those convicted under the obeah laws were no longer objects of fear. They might be a little mad perhaps, but they certainly could not be taken seriously. However, police supervision might be called for.

This story of an apparent increase in wisdom and tolerance is the most horrible example of all of the policing of a culture. The mix of the spiritual with the technical healing skills which obeah represented has been truly lost. First it was respected but repressed, then it became a stigmatized activity, and finally the attenuated practice became an object of ridicule, while simultaneously alternative healing and alternative cultural images were offered as more 'sensible'. In this case the cultural policing was successful. Those cultural knowledges have gone. Most black Trinidadians probably believe with de Verteuil, the white Trinidadian historian, that obeah is and was 'hocus pocus with white chickens and lots and lots of blood'. He forgot to mention blue glass.

Modern v. post-modern criminology: transcending the dichotomy for the Caribbean

If this were a textbook there would have to be the space for a detailed critical appreciation of the contributions to 'crime and development' theory by Fitzpatrick and Sumner, Seidman, Boehringer, and Pryce, the United Nations, and Lopez-Rey. But in this short discussion I want, with no disrespect to my various mentors and predecessors, to cut that short. Suffice it to say that however sophisticated the analyses, they are often rejected by Caribbean students and scholars such as Fanon and Pryce, because they do not address the experience of racism.[2] At the level of experience, racism defies explanation in terms of class position or interests. But the conflict approach for which Pryce argued served only to substitute 'colonialism' for 'capitalism', or to give the two phenomena equal status as ultimate negative causes. In the Caribbean, feminists tend to share the Pryce position, seeing their men and their violent domestic circumstances alike as outcomes of their colonial past. But everyone knows there is a lack of fit, everyone wants a specifically Caribbean theory which takes adequate account of the particular histories of the last five hundred years and the various cultures and relational patterns to which these particular histories, present circumstances, and political and personal choices have given rise. Colonialism as a concept is too far away, too general, to make sense of the variation or, it must be said, the effectiveness of the resistance, yet the continuing impact of colonialism is altogether too real and too obvious for explanations in terms of it to be thrown out either.

I propose to tackle this dilemma in reverse order, starting with the search for an adequate account of the policing of culture and then exploring connections with the policing of women, labour, and resistance. My premise is that any worthwhile theory must make sense of all of it.

Explanations for the policing of culture where they have been offered have typically been reductionist in that they have assumed that the culture had to be policed not because it was offensive or dangerous in itself but because of its impact on political or economic relations. Explanations of the policing of working-class leisure in the First World have seen that leisure as economically damaging (Harring 1982) or, in the Hall and Jefferson (1976) tradition, as a site of political resistance. In the Caribbean context it has been argued that obeah posed a threat to the very lives of the colonists, that drumming was dangerous as a means of communication, that the gathering together of large numbers of people leads to 'disturbances', and that the unity of the poor across ethnic lines would pose a political threat. These too are reductionist arguments, explaining the 'dangers' of cultural practices in terms of their effects. Such explanations connect readily with elaborated marxisms and those approaches which locate colonialism alongside capitalism as prime cause.

On the other hand, the tradition of post-modernism stemming from Foucault sees discourse, and by extension the rest of the symbolic world, as having *intrinsic* power, which is not derived from any other power source such as control over the means of life or the state, even by the longest route and the most complex chain of meditations. Power inheres in discourse/knowledge: and in other symbolic forms, for I would argue that the rhythm of the chac chac or the full low twang of the box base is also knowledge. The word, the sound, the line is a powerful thing. Not only poets and playwrights know this, but also administrators, politicians and lawyers. Cultural forms have power in themselves in the sense that they produce change or stability. Finding the phrase that touches the soul, whether in architecture, music or speech, is a powerful thing.

Arguing with Foucault that the powers of symbolic forms are internal to them is not a new departure, but it is a way of understanding so far overlooked in the 'crime and development' tradition. It is necessary, however, in order to make sense of the confused policing of obeah which Edwards (1976) has described. The legislation could not be formulated in the middle period because no specific evil outcomes were to be prevented. It was not clear who would be the injured party. Users of the obeah man or woman's services very rarely reported the offence. Until the category of fraud involving an unknowing victim was identified and applied, it was not clear why this (by now) perfectly harmless activity had at all costs to be stopped.

Only an understanding of a cultural practice as having intrinsic power can explain this. An alien cultural practice is a challenge at the level of identity, of consciousness even. It is the most fundamental challenge of all, albeit unintended. The insistent presence of the inconceivable cannot be tolerated. This is not because of organizational effects (which may be there, but on the other hand religions, like Spiritual Baptism, have been described as opiates); it is not because productivity will be affected; it is not because there is a hidden but translatable meaning, such as being a call to arms or other malign signal; rather it is precisely because a practice defies translation that it must be policed, for in this defiance it announces that the reality which has been constructed by you or me or the Caribbean colonists is not after all *the* real, but precisely a chimera. On this view, the policing of culture is an attempt to stave off the choice between chaos and an alternative reality.

The trouble in Trinidad is, of course, that capture and enslavement, the criminalization of being ill at work, not to mention imprisonment for resistance, are hard to describe as events resulting from purely symbolic challenges, possibly unintended. This makes even bigger nonsense than trying to find instrumental explanations for the policing of obeah after emancipation. Instrumental explanations do make sense as 'obviously' here as they failed to make sense in the cases discussed above of the policing of culture. An alternative position embracing, although of course resituating, these alternatives is needed. The neo-Kantian realism developed by Bhaskar (1979) and Code (1987) in particular provides part of the answer, as does Foucault himself (Foucault 1972; Cain 1993); but the Caribbean also forces me to attempt a unique account.

What is meant by the radical autonomy of discourse and other symbolic forms? It means two things. First, as I have argued above, it means that symbolic forms and cultural practices are powerful in themselves. Theirs is not a contingent power depending on the social location of the spokesperson/performer or the author of the symbol; it is an intrinsic power. Such forms and practices matter in themselves. Secondly, I want to argue for the radical uncausedness of symbolic forms and cultural practices. Indeed, the concept of cause can be distorting in sociological analyses, and (as I have argued elsewhere) a more modest conception of theory as a 'mapping' of relationships and practices allows better for the identification of exceptions, discontinuities, and patterns of articulation or disarticulation between configurations of relationship of lesser and greater scope.

However, to argue for the radical autonomy of symbolic forms and cultural practices in these two senses does not mean that they are floating about in social space. They can be 'mapped on' to relationships of other kinds in order to achieve a more complete understanding. In other words, autonomy does not entail primacy. There can be other uncaused phenomena, also with intrinsic powers. As I have argued elsewhere (Cain 1993), even Foucault was not arguing for the ontological primacy of discourse. Rather he emphasized its autonomy and its potency, as well as sketching in the ways in which its relations with the extra discursive might be conceived, and so studied (Foucault 1972: 44–6.) I share this view. It becomes necessary to examine what are these other kinds of relationships, for many would argue that all relationships between people are symbolic.

Bhaskar (1979) argues that a realist ontology, the belief in an independent reality, does not commit the knower to a positivist or absolutist epistemology. Code (1987) argues that the evidence for a realist ontology is at least as believable as the evidence for a purely ideal world, and that therefore to accept a realist ontology is to act as a responsible knower.

External, self-existent reality, however, can only be known by historically and socially located people suffering from all the cognitive and perceptual limitations of their kind. The art of knowing is both a selective and a creative one, always articulated with historical, social and symbolic relationships in uncaused ways which need to be explored. Knowledge is a way of shaking hands with reality which changes that which it reaches: it cannot be reality itself.

The problem for sociologists has always been that relationships, which are the objects of our discipline, are a form of reality with a very large knowledge component. This does not preclude the possibility of relationships which are not known, even by the people who constitute them. It may not be 'known' that domestic relations constitute part of a configuration of relationships of much larger scope, although many women do now know this to be the case. It certainly makes sense to argue that a sex/gender structure was real, existed, before anyone knew about it (see Harding 1983). Relationships which are not known none the less impact upon people's possibilities for knowledge and action.

What compounds the problem is: (a) knowing a relationship is inevitably incomplete at least; (b) as with all knowledge, there is no way of knowing whether the 'answer' (the knowledge itself) is adequate to the knower's purpose or not until after the event (given that reality and knowledge are incommensurable, truth is not a possible concept here); (c) the way the relationship is known may change the way people constitute the relationship. This being the way the world is, all one can do is attempt to produce good quality knowledge (Cain 1992) and in this way act as a responsible knower (Code 1988). But even these difficulties, and the acknowledgement of the symbolic component in known relationships, do not mean that relationships lack *any* reality independently of the symbolic.

A philosophical underpinning of this kind, which avoids a choice between modernism and post-modernism at the ontological level and accepts both reality, choice and permanent uncertainty, makes it possible to meet the demands of my students, among others, for a theory which sees the capture and enslavement of their ancestors as clearly serving the economic purposes of another race (and another class) of persons, while also making sense of the apparently pointless and wanton destruction of quite innocent and apolitical cultural forms.

The argument would then go like this. The constitution and control of the post-emancipation labour force must, whatever the specific characteristics of the occasion, be explained in a way which articulates the phenomenon with class relations as they themselves are articulated with and within first the colonial and then the post-colonial state, and always in the case of the Caribbean with the phenomenon of global capital. Similarly, a mapping of configurations of relationships of greater and lesser scope can explore the interface between East Indian plantation workers and Bajan policemen, and how it connects the local legislative council, the emergence of Tate and Lyle, and the British navy standing off San Fernando. The ways in which these relationships were discursively constructed is a part, but not the totality, of the way they may be understood, because the powers at play are relational *as well as* discursive.

This makes the task of theoretical mapping more complex, for if power is intrinsic to relationships as well as intrinsic to discourses and symbolic forms, the unity or dissociation of these two powers in the concrete practice must be examined; and this space for discrepancy, and disjunction at each moment, this permanent potential fracture is what creates the space for resistance which in the Caribbean has been so effective. (The African workers never did return to the plantations and many still do live outside the official economy; the work-force did manage to become strongly unionized on the plantations, in the oilfields, and in the public service; a black and 'mixed' middle class seized control of the state as the British withdrew, and the plantations and parts of the oil industry were nationalized.)

What I am arguing, then, is that relationships and discourses are analytically distinct although united and often reciprocally constitutive in the concrete situation. Both powers were deployed by the colonists with variable success. Both powers were used by the colonized too – sometimes to engage with the colonists and sometimes just to live.

Learning from the women

In the examples presented, relational and discursive powers appear both to occasion and to be deployed with equal force in the policing of women. Afro-Caribbean women, it seems to me, express their sexuality and their identity with a pride and directness which is quite different from the English pressure to attractiveness as a state of being. The way they walk is different, the way they sit is different, the way they present themselves to each other is different. They laugh (well, one did) at the simultaneous movement to approach and retreat of the English woman ('It's only me.'). There is nothing 'only' about an Afro-Caribbean woman's presentation of self. Today we know that the ways of doing genders are infinite. To the colonists, this mode of womanliness was other, different, alien, and to be policed – just like the drumming and the obeah. But there is evidence too that in the case of East Indian women, the new ways of being were a relational, political, challenge to East Indian men, led by a new relational independence which in the nineteenth century was not speakable or spoken. Oral historians are working on this,[3] but certainly the analysis will need a conception of dual power bases, in tension or alliance, in order to explore both the household particularities and the overarching patterns.

Perhaps, after all, I have not presented a method appropriate only for the Caribbean, but a method for everyone.

Conclusion

In this chapter I have argued that the colonial experience poses starkly the perpetual sociological dilemma of prioritizing structure in explanation or prioritizing communication. This dilemma persists even when causal analysis has been jettisoned. In the final section of this chapter I have presented an ontology which makes it possible to see both relationships and symbolic practices as having their own intrinsic and interdependent powers which may, in a concrete situation, be in tension or reciprocal support. In either event, the relationships and the symbolic practices must both be examined so that the manner of their articulations and disjunctions may be mapped.

This approach makes it possible to explain in the same way the policing of labour, the policing of politics and resistance, the policing of women, and the policing of culture.

Notes

[1] I allude to the work of my colleague Pat Mohammed who has been presenting papers and informal talks on the East Indian family over the last several years. I believe that she coined the term 'creolization' in this connection.

[2] See Boehringer and Giles 1977; Fitzpatrick 1980; Lopez-Rey 1970; Seidman 1966; Summer 1983; United Nations 1985. However, Fitzpatrick 1993 explicitly addresses the issue of the integral racism of the legal form.

³ In particular Mohammed, P. (1993) Ph.D. dissertation, Institute of Social Studies, The Hague, uses the concept of a 'negotiation of gender' to capture these complexities.

References

Abdullah, O. (1980). *The Commission of Enquiry Appointed to Enquire into the Existing Conditions of the Prisons and to Make Recommendations for Reform in the Light of Modern Penal Practices and Rehabilitation Measures*. Rt Revd C. O. Abdullah, chairman. (Government Printery, Port of Spain).

Anderson, D. and Killingray, D. (1991). *Policing the Empire* (Manchester, Manchester University Press).

Bhaskar, R. (1979). *The Possibility of Naturalism* (Brighton, Harvester).

Boehringer, G. and Giles, D. (1977). 'Criminology and neo-colonialism: the case of Papua New Guinea', *Crime and Social Justice*, (Fall–Winter), 58–63.

Breton, B. (1979). *Race Relations in Colonial Trinidad: 1870–1900* (Cambridge, Cambridge University Press).

Cain, M. (1989). 'Feminists transgress criminology' in Cain, M. (ed.), *Growing Up Good* (London, Sage).

Cain, M. (1992). 'Realist philosophy and standpoint epistemologies, or feminist criminology as a successor science' in Gelsthorpe, L. and Morris, A. (eds.), *Feminist Perspectives in Criminology* (Milton Keynes, Open University Press).

Cain, M. (1993). 'Foucault, feminism, and feeling: what Foucault can and cannot contribute to feminist epistemology' in Ramazanoglu, C. (ed.), *Up Against Foucault* (Routledge, London).

Cain, M. and Birju, A. (1992). 'Crime and structural adjustment in Trinidad and Tobago', *Caribbean Affairs*, 5(2), 141–53.

Code, L. (1987). *Epistemic Responsibility* (Hanover, University Press of New England).

Craig, S. (1988). *Smiles and Blood* (London, New Beacon Books).

Craig, S. (n.d.). Unpublished research materials, read in draft form by the author.

Dadzie, S. (1990). 'Searching for the invisible woman: slavery and resistance in Jamaica,' *Race and Class*, 32(2), 21–38.

Deosaran, R. (1993). *A Society Under Siege: a Study of Political Confusion and Cultural Mysticism* (St Augustine, McAl Centre for Psychological Research).

de Verteuil, A. (1992). *Seven Slaves and Slavery: Trinidad 1777–1838* (Scrip J. Printers Ltd, Port of Spain).

Dodd, D. (1979). 'The role of law in plantation society', *International Journal of the Sociology of Law*, 7(3), 275–96.

Donzelot, J. (1979). *The Policing of Families* (London, Hutchinson).

Edwards, A. (1976). 'The evolution of the obeah laws of Jamaica', *Jamaican Law Journal*, 19–25.

Fanon, F. (1968). *The Wretched of the Earth* (Harmondsworth, Penguin).

Fitzpatrick, P. (1980). *Law and State in Papua New Guinea* (London, Academic Press).

Fitzpatrick, P. (1993). *Mythology of Modern Law* (London, Routledge).

Foucault, M. (1972). *The Archaeology of Knowledge* (London, Tavistock).

Foucault, M. (1978). *The History of Sexuality Vol. 1* (Harmondsworth, Penguin).

Hagley, L. (1993a). 'Crime and structural adjustment: on the exercise of judicial discretion', *Caribbean Affairs*, 6(1), 147–54.

Hagley, L. (1993b). 'In search of a penal policy: the case of Trinidad and Tobago'. Paper presented to 6th International Conference on Penal Abolition (ICOPA), Costa Rica, June.

Hall, S and Jefferson, T. (1976). *Resistance Through Rituals* (London, Hutchinson).

Harding, S. (1983). 'Why has the sex/gender structure become visible only now' in Harding, S. and Hintikka. M. (eds.), *Discovering Reality* (Boston, D. Reidl Co.), 311–24.

Harring, S. (1982). 'The police institution as a class question: Milwaukee socialists and the police 1900–1915', *Science and Society*, XLVI(2), 197–221.

Lopez-Rey, M. (1970). *Crime: An Analytical Appraisal* (London, Routledge).

Lovelace, E. (1982). *The Wine of Astonishment* (London, Andre Deutsch).

Mahabir, C. (1980). 'Crime and nation building: the Emergency Powers Act, 1970', *International Journal of the Sociology of Law*, 8(2), 129–48.

Mahabir, C. (1988). 'Crime in the Caribbean: robbers, hustlers, and warriors', *International Journal of the Sociology of Law*, 16(3), 315–88.

Mair, L. (1986). 'Women field workers in Jamaica during slavery', Elsa Goveia Memorial Lecture, Department of History, Mona, UWI.

Morrison, T. (1987). *Beloved* (New York, Knopf).

Norman, H. W. (1885). *Correspondence Respecting the Recent Coolie Disturbances in Trinidad at the Mohurrum Festival with Report Thereon by Sir H. W. Norman, KCB* (London, Eyre and Spottiswoode).

Ottley, C. R. (1964). *An Historical Account of the Trinidad & Tobago Police Force from the Earliest Times* (Private Publication, Port of Spain).

Pryce, K. (1976). 'Towards a Caribbean criminology', *Caribbean Issues*, 11(2).

Ryan, S. (1991). *The Muslimeen Grab for Power: Race, Religion, and Revolution in Trinidad and Tobago* (Port of Spain, Inprint Caribbean).

Seemungal, L. (1974). *Report of the Commission Appointed to Enquire into the Circumstances Surrounding the Outbreak of the fire at the Royal, Goal on the 1st January 1976*, Mr Lional A. Seemungal QC, chairman (Government Printery, Port of Spain).

Seidman, R. (1966). *A Source Book of the Criminal Law of Africa* (London, Sweet and Maxwell).

Singh, K. (1988). *Bloodstained Tombs: The Muharram Massacre of 1884* (London, Macmillan Caribbean).

Summer, C. (1983). *Law, Crime, and Underdevelopment* (London, Heinemann).

Trotman, D. (1984). 'Women and crime in late nineteenth century Trinidad', *Caribbean Quarterly*, 3 and 4, 60–72.

Trotman, D. (1986). *Crime in Trinidad* (Knoxville, University of Tennessee Press).

United Nations (1985). 'New dimensions of criminality and crime prevention in the context of development' A/conf/121/20.

Willis, J. (1991). 'Thieves, drunkards, and vagrants: defining crime in colonial Mombasa, 1902–32' in Anderson and Killingray (eds.), *Policing the Empire*, 219–35.

Policing and prosecution

6

The end of public policing? Police reform and 'the new managerialism'

EUGENE MCLAUGHLIN AND KARIM MURJI

> The old is dying and the new cannot be born – in the interregnum there arises a great diversity of morbid symptoms. (Antonio Gramsci, *Prison Notebooks*)

> Of all the public services, the police are the most over-ripe for reform. (Howard Davies, *Fighting Leviathan*)

Introduction

'Crisis' has been an overused word in relation to the police in recent years, but events in 1993 may indicate that new dimensions have been added to the familiar problems. The police's hitherto 'sacred' role has been called into question by the chief inspector of constabulary and they have found themselves in open conflict with the Conservative government.

The source of the 'crisis' lies in the loss of credibility suffered by the police as a public sector bureaucracy in the last ten years. First, there has been an impression that they have retreated from the public sphere, no longer making arrests because of disillusionment with 'revolving door' cautioning policies and a lack of support from the rest of the criminal justice system. Whether this is true or not, there seem to be plenty of takers willing to fill the spaces left by the police. For instance, there has been widespread publicity about vigilantism, community self-help and private security services. These have taken a variety of more or less edifying forms, from community self-defence initiatives (in the case of racial attacks for example) to proactive patrols, as well as the dispensation of summary 'popular' justice. Increased respectability was accorded to vigilantism by a BBC *Panorama* poll showing considerable public backing for 'avenging angels'. Further support was lent by the chairman of Dixons who said that there was a need 'to legitimize the meaning of vigilantism' and the admission that his stores had resorted to the use of vigilantes to protect themselves during a crime wave.

At the same time other players have emerged to take on quasi-policing roles. Some local authorities are pioneering new developments in the policing of 'problem' estates. In Sunderland, for example, private investigators are being used as 'professional witnesses' by the local authority, and in Hackney the council has resorted to using civil injunctions against 'criminal' residents and their families. Meanwhile, in Sedgefield, the local authority has gone so far as to set up its own 'shadow' police. Other local authorities have also looked into the possibility of developing their own community safety services.

Not surprisingly, private security firms have also stepped into the breach. There have been well-publicized reports from Greater Manchester, Dorset and Bristol, for example, of communities and neighbourhoods deciding (in certain instances with police support) to employ private security firms for routine patrolling purposes. Private policing also received a boost in April 1993 when it was announced that the Treasury was pushing for the externalization of certain 'marginal' (or non-core) policing functions. Two police forces have responded to the pull of market forces by announcing that they are giving serious consideration to setting up their own private security units to compete with local private security firms. Meanwhile, concern about rural crime led the magazine *Country Life* to launch a campaign to restore the ancient office of parish constable. The home secretary signalled approval by calling for ideas about the job description of such constables to be sent to the Home Office.

Secondly, there was increasing evidence (especially from the Audit Commission) of inefficient and outdated working practices. Finally, in tandem with rising crime and declining clear-up rates, Conservative perceptions of the police were changing. In the wake of a number of miscarriages of justice, new doubts about the police were emerging from within hitherto loyal constituencies. As Assistant Chief Constable Elizabeth Neville conceded:

> Quite ordinary people simply assume that police officers don't tell the truth. Middle-class people who vote conservative think the police are not corrupt in the sense of taking money but not trustworthy. (*The Guardian* 27 November 1992)

It was these concerns that finally prompted the then home secretary Kenneth Clarke to announce at the 1992 conference of the Association of Chief Police Officers (ACPO) that reform would be necessary to win back the confidence of 'middle England' (*The Guardian*, 11 June 1992). As we all now know, the reform proposals took two forms, the *Inquiry into Police Responsibilities and Rewards*, chaired by Sir Patrick Sheehy, and the Government White Paper, *Police Reform*, both published in June 1993. Together they signalled the government's intention to modernize British policing. If Sheehy was to bring about the internal reform of the organization, then the White Paper complements it by proposing reform of police authorities.[1]

The reform package generated an extremely critical reaction which included a mass gathering of police officers at a Wembley rally and regular full-page newspaper adverts asking people to encourage their MPs to oppose the proposals. Newspapers commented freely that the long-presumed love affair between the Conservatives and the police had ended with a bang. Police officers spoke of feeling betrayed by a government which had previously identified itself as a staunch supporter of law and order. A variety of commentators saw the reform package as basically market-driven centralizing measures which would add to the loss of local democratic control of the police (Reiner and Spencer 1993; Dingwall and Shapland 1993). It is with this critical response that we take issue in this paper. While there are undoubtedly elements of centralization and de-democratization present, focusing solely on these leads to an underestimation of the underlying managerial nature of the proposed changes. Instead of looking at the details of Sheehy and the White Paper in isolation, we argue that the reform package is better understood as part of the ongoing *managerialization* of the public sector. We attempt to show how 'the new managerialism' can be used to 'read' both Sheehy and the White Paper in a rather different light to those viewpoints which have received most attention. Managerialism is becoming an increasingly familiar part of the public sector and at the end we speculate a little about the possibilities for reform which it raises in regard to the police and policing.

Responses to the reform agenda

The publication of the White Paper and the Sheehy Report triggered a series of critical responses which quickly coalesced around two themes. There was widespread agreement that the proposals were part of 'a single centralising package' (P. A. J. Waddington, *The Independent*, 1 July 1993) and doomed to failure. These are some of the main criticisms made of the White Paper and the Sheehy Report:

The White Paper on police reform

The White Paper managed to unite the police and the local authority associations in opposition to the plans to reform police authorities. The arguments of the opponents can be arranged under two interrelated headings. First, the proposed reforms would mean further central control of the police and second, that there would be a corresponding loss of local democratic accountability. Thus, the president of ACPO, John Burrow, stated:

> We seriously question the need to reconstitute police authorities. The essence of policing is its relationship with the local community and this relationship is made legitimate through the police authority's accountability to the local electorate. No matter how this package is presented as reinforcing local accountability it is in fact a shift to greater national control. (*Local Government Chronicle* 2 July 1993)

More specific arguments made against the White Paper included:

1. Reform of the police authorities would accentuate the historical trend towards greater central control of the police. For David Rose of *The Observer* (4 July 1993) the White Paper was 'the most centralising measure in the history of British policing, amounting to a basic constitutional shift'.

2. 'Creeping centralization' would mean that decisions about policing would become 'more secretive, less accountable and less in touch' with local people (*The Guardian* editorial, 29 June 1993).

3. Another 'local' service would become divorced from local government. For the county, metropolitan and district council associations the restructured police authorities would, as quangos, become 'the agents of central government instead of the legitimate voice of the community'.

4. The essence of British policing would be irrevocably harmed and the 'war on crime' seriously damaged.

5. Achieving the national objectives set by the Home Office would be 'distorted' by periodic moral panics.

The inquiry into police responsibilities and rewards

The Sheehy proposals were viewed as giving the seal of approval to the government's centralizing ambitions. The soft version of this argument attributes this to the fact that Sheehy worked uncritically within the general framework laid out by the White Paper, while the more conspiratorial view asserted that Sheehy's talk of managerial flexibility and devolution was, at best, an illusion and, at worst, a masking exercise for the centralization agenda. The report was also criticized on the grounds that it was fatally flawed in its analysis, being more suited to the world of commercial management than policing. Consequently, it was argued that it could not bring about desired improvements in police effectiveness and efficiency. Instead, as speakers from the respective police staff associations informed the mass rally at Wembley, Sheehy was a 'blueprint for disaster'. Dick Coyles of the Police Federation subsequently argued that:

> Sheehy has no place in the present or the future of policing. He and his colleagues speak the language of an alien culture, which never begins to understand the real significance of policing in society. (*Police Review*, 1 October 1993)

A variety of apocalyptic warnings were made to back up this claim:

1. Reducing the ranks was a retrograde, unwarranted and unproductive step because rank confers prestige and status and is organizationally important as a motivator – maybe more so than money – and a necessary component of effective supervision.

2. Organizational change on its own could not have any impact on the effectiveness of policing. Cultural change is the key to reform.

3. Performance measures would be likely to have an adverse effect on the quality of service over a whole range of issues, encouraging 'short termism', bad police work and endangering the public.

4. The idea of setting targets is premised on the misconception that

policing can be policy driven. It cannot: day-to-day policing is demand driven, responding to the demands of the public.

5. New contracts and working conditions would seriously hinder recruitment, retention and motivation.

6. It would change the ethos of the job and reduce the service from being a dedicated vocation and a 'calling' to an ordinary job, leading to a loss of moral legitimacy.

7. It would undermine morale by (a) 'emasculating' the negotiating rights of the rank and file; (b) exacerbating tensions which exist within the organization by encouraging unhealthy competition between forces and officers; and (c) being imposed from without.

8. Police culture would not change, rather it would absorb the changes and learn to cut new corners.

9. It would lead to fire-brigade policing and a decline in preventive and detective work.

Criticizing the critics

There are serious problems with the critical views outlined above. An initial criticism is that the appeal to 'local democracy' and 'democratic accountability' sounds hollow and, frankly, cynical. More problematically, the argument that the police are already locally accountable suggests a scenario in which the tripartite structure represents a 'pure' form of democratic accountability and police authorities are the embodiment of the 'democratic will'. The fatal flaws of the 'tripartite structure' of police accountability were delineated in painstaking detail in the 1980s (Jefferson and Grimshaw 1984; Spencer 1985), but the lessons of that decade have either not been learnt, or are simply being ignored. The same applies to the Conservative government's restructuring of police authorities and the defeat of campaigns for meaningful local democratic accountability.

Only the *Local Government Chronicle* (editorial, 2 July 1993) seemed willing to acknowledge that police authorities and their supporters were on shaky grounds in their evocation of democracy when it stated that the reform proposals would probably not generate much controversy in local communities because of 'the failure of police authorities to have a clear local profile'. This is not surprising when Stephen Murphy, the chair of Greater Manchester Police Authority proudly informs the media that there should be no change to the *status quo* because the authority has not taken a 'political' decision in recent memory! If nothing else, the proposed restructuring of police authorities will lay bare the myth of local democratic accountability and the cosy 'non-political' set of relationships that were established after 1985. We would argue that a transparent lack of democracy is better than a beguiling mirage of democracy.

A further problem with the critical response is that the sole concentration on centralization is misleading. We shall argue that a more complex and contradictory process is in motion. The key signal of this process is the gap between the three police staff associations. While the Police Federation and the Superintendents' Association remained resolute in their opposition, ACPO gradually made it clear that – while they opposed performance-related pay and fixed-term contracts for the rank and file – they were in favour of other proposals. For example, ACPO welcomed proposals in the White Paper to give greater autonomy to chief constables. This qualified acceptance should surprise few people, because the core principles of the White Paper and the Sheehy Report deliver what many progressive senior officers have been aiming for some years: greater managerial control over their organizations, budgets and personnel. Thus, a fundamental difference between ACPO and the Police Federation was that while the latter opposed the proposals, police managers were inclined to negotiate and disagree *within* the managerial framework laid out by both the Sheehy Report and the White Paper. It is this contradictory response which leads us to argue that the reform agenda being laid before the police should be read as being part of a wider process of the *managerialization* of the public sector in Britain, rather then simply one of centralization.

The new managerialism

There is now a substantial body of work available which delineates the impact of the new managerialism on the public sector in this country and elsewhere (Hood 1991; Massey 1993; Pollitt 1993; Farnham and Horton 1993; Clarke, Cochrane and McLaughlin 1994). It is something which police managers and others have clearly been aware of for some time (for example, see Newman 1984; Butler 1992; Bradley, Walker and Wilkie 1986; Horton and Smith 1988). Consequently, we shall not repeat debates about the complicated genesis and intellectual provenance of this set of ideas. For our analysis what is important is the general agreement that this development is more than a passing fad. It is closely linked with wider developments in the reconstruction of the public sector (Le Grand and Bartlett 1993) and with the kinds of changes which the government has introduced into other areas of the criminal justice system (for example see Jones 1993; Leishman and Savage 1993a; McLaughlin and Muncie 1993; Spencer 1993). The new managerialism undermines the traditional barriers between the private sector and the public sector. Farnham and Horton (1993) argue that it involves the use of economistic, rationalist and generic frames of reference (which is in contrast to the older public sector model of administration based on bureaucracy, incrementalism and particularism). Taking each of these frames of reference in turn we can briefly illustrate how the reform proposals dove-tail with the new managerialism. Read in this light it should become apparent that they are part of the wider dynamic of managerialization, already injected into public services during the 1980s and 1990s. We shall also argue that the police themselves are already actively engaged in a managerialization process which leads in much the same direction. Ironically, in the long term it is this which places the police in a no-win position in relation to the reform agenda.

Economism

The essence of economism is the application of accountancy principles to public services. This includes the well-known 'value for money' slogan and the delegation of financial responsibility lower down the line (as in the setting up of governmental agencies, or in locally managed schools or hospital trusts). It is not difficult to see that the police have already travelled a long way down this road. Since the famous Circular 114/83 value for money considerations have underlain much police thinking and initiatives (Horton and Smith 1988). This has been pressed home by subsequent Home Office circulars, more focused monitoring by the Inspectorate and, crucially, evaluative reports emanating from the Audit Commission which identified waste, archaic working practices and non-management.

The reform package offers a framework to deepen and extend this process, by providing the practical means to break the rigid financial paradigm that drives the costs of policing inexorably upwards. For example, in order to promote value for money they propose cash limits on police budgets and giving chief constables greater freedom over how to allocate that money.

> Thus we have sought both to empower and to make chief officers accountable for how resources are managed and service is delivered, freeing them to direct resources so as to meet changing demands. (Sheehy Report, para. 15.3)

Sheehy also outlined a blueprint for police managers to make considerable savings through the removal of statutory regulations 'in favour of local discretionary arrangements which will free management to manage flexibly according to local needs, circumstances and priorities' (para. 11.9). Local managers would have the freedom to decide the appropriate expenditure on officers, civilian staff and equipment and be further empowered through the proposed restructuring of the rank structure, salary levels, pensions and allowances. Managers would be forced to manage and ultimately this would mean exercising the power to hire and fire. Thus, in Sheehy we find proposals which provide the means for more cost-effective local policing to become a reality.

Rationalism

Rational management consists of breaking the managerial task into operational and strategic components. It is upon the strategic aspect that we want to concentrate here. The use of mission statements and the setting of strategic goals have become a familiar part of life in the public sector. As a result of the reforms initiated by chief officers such as Sir Kenneth Newman and Sir Peter Imbert, the police also adopted a corporate management style and the ideas of management by objectives (or policing by objectives) (see Newman 1984). In the 1990s strategic management will become a central feature in all forces. What is novel is that the White Paper extends this rational strategic approach to all actors in the policing process. At the broadest level, policy will be set by the Home Office's national objectives for the police. Within this framework the restructured police authorities would have to establish costed local policing priorities based on consultation with local communities. They would also have an oversight role in the monitoring of police performance.

Policy implementation would be the responsibility of chief constables. With the separation of police authorities from local government, any view of chief constables as being the equivalents of a director of education or social services in a local authority vanishes; instead, as chief police officers are recognizing, they become analogous to the chief executive of the local authority or the health authority. As Keith Hellawell, chief constable of West Yorkshire said in response to Sheehy:

> I look forward to the changes. I think we should be paid in accordance with the kind of money paid to the heads of large corporations; we are moving further away from being chief officers and becoming more like chief executives. In return we should be allowed the freedom to run our organisations and generate our own income. (*The Independent* 1 July 1993)

Chief constables would then be in a position to devolve budgets and clearly defined managerial responsibility down to divisions and basic command units, the managers of which are responsible for day-to-day operational matters and meeting both force and local policing priorities. Sheehy supported this localization on the grounds that devolving operational responsibility to a flattened middle and lower management span would generate innovation, thus improving organizational effectiveness and providing a firm basis upon which to assess and evaluate personal performance.

Hence, while there are undoubtedly elements of centralization and local de-democratization embedded in the reform agenda, the overall rational management approach also provides for, at one and the same time, elements of local empowerment and different forms of decentralization.

Genericism

The third axis of the new managerialism consists of four strands:

— managers facilitate change rather than resist it;
— management is driven by objectives rather than problems;
— managers become customer-focused;
— managers are likely to be generalists rather than specialists.

It is possible to detect these strands already taking hold in certain forces. Individual senior police officers and ACPO are, for example, making concerted efforts to project a positive image of themselves as the carriers of dynamic and innovative change. Police forces are already engaging in surveys of customer opinion and the level of satisfaction with services. Indeed forces are pushing ahead with this as a way of implementing the Citizens Charter. Certain forces are now delivering to every household a 'statement of expectations' concerning the standard of policing services that will be delivered in that locality. Corresponding to this shift has been the adoption of the language of consumerism and quality of service as the police have sought to re-present themselves in public. The reform agenda with its emphasis on local consultation in the setting of local policing priorities seems set to further this process.

The use of management by objectives principles by the police has already been mentioned. It seems likely, therefore, that the impact of the reform process will result in policing becoming more objective-driven, since this will be the basis for evaluating performance. Successful, proactive, customer-oriented managers will be rewarded, while underperforming officers, chief constables and police authorities may find that they are ripe for 'take-over' as the home secretary exercises new powers of amalgamation. Perhaps just as worrying for some is the intriguing idea that the government's reforms open the door to the direct recruitment of police managers who have no previous background in the force (Wall 1993; Leishman and Savage 1993b).

For some critics the reforms are inadequate because they bring about structural changes in rank and rewards but do not produce corresponding cultural changes in management style. This argument is wide of the mark. The reform proposals are designed to deliver a package of structural *and* cultural changes in which new managerial principles, if implemented, are intended to run through everything the police do. Policing is already guided by the need for economy, effectiveness and efficiency, meeting clearly defined objectives and thinking of the public as customers of police services. The proposed reforms are intended to deepen these objectives by 'loosening the shackles' – they release police managers from the grip of local and central government, and make it easier to get rid of the 'dead wood' in the organization. What all of this means is that chief police officers can become the masters of their own destiny – setting 'their' targets, evaluating the performance of 'their' organization against those objectives and 'benchmarking' themselves against other organizations operating in the same sector of the market. Members of ACPO who have been toying with these ideas now have the opportunity to put themselves to the test as *real* managers. But to what extent will this vision of managerialism be realized?

Can the police resist managerialism?

During 1993 the Police Federation declared war on Sheehy through its media campaign and shaman-like show of strength at Wembley. But it is interesting to note the response of traditionally pro-Conservative newspapers to the Wembley rally. The *Daily Telegraph* (21 July 1993), for example, argued that the public was entitled 'to expect a more detached and professional, less narrowly mercenary, response from the Police Federation to the present debate'. While the *Daily Mail*, (19 July 1993) informed the home secretary that it was his 'unenviable ministerial duty to stand *up to* as well as *for* the police'. While these views indicate that there may be less support for the police than some officers seem to imagine, it is none the less possible that the police campaign will muddle or at least delay the reform process. However, we doubt that longer-term reform of the police along managerial lines can be derailed for three principal reasons.

First, Sheehy's opponents continue to rest their case on the argument that the reforms will not work because they are inappropriate to the 'vocational nature' of policing and would, if implemented, destroy the 'special status' of the British police. We do not set much store by the idea that policing is 'special'. This argument has been effectively debunked by a generation of police research. As the Sheehy committee stated: 'there has been a tendency on occasion – some feel an exaggerated tendency – to claim special status for police officers when this is not justified' (para. 1.7). Police work, for the most part, remains a mundane set of activities which have been subject to much mystification. And, as the events mentioned at the beginning indicate, it is not at all inconceivable that many of the tasks now carried out by the police could legitimately be hived off to other public, as well as private and voluntary agencies. This would leave the police with clearly defined 'specialist' core tasks, a process which both the White Paper and the Sheehy Report (and indeed the Audit Commission) support. None of this has to mean that ordinary police officers will be reduced to being the 'poor relations' of a detective élite or the equivalent of private security guards:

Anyone who really has a vocation can still make the police service a 'job for life' and, moreover, the service will reward their expertise and dedication, better than it does at present. (Sir Patrick Sheehy, *Financial Times* 26 July 1993)

Secondly, we have argued that the police have already embraced managerialism during the 1980s in an attempt to put their own house in order. There is little doubt that a managerialist culture exists and has taken root. The issue then becomes not one of whether or not there will be managerialism, but of how far it will (or ought to) go. On what legitimate grounds can the police now resist further steps in this process? It seems fair to say that once the managerial imperative is placed at the heart of an organization it is very difficult to go back to the old order.

A third weakness in the case of those attacking the reform proposals is the problem of credibility. Does anyone really believe that the *status quo* is defensible? The idea that policing is a 'special vocation' does not stand up to examination when viewed in the light of recent abuses of power. Radical reform of the police would seem to be a minimum demand given the 'job for life' mentality, the restrictive practices and the existence of inefficient and corrupt officers. Any semblance of a 'sacred' consensual social contract between the police and the community was ripped apart in the course of the 1980s as officers eagerly accepted the sponsorship of the Conservative government. But such patronage has costs as well as benefits and the police have had to come to terms with its consequences, including the gradual imposition of a market culture. As the government's 'long march through the institutions' takes its toll there seems little or no prospect of returning to an older (idealized) order. As the chief inspector of constabulary has conceded, 'In this doubting age, the service may never again return to the post-war position of being a national institution' (Woodcock 1992).

The wider point is that the new managerialism is part of the 'revolution in government' which looks as if it is here to stay. It may have been initiated by a radical Conservative government to break the older bureaucratic ethos of public administration. However, there is also an emergent consensus that the 'apolitical' *ideology* of new managerialism will outlast radical right regimes because the promise and meaning of a more business-like public sector is attractive to a wider constituency. As Pollitt states:

'better management' sounds sober, neutral, as unopposable as virtue itself. Given the recent history of public-service expansion the productivity logic has a power of its own which stands independently of the political programme of the new right. (Pollitt 1993: 49)

Conclusion

The White Paper and the Sheehy Report have been received as summoning forth spectral visions of the end of policing as a 'vocation' and a politically directed police force. If the scale of the critical reaction is not surprising (the police are after all merely defending their patch, much as any other self-interested group would), its terms are more questionable. In our view it would be misleading to see 1993 as marking a sudden departure from what has been the case to date. Indeed, in two ways, the reform proposals marked a continuation rather than a radical departure from the government's approach. First, they indicate the culmination of increasing government dissatisfaction with the police. Signs of this are obvious from at least 1988 onwards, as evidenced by reports into virtually every aspect of policing emanating from the Audit Commission, the debate about the need for the separation of local and national policing (including the call for a national detective agency), the more active role taken by the Inspectorate, as well as the debate about the entry of an 'officer class' into the hierarchy of police management (Audit Commission 1990; Reiner 1992; Leishman and Savage 1993a, 1993b). Secondly, the government's proposals for police reform are merely the latest in a long line which seek to apply the ethos and principles of the private sector to the public services. So the police are now invited to follow a similar path to that already followed by education, the health service, local government – and more pertinently, even the courts, the prison and probation services. All of this indicates that the reform agenda has been unfolding for some time. Sheehy and the White Paper are the 'next steps' in this process not a radical departure from it. Hence the reform proposals – seen as part of the managerialization of the public sector – is rather more complex than the critics have allowed for. This argument also suggests the need to step outside a narrow criminological perspective if we are to make sense of the politics of police reform. In this final section we speculate about where managerialism and the reform of the police could lead.

The impact of the new managerialism means that the logic of the market now runs deep within the new post-Thatcherite public sector culture. But what is emerging is not the privatization feared by many during the 1980s but rather a quasi-market approach. Here, while state funding is retained, the way in which services are provided is changed. Decision-making is decentralized as the state becomes a purchaser of services which are bought from independent providers competing in an internal or quasi-market (Le Grand and Bartlett 1993). The idea is that internal competition produces more efficient services at a lower price, while affirming consumer sovereignty. As workers in the public sector are only too aware, the scope for applying this approach is wide. The development of quasi-markets means that at least some of the most debilitating and paternalistic statist assumptions about the delivery of public services have been challenged and, in some instances, removed. The image of the central or local state as the monolithic provider of all people's needs and wants is passing into distant memory. What is emerging instead is a new set of relationships underscored by the discourses of the market and consumerism.

What are the implications of this ongoing revolution for the police? Broadly, one can speculate on two possible outcomes, which we label the 'last chance' and the 'end of public policing' scenarios. In the former, the reform proposals can be seen as the government's attempt to give a decisive spur to the internal reform process and to progressive senior officers. Sheehy and the White Paper invite chief officers to become *real* managers, with financial autonomy, clear performance targets and the contractual freedom to ensure that the work-force delivers – the power to hire and fire. Some of those who live by managerialism will presumably also die by it if they do not adapt to the new circumstances. There will also be a shake-out throughout the ranks, as a Victorian institution seeks to remake itself for the twenty-first century. In the process the culture, style and methods of policing will also undergo change, away from the paramilitary command style into the new professional service culture of 'new times'. While this vision may include a specialized national police force, what would also emerge, ideally *at the locale*, is a post-Fordist police 'dis-organization' based on flexibility, diversity and consumer sovereignty. This 'post-modern' vision of the future may be unwelcome to many police officers, but they may well prefer it to the second scenario.

Our 'end of public policing' scenario begins with the question of market competition. How far can or should there be a quasi-market in the provision of police services? Under the reform proposals, 'the police' will still remain as the monopoly providers of policing services. But the edges continue to blur because of the scale of involvement of the private sector, the hiving off of certain police tasks to other agencies and the increase in direct community self-policing. If this 'creeping privatization' continues, the police may find that their local role begins to crumble away, leaving them with élite national policing as their core responsibility. Market forces would find that the police are a bloated public sector bureaucracy ill equipped to cope with competition.[2] There are as yet no formal proposals to subject the police to open competition. But it could be argued that the logic of the reform process and the quasi-market approach means that the 'evaluative state' (in this case, individual police authorities) ought to be able to purchase the service it wants from among a range of competitive providers (see also Loveday 1993a, 1993b). In the immediate future, competition for policing contracts might be limited to existing police forces in a system of internal competition designed to exclude outsiders such as the private security industry.

But if a marketized future was to become a reality then this cosy 'internal market' could be challenged on the grounds that it restricts free competition. If the challenge was successful there is no reason why other European (or perhaps even transatlantic) police forces could not compete with local police forces for the delivery of particular policing services (see also Dorn 1993). Some would argue that, perhaps, there is no reason why communities and neighbourhoods could not choose to take on the direct role of purchasing their own specialist policing requirements or indeed opting out altogether in order to set up their own policing arrangements. A demarketization could also take place if the formal boundaries between the local police and other local services collapsed completely and multipurpose decentralized community safety teams were formed by local authorities. Whatever outcome ensues, it seems clear that the placing of an essentially *private* set of managerial imperatives and approaches at the heart of policing heralds the inception of reforms that will put an end to public policing as it has been understood in this country for over a century. In the process, critics of police reform would have to realize that there can be no going back to the securities of either the authoritarian or even the social democratic state-form.

Notes

1   In this paper we refer collectively to the Sheehy Report and the White
    Paper as the 'reform proposals'. This does not mean that we do not see
    differences between them, but they are taken together for the purposes of
    the argument presented here. Similarly, we shall also refer to them as the
    'government's proposals' even though the Sheehy inquiry does not
    constitute an official government report.
2   It may be that this realization is what underlies Sheehy's recommendation
    for cutting the starting pay and restructuring the pay scales.

References

Audit Commission (1990). *Effective Policing: Performance review in police forces* (London, HMSO).

Bradley, D., Walker, N. and Wilkie, R. (1986). *Managing the Police* (Hemel Hempstead, Harvester Wheatsheaf).

Butler, A. (1992). *Police Management*, 2nd edn. (Aldershot, Dartmouth).

Clarke, J., Cochrane, A. and McLaughlin, E. (eds.) (1994). *Managing Social Policy* (London, Sage).

Davies, H. (1992). *Fighting Leviathan: Building social markets that work* (London, Social Market Foundation).

Dingwall, R. and Shapland, J. (eds.) (1993). *Reforming British Policing Missions and Structures* (Sheffield, Faculty of Law, University of Sheffield).

Farnham, D. and Horton, S. (eds.) (1993). *Managing the New Public Services* (Basingstoke, Macmillan).

Home Office (1993). *Police Reform: A police service for the twenty-first century* Cm. 2281 (London, HMSO).

Hood, C. (1991). 'A public management for all seasons?', *Public Administration*, 69, (spring).

Horton, C. and Smith, D. (1988). *Evaluating Policework* (London, PSI).

Jefferson, T. and Grimshaw, R. (1984). *Controlling the Constable* (London, F. Muller).

Jones, C. (1993). 'Auditing criminal justice', *British Journal of Criminology*, 33(2).

Le Grand, J. and Bartlett, W. (eds.) (1993). *Quasi-Markets and Social Policy* (Basingstoke, Macmillan).

Leishman, F. and Savage, S. (1993a). 'The police', in Farnham, D. and Horton, S. (eds.), *Managing the New Public Services*.

Leishman, F. and Savage, S. (1993b). 'Officers or managers?', *International Journal of Public Sector Management*, 6(5).

Loveday, B. (1993a). 'The local accountability of police in England and Wales: future prospects', in Reiner, R. and Spencer, S. (eds.), *Accountable Policing: Effectiveness, Empowerment and Equity* (London, IPPR).

Loveday, B. (1993b). 'Management and accountability in public services: a police case study', in Issac-Henry, K., Painter, C. and Barnes, C. (eds.), *Management in the Public Sector: Challenge and Change* (London, Chapman Hall).

McLaughlin, E. and Muncie, J. (1993). 'The silent revolution', *Socio-Legal Bulletin* (La Trobe University, Melbourne).

Massey, A. (1993). *Managing the Public Sector* (Aldershot, E. Elgar).

Newman, K. (1984). *Report of the Commissioner of Police of the Metropolis* (London, HMSO).

Pollitt, C. (1993). *Managerialism and the Public Services*, 2nd edn. (Oxford, Blackwell).

Reiner, R. (1992). *The Politics of the Police*, 2nd edn. (Hemel Hempstead, Wheatsheaf).

Reiner, R. and Spencer, S. (eds.) (1993). *Accountable Policing: Effectiveness, Empowerment and Equity* (London, IPPR).

Sheehy, P. *et al.* (1993). *Inquiry into Police Responsibilities and Rewards* (London, HMSO).

Spencer, J. (1993). 'The criminal justice system and the politics of scrutiny', *Social Policy and Administration*, 27(1).

Spencer, S. (1985). *Called to Account* (London, NCCL).

Wall, D. (1993). 'Controlling the police', paper presented at the British Criminology Conference, Cardiff University, July.

Woodcock, J. (1992). 'Why we need a revolution', *Police Review*, 16 October.

7

Revising 'police powers': legal theories and policing practices in historical and contemporary contexts

DAVID DIXON

This chapter examines the nature of police powers in England and Australia. The focus is not on specific powers (although some are discussed as examples) but rather on 'police powers' as a concept. Issues discussed include the origins and development of police powers, the relationship between powers and duties, the role of powers in policing practices, the legal concept of police powers and the utility of changing police powers in response to concerns about crime and disorder. The argument running through what follows is that police powers cannot fully or even usefully be considered in legalistic isolation. What a power means is usually defined (at least in part) by how it is used. In this sense, police powers and policing practices cannot be clearly distinguished.

1. Histories of policing

There is difficulty in separating the history of police powers from the broader history of the police, especially when (as in Australia) historians have only recently begun to concern themselves seriously with police history. Sections 1–4 discuss police powers, and focus on their relationship to the reorganization of policing in England and Australia in the first half of the nineteenth century.

On a thumb-nail, the traditional account of English police history is as follows. The village constable was the product of a tradition of self-governing, responsible, local communities in the early Middle Ages. In the early modern period, the institution of constable declined into the caricatures provided by Shakespeare – Dogberry in *Much Ado About Nothing* and Elbow in *Measure for Measure*. By the eighteenth century, England was almost an unpoliced society. After years of combating dogged, irrational resistance, enlightened reformers led by Robert Peel succeeded in introducing a professional police force to London in 1829 which rekindled the office of constable and the relationship between police and community. There was no deep divide between police and people; rather, the police were merely 'citizens in uniform'.

In such accounts, the introduction of the 'New Police' is 'regarded as the social equivalent of the steam engine in the process of industrialization: the "heroic" invention which transformed the situation from one of persistent disorder to one of relative tranquillity' (Stevenson 1979: 321). Peel's Metropolitan Police set the example which provincial England, Australia and much of the common law world followed, while the rest of the world looked on in envy.

Social historians have exposed this account as being largely ideology and teleology, misleading in most significant respects (for reviews of this extensive literature, which is by no means homogeneous, see Brogden 1988 *et al.*: ch. 4 and 5; Emsley 1991; Reiner 1985: part 1; Robinson 1979). From their perspectives, the story is to be told a different way. The village constable was the product, not of arcadian self-government, but of the intersection of contrasting forms of political organization – the local Anglo-Saxon state and the increasingly centralized Norman state. This tension was felt subsequently, for example in the seventeenth century, as constables mediated between the norms of village communities and the central state's attempts to impose new standards of moral and social discipline (Wrightson 1980).

The constable's role was not policing in its modern sense; rather it involved much more general social ordering. This was reflected in the broad use of the term 'police' when it first entered the language in the eighteenth century. When people

> did use the word, they were referring to the general regulation or government, the morals or economy, of a city or country. The French word derived from the Greek *polis*, the root base of the words 'politics', 'polity', 'policy'. (Palmer 1988: 69)

Later, 'the word "police" began to be used, in its continental sense, to refer to the specific functions of crime prevention and order maintenance' (Johnston 1992: 4; see also on 'that strange word "police"', Radzinowicz 1956: 1–8). So 'policing' originally referred to the general functions of civil government. While this was much broader than the constables' duties, the constable in, for example, the seventeenth-century village engaged in a wide range of administrative duties (Kent 1986). The new police inherited or were subsequently allocated many such functions (Steedman 1984). Their Australian colleagues followed suit (Moore 1991: 116). Examples range from the duties of inspecting and licensing butchers' shops in the Sydney Police Act 1833 to modern police officers conducting driving tests in Australian country areas. Much more importantly, in some versions of 'community policing', police organize and co-ordinate public services such as housing and welfare. A significant strand of nineteenth- and twentieth-century police history has been the ambivalence of police about these administrative duties: on one hand, they distract from 'real police work'; on the other, they may justify the allocation of resources and other bureaucratic benefits and may soften the police image.

The role and activities of the constables of the 'old' (pre-nineteenth century) police must be assessed in their own terms (which changed over the centuries), not against standards and job-descriptions of modern policing (Kent 1986: 6; Philips 1980: 161). For example, social historians have shown how the apparently irrational and illogical aspects of eighteenth-century criminal procedure have to be decoded according to their, not our, logic and rationality (for example Hay 1975). The distinction between the civil and criminal aspects of a wrongful act were insignificant before 1800 (Lenman and Parker 1980: 12). Early modern constables are no more accurately portrayed as Dogberry or Elbow than early twentieth-century American police are portrayed as the Keystone Kops (Sharpe 1983: 2).

Far from there being a clear distinction between the old and the new police, there was considerable continuity. The old were more organized and efficient, and the new less disciplined and effective than traditionally suggested:

> The development of paid policing and police forces was happening long before the setting up of the Metropolitan Police in 1829, while professionalisation, central direction and standardisation remained weak long after that date. (Styles 1987: 18)

Meanwhile, 'the "new" police often turn out on closer examination to be akin to the old, in personnel, efficiency and tactics' (Gatrell 1990:

260 ; cf. Philips 1980: 160). The significance of the reorganization of English policing in the second and third quarters of the nineteenth centuries is that it was the central state's attempt to monopolize policing activity by its concentration in a 'professional', organized body. 'In the long view 1829 may be of interest mainly for the trend it revealed towards an ever increasing subjection of law-enforcement in all its aspects to central direction' (Gatrell 1990: 260). More generally, it was part of the long-running process in which the state took over the processing of disputes which would previously have been settled privately. This state monopolization of policing increasingly appears to be a historically discrete development. Before the new police, much police work was done by private individuals and organizations. The second half of this century has seen the re-emergence of a private security 'industry' and increasing pressures of privatization on police forces (Johnston 1992; Shearing 1992; Shearing and Stenning 1987).

The ideology of constables as 'citizens in uniform' has been important both as a legitimating device and as an impediment to proper consideration of the nature of police powers. In 1929, the Royal Commission on Police Powers and Procedure claimed:

> The Police . . . have never been recognised, either in law or in tradition, as a force distinct from the general body of citizens . . . (T)he principle remains that a Policeman . . . is only 'a person paid to perform, as a matter of duty, acts which if he were so minded he might have done voluntarily'. Indeed, a policeman possesses few powers not enjoyed by the ordinary citizen, and public opinion, expressed in Parliament and elsewhere, has shown great jealousy of any attempts to give increased authority to the Police. (1929: 6)

Such blinkered and inaccurate views contributed substantially to the lack of attention to the reality – a linear growth of special police powers – and were founded in the assiduously cultivated myth of the 'special relationship' between police and people in England and Wales (Weinberger 1991).

Far from achieving early acceptance, the new police operated as a disciplinary force in a deeply divided society. Consent to policing is not merely an ideological fiction: but equally, it is not a natural condition. Rather, the construction of consent to policing was a long-term, intensive, often deliberate, and never fully successful project of negotiation between police and people (for a summary of relevant research, see Dixon 1991c: 261–6). Such negotiations are carried out in part at a general level (for example the construction in post-war films and television series of a 'police image'). But they are also specific and must be related to the particular circumstances of policed communities: this is shown brilliantly in studies by Brogden of Liverpool (1981), by Hogg and Golder of Sydney (1987), and by Cohen of Islington (1979). This should warn against simplistic analysis of Australian policing as if it was just an extension of a homogenized new police. The very particular relationships between Australian police forces and publics still await proper historical treatment, although a start has been made (Finnane 1987; see also Byrne 1993: ch. 6; Neal 1991).

While traditional police histories treated London's Metropolitan Police as the path-breakers, recent historians have pointed out that other reorganized forces came earlier, notably in 1822 with the establishment of the Royal Irish Constabulary (RIC) (Palmer 1988). The particular significance of the RIC is that it provided a paramilitary model of policing which was at least as influential in the production of colonial police forces as the English model (King 1956; Palmer 1988: 543; note however Brogden's argument (1987a; 1987b) that this contrast understates the paramilitary ability and influence of the Metropolitan Police). Both forces provided models and personnel for early Australian police (Haldane 1986: 27).

2. Original police powers?

The revision of police history noted in section 1 has principally been concerned with issues of organization, constitutional position, and police-public relations. Relatively little attention has been paid to the nature of police powers. Indeed, in this respect there is little to distinguish old and new histories. Generally, both speak as if the old police (constables who were elected from within a community to serve for a year, although deputies were often employed) were restricted to common law powers: 'precisely because in legal theory he was a sort of delegate of the community, the constable exercised common law powers only' (Lustgarten 1986: 28). These were passed on to the new police (in England and Australia) and subsequently were strengthened by the addition of statutory powers. The history of police powers is ripe for a thorough reassessment. Here, it is possible only to suggest how such a project could begin.

The methodology of much writing about early policing is historically deficient because most authors tend to think about policing in modern rather than contemporary terms: they try to find evidence in the historical records of how the old police carried out functions characteristic of modern police. They distort history by using modern concepts of law and authority. Despite the emergence of published guides such as Lambard's *The Dueties of Constables* (1599), the extent of the early constables' authority was neither widely known nor clear. In the seventeenth century, 'The law was a maze to the unwary officer . . . many constables were "doubtful of what power they have," for the simple reason that "the law is very dark"' (Wrightson 1980: 28, quoting Worsley from 1655). The constables' authority stemmed more from practice than from powers which were legally defined by courts.

The modern concept of police powers was produced from the redefinition of state-society relations in seventeenth- and eighteenth-century England. It is in the eighteenth century that crucial developments in police powers emerge. These included the Constables Protection Act 1750, granting legal immunity to constables who acted under a magistrate's warrant: the late provision of this vital protection illustrates well that challenges to a constable's legal authority were the product of late-modern socio-political change. In 1765, *Entinck v Carrington* (2 Wils. KB 274) defined the modern concept of police powers premised upon the relations between the citizen and the liberal state. The central principles established in *Entinck v Carrington* were:

> every official interference with individual liberty and security is unlawful unless justified by some existing and specific statutory or common law rule; any search of private property will similarly be a trespass and illegal unless some recognised lawful authority for it can be produced; in general, coercion should only be brought to bear on individuals and their property at the instance of regular judicial officers acting in accordance with established and known rules of law, and not by executive officers acting at their discretion; and finally it is the law, whether common law or statute, and not a plea of public interest or an allegation of state necessity that will justify acts normally illegal. (Polyviou 1982: 9)

From 1765, it was not enough that police action was carried out at the direction of government, whether central (ministers) or local (justices of the peace). As Lord Chief Justice Camden stated in *Entinck v Carrington*, 'If it is law, it will be found in our books. If it is not to be found there, it is not law.'

Consequently, the process of providing police powers, of putting them into the law's books, got under way. For example, the early constable's legal powers of arrest were the same as the ordinary citizen's: reasonable suspicion was not enough and a felony had actually to have been committed. However, the assumption that early constables did not arrest on suspicion (for example Denning 1949: 19) is another example of transposing modern ideas to inappropriate historical contexts. It was challenges to the practice of arrest on suspicion which led to its legal formalization and development in *Samuel v Payne* ([1780] 1 Doug. 349) and *Beckwith v Philby* ([1827] 6 B & C 635). These cases established that people reasonably suspected of felonies could be arrested by constables, while the ordinary citizen's power to arrest continued to depend on the actual commission of an offence. It was only at this relatively late date that this distinction which is usually cited as the exemplar of the constable's common law powers was made.

3. Police powers after reorganization

The introduction of the new police in England was initially accompanied with the creation of few powers. The *Act for improving the Police in and near the Metropolis* which established London's Metropolitan Police in 1829 contained only two powers. Section 9 provided for police to grant bail, while Section 7 authorized a constable to apprehend 'all loose, idle, and disorderly persons whom he shall find disturbing the Public Peace, or whom he shall have just Cause to suspect of any evil Designs, and all Persons whom he shall find between Sunset and the Hour of Eight in the Forenoon lying in any Highway, Yard, or other Place, or loitering therein, and not giving a satisfactory Account of themselves . . .'

It has been suggested that 'the question of whether or not the new forces would require statutory powers or whether the traditional common law power would suffice' was generally ignored in the debates about policing in the first quarter of the nineteenth century (Brogden 1982: 125). In part, this was due to political considerations: the opposition to reorganization of policing might well have recovered its former strength if the new police had been provided with an array of powers. Issues of accountability and control were more significant than powers.

A related factor was that the primary mandate of the new police, as expressed in their initial instructions, was the prevention of crime:

> To this great end every effort of the police is to be directed. The security of person and property and the preservation of a police establishment will thus be better effected than by the detection and punishment of the offender after he has succeeded in committing crime . . . (1829 Metropolitan Police Instructions, quoted in Critchley 1978: 52–3)

In turn, this was a partly rhetorical gloss on the intention that the new police should be concerned primarily with public disorder. The Metropolitan Police gradually shifted from being a preventative force to one strongly committed to crime investigation (Weinberger 1991).

However, this standard account of the powers initially provided for the new police overlooks a crucial factor – the extensive statutory powers which were already available. From the early Middle Ages, statutes reacted to fears of deviance, crime and disorder. 'Forasmuch as from Day to Day, Robberies, Murthers, Burnings and Thefts be more often committed than they have been heretofore . . .' began the Statute of Winchester in 1285. While the language is archaic, these sentiments resonate with modern 'moral panics'.

Pre-eminent among such legislation were the Vagrancy Acts which were passed from the mid-fourteenth century. If policing is properly understood as being about order maintenance and the control of socially marginal groups as much as it is about law enforcement, the importance of the Vagrancy Acts becomes clear. From the Middle Ages, a long series of additions provided powers for the control of social deviance. The objectives of such control shifted from the protection of trade, to the disciplining of labour, and then to the suppression of incipient criminality (Chambliss 1964; but see also Adler 1989a; 1989b; Chambliss 1989). The Metropolitan Police Act 1829 did not need to include extensive powers because this had, in part, been done five years earlier when the Vagrancy Act 1824 reformed provisions for 'the Suppression of Vagrancy and for the Punishment of idle and disorderly Persons, and Rogues and Vagabonds'. This Act provided wide-ranging proscriptions of deviance. Failing to support or deserting one's family, prostitution, begging, fortune-telling, 'wandering abroad . . . not having any visible Means of Subsistence', displaying obscene pictures, indecent exposure, public gambling, and possessing implements with intent to commit a felony were just some of the prohibited activities. The power of arrest was available to any citizen, but was obviously most useful to police. In addition, Section 4 included a provision which was to become notorious (Demuth 1978). 'Every suspected person or reputed Thief, frequenting . . . any Street . . . or any Place of public Resort . . . with intent to commit Felony' could be arrested and punished as a rogue and vagabond.

These pre-existing powers of the new police in London were soon considerably extended by the Metropolitan Police Act 1839: this reflected an early decline of upper- and middle-class opposition to the new police, as it became clear that the police protected rather than threatened their interests. The 1839 Act provided power to arrest and to enter and search property in numerous instances. It also gave the Metropolitan Police Commissioner authority to issue regulations for the use of public streets. Many detailed offences were created, including sliding upon 'Ice or Snow in any Street to the common Danger of the Passengers' (Section 53(17)) and, much more importantly, the use of 'threatening, abusive, or insulting words or Behaviour . . . whereby a Breach of the Peace may be occasioned' (Section 53(13)), the origin of later public order summary offences. Power of arrest without warrant was provided to constables for all these offences, and in any case when an offender's name and address were not known (Sections 53 and 63). A constable was also empowered to arrest without warrant:

> all loose, idle, and disorderly Persons whom he shall find disturbing the public Peace, or whom he shall have good Cause to suspect of having committed or being about to commit any Felony, Misdemeanor, or Breach of the Peace, and all Persons whom he shall find between Sunset and the Hour of Eight in the Morning lying or loitering in any Highway, Yard or other Place, and not giving a satisfactory Account of themselves. (Section 64)

In addition, a power was created to stop and search vehicles and 'any Person who may be reasonably suspected of having or conveying in any Manner any thing stolen or unlawfully obtained' (Section 66).

Already, the Metropolitan Police had much more than common law powers. Police outside London were provided with local powers, which were consolidated in the Town Police Clauses Act 1847. This growth would continue in a process of *ad hoc* growth discussed in section 6.

4. Early provisions for police and police powers in Australia

Bland claims that the powers of Australian police were modelled on those in England and Wales (for example Chappell and Wilson 1969: ch. 1; Milte and Weber 1977: ch. 1) are misleading. Several points illustrate this. First, early Australian police were appointed as constables and had the constable's common law powers; but as noted above, these were not as clear as is often suggested.

Secondly, Australian police did not have a reservoir of statutory power such as the Vagrancy Acts. The first legislation to provide a statutory basis for Australian policing, the Sydney Police Act 1833, is routinely said to have been modelled on the Metropolitan Police Act 1829. While this was true in terms of the constitutional and bureaucratic structure of the new police organization, the Sydney Police Act 1833 also included a mass of detailed and specific rules for 'the greater regularity and convenience' of the town and a comprehensive battery of offences, many of them accompanied by a power to arrest without warrant. This was soon followed by the Vagrancy Act 1835, modelled on the English Act of 1824.

Thirdly, the social context of police in the new colony was quite different from that of their counterparts in England or Ireland (Neal 1991: 143. For an impressive analysis of the specificity of Australian policing, see Moore 1991). The first civil police in Australia, a night watch established in 1789, were themselves convicts. From the beginning, police powers (provided in Governor's Orders) were controversial. Marines (who had apparently been responsible for many of the property offences which the watch had been established to suppress) objected to being detained by a watch made up of convicts. What was recognized at the time as a power to detain on suspicion for questioning was amended so that soldiers could be stopped only if they were 'found in a riot, or committing any unlawful act' (Government and General Order, 9 November 1789, in HRA 1914: 139).

Apart from enduring problems of personnel, early Australian constables were policing a special kind of society and were provided with very extensive powers of discipline and surveillance. For example, a reconstituted night watch was instructed in 1796 to enforce Sunday observance, 'to apprehend all night-walkers, all disorderly and suspicious persons' and to 'interrogate all . . . found idling about in their division, not being inhabitants thereof, and oblige them to give an account of themselves' (Government and General Order, 9 November 1796, in HRA 1914: 701).

In 1811, Governor Macquarie reorganized the Sydney police and issued detailed regulations which criminalized 'a vast range of public conduct' (Brennan 1983: 44). This was legislation for a penal colony, a society which was deeply divided between free and convict, between civil and military, and in which fear of disorder merged with fear of insurrection. Surveillance was exemplified by the instruction to the chief constable to 'watch narrowly all prisoners and Suspected Persons, and make enquiry as to their different Modes of employing their own hours' and 'in general do his utmost endeavour to preserve Publick (sic) Decorum, and to report every Breach thereof' (Police Regulations 1811, Section 5(5 & 6) in HRA 1916: 409). He was to record the name and place of residence of all convicts in Sydney and to order constables 'to visit the Houses of such prisoners at certain Times during the Night' (Section 5(8) in HRA 1916: 410). The magistrate designated Superintendant (sic) of Police was directed to

> keep a Register, in which he shall Enter the Names and places of Abode of every Housekeeper in the Town of Sydney, or within One Mile thereof, and of every person comprising their respective families, and the situations which such persons fill therein. (Section 6(13), in HRA 1916: 411)

Convicts and householders were obliged to provide police with the information to be held in these registers (Section 6(10) in HRA 1916: 412)

The 'Idle, Disorderly or Suspicious' (including convicts, whom police were instructed 'strictly (to) stop') found in the streets after 9 pm were to be arrested (Sections 1(3) and 4(4), in HRA 1916: 406, 408). Convicts and 'labouring persons' were prohibited from being 'abroad or away from their houses' between 9 p.m. and dawn without 'reasonable Cause' (Section 6(1), in HRA 1916: 412). The chief constable was directed to arrest 'all Persons whom he shall see drunken, idle, or disorderly in the Streets, at any Time, and all persons who have no apparent Means of obtaining a livelihood' (Section 5(4), in HRA 1916: 409). Those 'breaking or profaning the Sabbath day' were to be also arrested (Section 5(7), in HRA 1916: 409).

The police were under the direction and control of a magistrate whose duties included not just 'the general Care, Superintendence and inspection of every thing and person connected with the police of the

Town of Sydney', but also the trial and punishment of offenders. Convicts found guilty of 'Wilful Neglect of Work, of being abroad during the Night after the limited hours, or of being intoxicated in the publick Streets at any time' could be sentenced to fifty lashes and hard labour for thirty days (Section 6(6), in HRA 1916: 410). The same punishments faced anyone who fell within the compendious description of 'idle and disorderly' persons: this included

> all poor persons not using proper means to get employment, or spending their money in Ale-houses or places of bad repute, or not applying a proper proportion to the maintenance of their families, or threatening to desert their families, or wilfully absenting themselves from their Work, or publickly breaking or profaning the Sabbath Day, or attempting to Commit any Felony or Misdemeanour, or to break any house, or shall refuse to assist any Constable in the execution of his Duty, or being out after hours at night without reasonable Cause, or being drunken or riotous in the streets during any time. (Section 6(9), in HRA 1916: 411)

That no specific powers were provided for the enforcement of such prohibitions seems hardly significant: it was clearly expected that the police would arrest suspected offenders. (The power to impose corporal punishment was disapproved by the government in England: see Earl Bathurst to Governor Macquarie, 23 November 1812, (in HRA 1916: 666–9, at 666). Macquarie replied, insisting on the need for such punishments: see Governor Macquarie to Earl Bathurst 28 June 1813, in HRA 1916: 707–30, at 720.)

Police also had extensive authority to enter and search property: they had 'a discretionary power of calling at houses where prisoners reside, or at any other Suspicious Houses, at any Time during the Night, to see if such prisoners or other Suspicious Characters are within, and if not, they shall examine the Master or Mistress of the house thereupon' (Section 4(5), in HRA 1916: 408). Licensed premises, which had to be closed by 9 p.m., could be entered thereafter if 'any riot or disturbance' was heard within (Section 4(10), in HRA 1916: 408). Houses suspected of being of 'ill-fame' or at which alcohol was sold illegally could also be entered. People found 'Tippling or Drunken, or misconducting themselves therein' could be arrested (Section 4(11), in HRA 1916: 409). Police were instructed to be 'diligent in pursuing, searching for, and apprehending all Felons, Burglars, Housebreakers, Riotous and disorderly Persons' (Section 4(12) in HRA 1916: 409). The breadth and detail of these prohibitions and powers reflected the special position of the early Australian police and the nature of the society in which they worked.

Fourthly, New South Wales was not only a penal colony, it was also a new society in a very material sense: in Sydney, a new city was being constructed (King 1956: 218). This emphasizes the need to see policing and police powers in their specific contexts, rather than as some generic activity or institution. As well as reorganizing the structure of the police and adding new provisions for 'the maintenance of the public peace and good order' (Section 1), the Sydney Police Act 1833 provided a code of rules for urban life, covering such matters as the permissible location of certain social and economic activities, 'the removal and prevention of nuisances and obstructions' (Section 1), permissible uses of public and private places and resources, town planning, and public safety. Rules, accompanied by offences for breach, were created for a range of matters such as cleanliness and use of water supplies, the regulation of carters, porters and boatmen, public preparation, sale and transportation of goods, disposal of refuse, traffic, keeping of animals, naming of streets, covering of coal-holes and cellars, provision of guttering. The town surveyor was responsible for supervision of many of these matters. Almost all were backed by offences of failure to comply.

A battery of specific offences was created. Section 25 alone prohibited the use of public places for, *inter alia*, beating carpets; flying kites; 'breaking, exercising or trying horses'; disposing of 'any ashes, rubbish, offal, dung, soil, dead animal, blood, or other filth or annoyance, or any matter or thing'; butchering animals; and using vehicles or animals on 'foot ways'.

Offences which were more serious or required immediate action in an emergent urban community were accompanied by specific police powers, usually of arrest without warrant. Constables were given this power to deal with a disparate range of offences. These included bathing in the harbour between 6 a.m. and 8 p.m. (Section 21); damaging roadways by hauling building materials (Section 27), breaking or extinguishing street lights (Section 36), and throwing dead animals into the harbour (Section 37).

The priorities of a growing urban community were expressed in the special provisions regarding disposal of 'night soil'. A person who emptied privies or drove a 'night soil' cart between 5 a.m. and 10 p.m. or who allowed its contents to spill could be arrested by 'any person or persons whomsoever' (Sections 33 & 34). The seriousness of the problem was expressed not only by the available punishment for emptying privies and transporting nightsoil outside permitted hours (a fine and thirty days imprisonment) but also by the instruction to constables that they were 'strictly charged' by the Act to arrest such offenders (Section 34). Similarly, traffic was already a perceived problem. 'Many accidents happen and great mischiefs are frequently done in the streets and public places . . . by the negligence or wilful misbehaviour of persons driving therein.' Powers were provided for constables and private citizens to arrest without warrant drivers of carts and other vehicles who, for example, did not keep to the left of the road or who 'by negligence or misbehaviour prevent, hinder or interrupt the free passage of any carriage or person' (Section 50)

The objects of social cleansing were human as well as material. Some types of people were made subject to police powers which were concerned with disturbances of public order and the supposed potential for other criminality. In a section drawing on the English Vagrancy Act 1824, police were authorized to arrest 'all loose, idle, drunken or disorderly persons' who were found between sunset and 8 a.m. 'lying or loitering in any street, highway, yard, or other place . . . and not giving a satisfactory account of themselves' (Section 6).

In a society such as early New South Wales, a person's status was vital. Some people were penalized for being in the wrong place at the wrong time: sailors found in public places (including pubs) between 9 p.m. and sunrise could be arrested unless they carried a pass from their ship's captain (Section 44). Similarly, convicts assigned to private service could be arrested and 'shall be deemed guilty of disorderly conduct' if found in a public place without a pass between sunset and sunrise (Section 55).

It is essential not to read such legislation as an inappropriate but expedient combination of police and other public matters: this is to impose a modern distinction. Instead, policing in the early colonial period has to be understood as a general enterprise of social ordering from which the responsibilities of a professional police only gradually emerged as a distinct area. The result was that specific police powers were scattered through the 1833 Act according to a logic which appears only in retrospect to be deficient. (Foucault's concept 'governmentality' may be found useful as a means of accounting for the role of the police in 'disseminating discipline' : Websdale 1991).

The subordination of police to judicial authority was an important feature of the early legislation, and another example of Anglo-Irish influence. Police were appointed by and under the direction of two justices of the peace who were the police magistrates. It was the latter's duty 'to suppress all tumults, riots, affrays, or breaches of the peace, all public nuisances, vagrancies, and offences against the law; and to uphold all regulations . . . for the management and discipline of convicts' (Section 4) and to 'cause to be dispersed' people playing public games in breach of Sunday observance rules (Section 11). They appointed police constables, who were sworn to 'obey all such lawful commands as they may from time to time receive from any of the said Justices for conducting themselves in the execution of their office' (Section 4). The extensive arrest powers noted above were for the purpose of bringing suspects before a Justice 'to be dealt with according to law'. Justices could provide warrants for police to inspect and give directions for the cleaning of butchers' premises (Section 26). They also approved applicants for carters' licences which police issued (Section 54). Magisterial involvement and control were central to early nineteenth-century conceptions of policing: as section 6(iv) will suggest, this was soon to change, at least in practice.

From its origins in Sydney, Australian policing gradually developed and spread. Forces modelled on that of Sydney were established in emergent towns in New South Wales, while a number of specialized forces were also set up:

> By the 1840s there were six separate forces in New South Wales. In addition to the Sydney City Police, a harbour-based Water Police authority and the rural constabulary, there were three rural forces: the Mounted, the Native and the Border Police. (Moore 1991: 110)

A similar process developed elsewhere:

> By the 1850s . . ., Australia's various colonies all had a number of police forces. The two largest colonies of Victoria and New South Wales had some ten police forces between them in addition to the many constables working solely on behalf of local magistrates. Forces were created not as a result of any grand plan but as a need arose and was recognised. (Moore 1991: 112)

Gradually, these were consolidated into unitary state forces: a centralized force emerged in New South Wales in the 1860s (Moore 1991: 116; Walker 1984: 25; for a summary of other state developments, see Chappell and Wilson 1969: ch.1). However, the basic structure of police powers remained the same. The pattern of *ad hoc* growth which was found in England and Wales continued to characterize Australian policing (Finnane 1987: 90).

5. 'Police powers'

In sections 5–10, the focus shifts from historical to conceptual discussion.

Police powers are not coterminous with the police. In some instances, they long predated organized police forces. In certain circumstances, they are available for use by people who are not police officers, both private citizens and state officials. Meanwhile, many police duties, responsibilities and activities are not facilitated by the provision of specific powers. The focus here is the coercive powers which are available to police officers, and their use thereof.

As a legal concept, 'police powers' are simply exemptions from criminal or civil liability for what otherwise would be unlawful acts. For example, a search of a person constitutes an assault unless a power is provided.

> It is in this sense, then, that search and seizure laws confer powers. More particularly, they confer *exceptional* powers, powers to do what an individual is, in ordinary circumstances, forbidden to do . . . Rules defining police powers have a specific function . . . they set out exceptions to the ordinary prohibitions against intrusions upon an individual's person, private domain and possessions. While this function is a critical one it is also in a sense quite modest. Our legal tradition does not purport to devise permissible enforcement strategies or define situations in which intrusions *should* be performed. Rather it establishes when intrusions *may* be performed, by requiring that when law enforcement officers determine to pursue an investigation through an intrusive action, they justify the intrusion, obtain the proper authorization and perform it within the limits set down in the law. (LRC Canada 1983: 10, 122)

If police officers do not have authority, their actions can be lawfully resisted just as if they were private citizens infringing another's interests. The result can be seen in cases in which people have been acquitted of assaulting police officers who have been found not to be acting within their duty in searching, detaining or touching. (For example *Pedro v Diss* [1981] 2 AER 59. Judicial discomfort with such results is evident in attempts to avoid the conclusion that the officer was not acting in the course of duty: see for example *Donnelly v Jackman* [1970] 54 Cr App Rep 229.) There is nothing special about the powers of the police from this perspective. Police powers are not conceptually distinct from, for example, a citizen's right to make arrests or the powers of a wide range of public officials (immigration officers, welfare officers, revenue officers, public utility officials) to enter property or to arrest in certain circumstances.

If a police power exists and is exercised:

> it transforms legal relations between state and individual. A peace officer who arrests an individual puts that individual in lawful custody, from which escape is an offence, and deprives the citizen of a right to resist what would, without the authority to arrest, amount to an unlawful assault. (LRC Canada 1985: 2)

However, it is important to note that this transformative process is not all negative: arresting a citizen may activate certain rights (for example to publicly funded counsel) which a person who merely 'assists officers with their enquiries' may not possess (Dixon *et al.* 1990).

A doctrinal corollary of this approach to police powers is that they should be clearly defined and specific, so that police and citizen alike know what is and what is not authorized. This is a traditional account of the rule of law, usually associated with A. V. Dicey (1902). As will be shown below, the considerable distance between concept and legal reality limits the validity of this approach.

The police do not need to have legal powers for everything that they do. Like other citizens, they may do anything that the law does not forbid. Indeed, most police work entails duties which do not involve the use of coercive powers:

> the police (contrary to popular mythology) do not mainly operate as crime-fighters or law-enforcers, but rather as providers of a range of services to members of the public, the variety of which beggars description . . . Crime fighting has never been, is not, and could not be the prime activity of the police. (Reiner 1985: 111–12, 171, and see 111–23 passim for a good summary of the police role which avoids simple dichotomies of 'force' and 'service').

Powers are only necessary when a person's identifiable interest is infringed. The common law's definition of such interests is limited. For example, a man whose telephone was being tapped sought an injunction against London's Metropolitan Police (*Malone v Metropolitan Police Commissioner* [1979] Ch. 344). This was refused on the ground that the telephone tapping did not involve any trespass or other unlawful act: the court could identify only the Post Office's property interest and not the man's interest in privacy, communication or the message communicated. It was for Parliament to legislate for the controls on telephone tapping which were needed to needed to satisfy obligations under the European Convention on Human Rights. (This unwillingness to extend a citizen's interests contrasts with the extension of police powers by English courts in recent times: see below. The Australian High Court has been more concerned to preserve rights: see for example *Williams v R* [1987] 66 ALR 385 and *R v Foster* (unreported, 1993) on pre-charge detention for questioning and *Petty and Maiden v R* [1991] 65 ALJR 625 on the right of silence.)

The limitations of a narrow legal conception of police powers are clear. Practices of arrest and search by organized police forces are much more than mere exemptions from legal liability.

> The . . . proposition that the police should not be subject to any special restrictions that don't apply to other people . . . is absurd, because the power (both legal and physical) that the police have makes them especially dangerous *as well as* useful. Acting within the state apparatus, officials can do things to citizens which are quite different in character from the sort of things citizens can do to one another. (Waldron 1990: 41, original emphasis: the question of resolving this 'absurdity' is considered below.)

In consequence, any useful discussion of police powers must break out of the limits set by legalistic definitions (see section 7).

Waldron's indication of the ambivalent nature of police powers reflects a discomfort which police officers often display in using the term 'police powers'. Several police officers have bridled when asked about aspects of their 'powers'. Similarly, the Queensland Police Service, in its submission to the Criminal Justice Commission's review of police powers, preferred to speak of 'policing authorities' rather than powers (Queensland Police Service 1991: 1). Such use of euphemisms is not uncommon in policing: they are used to present what is thought to be a more favourable aspect, as in the current English police fashion of describing charge rooms and cells as 'the custody suite'. In the present case, the sensitivity is misplaced: the use of the word 'powers' in the context of policing should have no pejorative implication, and 'powers' is a standard usage in legal discussion of public bodies.

The *Malone* case illustrates well another sometimes problematic consequence of conceptualizing police powers as exemptions from prohibitions. In legal systems such as Australia and the United Kingdom which lack constitutional measures such as a Bill of Rights, the relevant prohibitions are those specified in tort and, particularly, the criminal law: Malone's investigators did not need to consider the possibility that their actions might be unlawful by virtue of transgressing a constitutionally protected right to privacy. (Although they should have considered the European Convention on Human Rights: see *Malone v UK* [1984] ECHR series A, v.82.) They were simply doing something which was not unlawful. By focusing on prohibitions, this legal tradition sees the non-prohibited as a legal vacuum. Activities within it are private rather than public, as the discussion of 'consent' (in section 7, below) illustrates. The creation of a new offence simply reduces the area of the vacuum.

Limitations of this legalistic way of conceptualizing police powers and criminal law are apparent: the legal vacuum has social and political substance. When people object that a proposed extension of police powers or criminal law would infringe their 'rights', this is not a mistake, an expression of legal unsophistication. These kind of rights are much less clear than those specified in constitutional documents, but they are none the less significant (not least because the latter are often products of the former). At issue here are understandings of the limits of acceptable state intervention which are historical products of social and political disputes and negotiations. When Malone complained that his right of privacy was infringed by telephone tapping, the implicit reference was to a social and political understanding of the citizen's relationship with the state. This originated in the liberal democratic settlement which emerged from the social, political and legal conflicts of the seventeenth and eighteenth centuries. The potency of this concept of rights did not lie in its legal or even historical accuracy. For example, it relied on an account of the 'free-born' Anglo-Saxon Englishman (sic) and his subjugation to the 'Norman Yoke' which was largely mythical, but which was highly significant in the democratic movements of the eighteenth and nineteenth centuries (Hill 1954; Thompson 1963: ch. 3).

6. Types of police powers

This section presents an overview drawing on police powers in England and Wales, Canada, and Australia. While comparative material is useful, it is again important to note differences in national (and state) developments. As noted above, senior Australian and Canadian courts have been less willing than those in England and Wales to extend police powers (LRC Canada 1983: 47). Similarly, there are important differences in the extent to which criminal procedure has been legislated and codified.

i. Statute

As sections 3 and 4 above showed, a major source of police powers is legislation prohibiting an activity. While the primary focus of such legislation is the substantive criminal law, its corollary is an extension of police powers. This may result either explicitly when a statute provides a special power facilitating enforcement of a prohibition or, more commonly, implicitly when a statute, for example, designates an activity as an arrestable offence. Again, this designation may be explicit or implicit, for example by setting a penalty which is above the level at which certain police powers become available.

The distinction between offence and power is sometimes over-looked (or is practically irrelevant). A good example here is the controversy in New South Wales in the late 1970s and 1980s about public order laws. At issue were *offences* (notably, offensive language and conduct). However, the debate was conducted largely in terms of *powers*: police argued that their powers had been reduced when an offence had been statutorily amended and that they should be restored. (This legislation did include some powers, but these were not at issue in the controversy.) Similarly, the 1988 legislation which 'restored' police powers:

> contains only a single new provision that deals with police powers, allowing police to seize liquor from minors in a public place and administer a caution . . . The new Act does, however, expressly re-criminalise offensive language, further restricts soliciting for the purposes of prostitution, and increases the penalties for most offences. (Brown *et al.* 1990: 965).

The implications of this example are:

First, substance and process are so inextricably bound up, that to 'increase police powers' may actually mean 'to create substantive offences which make it easier for police to charge people' . . . Second, the enormous discretion which is vested in police to operate this system on the streets is bounded as much, or as little, by the prevailing ethos as by the 'requirements' of law. The 1979 and 1988 legislative shifts only marginally impinged on formal police powers. Of considerably more importance were the signals given to police and magistrates by those changes. (Brown *et al.* 1990: 965; see also Egger and Findlay 1988).

The linking of offences and powers has been influenced by the way in which statutes are written. As the examples cited in sections 3 and 4 demonstrate, the favoured style of legislative drafting in the nineteenth century was to define offences very specifically and minutely, rather than the broader generic drafting now adopted. Powers were attached to (or implied from) prohibitions. Similarly, when a perceived need for a power arose, it would be tagged on to other legislation. As in the case of Canadian search powers, the result was 'an assortment of powers' which was:

the product of a growth that has occurred in piecemeal fashion over the past 300 years. The tendency of legislators has been to enact a search power and append it to a particularized enactment when and where the need for one has been evident. Consequently, search and seizure powers have been regarded individually, as incidents of larger enactments, rather than collectively, as incidents of a category of powers . . . Procedural rules governing search have not so much developed as accumulated. (LRC Canada 1983: 8)

This approach was a corollary of the definition of powers as exemptions which has been discussed above. As Leigh suggests:

English law insisted strongly that invasions of liberty . . . had necessarily to be grounded in positive law . . . Government did not seek to create a comprehensive framework of police powers; instead, powers were granted on an ad hoc basis, sometimes grudgingly, sometimes as with the old Vagrancy Acts, entirely too readily, but generally with some reference to some demonstrable need. Unfortunately, and perhaps inevitably, the particular settlement arrived at became both cumbersome and in many respects illiberal. (Leigh 1985: 33, 35)

This incremental accretion of powers via prohibitions resulted in confusion and anomaly until significant codification of major police powers was provided in the Police and Criminal Evidence Act 1984.

ii. Common law and judicial interpretation of codes and statutes

English judges have often prided themselves as protectors of citizens' rights. This image is easier to maintain if attention is directed towards great eighteenth-century cases, such as *Entinck v Carrington* (see section 2, above). Their more recent record indicates a selectivity in their concern for citizens' rights. Courts became increasingly willing to extend police powers in the 1960s and 1970s, notably in search and seizure and pre-charge detention for investigation (Dixon 1992b). Canadian courts felt pressure to expand police powers in the same way. As in England, courts typically dealt with cases *ad hoc*. Discussion of the nature of powers and of the proper relationship between powers and duties was generally lacking. The result was 'a body of contradictory case authority for which the underlying principles remain unclear' (LRC Canada 1985: 37).

While principles and policies were never properly articulated, this tendency 'to construe the rules liberally in order to allow some scope to police inquiries' constituted a move 'tentatively towards an ancillary powers doctrine which would enable the police to perform such reasonable acts as are necessary for the due execution of their duties' (Leigh 1975: 31, 33). Similarly, Canadian courts have sometimes recognized ancillary powers, 'the notion that the duties conferred upon peace officers imply the powers necessary and incidental to their performance' (LRC Canada 1983: 14–15; 1985: 37, 39). A concern here was to align more closely police powers and police duties: an action might be considered as a police power (that is protected from the consequences of unlawfulness) if it was carried out justifiably in the course of police duties (LRC Canada 1985: 3). This potentially broadened police powers very considerably:

> The obvious problem with the doctrine is that general police duties are extremely wide, and a test of whether or not an action is a 'justifiable interference' with liberty or property is not sufficiently precise to be any real safeguard to fundamental rights and freedoms. (LRC Canada 1985: 39)

It is possible to distinguish between power ancillary to another power and power ancillary to a duty. This contrast may be drawn, for example, between allowing police during a search to seize articles which had not been specified in an authorizing warrant and, on the other hand, allowing police to cordon off a street or to detain witnesses or groups of people, for example in crowd control or as part of a major crime investigation. The latter type of action is so rarely challenged that its legal basis is not an issue of dispute in practice: its existence is assumed from necessity and practice. (The difficulties of providing an appropriate statutory power apparently discouraged the British government from following the Royal Commission on Criminal Procedure's recommendations on this: see RCCP 1981: para. 3.91–3.) This raises an issue which will be considered further in section 8 below: the interrelation of law and policing practice.

iii. Codified powers

While codification of criminal law has a long history, codification, or even extensive consolidation, of criminal procedure has received much less attention until recently. Since the 1970s, there has been increasing interest in the reform of criminal procedure in common law countries, notably in the work of the Canadian Law Reform Commission, the Royal Commissions on Criminal Procedure and on Criminal Justice in England and Wales, the Thompson Committee on Criminal Procedure in Scotland, the New Zealand Law Commission and Public and Administrative Law Reform Committee, the Australian and New South Wales Law Reform Commissions, and the Criminal Justice Commission in Queensland.

A notable feature of these has been a concern to develop principles upon which to base criminal procedure. (See, in particular, RCCP 1981: ch. 1 & 2; LRC Canada 1988). This is a deliberate shift away from the traditions of *ad hoc* change and challenges simplistic accounts of criminal justice as balancing police powers and suspects' rights. The major legislative product of this trend is the Police and Criminal Evidence Act 1984 (England and Wales) (PACE). As comments below will indicate, this legislation has, amongst other things, demonstrated that police powers and suspects' rights can be increased together, and that such change need not be at the expense of one or the other. However, the inadequacies of PACE which have emerged since 1986 show how fundamental restructuring of criminal procedure must be if it is to be successful.

iv. Controls on police powers

It is convenient here to comment on more general characteristics of police powers which serve as controls on their exercise.

A significant heritage of the old constabulary arrangements was the relationship between police and magistrates. As noted in section

4, nineteenth-century police in Australia and England and Wales were controlled and directed by justices of the peace. This general control was accompanied by specific controls built into police powers. Searches of property and arrests in many situations could be done only on the authority of a magistrate's warrant. Arrested suspects had to be taken before a magistrate without delay. More generally, requirements that powers be exercised only on reasonable suspicion or with good cause were intended to make possible an objective assessment by magistrates (and other judicial officers) of the legality of using a power when there had been no prior judicial authorization (LRC Canada 1985: 45).

A crucial factor which has been consistently underemphasized in criminal justice studies is that the relationship between police and magistrates upon which these control arrangements depended was fundamentally altered in the mid-nineteenth century. As police forces became more organized and 'professional', magistrates withdrew from the investigation of crime into a narrower judicial role. The shift was most significant in the area of arrest, charge and interrogation. Police took on responsibility for investigating crimes after arrests had been made. Practices evolved of police arresting suspects and taking them to a station for investigation and charging before presentation to magistrates. However, no provision was made in the law for this enormously significant change in practice (except in regard to police bail). The formally conducted process of in-station charging had no legal basis and was not recognized by many influential commentators until quite recently (for example Devlin 1960 and for a study of this history, see Dixon 1992b). The result of this disjunction between law and practice was seen, in Australia, in *Williams v R* when the High Court made clear that police had no common law power to detain suspects for investigative purposes. Belatedly, federal and some state legislatures have created powers of pre-charge detention.

Some modern legislation has continued to use magistrates as supervisors of police powers. For example, the Police and Criminal Evidence Act not only continues magistrates' responsibility for arrest and search warrants, but also involves magistrates in the authorization of pre-charge detention beyond thirty-six hours. However, other methods of control are also employed. Notably, the Police and Criminal Evidence Act relies heavily on supervision and management within police forces and on bureaucratic record-making. The latter may provide material for use by controllers both within the police and externally, including the courts. (On the effectiveness of these safeguards, see Dixon *et al.* 1990a; Bottomley *et al.* 1991; cf. McConville *et al.* 1991.)

The Police and Criminal Evidence Act also attempts to strengthen the control imposed by the 'reasonable suspicion' requirement by providing directive guidance in a Code of Practice which details what constitutes reasonable suspicion in the context of using stop and search powers (see Code of Practice A, Section 1). The effect of such provisions and of related record-making requirements has proved to be very limited (Dixon *et al.* 1989). This emphasizes the importance of distinguishing between powers exercised in public and those in the police station: the former may be considerably less amenable to control by bureaucratic and managerial methods, and more imaginative approaches to controlling them are required.

The controls provided in the Police and Criminal Evidence Act restricted some practices (for example of detention for questioning) which had previously been effectively legalized by the courts' acceptance of evidence produced from them, as well as by *Dallison v Caffery* [1964] 2 AER 610 and *Holgate-Mohammed v Duke* [1984] 1 AER 1054. While acknowledging that the Act extended some powers, police officers feel that others were reduced. Taking police powers away is rare: their growth is usually incremental. As Finnane suggests, the effective reduction in police powers by the changes to summary offences in New South Wales in 1979 was most unusual (1987: 102). This explains some of the anger which the legislative change produced (Egger and Findlay 1988).

v. 'Exceptional' powers

A category which would conventionally be included here is 'exceptional' or 'emergency' powers, that is those introduced to deal with a special situation in a way which does not accord with usual standards regarding suspects' rights. The Prevention of Terrorism Acts in England and Wales (which have been renewed repeatedly since the 1970s) are the usual example. Australia has some notable examples of exceptional powers: these include the Bushranging Act 1834, consorting and garrotting provisions (Crimes Act 1900 NSW Sections 546a and 37) , and public order laws.

However, it seems preferable to resist the dichotomous classification of normal and exceptional powers. It relies on a rosy view of 'normal' powers, usually associated with the account of common law powers which was criticized in section 3 above. It understates the strength of 'normal' powers provided by statute (see sections 3 and 4). Many 'normal' (or 'normalized') powers are the result of short-term moral panics (for example the recent Western Australian legislative reaction to young car thieves); but they stay in the statute book long after the panic has subsided. Garrotting, the Victorian equivalent of 'mugging' is a good example: see Davis 1980. It is better to conceive of police powers as being on a continuum, rather than as being neatly divided into 'normal and 'exceptional'.

7. Powers: the law/practice dichotomy

To this point, the analysis has been largely formalistic in implicitly defining police powers as specific authorities provided by statute or common law. However, a discussion of police powers as provided by case-law inevitably stretches this formalistic definition and demands consideration of the relationship between law and policing practice.

Judges can only develop (or limit) police powers when disputes about an existing police practice reach their courts. In this sense, a judicial decision is reactive rather than creative: it transforms practice into authority (or stamps practice as being illegitimate). So, as suggested in section 2, what came to be dignified as 'common law police powers' were in some important respects simply established practices which lacked formal judicial recognition.

> For example, the power to search arrested people is often assumed to be traceable to the earliest days of common law jurisprudence . . . In fact the *practice* of such searches clearly predated the existence of any specific authority for them . . . these searches seem to have been simply assumed over the course of time to be proper and valid. This is due in large part to the historical tolerance of intrusive and indeed violent acts towards persons accused of crimes. (LRC Canada 1983: 48)

Similarly, the Royal Commission on Police Powers and Procedure (England and Wales) found in 1929 that there was no clear authority for searching an arrested person's premises. However, 'the practice seems to have had the tacit approval of the Courts for so long that, in the opinion of the Home Office, it has become part of the common law' (RCPPP 1929: 14). This opinion was crucial: police forces would seek guidance on such matters and the Home Office's opinion would be decisive. In this sense, the executive was responsible for shaping the common law at least as much as the judges. Dignifying such practices by describing them as common law had clear legitimating effects.

Police powers can be increased by judicial inaction as well as action. If judges consistently refuse to exclude evidence obtained in some unlawful way, then that practice has a judicial imprimatur which is hard to distinguish from authorization. (While it is true to say that the practice is not fully legalized in the sense that it may found a civil claim, this possibility is usually not significant.)

A central example of this in Australia is detention for questioning. It appears that practices of detaining for questioning emerged in Australian jurisdictions which mirrored those in England and Wales. The previously accepted common law rule (that the requirement to take an arrested person before a magistrate without delay did not allow detention for questioning) was strongly reasserted by the High Court in *Williams v R*. As noted above, some states have provided statutory powers to detain for questioning. In the states which have not yet done so, methods have been adopted to allow the decision's effect to be sidestepped or ignored. For example, in the foremost commentary on criminal law in Queensland, the section dealing with the duty to take arrested suspects before a justice (Section 552 of the Criminal Code) gives as authority *Dallison v Caffery*, an English decision which the majority in the High Court hearing of *Williams* rejected. *Williams* is mentioned merely in passing (Carter 1992: 7388). This text is similar to NSW Police Instructions, which prefer *Dallison v Caffery* and the dissenting opinion of Gibbs CJ in *Williams* to the clear ruling of the High Court's majority (Dixon 1992b: 38–9).

If judges (and other actors, notably defence lawyers) condone legal fictions about police practices, they are substantially if not formally legalized. A major example here is the way in which restrictions on police powers may be avoided by obtaining a suspect's 'consent' to police activity (Dixon *et al.* 1990). The legal effect is to make irrelevant the officer's status: it is as if one private citizen were making a request of another.

> The advantages of resorting to consent as the basis of authorization for a search or seizure are many – a diminished likelihood of review, a possible psychological edge over the person searched, the less burdensome procedural requirements, and the absence of confinement to the usual 'grounds of belief'. (LRC Canada 1983: 159)

In Australia, the most significant issue in this area is the practice of 'voluntary attendance' by suspects at police stations which effectively provided Australian police forces with non-statutory powers to detain for questioning. It is beyond dispute that most attendances of this kind would not meet a developed legal definition of voluntariness, which would require knowledge of alternatives and active choice rather than the submission or passive acceptance of authority which usually characterize voluntary attendances (Dixon *et al.* 1990). Analyses of this issue often conclude that a clear distinction between consent and coercion cannot be made when policing activities are involved (Dixon *et al.* 1990; LRC Canada 1983: 160), and that consequently 'consensual' activities should be brought within a framework of legal regulation:

> It is important . . . to regard 'consent' searches as an intrinsic part of the scheme of police procedures and not as privately sanctioned transactions that fall outside the concern of the public law-maker (LRC Canada 1983: 159).

Examples of such provisions in force can be found in the Police and Criminal Evidence Act's Codes of Practice on search of premises and investigative detention, while recommendations for similar provisions are made in the New South Wales Law Reform Commission's 1990 report on police powers (NSW LRC 1990).

The argument advanced here is that a clear line cannot be drawn between law and practice in the police powers which have developed in jurisdictions based on or emergent from the common law. As Doreen McBarnet (1981) has argued, the appropriate distinction is not between law and practice, but rather between the law and practice on one side and legal rhetoric and ideology on the other. The vehicle for this combination of law and practice has been the case-law form, with its flexibility and adaptability (on McBarnet's discussion of this, see Dixon 1992b: 53–5).

Finally, powers cannot be considered in isolation from other features of criminal justice systems. For example, police powers of custodial interrogation are particularly significant in adversarial systems 'in which the surest way to "victory" is aborting formal combat – the trial – by obtaining the other side's surrender – a guilty plea or at least a confession' (Lustgarten 1986: 9). Powers which are conducive to producing confessions are also increased in importance when proof of intention is stressed in substantive criminal law. Juries may infer intention from actions; but the best evidence of it will always be a reliable confession. These factors provide the context for the emphasis which police have placed on interrogation and the significance to them of appropriate powers to detain for questioning. Similarly, if police are responsible for prosecutions (or have great influence on public prosecutors), then the power to arrest and charge assumes greater significance than when an effective screening of prosecutions is provided by a powerful and independent public prosecutor (Lustgarten 1986: 4–7). Police powers cannot be considered apart from the broader criminal justice system in which they are located.

8. The office of constable

Police powers are sometimes distinguished from those of other state officials by the nature of the 'office of constable':

> The essential feature which distinguishes Police organisations from most other organised bodies is that the Policeman's powers are not delegated to him by superior authority. (RCPPP 1929: 15)

Powers are said to be given to an officer as a constable, not as a member of a police force: 'in essence a police force is neither more nor less than a number of individual constables, whose status derives from the common law, organised together in the interests of efficiency' (Hailsham 1981: 107). The doctrine of the constable's office has been the subject of (and confused by) considerable controversy in British debates about police accountability (see for example Brogden 1982; Jefferson and Grimshaw 1984; Lustgarten 1986).

While it is true that officers must make their own decisions about, for example, whether they have reasonable suspicion necessary to exercise a power and *in this sense* cannot be ordered to exercise powers, this is not distinct from a general administrative law requirement that officials should exercise discretion given to them by law and must not act under dictation. There is nothing special about police or police powers in this regard.

Concentration on this legal requirement largely serves to ignore the reality of police organization and command, which does assign officers to tasks, including the exercising of powers. An administrative law requirement that a public official should make her/his own decision and not act under dictation is not inconsistent with the operation of a bureaucratic structure of this kind. It certainly does not provide the basis for the assertion of some unique constabulary independence. As Lustgarten suggests, the exceptional cases of officers persevering with prosecutions against orders in fact prove the rule rather than subvert it: subsequent prosecutions are brought by the officer as an individual, not as a member of a police force (1986: 11–13, 171).

9. What are police powers for?

A legalistic answer to this question would be specific and simplistic. For example, it is said that the power of arrest begins the process of bringing suspected offenders before the courts to be tried (Devlin 1960). The reality of arrest in policing practice is rather different. Arrest serves a number of functions. For example, it can be preventative. This is legally recognized in the power to arrest to prevent a breach of the peace and under statutory powers (such as suspected persons or loitering offences). In such circumstances, arrest is an expression of power, a demonstration of police control over a situation. Secondly, arrest can serve as punishment. It is now well recognized in criminal justice studies that the experience of arrest, detention and trial can be just as punitive as any formal punishment which a court imposes (Feeley 1979).

This perspective provides a way of understanding disputes about powers associated with public order offences. Those who argue that, for example, offensive language should not be an arrestable offence (as it is in New South Wales) on the grounds that a summons will usually be appropriate overlook (perhaps deliberately) the ways in which police use such a charge, especially in their control of Aboriginal people. Often, this is not (or not simply) to respond to an offence. Rather, an offensive language charge is a method of control, a justification for removing a person from a public place. This is particularly the case when, as so often happens, the victim of the offensive language is a police officer (Egger and Findlay 1988). Public order law provides clear examples of the breadth of police discretion, but similar analysis can be made of much policing activity:

> 'Enforcing the law', in the sense of arresting someone, may be only one of several resources available to policemen (sic) for handling incidents. From this point of view an arrest is not adequately explained by the evidence presented by the arresting officer to justify his use of the resource, i.e. his

use of his powers of arrest. For on other occasions when this power might have been invoked, an alternative resource may have been used to deal with the incident. (Chatterton 1976: 105)

Chatterton goes on to insist that we should suspend 'the conventional idea that laws are things to be enforced, and (think) of them instead as resources to be used to achieve the ends of those who are entitled or able to use them' (1976: 114; cf. Bittner 1970). These ends include resolving trouble, restoring public order, getting a suspect into custody so that other possible charges can be investigated, and punishing the blameworthy. So, arrest powers are not just the legal method of setting the criminal process in motion: the choice of their use is also to be seen as a tool of social discipline.

It is important to stress that this perspective requires abandoning the mythology in which crime-fighting is the sole police function (see section 10):

> The core mandate of policing, historically and in terms of concrete demands placed upon the police, is the more diffuse one of order maintenance. Only if this is recognised can the problems of police powers and accountability really be confronted in all their complexity, and perhaps intractability. In this light, the vaguely defined 'public order' offences . . . (which are such a scandalous embarrassment from either a crime control or due process approach) speak to the heart of the police function. (Reiner 1985: 172)

It is only in this context that, for example, Queensland police demands for a 'move-on' power can be properly addressed (Queensland Police Service 1991). To concentrate on the penalty for a failure to move on draws attention away from the central issue of how police contribute to social ordering, the diversity of behaviour which a society can tolerably encompass, and the relations between police and the socially marginal groups who are directly affected by order maintenance policing.

Similar issues arise in the case of powers to stop and search. Historically, stop and search has been used not just to investigate those suspected (reasonably or not) of having committed offences, but as a more general technique of social surveillance and discipline – checking on people whose appearance is incongruous because, for example, they appear to be in an inappropriate place at an inappropriate time (young people in a commercial area at night; a black person in a white neighbourhood). The use of such powers is justified as contributing to crime detection (even if only some 17 per cent of stops lead to arrests: Dixon *et al.* 1989: 190), to information gathering (particularly in the case of stops for suspected illegal drugs), and to crime prevention (deterrent stop and search is an important, if often unrecognized, part of a beat officer's activities). But these are only part of a more general use of a power for purposes of social surveillance and discipline. (For a discussion of these issues related to stop and search in England and Wales, see Dixon *et al.* 1989.)

The case of stop and search is an excellent example of how excessive use of a police power can be dysfunctional or counter-productive. A major pre-condition of the 1981 Brixton riots was the intensive use of stop and search powers which worsened relations between police and young black people. The result was serious rioting and the commission of many serious offences (Scarman 1981). Similar results have been produced by other instances of intensively using stop and search or 'field interrogation' in an aggressive patrol strategy. Studies in the United States and in England suggest that the level of some crimes may be reduced, but 'the price in alienation of some sections of the public (primarily young males, especially blacks) is very high' (Reiner 1985: 123). The lesson to be learnt is that any potential benefits which police powers may provide can be dissipated if they are used inappropriately. This is particularly significant given police reliance on information from the public in crime detection: this issue will be raised again in the context of police effectiveness in the next section.

Scarman's discussion of stop and search powers in his Brixton report insisted that police powers cannot be considered in isolation from their use or from the broader context of police duties and responsibilities. In an analysis which has been influential, Scarman argued that the primary police duty is the maintenance of social order. Enforcing the law is a secondary duty. It may be a means of achieving the former, but on occasions 'law enforcement puts at risk public tranquillity . . . (and) can cause acute friction and division in a community' (1981: para. 4.57). When a conflict between the duties arises, the maintenance of order must take priority. This is achieved by the use of the discretion which 'lies at the heart of the policing function' (1981: para. 4.58). The important link which Scarman makes is to stress that the balance between law enforcement and order maintenance will only be achieved when another, that between police independence and accountability, is successfully made. This balance in turn depends upon the police securing the consent of the communities in which they work (1981: paras. 4.59–60). Scarman's report showed clearly the indissoluble links between police powers, discretion and accountability (even if his social democratic analysis was flawed: see Hall 1982).

While stop and search attracted most attention in debates about policing in England and Wales in the early 1980s, the central issue in Australia in the early 1990s is custodial interrogation. From a legalistic perspective, the central purpose of police powers to detain for questioning is the collection of evidence for potential use in court. A more socially realistic perspective suggests that the division between investigative and judicial functions is too neat. Criminal justice systems which depend on very high rates of guilty pleas for their effective functioning have transferred the crucial site of determination from the court to the police station. When cases are effectively determined by a confession, then a power to detain and question is more, in practice if not in law, than an investigative power.

It may seem 'common sense' that providing new police powers by legal change means extending police power. This may not be the case, and (as noted in section 6(iv), above) one effect of legislating on police powers may be to control police power. This paradoxical result may be produced when police develop informal practices such as relying on 'consent' in order to search or question, or when more clearly coercive unlawful practices are not challenged in court, or when legal powers are used inappropriately (for example, when stop and search is carried out without reasonable suspicion). If a legislature provides formal legal powers, these may authorize less than was previously common practice.

This is well illustrated by contrasts in the reception of the Police and Criminal Evidence Act. Many civil libertarians and other critics complained vociferously that the Act introduced draconian police powers. Meanwhile, police officers could be heard complaining about the constriction of their powers. It was as if two quite different and conflicting statutes were being discussed. In fact, one side was comparing the Act to a (rather idealized) view of the previous law, while the other compared it to their practical experience of the law in policing practice. While the Act does significantly extend some powers (notably of arrest), its effect on stop and search should have been considerably to restrict previous practices (although as noted above success has been limited: see Dixon *et al.* 1989). The new regime for pre-charge detention provides much greater control over these crucial practices (even if this control is by no means ideal: see Dixon 1992; Dixon *et al.* 1990a; cf. McConville *et al.* 1991).

10. Police powers and police effectiveness

[A] constant call from police circles is for more powers to be able to deal with crime suspects. The assumption is that if more powers were available, the police would be able to detect more crime, successfully prosecute more offenders and thus significantly reduce crime levels. The implicit claim is that there exists a causal link between the powers provided and 'success' in the 'war against crime'. Apart from the fact that in many instances the police already exercise the powers that they are seeking (and in asking for changes to the law they are, in effect, asking for their present practices to be given legal status), short of granting quite draconian powers, what evidence there is raises very considerable doubts about the validity of the assumptions made by the police and others in arguing for more powers. (Sallmann and Willis 1984: 217)

How is police effectiveness influenced by a change in police powers? It is important to examine this question because an answer to it is usually taken for granted in calls for the extension of police powers. When a problem of crime is perceived, the remedy most commonly advanced is an extension of police powers to deal with it. As the Queensland Criminal Justice Commission's public hearings in 1992 on police powers demonstrated, some advocates of this remedy do not fully consider either the powers already available to police or the likely effect of extending powers on the perceived problem, or indeed whether measures other than police powers might be more effective. This suggests the crucial symbolic significance of police powers. As Reiner suggests,

Until relatively recently discussions about criminal justice policy and the police specifically, have been locked into the law and order mythology that given adequate resources and powers the police could tackle the problem of rising crime. The only opposition to the law and order lobby was on civil libertarian grounds that police effectiveness must not be bought at too high a price in the undermining of civil rights. However, a recent wave of . . . research in the US and Britain has begun to question the assumption that increased police power and resources *could* control crime. (Reiner 1985: 117)

The relationship between police powers and police effectiveness has received much less detailed attention than the relationships between police resources and policies and police effectiveness. It is helpful to note some of the lessons and conclusions which can be drawn from these debates, because they are in many respects comparable to our current concerns. First, crime rates cannot be used as a simple indicator of police success: 'one of the classic pitfalls of police performance analysis is the tendency to use crime statistics to measure effectiveness' (Grabosky 1988: 3). At base, they are no more than a record of the documented activities of police officers: their relationship with 'actual crime' is mediated through a series of policies and recording practices which fundamentally affect the result. Carefully analysed, they can still be useful sources of data (Bottomley and Coleman 1981; Bottomley and Pease 1986: ch. 2). What is clear is that a falling (or rising) crime rate cannot be simply read as denoting police success (or failure). The creation of a new police power (either directly or via a new offence) may lead to an increase in the crime rate (that is if police are able to deal with more suspects or if an activity is newly criminalized). Matters are rarely as straightforward as this; but the fundamental point is that increasing police powers may increase (officially recorded) crime.

Secondly, 'a significant proportion of police resources is devoted to tasks quite unrelated to the prevention of crime and the apprehension of offenders' (Grabosky 1988: 1). Meanwhile, most criminal activity is unaffected by the police either because it is not reported or is, to all intents and purposes, undetectable (Hough and Clarke 1980: 7–8). At levels of resources and power which can currently be contemplated, the police are too far removed from criminal activities for them to have a decisive impact. The classic example here is the Kansas City Preventive Patrol Experiment, in which very different styles of policing were found to have no significantly differential effect on crime or on fear of crime or on attitudes towards police: indeed, it seems that they were hardly noticed by many residents (Kelling *et al.* 1974; for a review of later research, see Reiner 1985: 117–19). Together, these factors mean that a change in police powers is unlikely to have a direct or substantial effect on crime.

Thirdly, fear of crime is a factor which should be taken into account in evaluating police effectiveness. For many people, fear of crime is at least as great a problem as the real likelihood of victimization. Police forces are important producers of knowledge, information and opinion about crime:

The popular image of the police battling with an almost intractable crime problem is arguably the main source of people's fear of crime – a fear justified neither by the risks nor by the nature of the vast bulk of crime. (Hough and Clarke 1980: 9)

When police officers complain that they cannot do their job properly because of a lack of powers, this is likely to increase public fear of crime. Consequently, considerable responsibility should be exercised in making such claims. There have been some unfortunate examples of irresponsibility, such as the advertisment placed in Sydney's *Daily Telegraph* in August 1979 by the NSW Police Association as part of its campaign over public order legislation:

> You can still walk the streets of NSW, but we can no longer *guarantee* your safety from harassment . . . What concerns Police is that you have families who use our streets and we can no longer guarantee them protection from harassment by the hoodlum element. But there is an even more alarming factor – there is a real danger that Police could eventually lose control of the streets . . . It is possible that the Offences in Public Places Act (1979) could be the seed from which a growth pattern of New York style street crime will be the future harvest? (quoted in Brown *et al.* 1990: 967)

Finally, a lack of powers does not emerge from relevant research as a significant factor influencing the effectiveness of the police. Research commissioned for the Royal Commission on Criminal Procedure concluded that 'There are no obvious powers which police might be given that would greatly enhance their effectiveness in the detection of crime' (Steer 1980: 125). The detection and clear-up of most crime depends, not on police powers, but on the provision of information by the public:

> the prime determinant of success is information immediately provided by members of the public (usually the victim) to patrol officers or detectives . . . If adequate information is provided to pinpoint the culprit fairly accurately, the crime will be resolved, if not it is almost certain not to be. This is the conclusion of all the relevant studies. (Reiner 1985: 121)

If the flow of such information is so crucial, it may be more useful to concentrate efforts on improving police-community relations than on increasing powers: indeed, if an increase in powers contributes to alienation between police and public, the result may well be counterproductive.

Calls for increasing police powers usually include as a corollary reducing suspects' rights. These rights, it is claimed, obstruct effective police work. Three points should be made here. (These are based on research in England and Wales, but the results are of relevance to Australian criminal justice systems.) First, suspects rarely exercise the rights which are supposed to be so obstructive. The prime example here is the 'right to silence', the target of concerted attacks from police since the 1960s. All empirical studies (reviewed in Dixon 1991a) show that very few suspects exercise this right. It is hardly surprising, given the difficulties of remaining silent, lack of knowledge of rights, and lack of legal advice. This is (or should be) well known. The conclusion must be that the right of silence has become an issue of symbolic rather than instrumental significance: it is the site on which general ideological conflicts about criminal justice are fought (Dixon 1991a).

Secondly, the legal status of these rights is often doubtful. The lack of legal substance for suspects' 'right' of access to legal advice in Australia (and in England and Wales before 1986) provides a good example. If 'rights' are not protected by the courts nor made real by the provision of services such as publicly funded duty solicitors in police stations, then they are of little value or meaning (Brown 1984).

Thirdly, the assumption that rights obstruct policing depends on a model of criminal justice that is balanced between police powers and suspects' rights: increase one, and the other must decrease. Research on the effects of the Police and Criminal Evidence Act 1984 shows how unhelpful such dichotomous thinking can be. The experience of England and Wales is that rights and powers can increase together, indeed that they can complement each other. A good example is the provision of legal advice to suspects in custody. Far from producing a (from the police perspective) disastrous increase in use of the right of silence, legal advice has had considerable benefits for police as well as for suspects: communication between police and suspects is eased and, in appropriate cases, earlier confessions are made. Use of the right of silence has not increased dramatically, is not 'abused' by professional criminals, and has little or no effect on the likelihood of a suspect being charged or convicted (Dixon 1991b; 1992a). Similarly, both police and suspects have benefited from the introduction of a clear regime for detention for questioning and the systematic tape-recording of interrogations (Dixon *et al.* 1990a). Reiner's authoritative review of the research literature concludes that:

It is not plausible that changes in police powers would significantly increase police effectiveness in crime control . . . There is no evidence that rules of criminal procedure allow a significant proportion of suspects to avoid conviction. (Reiner 1985: 173)

Such findings are a better basis for public policy than the rhetoric and misinformation which generally characterize debates about police powers.

In any case, to focus on a supposed lack of power (or any single) factor is misleading because neither policing in general nor law enforcement in particular are unitary activities. In order to understand the field, the focus must be much tighter, concentrating for example on factors such as varying detectability of types of crime, the likelihood of one detection leading to other crimes being cleared up (as offences 'taken into consideration' or 'written off'), the influence of relationships between suspect and victim, and between police and public (Bottomley and Coleman 1980: 85–98; 1981). In sum, policing is a much more complex activity than nostrums about the need for more powers would suggest. Claims for more powers need to be analysed specifically: what is the problem to be addressed? how would increasing police powers help to solve it? what are the alternatives? what would be the costs of increasing powers and might these outweigh the benefits?

The 'rational deterrent' model of policing implicit in 'common sense' discussions of police effectiveness has been properly criticized. Its concept of effective policing is unproblematic, but 'such clarity of vision is a form of myopia' (Hough and Clarke 1980: 2). Similarly, much discussion of police powers relies on what I prefer to call a legalistic/bureaucratic model of policing:

A central tenet of the police claim to legitimacy is their subordination to law. Police work is presented as being the application of an objective set of laws. The police are accountable to the law . . . Problems in policing arise because the law has become unrealistic and inadequate . . . It is assumed that law is the major determinant of police activity and consequently that legal change . . . will effect change in policing practice (and that) police institutions conform to an effective bureaucratic model, in which senior officers are able to direct the activities of their subordinates. (Dixon 1992a: 2–3)

This model has been shown to be inaccurate by the considerable number of empirical studies of policing which have been produced in the United States since the 1960s and the United Kingdom since the 1970s (for reviews, see Dixon 1992b; Reiner 1985). There is no reason to believe that, when substantial research comes to be done on policing in Australia, that the result will be any different. Crucially, the assumption that changing a police power will have a direct, intended effect on policing practices must be abandoned. Such legal changes are communicated and mediated through layers of organization and culture. Like a whispered message which is passed from person to person, they can be changed very considerably in this process. The effect of research to date has been largely critical: we know that law does not affect policing as the legalistic/bureaucratic model would suggest, but we do not yet have real understanding of how it *does* affect it. Many empirical studies, in reacting against received assumptions, have employed a culturalist approach which has its own limitations and deficiencies (Dixon 1992b: 3–4). There is a clear need for research which analyses specific instances of legal change and its effect on policing practices.

An extension of police powers is one of the clearest ways in which politicians can signify that they take public concerns seriously. When the demand is to 'do something about the crime problem', a change in police powers is an attractive option: it is likely to be popular, highly visible, and cheap. In such a context, more searching questions about the utility or likely effect of a change tend to be overlooked.

Pressure for changes in police powers often comes from the police themselves. The 'perennial clamour by law enforcement officials for increased powers' can be traced back to the earliest days of organized police forces in Australia (Haldane 1986: 15). Current concerns have to be seen in the light of their long history (Finnane 1987; 1989; 1989a). In recent decades, senior officers have become increasingly frequent and influential contributors to public debates about policing and a wide range of social matters. Clearly, the police have status as experts in areas of their specialization. However, it is equally clear that claims for increased powers are made by police not just as disinterested experts, but as politically aware bureaucrats. Claims for increased police powers are often linked to other bureaucratic interests, notably increased resources and establishments. Once again, claims for more police powers may have a very significant symbolic dimension, drawing attention to perceived crime threats or needs of police, or indeed drawing attention away from other public concerns such as police corruption or indiscipline.

This suggests that there is difficulty even at a superficial level in knowing what a change in police powers is intended to achieve. Some examples demonstrate that the measurement of intended effects is likely to be a highly complex matter.

A simple case is a police power to conduct random alcohol testing on drivers. Measures of effectiveness would include trends in convictions and road deaths. But a direct relation between the power (to carry out random breath-tests) and the result (declining alcohol-related road deaths) is confounded by other immeasurable factors, such as the effect of road safety advertising and, more generally, changing social attitudes towards drinking and driving.

Other examples are less straightforward. Police powers and their use in dealing with domestic violence illustrate the point. In a number of jurisdictions (notably in the United States), police have been directed to use arrest powers in dealing with incidents of domestic violence. (Although new arrest powers are not usually introduced, the effect is comparable to such a legal change.) The impact of such policies has attracted a great deal of research, probably more than on any comparable shift in police power and practice (Sherman 1992a). Early claims that such a policy reduced domestic violence (Sherman and Berk 1984) led to their widespead adoption in numerous jurisdictions. However, it is now becoming clear that the effects are much less certain and desirable than the initial studies suggested. Far from reducing domestic violence, mandatory arrest policies have increased arrests in half of the cities where the original research has been replicated. It is suggested that arrest has different effects on different kinds of people (see Sherman 1992: 203–12 for a summary of this research).

Such research raises methodological problems which are common to projects relying on crime statistics and official data. The measurement is of arrests, not of incidence of domestic violence. The relationship between arrest and incidence is complex: for example, the previous record of suspects may be decisive. More fundamentally, questions may be asked about measures of 'effectiveness': while arrest rates are easy to calculate, women's feelings of security and empowerment (which may result from knowledge of presumptive arrest policies) are much less so.

A final example is the effect of the Police and Criminal Evidence Act 1984 on the investigation of crime in England and Wales. As noted above, irreconcilable predictions were made about the likely effects of this legislation. Subsequent empirical studies of its effects have reflected these expectations (Dixon 1992a). Brown's study of the impact of the Police and Criminal Evidence Act on investigations of domestic burglary provides useful insight into these problems of evaluation. It was commissioned in response to 'a fall in the number and percentage of crimes cleared up by the police' in 1986 (the first year that the legislation was in force) which 'some took . . . to indicate that PACE had indeed given the balance of advantage to the suspect' (Brown 1991: vi). After 1986, the statistics returned to their previous pattern and it appears that the 1986 dip was 'a temporary aberration' which was largely due to officers' unfamiliarity and caution in operating new procedures (Brown 1991: vi, 85). However, this does not mean that the Police and Criminal Evidence Act did not change policing, but rather that its impact cannot be adequately grasped at the level of generalities. Brown examined the way that the Police and Criminal Evidence Act affected burglary investigations at three stations which contrasted sharply in their investigative methods: one 'cleared a high proportion of burglaries through interviewing convicted offenders in prison about other offences'; at the second, suspects were frequently interviewed at the station for offences that might be taken into consideration (TICs) along with the main charge; while at the third 'the policy tended to be to charge offenders and lay little emphasis on interviewing about further offences' (Brown 1991: vii). The research found that these contrasting practices significantly affected the impact of the Police and Criminal Evidence Act which varied from station to station, but that there was 'no evidence that PACE led to any consistent reduction in police effectiveness against burglary' (Brown 1991: xi). It also emphasized other differences between the stations, notably 'in the standard of evidence considered necessary to justify an arrest and subsequent detention at the police station' (Brown 1991: xii). Brown makes clear the difficulty in disentangling the effects of the Police and Criminal Evidence Act (which itself is complex and multifaceted) from other contemporary changes, many of which are immeasurable, some of which may be imperceptible. These range from changes of personnel at the research sites to other legislative changes (notably, the introduction of the Crown Prosecution Service), to broader social and political changes (Brown 1991: 8).

Such vital considerations tend to be overlooked when legislative changes are discussed. In such debates, there is a good deal of loose talk about legislative 'intention'. Indeed, legislation is sometimes anthropomorphized, as when people talk about the Police and Criminal Evidence Act 'trying' or 'intending' to achieve some objective. While this is, of course, largely a matter of shorthand, it threatens to oversimplify matters. To ask whether the Police and Criminal Evidence Act achieved its objectives is a misleading question: such complex, multidetermined legislation can only in a very qualified sense be said to have 'intentions' (Dixon 1992a).

These examples suggest the need for great care and specificity in making claims about the effects of proposed or actual legislative changes in police powers. Sweeping generalizations and unfounded assumptions need to be replaced by thorough, well-grounded research. The outcome need not be an accumulation of specific case-studies without more general relevance. Brown provides an examplar of how broader lessons may be drawn from closely focused studies (Brown 1991: ch. 8).

11. Conclusion

It is hoped that this paper makes clear the need for considerable re-evaluation of the topics which have been considered. While the history of police powers awaits the depth of historical revision to which other aspects of policing have been subjected, it is clear that received wisdom about constables' original common law powers needs to be revised by greater attention to the historical contexts, notably the seventeenth- and eighteenth-century ideological shifts. Provision of wide-ranging statutory powers is no modern development, but can be traced back to early vagrancy legislation. Social and national contexts are also vital: the nature of early Australian society transformed the imported traditions of Anglo-Irish policing.

A proper understanding of police powers requires attention to be paid to the interactive relationship between law and practice. Rhetorical generalizations need to be abandoned in favour of specific, informed analysis of what particular police powers are, how they are employed, and what their use can achieve.

References

Adler, J. S. (1989a). 'A historical analysis of the law of vagrancy', *Criminology*, 27, 209–29.

Adler, J. S.. (1989b). 'Rejoinder to Chambliss', *Criminology*, 27, 239–50.

Bittner, E. (1970). *The Functions of the Police in Modern Society* (Maryland, NIMH).

Bottomley, A. K. and Coleman, C. A. (1980). 'Police effectiveness and the public: the limitations of official crime rates', in Clarke, R. V. G. and Hough, J. M. (eds.), *The Effectiveness of Policing* (Farnborough, Gower), 70–97.

Bottomley, A. K. and Coleman, C.A. (1981). *Understanding Crime Rates* (Farnborough, Gower).

Bottomley, A. K and Pease, K. (1986). *Crime and Punishment: interpreting the data* (Milton Keynes, Open University Press).

Bottomley, A. K., Coleman, C. A., Dixon, D., Gill, M. and Wall, D. (1991). *The Impact of PACE: policing in a northern force* (Hull, Centre for Criminology and Criminal Justice).

Brennan, F. (1983). *Too Much Order with Too Little Law* (St Lucia, University of Queenland Press).

Brogden, M. (1981). 'All police is conning bastards: policing and the problem of consent' in Fryer, B. *et al.* (eds.), *Law, State and Society* (London, Croom Helm).

Brogden, M. (1982). *The Police: autonomy and consent* (London, Academic Press).

Brogden, M. (1987a). 'An Act to colonise the internal lands of the Island: empire and the origins of the professional police', *International Journal of the Sociology of Law*, 15, 179–208.

Brogden, M. (1987b). 'The emergence of the police – the colonial dimension', *British Journal of Criminology*, 27, 3–14.

Brogden, M., Jefferson, T. and Walklate, S. (1988). *Introducing Policework* (London, Unwin Hyman).

Brown, D. (1984). Review of Sallmann and Willis: 1984 *Legal Service Bulletin* (August), 186–90.

Brown, D. (1991). *Investigating Burglary: the effects of PACE* (London, HMSO).

Brown, D., Farrier, D., Neal, D., and Weisbrot, D. (1990). *Criminal Laws* (Annandale, Federation Press)

Byrne, P. J. (1993). *Criminal Law and Colonial Subject* (Cambridge, Cambridge University Press).

Carter, R. F. (1992). *Criminal Law of Queensland* 8th edn. (Sydney, Butterworth).

Chambliss, W. J. (1964). 'A sociological analysis of the law of vagrancy', *Social Problems*, 12, 67–77.

Chambliss, W. J. (1989). 'On trashing Marxist criminology', *Criminology*, 27, 231–8.

Chappell, D. and Wilson, P. R. (1969). *Police and the Public in Australia and New Zealand* (St Lucia, University of Queensland Press).

Chatterton, M. (1976). 'Police in social control', in King, J. F. S. (ed.), *Control without Custody?* (Cambridge, Institute of Criminology), 104–22.

Cohen, P. (1979). 'Policing the working-class city', in Fine, B., Lea, J., Picciotto, S. and Young, J. (eds.), *Capitalism and the Rule of Law* (London, Hutchinson), 118–36.

Critchley, T. A. (1978). *A History of Police in England and Wales* 2nd edn. (London, Constable).

Davis, J. (1980). 'The London garotting panic of 1862', in Gatrell *et al.* (eds.), *Crime and the Law.*

Demuth, C. (1978). *'Sus': a report on the Vagrancy Act 1824* (London, Runnymede Trust).

Denning, A. (1949). *Freedom Under the Law* (London, Stevens).

Devlin, P. (1960). *The Criminal Prosecution in England* (London, Oxford University Press).

Dicey, A. V. (1902). *The Law of the Constitution* 8th edn. (London, Macmillan).

Dixon, D. (1991a). 'Politics, research and symbolism in criminal justice', *Anglo-American Law Review*, 20, 27–50.

Dixon, D. (1991b). 'Common sense, legal advice and the right of silence', *Public Law,* 233–54.

Dixon, D. (1991c). *From Prohibition to Regulation* (Oxford, Clarendon Press).

Dixon D. (1992a). 'Legal regulation and policing practice', *Social and Legal Studies,* 1(4), 515–41.

Dixon, D. (1992b). *Detention for Questioning in Australia and England* (Hull, Hull University Law School Studies in Law).

Dixon, D., Bottomley, A. K., Coleman, C. A., Gill, M., Wall, D. (1989). 'Reality and rules in the construction and regulation of police suspicion', *International Journal of the Sociology of Law,* 17, 185–206.

Dixon, D. (1990a). 'Safeguarding the rights of suspects in police custody', *Policing and Society,* 1, 115–40.

Dixon, D., Coleman, C. A., and Bottomley, A. K. (1990). 'Consent and the legal regulation of policing', *Journal of Law and Society,* 17, 345–62.

Egger, S. and Findlay, M. (1988). 'The politics of police discretion' in Findlay, M. and Hogg, R. (eds.), *Understanding Crime and Criminal Justice* (North Ryde, Law Book Company), 209–23.

Emsley, C. (1991). *The English Police: a political and social history* (Hemel Hempstead, Harvester).

Feeley, M. (1979). *The Process is the Punishment* (New York, Russell Sage).

Feldman, D. (1986). *The Law relating to Entry, Search and Seizure* (London, Butterworth).

Finnane, M. (1987). 'The politics of police powers: the making of the Police Offences Acts', in Finnane (ed.), *Policing in Australia: Historical Perspectives,* 88–113.

Finnane, F. (1989). 'Police and the political process in Australia – the case for historical revision', paper for the ANZ Society of Criminology Conference.

Finnane, F. (1989a). 'Police rules and the organisation of policing in Queensland', *ANZ Journal of Criminology*, 22, 95–108.

Finnane, F. (ed.) (1987). *Policing in Australia: historical perspectives* (Kensington, NSW University Press).

Gatrell, V. A. C. (1980). 'The decline of theft and violence in Victorian and Edwardian England', in Gatrell *et al.* (eds.), *Crime and the Law*, 238–96.

Gatrell, V. A. C. (1990). 'Crime, authority and the policeman-state', in Thompson, F. M. L. (ed.), *The Cambridge Social History of Britain 1750–1950*, volume 3 (Cambridge, Cambridge University Press), 243–310.

Gatrell, V. A. C., Lenman, B. and Parker, G. (eds.) (1980). *Crime and the Law* (London, Europa).

Grabosky, P. (1977). *Sydney in Ferment: crime, dissent and official reaction* (Canberra, Australian National University Press).

Grabosky, P. (1988). *Efficiency and Effectiveness in Australian Policing*, Trends and Issues paper no. 16 (Canberra, Australian Institute of Criminology).

Hailsham, L. (1981). *Halsbury's Laws of England* 4th edn., volume 36 (London, Butterworth).

Haldane, R. (1986). *The People's Force, a history of the Victoria Police* (Brunswick, Melbourne University Press).

Hall, S. (1982). 'The lessons of Lord Scarman', *Critical Social Policy*, 2(2), 66–72.

Hay, D. (1975). 'Property, authority and the criminal law', in Hay, D., Linebaugh, P., Rule, J. G., Thompson, E. P. and Winslow, C. (eds.), *Albion's Fatal Tree* (Harmondsworth, Penguin) 17–63.

Hill, C. (1954). 'The Norman Yoke', in Saville, J. (ed.), *Democracy and the Labour Movement* (London, Lawrence and Wishart).

Hogg, R. and Golder, H. (1987). 'Policing Sydney in the late nineteenth century', in Finnane (ed.), *Policing in Australia: Historical Perspectives*, 59–73.

Hough, J. M. and Clarke, R. V. G. (1980). 'Introduction', in Clarke, R. V. G. and Hough, J. M. (eds.), *The Effectiveness of Policing* (Farnborough, Gower), 1–16.

HRA (1914). *Historical Records of Australia: series 1: Governors' Despatches to and from England, volume 1* (Sydney, Library Committee of the Commonwealth Parliament).

HRA (1916). *Historical Records of Australia: series 1: Governors' Despatches to and from England, volume 7* (Sydney, Library Committee of the Commonwealth Parliament).

Jefferson, T. and Grimshaw, R. (1984). *Controlling the Constable* (London, Frederick Muller/Cobden Trust).

Johnston, L. (1992). *The Rebirth of Private Policing* (London, Routledge).

Kelling, G. L., Pate, T., Dickerman, D. and Brown, C. (1974). *The Kansas City Preventive Patrol Experiment* (Washington DC, Police Foundation).

Kent, J. R. (1986). *The English Village Constable 1580–1642* (Oxford, Clarendon Press).

King, H. (1956). 'Some aspects of police administration in New South Wales, 1825–1851', *Journal of the Royal Australian Historical Society*, 42, 205–30.

Lambard, W. (1599). *The Dueties of Constables, Borsholders, Tythingman, and such other lowe and lay Ministers of the Peace* (London).

Leigh, L. H. (1975). *Police Powers in England and Wales* (London, Butterworth).

Leigh, L. H. (1985). *Police Powers in England and Wales* 2nd edn. (London, Butterworth).

Lenman, B. and Parker, G. (1980). 'The state, the community and the criminal law in early modern Europe' in Gatrell *et al.* (eds.), *Crime and the Law*, 11–48.

LRC Canada (1983). *Police Powers – Search and Seizure in Criminal Law Enforcement*, Working Paper 30 (Ottawa, LRCC).

LRC Canada (1985). *Arrest*, Working Paper 41 (Ottawa, LRCC).

LRC Canada (1988). *Our Criminal Procedure* Report 32 (Ottawa, LRCC).

Lustgarten, L. (1986). *The Governance of Police* (London, Sweet and Maxwell).

McBarnet, D. (1981). *Conviction* (London, Macmillan).

McConville M., Sanders, A., and Leng, R. (1991). *The Case for the Prosecution* (London, Routledge).

Milte, K. L. and Weber, T. A. (1977). *Police in Australia* (Sydney, Butterworth).

Moore, D. B. (1991). 'Origins of the police mandate – the Australian case reconsidered', *Police Studies*, 4, 107–20.

Neal, D. (1991). *The Rule of Law in a Penal Colony* (Cambridge, Cambridge University Press).

NSW LRC (1990). *Police Powers of Detention and Investigation after Arrest* Report no. 66 (Sydney, NSW LRC).

Palmer, S. H. (1988). *Police and Protest in England and Ireland 1780–1850* (Cambridge, Cambridge University Press).

Philips, D. (1980). '"A new engine of power and authority": the institutional-isation of law-enforcement in England 1780–1830' in Gatrell *et al.* (eds.), *Crime and the Law*, 155–89.

Polyviou, P. G. (1982) *Search and Seizure* (London, Duckworth).

Queensland Police Service (1991).'Submission to the Office of the Minister for Police and Emergency Services and the Criminal Justice Commission in response to the issues paper: "Police Powers in Queensland"'.

Radzinowicz, L. (1956). *A History of English Criminal Law and its Administration from 1750: volume 3* (London, Stevens).

RCCP (1981). *Report of the Royal Commission on Criminal Procedure* Cmnd. 8092.

RCPPP (1929). *Report of the Royal Commission on Police Powers and Procedure* Cmd. 3297.

Reiner, R. (1985). *The Politics of the Police* (Brighton, Harvester).

Robinson, C. D. (1979). 'Ideology as history: a look at the way some English police historians look at the police', *Police Studies*, 2, 35–49.

Sallmann, P. and Willis, J. (1984). *Criminal Justice in Australia* (Melbourne, Oxford University Press).

Scarman, L. (1981). *The Brixton Disorders* Cmnd. 8427 (London, HMSO).

Sharpe, J. (1983). 'Policing the parish in early modern England' in Past and Present *Police and Policing* (Oxford, Past and Present Society), 1–25.

Shearing, C. D. (1992). 'Policing: the relationship between its public and private forms', in Tonry, M. and Morris, N. (eds.), *Modern Policing* (Chicago, University of Chicago Press).

Shearing, C. D. and Stenning, P. C., (eds.) (1987). *Private Policing* (Newbury Park, Sage).

Sherman, L. W. (1992). 'Attacking crime: police and crime control', in Tonry, M. and Morris, N. (eds.), *Modern Policing* (Chicago, Chicago University Press), 159–230.

Sherman, L. W. (1992a). *Policing Domestic Violence: experiments and dilemmas* (New York, Free Press).

Sherman, L. W. and Berk, R. A. (1984). 'The specific deterrent effects of arrest for domestic assault', *American Sociological Review*, 49, 261–72.

Steedman, C. (1984). *Policing the Victorian Community* (London, Routledge, Kegan Paul).

Steer, D. (1980). *Uncovering Crime: the police role* (London, HMSO).

Stevenson, J. (1979). *Popular Disturbances in England 1700–1870* (London, Longman).

Styles, J. (1987). 'The emergence of the police', *British Journal of Criminology*, 27, 15–22.

Thompson, E. P. (1963). *The Making of the English Working Class* (Harmondsworth, Penguin).

Waldron, J. (1990). *The Law* (London, Routledge).

Walker, R. (1984). 'The New South Wales Police Force, 1862–1900', *Journal of Australian Studies*, 15, 25–38.

Websdale, N. (1991). 'Disciplining the non-disciplinary spaces', *Policing and Society*, 2, 89–115.

Weinberger, B. (1991). 'Are the police professional? An historical account of the British police institution', in Emsley, C. and Weinberger, B. (eds.), *Policing Western Europe* (Westport, Greenwood Press), 74–89.

Wrightson, K. (1980). 'Two concepts of order: justices, constables and jurymen in seventeenth century England' in Brewer, J. and Styles, J. (eds.), *An Ungovernable People* (London, Hutchinson), 21–46.

8

Political autonomy, accountability and efficiency in the prosecution of serious fraud

MICHAEL LEVI

Introduction

For those pragmatists and consequentialists who do not adopt a 'pure' rights-based approach, their level of trust in law enforcement agencies – not only now but in the future – remains central to responses to policing powers: the term 'policing' here is used to include non-police agencies. This article focuses upon a particular sub-set of 'the trust issues', the prosecution of serious fraud, which came to the political fore in November 1992 and early 1993 with two extraordinary events. The first was the prosecution by HM Customs & Excise of three directors of a company called Matrix-Churchill for allegedly violating prohibitions on the export of arms components to Iraq by *deceiving* the Department of Trade and Industry into granting export licences. The second was the extraordinary sending of a watch inscribed 'Don't let the buggers get you down' by Michael Mates MP – then minister of state for Northern Ireland – to Asil Nadir, after the latter had been charged by the Serious Fraud Office (SFO) with defrauding Polly Peck International of over £30 million (in specimen charges): the 'buggers' clearly were the SFO. In his resignation speech following the revelation of his watch-sending to Nadir, who fled bail to the non-extraditable, diplomatically unrecognized republic of North Cyprus (his home and the site of many of his business operations), the former minister for Northern Ireland fulminated against violations of civil rights and the need to make prosecutions accountable. The problem is, as it always is, 'accountable to whom for what?'.[1] *Inter alia*, these and some other fraud cases involving powerful defendants and potential defendants have opened up interesting issues such as the relative autonomy of the *prosecution* as well as the *policing* process from 'the government': the arms-for-Iraq inquiry conducted in 1993–4 by Lord Justice Scott has highlighted the enormous amount of intra-governmental 'politicking' that can occur in some high profile cases – though it seems unlikely that many will have that degree of politicality – as well as the ambivalent role of the attorney-general as both party politician and senior law officer with 'accountability' to Parliament for prosecutions and the constitutional power of stopping them by entering a *nolle prosequi*.[2]

Legislation on powers to investigate white-collar crime seems often to diverge from that of 'ordinary' crime, largely because it is seen as analytically separable from it and does not attract significant civil rights lobbying: businesspeople's rights do not interest many on the political left, and because of their social status and articulate familiarity with verbal combat, they are not seen to be at risk of miscarriages of justice (Levi 1987; 1993). They are, in a sense, the most unappealing group among those who might lay claim to 'victim status' (Levi and Pithouse, forthcoming). For these reasons, paradoxically, there have been relatively few challenges to the unalloyed use of the 'crime control' (as opposed to the 'due process') model to combat 'white-collar crime'.[3] Not long after the Police and Criminal Evidence Act 1984 (PACE) settled the rights of suspects and the Prosecution of Offences Act 1985 institutionalized the separation of the investigative from the prosecution functions by establishing the Crown Prosecution Service (CPS), Lord Roskill's Fraud Trials Committee (reporting in 1986) asked primarily *efficiency*-oriented questions about how to reduce the extent to which the approach to major fraud investigations wasted police and court resources in cases that led to No Further Action decisions or to acquittals in the Crown Courts. Roskill proposed interdisciplinary task forces, with early legal and other expert input, buttressed by inquisitorial powers to obtain information: if this did not happen, customer and professional confidentiality would prolong investigations unduly and/or fail to provide investigators with information that would help their search for an accurate explanation of events. This looked like, and was, a rational approach to 'discovering the truth' of a sort which has led many to favour the continental *juge d'instruction* model, at least as it looks to those who do not have to experience it. (See Leigh and Zedner 1992 on mainland European prosecutions.)

Roskill had broadly intended a fully fledged inquisitorial regime in which, as in DTI (Department of Trade and Industry) investigations even at present, self-incriminating answers obtained under compulsion would be admissible unless specifically oppressive.[4] Committal proceedings were to be replaced by preparatory hearings at which the accused would be required to present their detailed defence to the prosecution's allegations, to iron out most areas of dispute before the trial began. However, under pressure from Jeremy Hutchinson – a leading QC in the House of Lords – *inter alia*,[5] a Home Office minister watered down the proposal to the present compromise in which although it is a specific offence to lie to the SFO, statements made under compulsion under Section 2 of the Criminal Justice Act 1987 can be admitted in evidence only if the defendant makes statements in the witness box which are inconsistent with his or her earlier remarks. Since few defendants give evidence (and few would be advised by their lawyers to give evidence whatever the powers of the SFO), this is mainly irrelevant in practice (Levi 1993).[6] Section 2 interviews are restricted to SFO lawyers and, somewhat to the surprise of several former members of the Roskill Committee, to SFO accountants (some of whom are seconded from large City firms) who have little training in interviewing apart from a short course by the City of London police: the Royal Commission (1993) has recommended that this power to interview under compulsion be extended to the police *in SFO cases only*. In affirming the right to silence for most defendants, the Royal Commission has retained the existing gap in the powers to deal with 'ordinary' suspects and those to deal with those suspected – reasonably or not – by the SFO and the DTI (in Companies Acts inspections). One intriguing issue that has remained undiscussed outside of the Guinness and Nadir cases, however, is what jurisprudentially is required before these powers can be triggered: the legislation requires that the case be 'serious' *or* 'complex', but does not define these terms, and the current guidelines issued by the director of the SFO to indicate what sort of cases he will consider taking on state vaguely that cases would normally involve over £5 million *and/or* be of significant public interest.[7]

Miscarriage risks in serious fraud prosecutions

In *The Case for the Prosecution*, McConville *et al.* (1991) make out their argument that cases are *constructed* by the prosecutor on the basis of police perceptions of 'what happened', in which the police reform witnesses' statements into their own reified amalgam of conviction-supporting material. Hypothetically, serious fraud cases – to which they make no reference – would not be expected to look like this, for their density and the élite status of suspects should protect them from the strong arm of the law, while prosecutors are involved in the supervision of the police fraud investigations in a way that seldom happens elsewhere, even in murders (Maguire and Norris 1993). Serious fraud cases – of which cases dealt with by the SFO are only a sub-set, since the Customs & Excise, DTI, and Inland Revenue prosecute their own cases, while the CPS processes many equally serious police investigations conducted under PACE powers – would be expected to involve lengthy negotiation over access to documents, over interpretations of what had happened, and over the decision to prosecute itself rather than to impose administrative penalties. (For American illustrations of this filtering, see Mann 1985.)

What actually happens, and is there a risk of miscarriages of justice in serious fraud prosecutions? In the 'famous' cases that generate the most attention, cases are poured over in fine detail, with the lawyers who will eventually prosecute the case being brought in at an early stage to guide the investigation: a role many SFO lawyers and outside counsel admitted that they find alien, since the culture of the Bar is more directed at cross-examination skills than in strategic planning and project management, and because they are more used to the detached, post-investigative role *required* by the CPS as part of its mandate of independence from the police.[8] Though this may change if the police are given the power to interview suspects and key witnesses under Section 2, unlike any other major crime investigation (Maguire and Norris 1992) the police are often treated (and certainly feel themselves to be treated) as 'gophers' by the SFO lawyers and accountants, and the cultural divide between 'professionals' and police remains strong: in accordance with the class metaphor, the police are positioned on lower floors of the SFO building and, except at formal functions, seldom mix socially with the lawyers and accountants whose offices are on the higher floors.

Observations of live SFO case conferences suggest that the police are often asked for their opinion about the credibility and strength of witnesses, whom they saw at some stage, whether on a voluntary basis or when taking witness statements for evidential purposes from those who had been required to talk to SFO lawyers and accountants. This was a largely untapped theme of research for the Royal

Commission on Criminal Justice: that police influence over *witness* statements can transform the complexity of the real world into a reified one in which witness culpability is minimized while suspects' culpability is maximized.[9] It is also an article of faith rather than evidence that professional status will immunise interviewers against taken-for-granted 'frames' within which the evidence and their interviews are viewed. What the SFO regime does is to ensure that interviews with key professional witnesses (under Section 2) are taped and are conducted by lawyers and accountants, removing one layer of such unsupervised steering. However, it remains deeply problematic to know which witnesses are telling the truth and, more especially, how 'blameworthiness' is distributed. For example, accountants may find it more convenient if they are sued later for professional negligence if it is believed that they were told lies by the directors than if they failed to check things without being told lies or even suggested serious 'dodgy' manoeuvres; it is also less damaging professionally to their reputations for competence. What is *anyone* who was not actually there at the time to make of conflicting interpretations of what was said (given that, unlike ordinary police cases, the SFO can make them *have* to say *something* unless they have a – tightly circumscribed – 'reasonable excuse' not to answer)?[10] Simply because fraud has a lot more documentation than other crimes does not mean that the interpretation of roles and who knew (or was told) what is unproblematical. The most public illustration of this is the undercurrents that have emerged about the drafting of witness statements by civil servants and ministers regarding the part of the Scott inquiry that has dealt with the Matrix-Churchill export licences. Whatever the disputes about Lord Justice Scott's interpretation of 'what happened', it cannot reasonably be denied that prosecution witnesses radically reframed events in order to fit the prosecution's theory to enable conviction to take place. Had the background documentation that the ministers' Public Interest Immunity certificates sought to hide not been made available to the defence, as it eventually was, there is every probability that the Matrix-Churchill directors would have been wrongly convicted for deceiving the DTI export licence department into believing that the arms components were made for civil use.[11]

During the course of my research in 1992 – though not caused by it! – the SFO came under increasing attack. One basis (or pretext) for these attacks is that the SFO levy 'scattergun' charges. The number of charges reflects an initial 'maximum bid' designed to give flexibility at a relatively early stage in the process, to see what the defence line will be in response, and it is expected that these will be whittled down at the preparatory hearings. Indeed, it is the *appearance* of ruthless pruning by the judge of the prosecution's initial charges in the Nadir case that gave rise to some surface plausibility in the allegation that the SFO was trying to get the judge removed and was using the accusations that Nadir's associates had tried to bribe the judge as a pretext for so doing.[12] (In reality, what happened was that a large number of charges were dismissed by the trial judge on technical grounds, subject to a pending House of Lords' ruling on the meaning of 'appropriation' in *Gomez*. Following their lordships' decision, the charges were reinstated and the prosecution then selected a sample of those original charges to continue with.)

The SFO was established under the Criminal Justice Act 1987 to streamline its cases more efficiently than the previous system in which full police enquiries preceded prosecution decisions. However, particularly given that most of its staff were recruited from the civil service in 1988 and external counsel act in a variety of cases, the core legal culture has been retained. Many prosecuting counsel still seek 'to reflect the full criminality of the case' not only in their charges but also in asking for many allegedly inessential further enquiries to be made: their personal 'performance indicators' reflect the success of the court case, and most counsel have been brought up in a cost-unconstrained environment. Partly because of their extra powers and élite status, SFO 'case controllers' – in-house lawyers who are cradle-to-grave case managers – unconsciously or consciously feel that the amount of money involved in the charges must be over a million pounds. If not, they plausibly believe that they will be criticized for 'scraping the bottom of the barrel' and using the sledgehammer powers of the SFO to crack what is in essence a minor case. What Roskill and others failed to predict was that the early involvement and higher status and experience of outside counsel would eclipse the role of case controller where there was a dominant counsel. Civil service staff – particularly those recruited from other departments in an era where there was a strong rising private sector demand – have comparatively little trial experience, and the absence of rights of audience to appear in the Crown Court and the High Court does not give them any opportunity to develop any trial experience.

In essence, except for the grafting on of the SFO, which deals with about sixty cases and conducts about twenty trials a year, the system as it is now is little different from what it was pre-Roskill. The expansion in the number and size of fraud cases means that the Headquarters Casework Division of the CPS is dealing with many of the sorts of prosecutions that Roskill envisaged should be the preserve of the SFO, most of which CPS cases have been conducted using the limited police powers to seek answers from suspects (though documents can be obtained pre-arrest via PACE Production Orders). The Royal Commission (1993) recommended a review of the overlap between CPS and SFO, which might dramatically extend the range of cases to which the extra powers would apply, and this review is now complete, encouraged by subsequent cases which have collapsed or have led to non-custodial sentences following plea bargains. The revenue departments continue with their focus on financial settlements as an alternative to prosecution: in cases where their targets are (offshore) donors to the Conservative party such as Mr Octav Botnar, then chairman of Nissan UK and currently a fugitive in Switzerland from later UK tax evasion charges, this preference for money recovered over criminal convictions is obviously 'sensitive' (if discovered by the public). Despite various actual and anticipated pressures, however, the prosecution of Botnar (and a co-director and auditors, by the Inland Revenue), Nadir (by the SFO), and the Matrix-Churchill directors (by HM Customs & Excise) lends support to those who argue that law enforcement officials enjoy relative autonomy from the government, despite the complex liaison between heads of prosecution departments and the attorney-general. Indeed, there is a sense in which the determination of Custom & Excise to go ahead with its prosecution of the Matrix-Churchill directors may be read as a reflection of that political and institutional independence: it appears that unlike the 1990 case in which allegations of supplying components to Iraq for a 'supergun' were dropped on the advice of the attorney-general, no such formal advice was given by the attorney-general over Matrix-Churchill, though he was active in seeking to promote Public Interest Immunity certificates which would have denied important information to the defence. No fraudsters are targets of police retributive sentiments to the extent of terrorists or the Medellin cartel, but who would argue that the Maxwells or Peter Clowes (of investment fraud Barlow Clowes) are viewed more favourably than any of those allegedly maltreated by the West Midlands Serious Crime Squad (though there are no serious fraud 'confessions' during the ride to the police station)? In the Barlow Clowes, Blue Arrow, Guinness, Polly Peck, and Maxwell cases, there were very high profile arrests in the glare of publicity, accompanied by allegations that 'the SFO' (treated anthropomorphically and mistakenly as a coherent institution) *deliberately* used this as a prejudicial public relations stunt. (Since his victims were 'only' shareholders – many of them institutional ones – Nadir, unlike Clowes or the Maxwells, was unlikely to have been a populist hate figure before his dramatic flight, and perhaps even after it.)

Fraud investigations, prosecutions, and trials have highlighted some key dimensions of our criminal justice system. The resource costs of investigations can be reduced if early decisions are made to go for modest charges: but this will reduce the sentence and entail greater risks of failure if the defence generates accounts of events which call the prosecution's frame of reference into question. In fraud cases, as in some homicides that are not simple family dyads, it is often difficult to be certain who should be giving evidence and who should be in the dock. Insiders – from the bankruptcy fraudsters who gave evidence against the Richardson and Kray 'gangsters' in the 1960s, to finance director Olivier Roux in Guinness – could plausibly be treated as accomplices or even as instigators who supply the authorities with 'big names' to get out of the frame themselves. The extraordinary unravelling of the Italian political system which is being precipitated by the criminal conspiracy allegations in *tangentopoli* makes (or should make) us confront the reliability of testimony given under pressure of self-exculpation, whether by professional criminals or those of 'good character'. There is no equivalent of the 'black box' fraud recorder: we cannot be certain that we have recaptured objectively the words that were used, and the possibly quite different understandings that people had of what was said. This is so even where civil servants and ministers are not 'economical with the *actualité*', as former minister for defence Allan Clark admitted he was when providing witness statements prior to the Matrix-Churchill case. The subsequent arms-for-Iraq inquiry under Lord Justice Scott has revealed just how complicated the attribution of 'guilty knowledge' can be, and how inevitable it is to make partially subjective judgements about the plausibility of different accounts.

In every realm of criminal justice, even where there is undercover infiltration or covert surveillance, imperfect approximations are made regarding 'what happened'. The police and regulators have their interpretations, which may reflect their cynical lack of empathy with the 'commercial community': the jury have theirs, which may reflect dislike of rich Jews or excessive respect for their social superiors as much as the evidence. (See Levi 1987, ch. 3; and Levi and Pithouse, forthcoming, for some evidence on public attitudes to fraud.) Abolishing the right to silence, as has already happened in SFO and DTI cases (which have been generally ignored by mainstream police researchers), does not magically reveal 'the truth'.[13] There is more pressure from police committees and the home secretary to deal with crime on the streets than crime in the suites: but the place of Britain in a global economy, as well as the security of retirement pensions and redundancy payments, depends also on Britain's reputation for dealing with financial misconduct. That, of course, creates its own pressures to get convictions, to show other countries that 'we' deal with our fraudsters effectively.

Reasonable people can disagree over whether or not they have discovered a 'smoking prosecutorial gun', and so far Asil Nadir has failed to come up with the tapes or records that will substantiate his case that 'they' wanted him out of the way to assist in a peace settlement regarding the Turkish Republic of North Cyprus. Likewise, how did the interests of the Conservatives in cracking down on City crime (and in forestalling commercially competitive US leaks about 'untouchable' British City crooks, arising out of US Securities and Exchange Commission and US Department of Justice interviews with insider trader Ivan Boesky) lead senior officers in the Metropolitan Police Fraud Squad to arrest Guinness Chairman Ernest Saunders, but not other 'City criminals' who presumably could equally have been arrested to satisfy the Conservatives' alleged pre-1987 election political white-collar blood-lust? These functionalist 'explanations' of prosecution decision-making in white-collar crime cases do not appear to work at the level of agency.

The closest fit for the paranoid conspiracy theorists of prosecution decisions might appear to be Matrix-Churchill, at least in terms of reflecting the desire to show the public that Britain had *not* willingly provided the weapons used to kill its own soldiers in the Gulf War:[14] some support for this explicitly political 'reading' is that Margaret Thatcher wrote congratulating the Customs & Excise for an earlier successful prosecution of two people who had allegedly supplied arms components to Iraq.[15] Yet even the determination to go ahead with the prosecution of Matrix-Churchill seems to have more to do with the resentment of Customs & Excise at what they viewed as political interference with their earlier planned prosecution over the supply of 'Supergun' components to Iraq.[16] But how generally do we decide on whether a prosecution or non-prosecution decision is affected by explicit political factors (or, for that matter, by the cultural attitude more common in Britain than in the US or Australia – the desire not to 'rock the boat')? 'Methodic suspicion' often leads to the ignoring of counter-evidence, but 'insider researchers' (as I have been in some serious fraud cases) are confronted with the classic Cicourel (1968) problem of being torn between our personal judgement that x would never have conspired to do y, and the risk that we too have 'gone native' and have been misled by excessive familiarity with our research subjects. If John Le Carre had written a novel about Matrix-Churchill, many might have found it to be an unrealistic portrait of shiftiness and ineptitude on the part of some civil servants and ministers. But to demonstrate that state institutions sometimes behave like that does not mean that *all* paranoid or self-serving allegations of political conspiracies are true. Though far less involved in the specimen charges in the indictment, the amount of money missing from Polly Peck – whose absence has still not been explained and some of which has not been satisfactorily traced – is equivalent to the total net losses from car crime in England and Wales that year: granted that people thought by the prosecutors and by the civil investigating accountants to be Nadir's nominees may not actually be so, it is unsurprising that prosecutors and investigators at the SFO should have come up with the hypothesis that a man who transferred so many millions to an offshore company acting on lawful authority but without any apparently good business reason might have been intending to steal it! Since Nadir currently (1994) shows no sign of allowing 'the buggers' to 'get him down' in the courtroom, the public will probably not have the opportunity of holding either him or the SFO to 'proper' account for the fairness of the decision to prosecute.

Even when there is no explicitly political 'spin' to a case, what does seem highly plausible is that once the team of lawyers, accountants, and police focus upon a case, a momentum builds up in which it becomes hard to call off a prosecution. There are no statistics on how many cases initially accepted after 'case vetting' by the SFO staff are subsequently not prosecuted, but case controllers possess low status compared with external counsel, and some tend to be deferential towards their recommendations when they advise prosecution. Although the case vetting officer is not normally the case controller, unlike some other cases (except, from a police perspective, major enquiries), so much money is poured into the investigation of an SFO case that it looks like incompetence and a vast waste of money, or even a 'cover-up'[17] if no prosecution results. If – as has happened up to a point over the manipulation of the stock market in the Blue Arrow and Guinness cases – independent counsel acting for the Crown appear to be waging a cultural war against what they view as corrupt accepted practice within the 'Establishment', the momentum of the prosecution is carried along in a wave of enthusiasm, and one arrives at the prosecution of large numbers of defendants.

The emotional contradiction many people experience when reviewing the prosecution of white-collar crime is that 'getting those rich buggers' may be seen as a necessary prerequisite of 'equal justice'. This is brilliantly captured in *Bonfire of the Vanities*, where the prosecutors long to put some rich white guys in jail, instead of the poor blacks whom they feel deep down have little real alternative to crime (Wolfe 1987). My observations of SFO work make it easy to visualize how they might get it wrong either in imagining possible lines of defence or in imputing culpability.[18] On the other hand, the depth of prejudicial publicity which follows a corporate collapse is a powerful impetus to carry people forward. The prosecution of white-collar crime, as much as any other, entails the perpetual refrains of 'was he behaving dishonestly?' and 'what did he know and what was he told about transaction n?' The criminal law bifurcates people into the crude binary division of 'guilty' or 'innocent', and in the complex world of corporate actions where there are so many people who potentially are indictable, this yields strange and bitter fruit, in which many of the witnesses are as unattractive and prone to generate disinformation as are the defendants. (Perceived misconduct by prosecution witnesses sometimes leads to acquittals following cross-examination.)

Much debate has gone on about the role of informants in the criminal justice process (Maguire *et al.* 1992; Audit Commission 1993), but it is a rare case where, as in the first Guinness trial in 1990, the judge has to give a massively complex set of jury instructions which revolve around whether the finance director, Olivier Roux, was really an unindicted accomplice or was merely a key witness (source: trial transcript). Likewise, it is a curious system in which, because the

SFO – which determines its own workload – considers itself to be 'full up' with cases such as Maxwell and BCCI, a vast fraud is dealt with by the police under ordinary police powers, going on to the CPS, which the week before or after might have attracted the extra powers (and financial resources) of the SFO. Even if the attorney-general had decided in 1994 to merge the headquarters fraud division of the CPS with the SFO, this line-drawing problem of seriousness and complexity would not have disappeared.

Conclusions

The important issues of accountability raised by serious fraud prosecutions are unlike most faced in other arenas, and arise principally because of the political (with a small or large 'p') ramifications of particular cases. These include party political donations from businesspeople – on which the heavily indebted Conservative party became highly dependent during the 1980s and 1990s to finance its campaigns and its headquarters – who sought favours such as well-photographed dinners with the prime minister, used by them for subsequent public relations purposes to impress people overseas as well as in the UK. They also include broader conceptions of 'public interest' which are difficult to unpack. In theory, prosecution decisions are made by crown prosecutors, by the director of the SFO, and by the prosecution divisions of Customs & Excise, DTI, and Inland Revenue autonomously from their political heads. However, the director of the SFO and the DPP are answerable to the attorney-general who in turn is answerable to Parliament. In practice, it is rare for answers to be given to current cases, but concern from MPs (including ministers) can transmit across to those dealing with the case. My brief research period – and longer observations and interviews over the past two decades – did not enable me to disentangle whether the non-prosecution of senior industry or governmental persons was due to 'influence' or merely to the well-attested fact that remoteness from actual decisions makes it hard to convict people for corporate crime (and therefore, consistent with the Code for Crown Prosecutors, arguably improper to prosecute them) (Wells 1992; Cullen et al. 1987). A good illustration is the problem of ascertaining the role played by former home secretary Reginald Maudling in the corrupt building scandals of architect John Poulson and in the investment 'scams' of American Jerome Hoffman (Gillard

1974), where a 'professional' judgement of the probability of conviction is hard to separate from a 'political' judgement of the downside risks of acquittal (or, for that matter, of conviction). Though their overall conviction rate (including guilty pleas) varies between two thirds and 80 per cent, the low conviction rate in 'famous name' SFO prosecutions makes the law officers of the Crown as well as the case lawyers look bad, and this is something they normally seek to avoid: bureaucracies need the support of politicians (including the attorney-general) for resources, and there has been a major campaign against the SFO under the rubric of cost-effectiveness, whose deeper motivation may lie in the ambivalent feelings of politicians and businesspeople about the *desirability* of the effective prosecution of fraud.

Notes

[1] Given what the media revealed during 1993 about the offshore nominee accounts that are used by the Conservative party to enable the donation of funds that – whether proceeds of crime or not – are undisclosed to *shareholders* or the general public as *party* political contributions, this looks like a classic case where it is obscure to which political constituency police and prosecutors *should be* accountable. (For police accountability see, more generally, Reiner, 1992.)

[2] This power was used to stop what would have been 'Guinness 3' when, to the consternation of the police, it was decided that following a confidential submission by the defence, there was insufficient evidence to support a prosecution against a senior partner in the major stockbroking firm, Cazenove. One interpretation of this decision to drop charges is that it was a 'political' decision to avoid prosecuting the most élite of those charged in Guinness: another, which I find more plausible, is that the submission made it likely that key prosecution witnesses would be discredited in the subsequent trial, leading it to collapse.

[3] A term that over-homogenizes a very diverse set of behaviours.

[4] Whatever 'oppressive' now means after the successful appeal by 'the Cardiff Three' against convictions for murder, during which the Court of Appeal criticized the South Wales Police for 'repetitious bullying': *R v Miller, Parris, and Abdullahi* [1992] 97 Cr. App. R. 99. Such a monotonic approach is most unlikely in a company or serious fraud investigation.

[5] The Law Society, in the form of Walter Merricks, a dissenting member of the Roskill Committee, lobbied hard with the media to suggest that the proposals were too draconian.

[6] Indeed in some respects, it may act to the defendant's *advantage*, since it

creates a pressure not to give evidence which otherwise s/he might be tempted to give!

7   There is currently no case law on what constitutes reasonable suspicion by the SFO on which their powers may be triggered, though if there was an obvious and gross departure from published guidelines, judicial review might be obtained. The minimum cost figure before the SFO will investigate has gradually crept up from £1 million in 1988 to £5 million in 1992, but many cases dealt with by the CPS and DTI involve more than £5 million. The conceptual latitude here is considerable, though in practice the use of powers is limited because the SFO restricts itself to some sixty cases under investigation at any one time (Levi 1993). It seems extraordinary, however, that the powers of the state to require the suspect's co-operation should depend on the existing caseload of the SFO rather than on any inherent qualities of the case to be investigated.

8   I am not assuming that this mandate is carried through in practice: obviously many CPS decisions are structured and pre-empted by what the police have done in their investigation, particularly given that the CPS seldom suggests (and cannot require) substantial reinvestigation.

9   As the Scott inquiry showed, the careful 'manufacture' and harmonization of civil servants' witness statements was a crucial part of what plainly would have been a miscarriage of justice had they been convicted. However, the 'negotiation' of statements was carried out by civil servants themselves rather than by police or even by the investigations division of Customs & Excise.

10 I am not arguing here for the sort of libertarian 'freeze' that (by inference) McConville et al. (1991) get into, where because one cannot be certain that x did y, we should prosecute or convict almost no one. That will simply lead to mass vigilantism, with the sort of respect for due process and evidence afforded by the Ku Klux Klan.

11 The vendors of arms to Iraq, whether encouraged by the security services or not, make unlikely heroes for civil libertarians!

12 I have no evidence that would enable me to test the accusations, but the assertion by Nadir's counsel that no High Court judge is bribable because none has been accused in the past is unimpressive logic. Those who initially made the allegation to the police have now fled to Nadir's hideaway in the Turkish Republic of North Cyprus, alleging now that the police put them up to it (which unsurprisingly is strongly denied): it seems reasonable to question what the motivation of the police would be for such action. However, the possibility of such allegations – and the conviction of several county judges in a long-running undercover investigation in Chicago – was one reason why I recommended that defendants should have been able to opt for trial without jury subject to the consent of both judge and prosecution. (This route away from possible jury prejudice was ignored by the Royal Commission.) The DPP's Office – the DPP having herself been director of the SFO at the time of the main

investigation – has subsequently decided that there should be no prosecution of those alleged to have been involved in the plot.

[13] Its use in criminal trials also may be prohibited in time, as the European Court has held in 1994 that the former Guinness Chairman, Ernest Saunders, has an admissible case that his trial – which included compulsory testimony from DTI transcripts – was a violation of Article 6 of the European Convention of Human Rights.

[14] It is hard to believe that this prosecution decision, taken by HM Customs & Excise, was undertaken with top-level governmental approval, since many outside that department appreciated the risk that 'the wheel would come off' (as it did), and would have judged it not worth that symbolic gain. Once taken, it may have seemed too hard to work out how to stop the prosecution. However, what is crucial is that the charges involved *deception* of the DTI officials, and it is devastatingly obvious that they were not deceived about the export licence applications.

[15] The convictions were later quashed by the Court of Appeal: *R v. Daghir, The Guardian*, 25 and 26 May 1994.

[16] The overlap between political interference and 'legal advice' arises from the dual role of the attorney-general.

[17] During 1994, after a preliminary investigation and review of extensive evidence provided by a private investigator on behalf of (formerly) wealthy Lloyd's 'names', the SFO controversially decided that there was insufficient evidence to justify their proceeding against those involved in managing the Gouda Walker syndicate. This was viewed by some as the 'Establishment' closing ranks, and some of those allegedly defrauded who had seen the original report remained dissatisfied by the SFO decision. How can we tell who was right?

[18] As Braithwaite (1984) and Fisse and Braithwaite (1993) demonstrate, it is astonishing how lines of accountability that are clear for managerial purposes suddenly become opaque when interrogated critically by outsiders. The apparent ignorance displayed by all senior Cabinet ministers except Michael Heseltine of the change in policy over the supply of arms to Iraq is another case in point.

References

Audit Commission (1993). *Helping with their Enquiries* (London, HMSO).

Braithwaite, J. (1984). *Corporate Crime in the Pharmaceutical Industry* (London, Routledge).

Cicourel, A. (1968). *The Social Organisation of Juvenile Justice* (New York, John Wiley).

Cullen, F., Maakestad, W. and Cavender, G. (1987). *Corporate Crime Under Attack* (Cincinnati, Anderson Publishing Co.).

Fisse, B. and Braithwaite, J. (1993). *Corporations, Crime, and Accountability* (Cambridge, Cambridge University Press).

Fraud Trials Committee (1986). *Report* (London, HMSO).

Gillard, M. (1974). *A Little Pot of Money* (London, Private Eye and Andre Deutsch).

Leigh, L. and Zedner, L. (1992). *Report of the Administration of Criminal Justice in the Pre-Trial Phase*, Royal Commission on Criminal Justice Research Study No. 1, (London, HMSO).

Levi, M. (1987). *Regulating Fraud: White-Collar Crime and the Criminal Process* (London, Routledge).

Levi, M. (1993). *The Investigation, Prosecution and Trial of Serious Fraud*, Royal Commission on Criminal Justice Research Study No. 14 (London, HMSO).

Levi, M. and Pithouse, A. (forthcoming). *The Victims of Fraud* (Milton Keynes, Open University Press).

Maguire, M., Noaks, L., Brearley, N. and Hobbs, D. (1992). *Assessing Investigative Performance* (Cardiff, School of Social & Administrative Studies Research Paper, University of Wales College of Cardiff).

Maguire, M. and Norris, C. (1992). *The Conduct and Supervision of Criminal Investigations*, Royal Commission on Criminal Justice Research Study No. 13 (London, HMSO).

Mann, K. (1985). *Defending White-Collar Crime* (New Haven, Yale University Press).

McConville, M., Sanders, A. and Leng, R. (1991). *The Case for the Prosecution* (London, Routledge).

Reiner, R. (1992). *The Politics of the Police* (Hemel Hempstead, Harvester Wheatsheaf).

Royal Commission on Criminal Justice (1993). *Report* (London, HMSO).

Wells, C. (1992). *Corporations and Criminal Responsibility* (Oxford, Clarendon).

Wolfe, T. (1987). *Bonfire of the Vanities* (London, Paladin).

9 ~ Authors meet critics I
The case for the prosecution and administrative criminology*

MIKE McCONVILLE AND ANDREW SANDERS

The research which formed the basis of *The Case for the Prosecution* was based primarily on police and prosecution papers and interviews of key decision-makers in a random sample of over 1,000 cases, largely from the point of arrest. We also conducted wide-ranging interviews and made general observations in our main fieldwork settings (courts, police stations and prosecutors' offices). We could have adopted other methods and sought other data sources, and we have been criticized for not doing so.[1] Our methods and data sources were chosen carefully, though: there is only so much that can be done in depth in a given time; securing the confidence of both sides at the same time in a longitudinal study of an adversarial system is almost impossible; and by utilizing 'official' sources we ensured that our analysis of the system was not derived from those who might be thought to harbour an animus towards it. Whatever we found from official sources about the system not living up to its rhetoric would, in consequence, be more likely to understate than to overstate the position.

In the book itself we set out to do three linked things. First, to develop the theoretical perspective of social construction as an aid to understanding the criminal justice system. This theory, oddly characterized as 'new left pessimism' by David Dixon, is in fact neutral in terms of social effects; as we put it in our book:

The essence of *social construction* is that its purpose is not necessarily to

---

*Revised version of remarks prepared for the 'Authors meet Critics' session of the British Criminology Conference 1993 which Mike McConville was unable to attend because of a last-minute emergency.

fulfil some assumed objective of the law, but to attempt to achieve a particular objective through the use of *the legal form*. Construction does not require or imply that cases are necessarily unworthy, unmeritorious or against the interest of the object of the construction, the suspect or defendant. (*The Case for the Prosecution*: 11, original emphasis).

Second, to apply this theory to the organization of criminal investigations and prosecutions by presenting a large amount of factual material on the criminal justice process from street discretion through to trial. Our view on this, as clearly set out in the book, is that whilst case construction is a feature of any criminal justice system, the adversarial system 'makes case construction a particularly partial and partisan process' (ibid., 11). Third, to evaluate the effects of recent legal and policy changes and the prospects for further changes in this area. This response will tackle some of the criticisms which have been made in respect of each of these three objectives.

Before addressing these issues, however, it is necessary to make an important point about the role of research and of researchers which this present debate brings into focus: current socio-legal scholarship is heavily dependent upon layers of knowledge set down by previous researchers and theorists, the status of which is provisional to be tested constantly through further research, theorizing and debate. Thus, our own research, whilst critical of Doreen McBarnet, is enormously indebted to her path-breaking theoretical work. We see this as advanced, and not overturned, through discussion and critique. This dialectical process can only result in future progress, however, if debate is informed and intelligent. It is, therefore, a matter of regret to us that much of the comment directed at our book is neither informed nor intelligent. By way of example, let us take head on the critical assertions of Rod Morgan. The gravamen of his charge is introduced in the following way: 'The fundamental question to be asked of this text concerns the degree to which the conclusions are empirically grounded. Whether they flow from the data, or are reached in spite of them?' His answer is clear: 'The book contains significant methodological shortcomings which some may judge to comprise sleight of hand.'

Morgan's first bit of evidence concerns an incident, described at page 49 of the book, in which a custody officer says to a suspect, 'Sign there to say that I've given you these forms', and who then indicates that the suspect is to sign the box on the form meaning that he does not want a solicitor. 'This incident', writes an astonished Morgan, 'is seriously offered as evidence of police power to ignore legal requirements.' Contrary to Morgan's view, this incident *is* evidence of police power to ignore legal requirements. Indeed, it is hard to see how it could be otherwise, and it is disturbing that those who involve themselves in, or seek to evaluate, empirical research fail to see this. Moreover, seriously or otherwise, it is significant not only as evidence of police power to ignore legal rules but also for the quite separate proposition that, even in extreme situations involving potentially substantial adverse consequences to themselves, people may sign documents without reading them carefully, a psychological propensity to which, as Morgan neatly demonstrates, academic criminologists may themselves be prone.

His next bit of evidence concerns our discussion of legal representatives at the police station which, according to him, ignores or downplays countervailing evidence. Based upon two sentences from page 53 of the book, Morgan charges us with setting up a 'negative stereotype . . . [which] is clear', namely: 'Legal advisers are either co-opted or ineffective', which leads Morgan to wonder idly 'why the police apparently go to such lengths to prevent their intrusion'. Had he read the previous page he would have had his answer. We explicitly state (at page 52) that one reason for the police isolating the suspect is 'to limit the constructive potential of the defence' as can occur where the suspect is 'advised to exercise silence, to refuse to answer police questions'. The dichotomy advanced by Morgan is not in the text but rather is attributed to us for the purposes of caricature rather than informed debate. Our subsidiary point is that the presence of a legal adviser during interrogations is no guarantee that police pressure on the suspect will be resisted or, even, that legal advisers will not join hands with the police in persuading the suspect to confess. This has been amply demonstrated in a range of empirical studies.

Morgan, more than any of our other critics, fails to grasp our central argument. He adheres to a quantitative fetish in which the constant refrain is for more examples, more figures and more statistics. Sometimes, of course, statistics are needed, and we attempted to supply them wherever we judged they helped the reader. But his requests for statistics are almost always misplaced. Thus, Morgan's concern is to count how often the police breached Home Office guidelines on cautioning (as if this were knowable), whereas ours, in this instance, is to demonstrate that the cautioning process 'enables [the police] to create any necessary pre-conditions, such as the "consent" which the suspect is required to give prior to being cautioned' (p. 81). It is the *capacity* of the police to manipulate or violate rules which we regard as of primary sociological importance and not simply the (revealed) frequency with which they engage in such practices.[2]

From the particular we turn to the general and, first, to the question of theory. It is unsettling, writing in 1994, to discover that not every academic researcher would agree that theory is necessary or desirable or even, to put it at its lowest, unavoidable. An implicit distrust, even rejection, of theory seems to underlie the comments of some of our critics. Yet even the most unreconstructed positivist might allow that theory is not incompatible with social science. If this is accepted, the problem is then sorting out the relationship between 'theory' and 'facts'. Anti-positivist perspectives all agree on one thing: that 'facts' are not objective neutral things lying around waiting to be observed and assembled. Facts are constructions which require interpretation in the light of one's understanding of the context in which they occur. Even if this were not so, the very process of selection and assembly (based on that understanding) creates an interpretation. Our position, then, is that no fieldwork can be done by *tablua rasa* researchers. Theory, whether implicit or explicit, always provides a prism through which the social world is observed.

All this should hardly need spelling out here, particularly as we do this in the book itself, acknowledging that 'Research, like the world of its subjects, is a process of construction' (p. 13). Yet several critics point out that our book could be viewed as a 'case' (that is an argument for a position) rather than an impartial review of the facts, as if this were a novel and damning insight.[3] Davis goes further and enjoins socio-legal researchers to 'let the evidence speak', a vacuous proposition which fails to understand that facts have no voices and that their bodies are continually constituted and reconstituted by social processes which themselves are important objects of investigation. If Davis and Morgan[4] really believe that facts speak for themselves they should try to defend this (now isolated) position and tackle (rather than ignore) our stated position to the contrary.[5]

David Dixon, on the other hand, does acknowledge that 'the issue is not solely or fundamentally an empirical one'.[6] This is particularly true for policing, a low visibility activity in which the mapping of empirical reality is intrinsically problematic. Moreover, insofar as research attempts to assess the extent to which legislation alters police behaviour and as the officers being researched are reluctant to reveal the extent to which that legislation is being resisted, the degree to which particular patterns unearthed by research are characteristic of policing will be unknown. One example of this – the use of 'ploys' by custody officers – will be discussed later. Another is illicit informal interviewing which – by definition – has particularly low visibility. Officers have good reasons to keep it that way. Any unearthing of it by research will demonstrate its existence, but its known presence in, say, 1 per cent of cases gives no clue in itself as to more extensive prevalence.[7] Further, facts about policing are not of equal weight. Legislation might seek to change ten aspects of policing with a view to, for instance, eliminating coercion in interrogation. If it succeeds in five this does not mean that the legislation is 50 per cent effective. The five most coercive aspects of policing may be the ones which are unchanged (or vice versa). Thus the significance of different sets of empirical facts produced by research has to be assessed, and that requires some theoretical understanding of the system as a whole.

It follows that to attempt to understand policing merely from known facts is an intellectually empty exercise. As Dixon says in his longer critique, many of our empirical results are similar to his, and so the difference must lie in the theory used to interpret the facts.[8] His theoretical position is neither ours nor that of the 'sea change' theorists who argue that legal rules are almost entirely determinative of police and prosecution practice. Echoing the 'Nothing works/Some things work' controversy in penology, Dixon argues that some legal rules do 'work'. Like the similarly caricatured Robert Martinson, we would not disagree. The question in this debate, is about the effects of these *particular* legal changes (namely, the Police and Criminal Evidence Act (PACE) and the Crown Prosecution Service (CPS)). Other types of change, which do not rely on police officers and prosecutors for their effectiveness, would be another matter entirely. Thus even in *The Case for the Prosecution* we argue for changes which would enhance adversarialism, and we elaborate on this elsewhere.

Even as far as PACE is concerned we do not deny that some changes have occurred. Where we and Dixon differ is on the *significance* of these changes. But how are we, Dixon, or anyone else, to assess significance? Only in the light of some general understanding of social processes and the institutions under scrutiny which is then tested against empirical findings, leading to refinement of initial understanding and so on. Since this process is not one susceptible to positivistic notions of proof, on any given set of 'facts' there will be room for legitimate disagreement. It is to be expected, then, that not all critics will share our perspective and that, therefore, their interpretations will differ from ours. What is not acceptable, though, is for Morgan and Davis to imply that their interpretations are superior to ours because, in some unspecified sense, they engage in less interpretation than we do.

It is, of course, entirely reasonable to claim that one interpretation makes more sense than another. One basis for such a claim (and there could be many) is that it fits the known facts better. This is the main thrust of Dixon's critique and, to some extent, that of Morgan, and it takes us on to the factual terrain of the book. Dixon argues that we wrongly attribute manipulative motives to the police when, *inter alia*, dealing with suspects' rights, and that we overgeneralize about police practices which vary considerably in many respects. In his longer critique he points, for instance, to an apparently dramatic variation between police stations: 'As regards telling suspects that legal advice is free, practice in the stations in Sanders *et al.*'s sample ranged from 0 to 94.4%.'[9] These figures relate to the provision of a leaflet informing suspects that, among other things, advice is free. What Dixon fails to relate is that study's findings that suspects were rarely given time to read the leaflet until after they signed their rights away, and that there was virtually *no* variation as regards the genuine telling of suspects that advice is free (that is orally). Suspects were orally informed that advice was free in just 5.5 per cent of cases, and this was usually only when suspects asked. Provision of the leaflet was not correlated with requests for advice, but oral provision of information was.[10] Clearly the latter is far more important than the former.

This is one aspect of the vexed question of 'ploys'. Of course Dixon is right to say that discouraging requests for legal advice is not *always* malevolent, and selective quotation of isolated sentences can give the impression that we adopt a rather broad-brush approach to this.[11] But anyone who is sufficiently interested in the detail can read our longer reports.[12] The question for a more general book like *The Case for the Prosecution* (and its generality – its attempt to understand the unity of the criminal justice process – is one of the main points of our book) and a broader critique such as Dixon's is what the general underlying working rules are. To imply, as Dixon does, that several factors jostle together with no sense of priority is to give up the search for underlying explanations. As it happens, new data sheds some light on this. Brown *et al.* found that there were very many more requests for legal advice when they were observing custody officers than when they were not.[13] We cannot think of any bureaucratic or legal reason for this, but it is entirely consistent with the general argument in *The Case for the Prosecution* about partially-hidden police practices in which deliberate ploys are important components.

Morgan alleged that we 'try to tarnish' the police through accusations of extensive use of ploys for which the evidence is 'weak' (he says that several researchers found little evidence of ploys) and by ignoring the fact that those ploys which are observed appear to have little effect on advice rates. Morgan turns a blind eye to the disparity between advice rates in Brown *et al.*'s observed and non-observed cases. *The Case for the Prosecution* has a far better implicit explanation for why advice rates are sometimes lower than at other times than Morgan's analysis would be able to offer. This disparity also tells us something about the relatively low number of ploys which Dixon and Morgan discovered.

Dixon's longer critique also castigates us for ignoring the effect on suspects of different systems of choosing custody officers in different areas. Apparently this is an example of the way we overgeneralize and ignore 'best practice'.[14] This is illustrative of a tendency by him and our other critics to assume that legal and procedural variations are of sociological significance. For the record it needs to be said that whilst Dixon records variations in these and other respects in his research reports, he does not attribute any significance, sociological or otherwise, to them there. Again, this is not simply a question of the attribution of weight to different types of facts, but also a question of theory: our theory leads us to believe that such variations are relatively insignificant in comparison with such matters as the brute facts of powers of detention, interrogation, and so on. For Morgan this is being 'led by the nose'. For us it is a matter of how to allocate scarce resources when there is so much else worthy of comment. Fortunately, because they were interested in this kind of minutiae, we can call on Brown *et al.* again. They found, as we would have predicted, that it makes absolutely no difference what the custody officer arrangements are.[15]

Dixon could have given other examples of geographical variation such as the dramatically different ratio of 'volunteers' to detainees in different stations or variations in the use of Section 1 stop and search powers. Perhaps he did not give these examples because he knew how *insignificant* in policing terms these differences are. When all suspects brought to the station are, or would be, held by the police it matters little – except to a black-letter lawyer – if one is officially a volunteer or not, and when 'consent' searches are routinely used to evade Section 1 it is the pervasive and patterned use of stop and search in any form which really matters. Here the reader need not take our word for it. Dixon and his colleagues convincingly make this exact argument themselves.[16]

The point about these examples is not just that they suggest a lot about police motivation in general, but that they illustrate how thoroughly misleading it can be to let 'the facts' speak for themselves. Dixon surely knows better, even if Davis and Morgan do not. It illustrates the necessity of weighing up and determining the significance of different sets of 'facts'.

A common criticism of *The Case for the Prosecution* is that there are not enough statistics. Reiner's generally very generous review asks why we do not tell the good news, such as the undoubted rise in advice rates, as well as the bad. And Morgan purports to report one of us as saying that it does not matter whether police malpractice occurs once or often. Of course we do not believe that if the police do something wrong once it shows that they can do it 'with impunity whenever it suits them'. Had Morgan read the book carefully he would have seen that we make precisely the opposite point: that police behaviour is not 'unbounded and the activities of individual officers are in important ways shaped by the law, by the need for self-protection and by practical and moral considerations' (p. 190, and the discussion at pp. 182–190). Nor do some of our critics appreciate the rather elementary point that statistics are meaningless outside the context in which they are generated, and that whether something happens a 'lot' or a 'little' is not the only, or even the more important, determinant of sociological importance.

We have seen that Dixon, for instance, ascribes great significance to the fact that much or even most of the time custody officers tell suspects their rights in a straightforward way. Many people do not want legal advice and in many other cases the police evidence is sufficiently strong for advice to be of little assistance to the suspect. So it is not surprising that frequently custody officers are not obstructive. This does not undermine our argument if, as we believe we show, custody officers are able and willing to be obstructive whenever investigating officers wish them to and/or need them to be. Similarly, it is possible to accept Evans's findings that most formal juvenile interviews do not employ 'tactics' in light of the fact that most juveniles confess readily anyway.[17] Of course, an important statistic, which none of us know, is how often formal and informal interviews employ tactics when juveniles do not readily confess.[18]

The fact that the police do not behave in manipulative ways when it does not assist crime control functions would undermine an argument that police working rules are based on malevolence, unlawfulness or corruption. But that is not our argument. And if, as it would seem from the data of Brown *et al.*, the police conceal many of their ploys from researchers, what is the point of counting those which are observed? All it provides is a minimum figure.[19]

Finally, we come to the question of reform about which the critics are seriously confused. Morgan and Dixon are concerned that the book is too dismissive of the power of law to alter specific practices (though Dixon does acknowledge that in other writings all three of us have actively engaged in lobbying for various reforms). We would argue, on the other hand, that the book as a whole – and our general perspective, individually and collectively – does give the law a serious role in structuring and legitimizing police actions. It is therefore common ground that some legal changes will have more effect than others and that some legal changes will have unexpected effects.

But this misses the whole point of our argument. Our central concern is not, as Morgan and Dixon imagine, with the effect of changing particular legal rules (though we comment upon some examples) nor, as Morgan believes, with the plight of 'all practitioners in the criminal justice system'. Our concern, as the book makes clear, is at the level of theory, in particular with the concept of reform through law. This we argue is a problematic project, even counterproductive, if it leaves the underlying structure of society (race, class, economic inequality, police culture etc.) untouched. Nothing said by our critics bears upon this argument and nothing they advance is inconsistent with our analysis. Indeed, thoughtful contributions to this debate are equally sceptical of the prophylactic effect of rule changes which leave embedded structures unchanged. Take a micro-issue such as reasonable suspicion which Dixon and his colleagues examined. Though they found little evidence that reasonable suspicion constrained police behaviour, they urged against the pessimistic conclusion that 'the PACE concept of reasonable grounds for suspicion must inevitably fail' (Dixon *et al.* 1989: 192)[20]. But what might rescue it? Not, it turns out, rule-change but, in a passage which goes a long way to making our point for us, the following 'minimal conditions': (i) clear expression of the desired standards; (ii) effective training in order to modify police culture; (iii) favourable political circumstances; (iv) the backing of effective sanctions for non-compliance; and (v) public knowledge of rights and the limits of police powers (ibid., 192). Whilst this does not tackle some of the structural issues we would regard as important, and it look more like a plea for a new society it is hard to read this as anything other than a rejection of reform through law. This is the precise argument we make in the book.

It comes as a surprise, therefore, to see Dixon jumping from this position to the view (which he does not justify) that PACE presents the best practical 'source for reform proposals' available to jurisdictions with systems akin to the British pre-PACE system. What if PACE has accentuated, not ameliorated, the crime control drift of criminal justice? What if different legal changes could have radically unexpected effects? Although *The Case for the Prosecution* sketches our answers to these questions and tries to outline the likely effects of different kinds of change, we do not purport to do this systematically. But Dixon should not portray the book as having no reform agenda at all.

Morgan does acknowledge our reform agenda, but then seeks to rubbish it on the ground that it is inconsistent with our allegedly general nihilism. In passing, we might note that it is the reform agenda of Dixon and Morgan which fails to follow logically from their general analysis. For they assume that, because PACE appears to confer more rights to suspects it must be a good thing even though their own research exposes the charade which characterizes so many of these rights. They refuse to see that, far from our position being a nihilistic one of 'damned if they do, damned if they don't', it is simply one which argues for an analysis of legal change which takes into account, in its evaluation, the working rules and embedded structure of the system.

Whether our analysis is 'pessimistic' or not is hardly the point. The credibility of an argument is surely more important, to an academic, than its practical consequences. When the arguments of *The Case for the Prosecution* in relation to the Crown Prosecution Service were first trailed we were dismissed by some prosecutors as being biased. Now, according to the chief crown prosecutor who took part in the conference session, we were not wrong at the time, but the times are said to have changed.[21] Whether our argument remains applicable depends on whether the changed features of the system have supplanted the working rules which really structure the system. Our analysis suggests that fundamentals have not changed. This is, of course, debatable but our critics do not challenge us at this level.

The Case for the Prosecution is not just a book about the way the criminal process works. It is also about the hypocritical self-portrayal of that process as 'fair' and 'just'. It additionally has relevance in challenging a new band of administrative criminologists who confuse theory with dogma and who fail to see that, as Doreen McBarnet put it, 'Theory is as necessary for policy aims as data is for explanation'.[22] The book was written in a way which was intended to make these messages clear so that they could be debated intelligently. Whilst researchers can hardly complain if the subjects of their research respond to perceived criticisms with any old argument, they have the right to expect academic critics to confront the principal arguments rather than to traduce them. In this respect, the achievement of some critics has fallen below accepted standards and thereby served to inhibit progress.

One plausible explanation for this is the administrative criminological mind-set which views theoretical discussion as a threat to the policy repair kits that administrators from time to time apply to the criminal justice process. This leads administrative criminologists to depict theory as critical, if not malevolent, and to seek to minimize its impact by attacking the theorists rather than the theory. Here, this is done by accusing us of attributing motive to others (Dixon) and by attributing motives to us (Davis and Morgan). Whilst this line would not normally merit a response, a short discussion will be revealing.

Dixon gives as his 'best example' our treatment of the way in which custody officers accept suspects for pre-charge detention, almost all of whom they ritually detain. Our explanation of this in terms of the shared culture of custody officers and case officers is seen as one-dimensional because it leaves out of account the bureaucratic reality that 'procedures are designed for accepting suspects, not for turning them away'. This is not, despite the impression given by Dixon, an expression of the law. It is a bureaucratic response to the law, and bureaucratic expectations, far from being random or spontaneous, often express precisely the relations of power and knowledge which are so central in criminal justice. Whilst the emblematic representation of power may be sanction and force, power is 'typically at its most intense and durable when running through the repetition of institutionalized practices'.[23]

Of course, calling a practice a routine should not be a reason for obviating the need for inquiry; nor should calling a practice benign, even well-intentioned. By calling certain practices of custody officers 'ploys' we apparently offend Dixon in two ways: by attributing motive and by attributing bad motive. We do no such thing: Dixon has missed the obvious point that there was no attribution of motive because custody officers told us in interview why they behaved as they did. In seeking to respond to us, Dixon commits the sin of which he accuses us except that he, without such empirical grounding, attributes good motive: officers, we are asked to believe, make 'well-meaning but inappropriate' assessments of the suspect's best interest. Davis makes a similar allegation but has a different agenda. Davis 'strongly suspect[s]' that our theory predated our investigation and complains: 'It is also upsetting to me, as a researcher, to find the authors utilising very generous police access in order to construct what amounts to an anti-police diatribe.' It is a pity that, for some researchers, protection of access appears to be held above fidelity to the data, but that is precisely the position in which administrative criminologists constantly find themselves. Defence of the *status quo* becomes the organizing framework of their lives and, without any theoretical position except indeterminacy, criticisms can only be personal or enfeebled: 'Interrogations are not *only* "social encounters fashioned to conform and legitimate a police narrative" – they are also, quite simply, interrogations' (Davis, original emphasis). Well, there are not only intelligent criticisms there are also, quite simply, criticisms.

All this seems to us to be a pity. *The Case for the Prosecution* was written as a contribution to an important debate, as one step in the continuing struggle to make sense of a large and powerful process in which justice is a frequent casualty. As we would be the first to acknowledge, the book has significant shortcomings (even if they are not discussed by the critics). That some critics have attempted to place a wagon-train around the existing system seems to us blinkered and often unworthy. Like the wagon-train, their arguments are dated and hark back to a bygone age in which those who once aimed at the frontier now live in the backwoods.

Notes

[1] Implicitly by Morgan and explicitly Davis (review of *The Case for the Prosecution* in *Policing and Society*, 2, 1992, 322). Davis criticizes us for not doing the research he would have liked us to do without considering how viable that would have been. Davis's suggestion that we did little of the data collection research does not deserve a reply.

[2] The frequency with which the police engage in such practices is of interest when it is sought to measure the social and political temperature of law and order at any particular historical moment but that was not our primary concern on each detailed rule.

[3] Again, Davis, op. cit., suggests, and Morgan implies, that our views came first and that we ignored contrary evidence.

[4] As a matter of fact, Morgan is also confused about our own clearly stated theoretical position. Correctly he states that we list the competing analytical frameworks of positivism, interactionism and structuralism. He then adds that we adopt an integrated approach 'which draws on all three approaches', leading him to muse: 'whether this constitutes a step towards enhanced theoretical sophistication, or provides a looselimbed framework within which imagination (and prejudice) can range freely, is a matter on which not everyone will agree'. Whilst Morgan's conclusion is clear, his premiss is wrong. Far from embracing positivism we reject it in these terms: '. . . positivist analysis is ultimately unprofitable'(p. 9). When critics fail to read or understand clear propositions imagination (and prejudice) can range freely. This is a matter on which we assume everyone will agree.

[5] McKenzie, on the other hand (*International Journal of the Sociology of Law*, 1992), states that all social life is a construction and that we are therefore getting excited over nothing because – he wrongly states – we fail to recognize this. He ignores the important part of our argument, namely that cases are presented *as if* they are simple renditions of unconstructed fact.

[6] D. Dixon, 'Legal regulation and policing practice' *Social and Legal Studies*, 1 (1992), 515, 516.

[7] In fact informal interviewing is, as judged by even conservative and unreliable estimates, higher than most commentators have claimed. See D. Brown *et al.*, *Changing the Code* (HMSO, 1992) and S. Moston and G. Stephenson, *The Questioning and Interviewing of Suspects Outside the Police Station* (HMSO, 1993). The unreliability is such as to understate, but not overstate, its extent. How much of this interviewing is illicit is not possible to estimate.

[8] Dixon, op. cit., 522. Our other critics (such as Morgan, Davis and

McKenzie), who accuse us of selectivity in our use of empirical evidence in the pursuit of preconceived ideas, fail to acknowledge how similar our 'raw' findings are to those of many other researchers.

9 Dixon, op. cit., 527.

10 Sanders *et al.*, *Advice and Assistance in Police Stations and the 24 Hour Duty Solicitor Scheme* (Lord Chancellor's Department, 1989), 52–5.

11 Dixon, for example, often quotes our conclusions and summaries. Out of context, these inevitably sound like overgeneralizations. It is not possible to present a complex argument without summarizing along the way, and it is not possible to write a summary which does not oversimplify. Thus he quotes our summary of an argument about the way distorted record-keeping serves to legitimize certain police practices. Taken out of context in this way it looks as if our argument is as one-dimensional as he suggests. Yet two pages earlier in the book we acknowledge that 'certain types of inaccuracy in custody records are simply the result of work pressure' (p. 96).

12 Saunders *et al.*, op. cit.; M. McConville and J. Hodgson, *Custodial Legal Advice and the Right to Silence* (HMSO, 1993).

13 Brown *et al.*, op. cit.

14 Dixon, op. cit. 527–8.

15 Brown *et al.*, op. cit.

16 D. Dixon, C. Coleman, A. K. Bottomley, 'Consent and the legal regulation of policing', *Journal of Law and Society*, 17 (1990), 345.

17 R. Evans, *The Conduct of Police Interviews with Juveniles* (HMSO, 1993).

18 Whilst one of Evans's main objectives was to provide a more comprehensive qualitative and quantitative analysis of interviews with juvenile suspects than earlier studies (Evans op. cit. 6) he (rightly, in our view) does not attempt to quantify the occasions on which informal interviews took place, although he notes that officers freely admitted such practices and records 'some' instances where there was irrefutable evidence of prior discussion and questioning (ibid., 28).

19 See M. McConville, 'Videotaping interrogations', *Criminal Law Review* 1992, 532, for some insight into the unlawful behaviour in which the police engage – in this case, unlawful informal interviewing – when they think they are not being watched.

20 D. Dixon, A. K. Bottomley, C. Coleman, M. Gill and D. Wall, 'Reality and rules in the construction and regulation of police suspicion', *International Journal of the Sociology of Law*, 17 (1989), 185, 192.

21 This is similar to police arguments about rule-breaking. Ten years ago the police refused to admit that there was any systematic breaking of the rules. Now it is accepted that, in furtherance of 'noble cause corruption', they did so. Since research is always published some time after the period to which it relates this type of argument can be used to undercut the contemporary relevance of all research.

22 D. McBarnet 'False dichotomies in criminal justice research', at page 28 in

Baldwin and Bottomly, *Criminal Justice: Selected Readings* (Martin Robertson, 1978).

23 A. Giddens, *The Nation – State and Violence* (Polity, 1987).

10 ~ Authors meet critics II

Pessimism or professionalism? Legal regulation of investigations after PACE

ROGER LENG

A problem with 'Authors meet Critics' sessions is that the focus of enquiry shifts away from the social phenomenon which originally attracted research and towards the methods and theories of the researchers. Thus, although I do intend to answer some of the major criticisms of *The Case for the Prosecution*, particularly those of David Dixon (not only in his contribution to this volume, but also in his more sustained critique published in *Social and Legal Studies*), my main purpose is to return to the central issue of the extent to which police investigations are susceptible to legal and administrative control. That issue will be examined in the light of evidence, not only from our own research, but also from the major parallel study of police work conducted by David Dixon in conjunction with Keith Bottomley, Clive Coleman, Martin Gill and David Wall and published as *The Impact of PACE: Policing in a Northern Force* (Bottomley *et al.* 1991). In particular, I will consider the obvious gulf between our own 'pessimistic' conclusion that legal reform in the style of the Police and Criminal Evidence Act (PACE) will have only limited effect in *significantly* regulating police work, as compared to the encouraging conclusion of Dixon and his colleagues that PACE has ushered in a new era of police professionalism.

Loose talk about intention

Dixon strongly criticizes *The Case for the Prosecution* on the basis that it is too ready to attribute motive and intention. His discussion of this confusingly conflates the attribution of intention to (i) the PACE Act; (ii) the Royal Commission on Criminal Procedure; (iii) various actors within the criminal justice process.

In relation to PACE, Dixon implicitly links us to what he sees as a general tendency among commentators to attribute artificially various motives and intentions to the Act (Dixon 1992: 523–5). We would agree that 'complex multi-determined legislation which was the outcome of some 20 years of debate can only in a very qualified sense be said to have intentions'. However, notwithstanding the vigour of his critique on this point, Dixon provides only one example of such attribution of intention or motive to PACE. He suggests that 'McConville et al. talk as if PACE was intended to fail'. This is not a direct quote, no page references are given and indeed the book contains no such statement. The closest we come to such a proposition is a statement that the Royal Commission expected police behaviour to continue unchanged (McConville *et al.* 1991: 196). Whereas intentions cannot be attributed to statutes, intentions clearly can be attributed to Royal Commissions. In any event, this assertion was not of general application and was made in the limited context of a discussion of the 'reasonable suspicion test' as the basis for lawful stop and search, and was fully supported in our text by quotes from the Commission's own report.

In other areas we clearly concede that the Philips Royal Commission *did* expect that changing the law would change practice. For instance, we make clear that the Commission believed that enacting a right to legal advice in the police station would increase the extent of such advice.

It is also odd for Dixon to berate us on the ground of attributing intentions to PACE. A glance at Dixon's own work finds that it is peppered with such attributions, thus Dixon suggests that: 'it would appear that the objectives of the legislators have been (or are gradually being) achieved'; that 'PACE and the Codes were not entirely successful in communicating the intentions of the legislature'; that 'PACE was intended to change in a fairly fundamental way the police approach to stops and searches'; and that 'PACE set out detailed regulations and procedures intended to achieve these objectives' (Bottomley *et al.* 1991: 165, 170, 171, 178).

Research sources – police records and police opinions

In criticizing our reliance on police records, Dixon raises the broad issue of the proper approach to various sources of data. I would argue that whereas our use of records is defensible, a greater cause for concern is Dixon's technique of relying upon unsupported assertions of police officers even where these contradict his other data.

Dixon accuses us (in effect) of hypocrisy in describing the function of police records as being to present a picture of police compliance and to obscure police operational practices, and in then relying upon the same records as a principal data source (Dixon 1992: 523–4). This criticism is very strange. Record-keeping is the central regulatory mechanism of PACE. The records themselves therefore become a central object of research interest. Are we, as social science researchers, supposed to lap up the products of the record-keeping process whilst treating the process itself as unproblematic? If it is proper to interrogate the process of making records, could that be done without relying upon the records as a principal source of data?

An equally problematic issue is what significance should be attached to interviews with police officers. Our own findings suggest that whereas such interviews may be a valuable source of material this should be treated with care. Particular difficulties arise when discussing PACE, because the Act remains a continuing source of discussion in police circles and all officers have received specific training on its operation. These factors produce the twin dangers that the accounts of police officers may either simply repeat current myths, or reflect the officer's understanding of how PACE *should* operate. In view of these dangers it is important to test the reliability of police accounts against empirical data where possible.

Dixon's own research apparently falls into the trap of simple reliance on unsupported police interviews. Thus, it is reported that 'a majority (of officers) recognised that (the new rules) had resulted in beneficial effects, particularly for the suspect and in greater pressure on officers to hasten the initial process leading up to the charging or release of those held in custody' (Bottomley *et al.* 1991: 134). This 'finding' is posited in support of Dixon's claim of a 'new professionalism' sweeping through the ranks (of which more later). Unfortunately, the asserted beliefs of officers upon which Dixon relies are flatly repudiated by his own detailed findings on detention times which show that overall, periods of detention (and hence investigation) have increased under PACE.

Perhaps in this area the social scientist should acknowledge the wisdom of the adage of the criminal advocate – that the self-serving statement should be regarded with extreme scepticism. (I would not however recommend the traditional corollary – that confessions are necessarily intrinsically reliable.)

An implicit history of criminal justice

Dixon is critical of what he sees as our implicit history of criminal justice. Challenging our statement that: '"law reform" [that is the PACE Act] is largely a matter of empowering the police in relation to the suspect', Dixon argues that: 'The idea that PACE is simply or essentially an expansion of police power and discretion indicates theoretical and historical misconceptions' (Dixon 1992: 530).

Our approach to the history of PACE is that pre-1985 the law was vague in many areas, thus tempting the police to push at its boundaries in the interests of crime control. In so doing the police would expect or hope either that the appropriation of power by the police would not be challenged, or that if challenged, it would be vindicated *ex post facto* by the courts. By describing PACE as empowering the police we suggest that PACE not only widened police powers but also conferred on the police many of the powers which had already been appropriated by them, but which had yet to be clearly confirmed by the courts.

For Dixon our mistake lay in a 'failure to appreciate the true extent of police powers before PACE'. He cites detention which he describes as having been subject to the 'vaguest limits' – that is the power to detain was not specifically provided for but was subject to a handful of piecemeal *ad hoc* rulings. Bizarrely, Dixon refers to two cases *Holmes ex p. Shannon* [1981] 2 All ER 612, and *Gowan* [1982] Crim LR 821 which he claims indicate that PACE did not widen the law on detention. In the first of these cases the Court of Appeal resolved some of the uncertainty of the law by placing a clear 48-hour limit on police detention prior to first court appearance. In the second case a conviction was quashed on the basis that the defendant's detention had been illegal because it breached the former statutory rule that an arrested suspect should be either released or brought before a court as soon as practicable. In both cases the police had appropriated a power to detain which the court had then denied. Dixon mysteriously asserts that the officers involved in these cases would view PACE as limiting rather than extending their powers. The better view is that PACE empowers the police to detain in circumstances in which formerly detention was held to be unlawful.

On a general level Dixon produces no sensible evidence to support his insulting claim that we failed to understand the scope of police powers pre-PACE and no reasoned refutation of our argument that PACE extended police powers in relation to suspects.

The legal regulation of policing

The key to Dixon's criticisms of the pessimistic message of *The Case for the Prosecution* lies in his own research conclusions that PACE has had a *significant* impact on police investigations and stimulated a new professionalism within the ranks. However, a careful examination of Dixon's own detailed findings raises considerable doubts about the soundness of his conclusions. Thus, Dixon has chronicled the ineffectiveness of the reasonable suspicion test as a restraint on police stops (Dixon *et al.* 1989), has found that 64 per cent of custody officers would seek to influence a suspect's decision whether or not to request legal advice in some circumstances (Bottomley *et al.* 1991: 147–8), and has commented in relation to custody officers' recording duties that: 'Duties . . . to evaluate the grounds for pre-charge detention are met in practice by largely ritualistic entries of statutory formulae on custody records' (Bottomley *et al.* 1991: 116). These findings are, of course, fully consistent with our conclusion that the police retain considerable control over the conduct of investigations even under the PACE regime.

An important strand in Dixon's argument is that legal regulation of the police is effective because it is accepted (perhaps grudgingly) by them and has been incorporated into police culture. He sees our analysis of police attitudes as 'oversimplified', as 'overstating police resistance to controls' and as 'exaggerating' the commitment of the police to crime control (Dixon 1992: 523). He focuses his criticism on the following passage (constructed from quotes from two separate chapters):

> maximisation of control often becomes a police project. The task for the police is to mitigate the effect of the restriction . . . or to seek exemption from it altogether . . . The police are constantly striving to push out or extend the boundaries of 'legal' behaviour . . . (McConville *et al.* 1991: 37, 177)

This passage embodies one of the major messages of our book and reflects both day-to-day operational police practice as well as organized political lobbying at a national level.

However, our position is neither simple nor absolutist. Thus, in the paragraph from which the first part of the above-quoted passage is drawn we argue that certain types of police decision-making are semi-autonomous in the sense that they are subject to some control either by rules or external review. We also accept that changes in legal rules have had some effect on the behaviour of state officials and that further rule revisions and fine tuning might have a wider impact (p. 193 – see for instance the effect of the revision of Code C, Brown *et al*. 1992), and we concede that legality (that is the requirements of legal provisions) may place limits on the extent of illegal behaviour by the police (pp. 183–4).

Dixon's argument that PACE acts as a significant control on the police rests on his faith in the twin regulatory mechanisms of supervision by senior officers and record-keeping. This faith is undermined by his own evidence on the operation of the PACE provision which requires the police to inform a nominated person that the suspect is being held in custody ('intimation'). He found in all thirteen cases where intimation was delayed on the authority of a superintendent, that the ground for delay was recorded as 'personal grounds'. The fact that the police apparently feel no need to record the particular circumstances of the case which make delay necessary, indicates that no meaningful scrutiny is anticipated. The use of a standardized formula strongly suggests that PACE does not direct officers' minds to the specific criteria set out in the statute.

Dixon also recounts how in a number of cases intimations were deliberately delayed by the police but without resort to the official mechanism for doing so and without the delay being formally recorded. In most of these cases there was an operational reason for delaying the intimation with which Dixon apparently sympathized, hence his euphemistic description of this conduct as 'rule-bending' rather than rule-breaking (Bottomley *et al*. 1991: 141). Although Dixon and his colleagues interviewed many officers who had been involved in such 'rule-bending' there is nothing in the account of these interviews to suggest that any officer experienced or anticipated censure or sanction. It is difficult to imagine a clearer demonstration of the ineffectiveness of PACE as a means of controlling the police.

As well as his general criticism of our scepticism about the impact of legal regulation on policing, Dixon charges us with overgeneralization in a number of respects. In particular, Dixon challenges our view of the 'essential unity of police practice' and queries whether we are right to apply Bittner's explanatory theory – that the police use law as a resource – generally to police investigatory functions (Dixon 1992: 526). In his view, our findings are flawed by a failure to appreciate the distinction between functions which are carried out inside and outside the police station. Once again Dixon's blind faith in the regulatory mechanisms of PACE is apparent. Thus, he argues that whereas policing in the street is largely immune from a supervisor's oversight, policing in the station is much more amenable to regulation because supervisors are present (or potentially so) and accordingly 'record-making duties must be taken seriously'.

Although the Philips Royal Commission set great store by the regulatory potential of record-keeping and supervision by senior officers, none of the studies conducted since PACE have vindicated the Commission's faith in these mechanisms. This is clear from Dixon's own findings on in-station supervision of stops and searches. Only 14 per cent of officers who had conducted stops and searches referred to the checking of records when answering questions about supervision. Of senior officers questioned only about a quarter mentioned checking the paperwork after the event (Bottomley *et al.* 1991: 29–44). These findings clearly debunk Dixon's claims about the regulatory force of in-station supervision.

Dixon and his colleagues also claim success for the regime of time limits and reviews which govern detention. Almost half (41 per cent) of all officers interviewed said that the new time limits had not affected their work at all. The remainder indicated ways in which their work had been affected, which included: that investigations were conducted more quickly; that supervisors were more aware of cases; and that under PACE more evidence was required for arrest than formerly. From these unverified comments by police officers Dixon *et al.* conclude that 'there were signs that (the system of time limits) had engendered a new professionalism among some officers in the way they approached cases, from arrest to charge' (Bottomley *et al.* 1991: 133).

Unfortunately, the evidence upon which this conclusion is based does not stand up to scrutiny. Thus, whereas some officers believed that the time limits prompted quicker investigations, the evidence is to the contrary. Both Dixon's own study and that by Brown (1989) demonstrate that periods of detention have increased under PACE, thus indicating that investigations were being conducted more slowly rather than more quickly. Similarly, the claim by some officers that greater evidence was needed as a precondition of arrest is solidly refuted by Dixon's own study of the operation of the 'reasonable suspicion' test (Dixon 1989).

Indeed if the PACE regime of time limits and reviews had significantly limited the practice of detention it would be expected that officers with experience both before and after PACE would have noted some restriction on their activities. It is instructive therefore that when asked whether PACE had created any particular problems in their work, 70 per cent of officers denied that any such problems had been created. The minority of officers who identified problems focused on two: that investigations had to be rushed; and that there were sometimes difficulties getting hold of an officer of sufficient seniority to conduct the review. As noted above, the claim that PACE had shortened periods of detention is not supported by the evidence. The second problem relates to the purely practical problem of getting hold of a review officer. The very fact that no significant mention was made of review officers overruling requests to continue detention, perhaps indicates that the review operates as a justificatory mechanism, rather than as a real restraint upon detention.

In view of the importance which the police attach to confessions as a means of obtaining convictions, perhaps the key gauge of the impact of PACE is the extent to which it has significantly affected the conduct of police interviews. The scheme of regulation under PACE (and the Codes) provides for contemporaneous notes (and now tape recording) of everything said at interview; provides for legal advisers to be present if requested and provides for the exclusion of confessions which are unreliable, or obtained unfairly or by oppression. However, these mechanisms can operate effectively only if the formal interview includes all significant interactions between the suspect and the investigators. Thus, provisions which require reliable recording and render confessions inadmissible are worthless if threats or inducements can be made in unrecorded discussions prior to a formal set-piece interview.

As we argue in *The Case for the Prosecution*, for the police the key issue is to control the content of the interview and this may be achieved through informal off-the-record meetings. In this respect, Dixon's research supports our findings. Thus, he found that the majority of officers admitted to asking questions off-the-record often or sometimes. A number of officers described the advantages in off-the-record chats in terms of avoiding denials on the formal record, and permitting opportunities to negotiate about bail or the prosecution of others (Bottomley *et al.* 1991: 157–62).

Having carefully documented the prevalence and perceived usefulness of informal interviews Dixon then proceeds to discuss police officers' reactions to the requirement to record interviews. His finding that officers are predominantly in favour of both forms of recording is then treated as evidence of an 'encouraging new professionalism amongst officers' (Bottomley *et al.*: 166). One may query this interpretation. Whereas PACE has clearly had an impact in the police station, this has not necessarily changed the quality or content of interactions between police and suspect, but rather has promoted a clandestine bifurcation of such interactions into formal interviews and informal discussions (which in formal terms never took place).

Thus, far from restricting the activities of investigators, the PACE rule about recording interviews, serves the police interest in controlling the investigation. By legitimating the formal interview, the rule elevates that part of the total interaction which the police have chosen to emphasize, whilst obscuring and denying that which is less convenient to the police case. Viewed in this light, constabulary enthusiasm for recording becomes quite understandable.

Professionalism or pessimism?

There is no doubt that PACE has changed much about police work. However, the mere fact that elaborate systems of record-keeping are followed and that opportunities for supervision exist, tells us little about whether in fact legal and administrative provisions effectively regulate the conduct of investigations. It is very apparent that the police are keen to describe their new mode of working under PACE in terms of professionalism, and Dixon and his colleagues are equally happy to adopt this notion in their broad conclusions on the impact of PACE. Unfortunately, it is not explained precisely what this concept of professionalism involves. If for Dixon the concept connotes obedience to law and commitment to due process values then we must conclude that clear evidence of police professionalism is still wanting, and I for one will remain sceptical (or pessimistic) about the potential for meaningful legal regulation of police investigations.

References

Bottomley, A. K., Dixon, D., Gill, M. and Wall, D. (1991).*The Impact of PACE: Policing in a Northern Force* (Hull, University of Hull).

Brown, D. (1989). *Detention at the Police station under the PACE Act* (London, HMSO).

Brown, D., Ellis, T. and Larcombe, K. (1992). *Changing the Code: Police Detention and the Revised PACE Codes of Practice*, Home Office Research Study No. 129 (London, HMSO).

Dixon, D. (1992). 'Legal regulation and policing practice', *Social and Legal Studies*, 1, 515–41.

Dixon, D., Bottomley, A. K., Gill, M. and Wall, D. (1989). 'Reality and the rules in the construction and regulation of police suspicion', *International Journal of the Sociology of Law*, 17, 185–206.

McConville, M., Sanders, A. and Leng, R. (1991). *The Case for the Prosecution* (London, Routledge).

11 ~ *Authors meet critics III*
New left pessimism

DAVID DIXON

'Authors meet critics' sessions all too often slide towards one or other end of a continuum at which authors meet either sycophants or antagonists. By contrast, my intention in organizing this session was to provide a forum for critical but constructive discussion of this important book in terms both of its policy implications and, as suggested in my original letter to the participants, of 'its contribution to British criminology and the development of criminal justice studies'.

The scale of the project reported in *The Case for the Prosecution* was remarkable, at least in the context of British criminology. It is unprecedented for such a large sample of cases to be followed from arrest to disposition, to be studied by a combination of documentary analysis, observation, and interviewing, and to be located in an explicitly theoretical context. Assessing achievement must be relative to ambition. Although my disagreement with much of McConville, Sanders and Leng's analysis will be evident, their book stands as the most important study of the effects of the Police and Criminal Evidence Act (PACE) and the Prosecution of Offences Act (POA) completed to date, and includes acute discussions of the interrogation process, of legal rhetoric, and of crime as a constructed category. It raises important theoretical and methodological issues for British criminology.

I am grateful to Andrew Sanders and Roger Leng for participating so constructively, particularly because my letter of invitation to them was accompanied by a copy of an article which strongly criticizes their work (Dixon 1992), and also because they had to face some very sharp criticism at the session. The discussion concentrated on the issue of whether the arguments and conclusions in *The Case for the*

Prosecution were justified by the research. In addition, some criminal justice professionals (notably Andrew Prickett, chief crown prosecutor for Wales) argued, somewhat predictably, that problems initially experienced at the introduction of PACE and the Crown Prosecution Service (CPS) have been tackled and, by implication, that the book's findings were dated. Although the session was extended, there was not time for many important issues to be raised. In this comment, I will briefly summarize my criticisms of *The Case for the Prosecution* and then make some wider comments about the book and the debate which it has provoked.

McConville, Sanders and Leng's account is open to several fundamental criticisms. In brief, there are tendencies towards theoretical essentialism, overgeneralization, and political pessimism which find numerous expressions.

First, there is a consistent attribution to actors (Royal Commissioners, legislators, police) of motive and intention in a way which oversimplifies complex and sometimes inscrutable processes. One example is McConville, Sanders and Leng's discussion of record-making requirements. They claim that 'Every feature of policing which enters the official domain is grounded in and based upon a paper reality created to authenticate and legitimate the police version of events, and to insulate police action from critical review' (1991: 98). In such attributions of motive, the use of the passive sidesteps the thorny issue of agency: *whose* designs and intentions are so deliberate and effective? In another context, individual responsibility is made clear: suspects are deterred from requesting legal advice by 'ploys' used by custody officers (1991: 47–54; see also Sanders *et al.* 1989). In our observations of custody officers at work (Dixon *et al.* 1990; Bottomley *et al.* 1991), we encountered most of the activities which are categorized in this way. However, it seems to be misleading to call all of them ploys. Deliberate discouragement of requests is only one among several factors, including routine performance of familiar tasks without appreciating the suspect's dilemma, and well-meaning but inappropriate assessment that requesting legal advice would not be in a suspect's best interest.

Perhaps the best example concerns the way in which custody officers accept suspects for pre-charge detention. It is frequently observed that custody officers do not examine the need for detention (as PACE requires), but instead ritually authorize the detention of almost everyone brought to stations under arrest (Dixon *et al.* 1990:

129–30; Morgan *et al.* 1990: 17–20). McConville, Sanders and Leng explain this by arguing that 'custody officers, with some exceptions, readily go along with the wishes of the case officers because they are emotionally committed to believing their version of events, and because they share the instrumental goals of case clearance which underpins all policework . . . Group solidarity, police culture and professional friendships dictate mutual reinforcement of authority' (1991: 42, 44). This is a one-dimensional explanation. As Morgan *et al.* point out, another factor is the bureaucratic reality in which it is easier and safer to accept a suspect into custody than to refuse (1990: 18–19). Procedures are designed for accepting suspects, not for turning them away. Once a custody officer begins to write a custody record (by asking the suspect's name, even though the item 'reasons for arrest' precedes this on custody records), the bureaucratic expectation is that it will be completed.

In addition to cultural and bureaucratic factors, there are legal pressures to accept suspects. PACE has standardized custodial interrogation: it is expected that most suspects will be 'interviewed'; it is regarded as desirable that this should take place at a police station; and the pressure of custodial interrogation can be properly considered by officers in deciding to detain for questioning (*Holgate-Mohammed v Duke*). Consequently, officers can legitimately claim that the conditions of Section 37 (which allows detention for questioning if this is necessary to obtain evidence by questioning) will almost always be met. The importance of this example is that it is not simply countering McConville, Sanders and Leng's structural account with a bureaucratic one. (Cf. the contrast drawn between explanations in terms of 'bureaucratic' pressures or societal structures in Sanders 1994: 811). Rather, it suggests that their structuralism is not comprehensive, but that it tends to oversimplify complex processes which have several determinants. (Elsewhere, Sanders points correctly to another example of the law's role: different criteria govern arrest and detention for questioning, so that 'arrests can lawfully be made in circumstances where custody officers should decline detention and negate the arrest'. Not surprisingly, custody officers resolve the dilemma by authorizing detention: 1994: 784).

Secondly, potentially misleading generalizations are made about policing practice – functionally (notably, the need to distinguish between the potential for regulation of policing on the street and in the station), geographically (the significant variation in PACE practices both locally and regionally) and culturally (police culture is not impermeable, and is characterized as much by division and sanction as it is by more familiar characteristics such as cynicism and suspicion).

It is true, as Roger Leng has argued, that sociological explanation must look for patterns and generalities. But it must also take account of discontinuities and inconsistencies: it may be that *they* are the pattern. To take one example from those discussed in more detail elsewhere (Dixon 1992), a notable feature of PACE has been its uneven usage across the country: for instance, very long pre-charge detention, investigative methods, and rates of requests for legal advice all vary substantially. This invites caution about suggestions that there has been a unitary, culture-based response to PACE and that policing cannot be changed by legal reform. Identifying the factors which produce such variations will be an important task for future research.

Thirdly, their account relies on an implicit history of criminal justice which is inaccurate: the extent of police powers in practice before PACE is understated, and the pressures for reform in the interests of organizational (by which I mean structural, not just bureaucratic) efficiency (notably, a reduction in disputes about police evidence) are underestimated by the concentration on the drift to law and order. There seems also to be a lack of historical perspective in their analysis of police culture. No adequate history is available, but it is clear that policing has changed considerably in recent decades, and that police culture has changed with it. (Like most police researchers, their concept of 'culture' is theoretically deficient: cf. Shearing and Ericson 1991.) When officers speak of a new 'professionalism' in police work, their terminology may be questionable, but they do refer to perceptible change. Crucially, there has been a shift in evaluations of investigative methods: the tradition of arresting on hunches, interrogating, and giving weak cases 'a run' has been challenged by according status to officers who investigate more carefully before arrest and who find ways of working within the rules (Dixon *et al.* 1990). One has by no means replaced the other; but there is a significant tension which indicates shifts and variations within police culture. It is such tensions within a changing institution which are among the most sociologically significant themes in this area. Obviously, this is not a declaration of a simple faith in 'progress'. It is not necessary to say that things have changed for the better to accept that there has been change: change requires recognition (not necessarily applause) so that analysis can address the new situation.

Fourthly, their distinction between reform and more fundamental change is essentialist and leads to unnecessarily pessimistic political conclusions. Not surprisingly, the authors do not like the tag, 'new left pessimists', which I applied to them. Elsewhere, their concern has been to identify potential for progressive reform (for example, Sanders 1993; 1994) and to engage in 'reform' by, for example preparing research papers for the Royal Commission on Criminal Justice. As Andrew Sanders commented, the issue is not 'do reforms work?' but 'which reforms will work?'. However, in *The Case for the Prosecution*, the rejection of reformism does not allow for this distinction:

> When we began our research we anticipated as one tangible product a set of reform proposals . . . We do not, however, intend to pursue this kind of analysis because we think it counter-productive . . . Reformist strategies embody . . . the false promises of liberal legalism . . . Attention should be focused away from extending ineffective 'protections' to a captive and largely unchanging suspect population, and towards altering the composition of this suspect group, by removing the bias of state legality against the weak and powerless. Within the legal system a start in this can be made by overturning police culture, by redefining the policing mandate and by instituting new forms of accountability. (1991: 191, 205–6)

The hopelessness of this programme is soon acknowledged:

> It is, of course, hardly necessary to emphasise that there is no real possibility of major changes to police culture or forms of police accountability. Law reform does not have a dynamic separate from and independent of state interest . . . There is no constituency of any note for reform which involves real protections for vulnerable citizens or substantive changes to existing modes of policing. For the state, existing modes of law enforcement *work*. (1991: 208)

This is not mere scepticism (cf. Boyle 1993: 577): I find it impossible to interpret these statements as anything other than an anti-reformist, functionalist pessimism. Within such an account, it is difficult to see how the reforms which they propose elsewhere (Sanders 1993: 105–8; 1994: 791) could be effective.

These issues have particular relevance in the Australian context in which I now work. In New South Wales (and some other jurisdictions), criminal procedure is similar to the pre-PACE position in England and Wales. While police have no power to detain for questioning, suspects are routinely interrogated at stations by officers who rely on fictional 'consent' or the reluctance of courts to exclude unlawfully obtained evidence (Dixon 1993). Suspects have no right to legal advice. There is a long history of verballing, not just in notorious cases, but as a matter of routine. Elements of these forces make the West Midland Serious Crimes Squad look like the boy scouts (see, for example, ICAC 1994; Fitzgerald 1989). Significant moves towards change are underway, with fissures driven into these police organizations. I have been involved in advising state reform commissions on reforming criminal procedure (New South Wales Law Reform Commission 1991; Criminal Justice Commission 1993–4). In this context, it does not entail donning rose-tinted glasses to see PACE as a source for reform proposals. Of course, it cannot be simply transplanted, and continuing organizational and cultural change will be vital to any success. But it is hard (within the bounds of the political realism) to suggest better modes of legal regulation than, for example, custody officers, publicly-funded legal advice, comprehensive recording requirements, and time-limited detention. Those who reject such reforms are police whose traditional practices are threatened by it, lawyers with simplistic commitment to 'common law' rights and how things have always been done, and cynics who see any change as likely to be for the worse. Such a context requires some realistic analysis of what progressive reform really means.

This leads me to some more general comments on the book and its reception. A common criticism of *The Case for the Prosecution* has been that the authors do what they accuse police of doing – selecting facts and constructing cases. Gwynn Davis, for example, argued at the conference and in a review that:

> the book presents a powerfully argued case which appears only tenuously related to the empirical investigation which supposedly provides its underpinnings . . . It would be nice, sometimes, to be able to make one's own judgements on the basis of the case material, rather than to be constantly bludgeoned with an argument which . . . pre-dates this particular investigation . . . Socio-legal researchers . . . should let the evidence speak (1992: 323, 324).

This argument is in serious danger of degenerating into naive empiricism. It should hardly need pointing out that evidence never has its own voice: it is always selected and spoken by authors. Even if McConville, Sanders and Leng made their whole data set available, it would still be constituted by their investigation, selection and presentation. (They include an eloquent statement of this basic point in their introductory chapter: 'Research, like the world of its subjects, is a process of construction . . . the fact that researchers do not and cannot have unmediated access to the "truth" is not a strength or a weakness of the research and is not a deficiency in our method: it is an epistemological reality': 1991: 13.)

While they should not be criticized for constructing their case, they can be criticized for not clarifying the process of construction, for example, by giving more details of their samples and of how they chose their illustrative examples. More fundamentally, the relationship between theory and methodology is inadequate. The authors seem to shun complex statistical analysis as a consequence of their rejection of positivism. But, as Sandra Walklate has commented, 'the radical project of the book and statistical analysis are not mutually exclusive enterprises' (1992: 534). British criminology and socio-legal studies could learn from the United States, where some of the best work combines progressive politics, critical theory, and sophisticated quantitative (as well as qualitative) analysis (for example Daly 1994).

McConville, Sanders and Leng's work is founded in a combination of structuralist and interactionist theory, with a strong commitment to constructionism. But their theoretical account is not developed by, for example, placing their work in the context of other constructionist literature. In general, theory is sketched rather than presented in detail: this is a pity, because the sketches are tantalizing. An example is their critique of McBarnet's analysis of the due process/crime control dichotomy. This is perceptive and important, but it is dealt with too briefly. As Boyle comments, 'The writers locate themselves in at least some of the theoretical debates of their time, but on a very abstract level' (1993: 574).

These are, of course, academic gripes, and their limits are appreciated. I would like McConville, Sanders and Leng to have doubled the length of *The Case for the Prosecution*, but I doubt that Routledge would have agreed. More importantly, the book is not just an academic production but (as the cliché goes) a political intervention. The academic elaboration which I would have liked might well have dulled its impact. Currently, the official debate on criminal justice is dominated by the theoretical and philosophical inanity of the Runciman Report. Michael Zander told us at a conference plenary that it 'doesn't matter tuppence if you do or don't have theory'. Whatever one thinks of *The Case for the Prosecution*, it is a most important counterweight to such views.

References

Bottomley, A. K., Coleman, C. A., Dixon, D., Gill, M. and Wall, D. (1991). *The Impact of PACE: Policing in a Northern Force* (Hull, Centre for Criminology and Criminal Justice).

Boyle, C. (1993). 'Guilt, innocence and truth', *Criminal Law Forum*, 4, 573–80.

Daly, K. (1994). *Gender, Crime and Punishment* (New Haven, Yale University Press).

CJC (1993–4). *Report on a Review of Police Powers in Queensland* (Brisbane, Criminal Justice Commission).

Davis, G. (1992). Review of *The Case for the Prosecution*, *Policing and Society*, 2, 322–4.

Dixon, D. (1992). 'Legal regulation and policing practice', *Social and Legal Studies*, 1, 515–41.

Dixon, D. (1993). 'The legal (non)regulation of custodial interrogation in NSW', paper for the ANZ Society of Criminology Conference.

Dixon, D., Bottomley, A. K., Coleman, C. A., Gill, M. and Wall, D. (1990). 'Safeguarding the rights of suspects in police custody', *Policing and Society*, 1, 115–40.

Fitzgerald (1989). *Report of Inquiry into Possible Illegal Activities and Associated Police Misconduct* (Brisbane, Government printer).

ICAC (1994). *Investigation into the Relationship between Police and Criminals* (Sydney, Independent Commission Against Corruption).

Morgan, R., Reiner, R. and McKenzie, I. (1990). 'Police powers and policy: a study of the work of custody officers', report to the ESRC.

McConville, M., Sanders, A. and Leng, R. (1991). *The Case for the Prosecution* (London, Routledge).

NSW LRC (1987) *Police Powers of Detention and Investigation After Arrest* (Sydney, Law Reform Commission).

Sanders, A. (1993). 'Controlling the discretion of the individual officer', in Reiner, R. and Spencer, S. (eds.), *Accountable Policing* (London, Institute for Public Policy Research), 81–112.

Sanders, A. (1994) 'From suspect to trial', in Maguire, M., Morgan, R. and Reiner, R. (eds.), *The Oxford Handbook of Criminology* (Oxford, Oxford University Press), 772–818.

Sanders, A., Bridges, L., Mulvaney, A. and Crozier, G. (1989). *Advice and Assistance at Police Stations and the 24 Hour Duty Solicitor Scheme* (London, Lord Chancellor's Department).

Shearing, C. D. and Ericson, R. V. (1991). 'Culture as figurative action', *British Journal of Sociology*, 26, 481–506.

Walklate, S. (1992). Review of *The Case for the Prosecution*, *British Journal of Sociology*, 26, 533–4.

12 ~ Authors meet critics IV

Damned if they do, damned if they don't: The Case for the Prosecution

ROD MORGAN

I read *The Case for the Prosecution* with admiration. It is a typical product from what I have come to think of, despite Andrew Sanders's translation to Oxford, as the Birmingham/Warwick School: well written, trenchantly argued, critical, copious use of evidence, persuasive. A classic piece of academic adversarialism which, given the subject matter, may seem peculiarly appropriate. If the book is taken at face value the conclusion to which the reader is literally led by the nose – and I shall justify that phrase – is that the criminal justice system is guilty. Guilty of confirming by its decisions the class, race and gender inequalities in our society. Guilty of allowing the police to pursue 'crime control' values virtually unfettered by defence solicitors who are co-opted by the system or by the Crown Prosecution Service who are police-dependent, police-supportive and prosecution-minded. Thus a relatively powerful police, operating in a corporatist criminal justice system characterized by consensus rather than competing checks and balances, use their powers further to disenfranchise the weak and powerless and to protect the strong and influential.

The theoretical core of *The Case for Prosecution* is elegantly set out in the opening and closing chapters, 'Criminal justice in England and Wales' and 'The problems of law reform'. In Chapter One McConville, Sanders and Leng list the competing analytical frameworks of positivism (evaluation according to a given set of rules, thereby to measure departure from them), interactionism (evaluation which assumes the ambiguity and diversity of rules followed by different groups) and structuralism (evaluation of the rules themselves, and the mechanisms whereby they are realized in practice) and find all three wanting. They adopt an 'integrated' approach which draws on all three approaches:

We need to recognise the complexity of the micro-social world, the dynamic way in which cases reflect external 'realities' and the way that cases are *social constructions* which further broaden socio-political objectives. (p. 11.)

Whether this constitutes a step towards enhanced theoretical sophistication, or provides a loose-limbed framework within which the imagination (and prejudice) can range freely, is a matter on which not everyone will agree. What is clear is that having collected and analysed their data, the authors come to what many commentators will regard as very pessimistic conclusions. They repudiate 'legal reformism'. They think it counterproductive. They contend that it offers the 'false promises' of positivism, whereas in fact the scope for change through amendment is very restricted. The implication is that most of the procedural and legal changes that were recommended *to* the Royal Commission, and certainly nearly all that was recommended *by* the Royal Commission, will achieve little 'to limit arbitrary, selective and discretionary behaviour on the part of the police' and will fail to 'envelop the citizen in a protective canopy of law' (p. 192).

They do not say that legal reform brings no benefits. On the contrary they conclude that the legal changes of recent years, notably the Police and Criminal Evidence Act 1984, have 'had *some* impact upon the behaviour of state officials and further rule revisions might have wider impact by "correcting" behaviour thought to be improper or inappropriate' (p. 193). However, they argue that 'legal reformists' mistakenly and naively assume that 'the purpose of legal reform is *benign*', that 'legal rules have instrumental effect' and that 'legal rules can be accurately *targeted*' in such a fashion that practitioners will not 'adjust their behaviour so as to circumvent or subvert clear legal precepts' (p. 194). Moreover legal reformism tends, they maintain, to see the criminal justice process as segmental when in fact it is unified by the dominance of the police, who are able, the authors allege, substantially to circumvent the Crown Prosecution Service and the courts 'by taking decisions themselves which are unreviewable and by constructing the evidence in such a way as to maximise their control over future decisions' (p. 199).

What, then, can be done? Little or nothing it would appear. The adoption of elements of the continental inquisitorial system will not work because the police will just as easily 'mislead . . . through case construction' judicial overseers as they currently mislead the courts (p. 202). Nor is changed police recruitment or training likely to achieve much if the 'police mandate' remains as it is. The same negative conclusion is drawn about enhanced accountability mechanisms. They will be 'after-the-fact', worth very little if 'the police are able to *construct the fact*' (p. 207). The problem is 'endemic to liberal capitalist society' and:

> Law reform does not have a dynamic separate from an independent of state interest. The criminal justice process not only imposes order but reproduces a particular form of social order which involves class, race and gender biases and which differentially distributes opportunity, wealth and power between different groups in society . . . there is no constituency of any note for reform which involves real protections for vulnerable citizens or substantive changes to existing modes of policing. (p. 208)

Thus, in a phrase itself carefully designed for reproduction, the police will go on policing the streets rather than the suites, focusing on the crimes of the poor and weak rather than the rich and powerful (p. 206). There you have it.

Readers will readily see that though the passing references to legal reform, police training and constitutional accountability suggest an 'integrated' approach, in fact it is the structuralist, or rather the functionalist, approach which wins out in the analysis. Functionalist, because the repeatedly intoned connection with liberal capitalist society implies a necessary reproductive connection (though this is never explained) and because there is nothing here that suggests that much can be done to change the essence of policing, and thus the criminal justice system, of any society. Further, since all developed societies, whatever their political rhetoric, are more or less unequal in terms of class, race and gender, one is drawn to the conclusion that whatever the dynamics of change are taken to be – and ultimately there is no optimism that change is on the agenda – reform of the criminal justice system will not be a key component. However, the fundamental question to be asked of this text concerns the degree to which the conclusions are empirically grounded. Whether they flow from the data, or are reached in spite of them?

The Case for the Prosecution is essentially an empirical research monograph, and it is on that basis that it should first and foremost be judged. The study involved sampling case files – 120 adults and sixty juveniles – in each of six police subdivisions, two in each of three police forces. The subdivisions were selected to represent 'different crime problems in inner-city, suburban and rural areas' (Appendix,

p. 209). In all cases, relevant documentary evidence, including that contained in custody records, was collected and interviews sought with key decision-makers. Success in interviewing arresting or reporting police officers was very high (generally 90 per cent or above) and moderately high with respect to custody officers, prosecutors or advocates (generally between one and two thirds). It is important to note that data collection occurred on either side of the implementation of the Prosecution of Offences Act 1985, so that any conclusions about the present performance of the Crown Prosecution Service must be regarded with caution. The main body of the text deals with decisions to detain, interrogation, building cases, reviewing cases for prosecution and acquittals and convictions in successive chapters.

There is not space here to consider all of the principal findings. The key issue concerns the degree to which the data sustain the authors' damning conclusions regarding legal reformism. In this respect it has to be said that the book contains significant methodological shortcomings which some may judge to comprise sleight of hand. A few illustrations will suffice to establish the point.

It is maintained that the Police and Criminal Evidence Act 1984 has made no real difference to police practice (with respect to stop and search this contention is supported by reference to other research studies), and even when it appears to have made a difference, that difference is said to be illusory. Thus, regarding detention and a suspect's rights to have someone informed of their detention or to seek legal advice, the fact that the custody records showed that in some 95–98 per cent of cases the suspect had been advised of his or her right, is said to mean little on the basis of Sanders's earlier study of legal advice in police stations (Sanders *et. al.* 1989). Sanders's negative conclusion is supported by a description from the present study in which a custody officer says to a suspect, 'Sign there to say that I've given you these forms', and who then indicates that the suspect is to sign the box on the form meaning that he does not want a solicitor. Nothing is read out and when subsequently asked about his practice the custody officer says that 'he never read suspects their rights and has never heard any other custody officer do so' (p. 49).

This incident is seriously offered as evidence of police power to ignore legal requirements. But this is manifestly an evidential travesty, unless academic discourse is to be conducted on the same basis as in an adversarial trial (a mode for which the authors profess distaste),

namely, try to tarnish one's targeted victim – in this case the police –
with any piece of evidence, however weak, suspect or rare, that comes
to hand. Thus there is no mention that other researchers have not
found 'ploys' to be used to prevent suspects gaining access to legal
advice to the extent that Sanders and his colleagues claim to have
found. Nor is there any reference to the fact that Sanders *et. al.* did
not find that the use of alleged 'ploys' influenced the rate at which
legal advice was asked for or obtained, or to the fact that access to
legal advice has very substantially increased since the Police and
Criminal Evidence Act was introduced.

A few pages later it becomes clear why this countervailing evidence
might not have been mentioned. Though the police are said to use
ploys to reduce the likelihood that legal advice will be obtained in
order to maintain suspect vulnerability to police pressure, nevertheless, paradoxically, if legal advisers do attend they are apparently
likely to be co-opted to the police viewpoint. 'Some' solicitors (we are
not told how many):

> will advise the client to speak, even when the answers given constitute, a
> full admission to the offence under investigation. And some, while
> expressing the intention to protect the client through the use of the right of
> silence, are ineffective. (p. 53)

The negative stereotype – it now seems proper to employ the same
pejorative language which the authors use to describe the police – is
clear. Legal advisers are either co-opted or ineffective, which makes
one wonder why the police apparently go to such lengths to prevent
their intrusion. Unfortunately, we do not have the legal advisers'
version of these events. They were not interviewed nor were their
advice sessions with clients observed.

I am suggesting that McConville and his colleagues occasionally
employ an 'adversarial methodology' remarkably similar to that
which they claim is used by the police. They build their critique by
highlighting evidence which supports their argument, and by ignoring
or downplaying countervailing evidence. Take, for example, their
discussion of the police use of cautions and informal warnings. Three
cases are cited in the text (pp. 81–3) where cautions or informal
warnings appear to have been recorded by the police in breach of
Home Office guidelines, no admission of guilt having been obtained.
Given that this practice is said to enable the police to build up long
records with potentially injurious consequences on individuals

against whom there is no case with evidential substance, it is odd that we are not told how many such cases were found. Were there only three, or were there more?

Or, to take another example, there is discussion in Chapter Six of the various reasons why no further action is taken in about a quarter of the cases in which suspects have been arrested and detained. The reasons given range from administrative convenience (getting rid of cases when officers are burdened with a heavy workload) or the need to protect informers, to officers concluding that suspects are innocent, or that social justice will best be served by taking no further action. These are very different reasons. But again no indication is given as to their relative importance, quantitatively or otherwise. Nor, when it comes to cases where the authors suggest that a 'prosecution at all costs rule' prevails, alongside an assertion that prosecution serves police objectives, is it clear what the origin of these objectives is.

Once again the authors' technique is strikingly similar to that of which they accuse the police. Between the pages of *The Case for the Prosecution* are the conventional references to 'samples' and claims to 'representativeness' in order that social science legitimacy be accorded. But subsequently, if Andrew Sanders's riposte at the Cardiff conference is to be at face value, it apparently matters not whether there was one or many cases of police rule-violation. There is no need to cite the extent of the evidence: the fact that rule-violation happened once is evidence that police breach the rules, and that they are able to do so with impunity whenever it suits them. This conclusion manifestly does not follow.

The Case for the Prosecution is without doubt a landmark study which deserves close attention. The data collected are vital to the contemporary debate about police powers and procedure and the authors accompany their analysis with a theoretical vigour of the sort lacking in the report of the Runciman Royal Commission. But they lead their readers by the nose, and not always in the precise direction in which one suspects fuller exposure of the evidence would point. Evidence of the police or prosecutors 'failing' or encountering 'resistance' (though it is not at all clear what 'failing' or 'resistance' would comprise and how the authors would recognize it – do police recognition that a suspect is innocent, or the Crown Prosecution Service declining to prosecute on public interest grounds, constitute 'failure'?) would apparently cut no ice with the authors. It would merely be an example of the 'system winning by appearing to lose' – a

Marxist phrase (if you will excuse the pun) of which the authors are particularly fond (Sir Robert Mark quoted in Reiner 1992: 64). The appearance or 'possibility of resistance' is, they argue, a requirement of an 'effective legal system'. It establishes the system's credibility, legitimacy and thus hegemony. Moreover, it provides the ultimate Catch 22 for all practitioners in the criminal justice system: damned if they do, damned if they don't.

References

Reiner R. (1992). *The Politics of the Police* (London, Wheatsheaf).

Runciman Report (1993). *Report of the Royal Commission on Criminal Justice*, Cm 2263 (London, HMSO).

Sanders A., Bridges L., Mulvaney A. and Crozier G. (1989). *Advice and Assistance at Police Stations and the 24 Hour Duty Solicitor Scheme* (London, Lord Chancellor's Department).

13 ~ Authors meet critics V

The case for the prosecution: police suspects and the construction of criminality

ROBERT REINER

When *The Case For the Prosecution* was published in 1991 I wrote a review of it for *The Times Higher Education Supplement* which was fundamentally very positive, although I demurred from some of the interpretations and conclusions. I agreed to participate in the Cardiff conference 'Authors Meet Critics' session on the understanding that critic did not necessarily mean hostile or negative critic. I did not reject any of the initial enthusiasm of my earlier review and used it as the basis of my contribution to the panel.

The most practical significance of McConville, Sanders and Leng's timely book is that it is the first comprehensive empirical examination of the momentous changes in the criminal justice process ushered in following the 1981 Report of the Royal Commission on Criminal Procedure chaired by Sir Cyril Philips. The recent Report of the Runciman Royal Commission on Criminal Justice, published in July 1993, can at best be described as a set of footnotes to Philips in so far as it tackles the issues of police powers and safeguards over their abuse in the first two substantive chapters. This makes the powerfully and convincingly argued thesis of this book still pertinent. McConville, Sanders and Leng suggest not only that the Royal Commission on Criminal Procedures package failed to achieve its avowed objectives, but that such a fate awaits any reforms which concentrate only on the criminal justice system itself.

McConville, Sanders and Leng tracked a large sample of cases through the criminal justice system, in two police subdivisions in each of three forces. For each of these six research sites they collected the first 120 adult and sixty juvenile cases arrested or reported for summons (a comparatively rare occurrence) from a set date after the research began in March 1986. The study tracks the course and outcome of these cases, in terms of whether it was decided to caution or prosecute, how suspects were handled by the police, how they exercised their rights, how they pleaded, and what the final verdict was. It also probes the decision-making of the key official actors of the pre-trial process, the police and prosecutors, by interviews about the cases with the arresting, investigating and custody officers, and the Crown Prosecution Service (CPS) personnel who handled them. All this amounts to the most wide-ranging data yet produced on the working of the criminal justice system since the Police and Criminal Evidence Act (PACE) and the CPS were introduced.

The material is analysed in terms of a comprehensive theory of the role and functioning of criminal justice. The perspective they offer is not a particularly original one, and derives from approaches which illuminated the best of the pre-PACE research. However, the main policy message of the book is precisely to underline the continuity of the determinants of police and prosecution practice despite the seemingly profound reorganization entailed by PACE and the Prosecution of Offences Act (POA). The theoretical approach they adopt is spelled out more clearly and cogently than it has been in earlier work, and is far better integrated into the analysis of empirical data.

Socio-legal research on criminal justice has always been critical of the positivism which constitutes the dominant ideology of the police and legal practitioners. It has challenged the view that the legal system is a neutral processor of facts in cases which are presented objectively for rational adjudication according to clear rules. However, the critique has itself polarized into two camps. 'Interactionists', using micro-sociological observational methods for the most part, have emphasized how the police and other officials deviate routinely from the rule of law and are governed by the values and beliefs of their own autonomous canteen culture. 'Structuralists' share the same view of police practice, but see the source of police adherence to crime control, rather than legalistic, due process values, as lying in the law itself, which is deliberately formulated in a 'permissive' way by state élites so that the police have a free hand in cracking down on the socially powerless. McConville, Sanders and Leng attempt to synthesize these two critical approaches. They emphasize that the police inevitably carve out considerable practical autonomy, and thus their beliefs and working routines are crucial for understanding law in action. However, cop culture is itself structured by the nature of their role in a particular social and political order.

The result is the social construction of criminality out of a target population, who constitute what Claude Rains playing the police chief in *Casablanca* memorably described as 'the usual suspects', to be rounded-up routinely. The social group who are the regular property of the police are the economically and socially marginal young men of the inner cities, nowadays disproportionately likely to be black. They are overwhelmingly the majority of those who are processed by the police. What McConville *et al.* show is that the construction of cases is heavily determined by the initial filter, the rank-and-file police, who are able to load the odds for decision-making at subsequent stages, notably by the formally independent CPS and the supposedly adversarial defence lawyers, through the packaging they produce at the outset of the process. Case failure is a rare occurrence and is due to occasional defects in police craftsmanship rather than the intrinsic characteristics of cases.

This picture will have a familiar ring to all who are acquainted with the classic research literature on policing. But this *déja vu* is precisely McConville *et al.*'s central message. Despite the complex paraphernalia of rules and safeguards introduced by PACE and POA there is a basic continuity of traditional cop culture with its crime control values effectively dominating the process. This will not be touched by any subsequent rule-changes either, but is an inescapable consequence of the police mission of being moral street-sweepers, charged with regulating the social flotsam and jetsam who threaten the order of public spaces. Only a fundamental restructuring of the police mandate, giving for example equal if not greater weight to suite as to street crime, could alter these basic constants. And this would require yet more fundamental political change (here the authors are understandably rather vague).

Although the basic thesis is compelling, and the material well organized to support it, this leads to finessing of some complexities which might dilute the force of their conclusions. Partly this is the old problem of whether to describe a glass as half full or half empty. Thus they emphasize (as do all other research studies since PACE) that over two-thirds of suspects detained in police stations do not exercise their right to see a solicitor. However, this is a doubling of the proportion who do see a solicitor compared to pre-PACE experience. The new procedures have led to a substantial change, although McConville *et al.* accentuate the negative. Throughout the presentation of data there is a similar tendency to stress the bad news. Thus most other evaluations of PACE have expended considerable effort in trying to explain what is a marked variation between areas in the impact of PACE, hoping to identify the sources of preferable practice. This book concentrates on the broad overall pattern, no doubt because the marginal difference which can be achieved by detailed police organizational reforms are seen as the equivalent of rearranging deck-chairs on the Titanic.

It is possible to quarrel with details of the authors' interpretation of data. It is also plausible that the safeguards represented by PACE and the CPS have become marginally more effective since the early teething period which is what the McConville, Sanders and Leng data tap. However, this does not detract from their overall achievement. This is a book which is of enormous value for its empirical, theoretical and policy contributions. It will be a landmark in socio-legal studies for some time to come, as is indeed reflected in its selection as the basis for this session.

Criminal justice issues

14

The supervision of offenders – what works?

CHRISTOPHER TROTTER

Background

For many years there has been controversy regarding whether or not probation or other community supervision programmes, whether with adults or children, can be effective in rehabilitating offenders. It has been argued both that such programmes do not work (Martinson 1974; Whitehead and Lab 1989) and that some programmes do work (Andrews *et al.* 1979; Gendreau and Ross 1979).

A study undertaken in the United States in the early 1970s (Martinson *et al.* 1975) which reviewed research on the issue up to that time has been widely quoted in support of the view that nothing works. In Martinson's words, 'With few and isolated exceptions the rehabilitative efforts that have been reported so far have had no appreciable effect on recidivism' (Martinson 1974: 25). This view has continued to receive support. Whitehead and Lab (1989) used an approach to analysing research studies known as meta-analysis. This approach can be described as a 'method of aggregating and statistically analysing the findings of several studies' (Fischer 1990: 297). After examining a range of studies relating to the effectiveness of correctional treatment of juveniles, including community-based programmes, they concluded that: 'The results show that interventions have little positive impact on recidivism and many appear to exacerbate the problem' (Whitehead and Lab 1989: 1).

On the other hand, it has been argued that, whilst the overall impact of correctional programmes may be minimal, this in fact disguises positive and negative effects. Some programmes or supervision approaches work and others are harmful (Andrews *et al.* 1990; Gendreau and Ross 1979; Lipsey 1991). It is suggested that the more successful approaches to supervision can result in reductions of about 50 per cent in reoffending rates, among both adult and juvenile offenders (Andrews *et al*. 1990).

Some research studies, mostly undertaken in North America, have suggested that effective supervision of offenders in the community is characterized by certain factors. These include focusing on high-risk offenders and the use by the supervising officer of pro-social modelling, structured problem solving and empathy (for example Andrews *et al*. 1979; Gendreau and Ross 1979).

Several studies and reviews of studies have found that probation supervision is most effective when more intensive services are given to high-risk offenders and less intensive services are given to low-risk offenders (Andrews *et al*. 1986; Andrews *et al*. 1990; Fo and O'Donnell 1975; Lunden 1990). It is argued that whereas high-risk offenders are likely to benefit from intensive services, low-risk offenders are relatively unlikely to reoffend and may be stigmatized by receiving more intensive services.

Numerous studies, and reviews of studies, have suggested that the adoption of a pro-social approach by supervising officers is related to reduced recidivism (Andrews *et al*. 1979; Andrews *et al*. 1990; Ferguson 1983; Fo and O'Donnell 1974, 1975; Gendreau and Ross 1979; Schwitzgebel cited Martinson 1975; Trotter 1990). These studies suggest that more effective supervisors have a more pro-social orientation, they present themselves as pro-social models and they encourage and reinforce the pro-social actions and expressions of their clients. In presenting themselves as pro-social models, supervising officers are more likely to be punctual, reliable, honest, friendly and to demonstrate concern for other people. They are more likely to express views about the value of a non-criminal lifestyle and about the value of pro-social pursuits such as work and social and personal relationships. They are also more likely to be optimistic about the chances that their clients can develop a non-criminal lifestyle.

In encouraging pro-social actions and expressions by the client the supervisor would be more likely to use praise or other rewards for those actions and expressions. This might involve praising the client for keeping appointments, being punctual, completing unpaid community work, discussing issues in an open manner or recognizing the harm that criminal behaviour can cause. It might involve reducing the frequency of appointments, because the client is maintaining the conditions of the probation or community corrections order.

Several studies have indicated that the use of structured problem-solving approaches by supervising officers are related to reduced offending by clients (Andrews *et al*. 1979; Ferguson 1983; Goldberg *et al*. 1984). Problem-solving approaches are outlined in a range of texts (for example Doel and Marsh 1992; Reid 1978; 1992). The basic components of the problem-solving approach include the clarification of role; surveying, ranking and exploring of problems; setting goals; developing strategies or tasks to address the problems; and ongoing monitoring of progress.

An important factor, which some research suggests may be related to reduced reoffending, relates to the use of empathy by the supervising officer, or the supervising officer's capacity to understand the client's point of view (Andrews *et al*. 1979; Truax, Wargo and Silber 1966). It is suggested in one study, however, that the supervisor's empathy is only related to reduced client offending where this is accompanied by the pro-social and problem-solving approaches referred to above (Andrews *et al*. 1979).

The research in relation to the value of empathy and reflective listening in correctional settings is limited and equivocal. Empathy is, however, an important component of many training courses for community corrections officers and probation officers, as well as being an integral factor in many general counselling models (for example Carkhuff and Berenson; Egan 1986).

The study reported on in this article aimed to consider whether the application of these principles, in a probation or community corrections setting in Australia, would result in reduced reoffending rates among clients.

Purpose of study

This study involved the training of a group of community corrections officers (CCOs) in community-based corrections in Victoria, Australia, in each of the principles or approaches which the research suggests may be related to reduced recidivism among clients. These include: the targeting of high-risk offenders; the use of a pro-social approach; the use of problem solving; and the use of reflective listening or empathy. The study aimed to consider whether or not those trained in the principles would actually use them in the supervision of their clients, and whether those trained in the supervision model had clients with lower recidivism rates than clients of other community corrections officers.

Method

Design

A one-week training course in effective supervision skills was advertised in all offices of the Community Based Corrections Department in Victoria. The course was available to all staff on a voluntary basis. Thirty-two CCOs enrolled for two courses which were held in March 1990 and June 1991. All those who volunteered for the courses were accepted. At the completion of each course the CCOs were invited to take part in the research project. This involved them supervising the next twenty clients allocated to them using the model which had been taught in the training course, attending ongoing training days and receiving some supervision/consultancy from research staff. Only two CCOs initially indicated that they did not wish to participate in the project. However, for various reasons such as leaving the department, resistance from management staff in the Community Corrections Centres, the CCO being promoted, or working in a specialist community work programme, only twelve CCOs continued with the project for more than six months. These CCOs and their clients were included in the experimental group.

Clients of CCOs in the experimental group were then followed up through an analysis of client files. The file analysis aimed to consider the extent to which file notes reflected the use of the supervision model and the recidivism rates of the clients. Data were also gathered through the file analysis in relation to two control groups. Control group 1 consisted of CCOs (and their clients) who participated in the initial training course but did not continue with the project. Thirteen CCOs in this category continued to supervise offenders. Control group 2, the primary control group for the study, consisted of CCOs and their clients, selected by systematic or interval random sampling (Seaberg 1988) from the same offices as those who completed the training course.

The three groups were then compared regarding the extent to which they used the model and regarding the recidivism rates of the clients. A range of data was also gathered in relation to client risk levels and CCO education and training levels, in order to determine whether certain intervening variables might account for the differences between the groups.

The design of the study is best described as quasi-experimental or descriptive. It was not possible to use a true experimental design because of the inability to assign randomly CCOs or clients to control and experimental groups (Grinnell and Stothers 1988).

Population

Victoria is an Australian state of about four million people. Some 7,000 offenders were on Community Based Corrections programmes at the time this study was undertaken. Community-based orders replaced probation some years ago in Victoria. They are similar to probation but, in addition to supervision, the courts can impose community work or other conditions as part of the order. Offenders may be placed directly by courts on community-based orders or they may be placed on parole by the Victorian Parole Board following their release from prison. Offenders on community-based orders and parole were included in this study.

The clients in the study had an average age of twenty-seven years; 83 per cent were male; 41 per cent were employed at the time of receiving their order; on average they had been convicted of twenty-nine prior offences and had appeared in court seven times; 41 per cent had a history of illegal drug use; 36 per cent had been previously imprisoned; and 26 per cent were first offenders.

Twenty-three per cent of the CCOs in the study were qualified in social work or welfare; 29 per cent had social science degrees; 14 per cent had postgraduate qualifications; and 19 per cent had no formal qualifications.

Training

The training course focused on four principles. Participants were asked to provide high levels of supervision to high-risk offenders, if possible, 45-minute interviews once a week in the first two or three months of the order. They were asked to see low-risk offenders for only short periods, about five minutes every two to four weeks and not to offer them counselling.

Offenders were categorized as high or low risk, on the basis of their score on the Community Based Corrections Intake and Assessment form. This form was initially developed in Canada where a number of studies have suggested that it is an effective predictor of client recidivism levels (Andrews 1982; Andrews and Robinson 1984; Motuik, Motuik and Bonta 1992). The form has been modified and further evaluated in Victoria (Saunders *et al.* 1987).

The principles of pro-social modelling and reinforcement were introduced to the participants, although to a large extent the approach was developed by the participants themselves. Discussion was held about how to present oneself as a pro-social model, client pro-social actions and expressions which should be encouraged, and the methods of encouraging or reinforcing those actions or expressions. Some use was made of training material developed in Canada (Andrews 1982).

The principles of problem-solving, which have been developed in a variety of texts, were outlined to the participants (for example Keissling 1982; Reid and Laura 1972; Reid 1978, 1992; Compton and Galaway 1989; O'Connor *et al.* 1991).

The principles of empathy and reflective listening have also been developed in a range of texts (for example Carkhuff 1969; Egan 1986). Essentially, reflective listening involves purposefully responding to content and feeling levels of clients' communications. Most of the participants were already familiar with this material and they were simply asked to make use of it consciously, along with the other principles of the model, in the supervision of their next twenty clients.

Data collection

A file analysis was undertaken on 366 files, 104 in the experimental group, 105 in the first control group (clients of CCOs who undertook the initial training course but did not continue with the project), and 157 in the second and primary control group selected from the same Community Corrections Centres as the other clients. Ten clients were selected, using a method of systematic random sampling, from the first twenty clients allocated after the training course to each of the CCOs who participated in the course. Where less than ten clients had been allocated after a period of three months, all clients allocated to those CCOs were included. Control group 2 was systematically selected, using a two-thirds ratio, from the clients allocated during the same period, and in the same offices as those of the experimental group and group 2.

Recidivism measures

A range of recidivism measures were used in the study, but they were closely correlated for the most part and only three measures are reported in this article. These include official breaches, that is where clients were returned to court for breaching their orders, either because they committed another offence within the period of the order or because they failed to comply with conditions (such as undertaking unpaid community work). The second measure reported here is imprisonment. This involves the client receiving a sentence of imprisonment for a breaching offence committed during the period of the order. Imprisonment includes instances where the sentence is suspended and only required to be served if another offence is committed. A third measure relates to the seriousness of the penalty the clients received for the breaching offence.

The follow-up period is one year. Whilst it might be argued that this is a short period, over 90 per cent of the offenders had orders which were for one year or less. Other studies have found that the majority of offenders who offend within three years will have done so within one year (Gendreau and Leipciger 1978; Cochran *et al.* 1981).

Results

Use of the model by the experimental group

It was anticipated that CCOs in the experimental group would make more use of the supervision model than CCOs in either of the control groups. Research staff gave a rating, on each of the 366 files, for the extent to which the files reflected the use of the model. A score of 5 or more reflected some or considerable use of the model, whereas a score of 4 or less reflected less use of the model.

Table 1 Scores of 5 or above for the use of the integrated model

Exp Gp (n=104)	Control 1 (n=105)	Control 2 (n=157)
44% (46)	21% (22)	16% (25)

(p=<.000 for Exp/Control 2)
(p=<.000 for Exp/Control 2)

Table 1 indicates that CCOs in the experimental group were more likely to show evidence of using the model than the two control groups. This was statistically significant well within conventional levels. Note that a one-tailed test of significance is used for this and subsequent tables because a direction for the results has been specified (Weinbach and Grinnell 1987).

It is also interesting to note that control group 1, those who undertook the initial training but did not agree to participate in the project, were more likely to show evidence of using the model than control group 2, who had no exposure to the model. The differences between the two control groups are not significant, however, and this may simply be a chance occurrence. On the other hand, it may be that those who withdrew from the project did in fact learn something from the training. It is clear that the CCOs who undertook the training course and agreed to participate in the project, did in fact make more use of the model in the supervision of their clients, in comparison to the control groups.

Recidivism rates
It was anticipated that the recidivism rates of the clients in the experimental group would be lower than those in the control groups. As illustrated in Table 2 this is the case using the official breach measure. This table includes both offence and conditions-related breaches (for example, failure to report). Clients in the experimental group had lower breach rates for both offence and conditions-related breaches. The breach rate is also significantly lower for the experimental group using the imprisonment measure as shown in Table 3.

Table 2 Official breaches within one year

Exp Gp *(n=104)*	*Control 1* *(n=105)*	*Control 2* *(n=157)*
(26%) (25)	(40%) (42)	(37%) (58)

(p=.022 Exp/Control 2)
(p=.016 Exp/Control 1)

Table 3 Imprisonment rates for the experimental and control groups

Exp Gp *(n=104)*	*Control 1* *(n=105)*	*Control 2* *(n=157)*
12% (13)	(19%) (20)	21% (33)

(p=.039 Exp/Control 2)
(p=.099 Exp/Control 1)

Recidivism rates taking other variables into account

It could be that the clients' level of risk, or the supervising officers' level of experience or education, could account for the differences between the groups. Or it could be that the supervisors in the experimental group were more likely to attend training courses than the control groups and that it was therefore a special group.

Logistic regression is a statistical technique which enables the 'probability of a dichotomous outcome to be predicted from a set of independent variables' (Microsoft Corp 1992). That is, it can provide information about the extent to which the differences between the groups can be explained by other variables.

Table 4 Logistic regression analysis of the relationship between official breaches and group membership by level of risk of clients, and CCO education, experience and training*

Variable	B	Standard error	Significance
Experience	.0354	.0681	.6034
Education	.2061	.3235	.5240
Training	.0180	.0321	.5752
Riskscore	.0827	.0248	.0009
Exp Gp	-.5950	.3269	.0344
Control Gp1	.1906	.3259	.5586
Constant	2.0509	.8193	.0123

*The impact of the experimental group and control group 1 are compared to control group 2. A one-tailed test of significance is used for the experimental group.

Table 5 Logistic regression analysis of the relationship between imprisonment rates and group membership by level of risk of clients and experience, education and training of CCOs

Variable	B	Standard error	Significance
Riskscore	.1079	.0313	.0003
Experience	-.0333	.0878	.7042
Education	-.0182	.4127	.9649
Training	.0336	.0370	.3632
Exp gp	-.7649	.4404	.0412
Control gp1	-.1054	.4201	.8018
Constant	-2.5966	1.0410	.0126

Table 4 shows that the official breach rate for clients in the experimental group is lower than for clients in control group 2, and that this difference is statistically significant even when allowance is made for other variables. These variables include the riskscore of the clients, the level of education of the CCOs (no formal education compared to a degree or diploma), the years of experience of the CCOs and the number of training courses which the CCOs had undertaken in the past three years. A similar significant difference was seen in relation to the imprisonment measure as seen in Table 5.

Recidivism rates of clients of CCOs who undertook the initial training course

It seems likely that if this course were to be repeated, there may again be dropouts. The overall impact of training is relevant, therefore, in considering the effectiveness of the training programme.

The clients of those CCOs who completed the initial training course (combined experimental group and control group 1) had lower recidivism rates in relation to each of the measures used in this study. Table 6 indicates that the differences between the groups is not statistically significant for the official breach measure, but is within the .10 level for the imprisonment measure.

Table 6 Official breach and imprisonment rates for clients of CCOs who undertook the initial training course

	Trained group (n=209)	Control group (n=157)
Official breach p=.165	32% (67)	36% (58)
Imprisonment p= .099	15% (33)	21% (33)

A regression analysis taking account of client risk scores and CCO experience, training and level of education revealed similar trends. Table 7 shows that clients who were supervised by CCOs who undertook the initial training course were also significantly less likely to commit serious offences, in comparison to the systematically selected control group.

It is apparent, therefore, that even though some CCOs did not continue with the project there was an overall positive impact on

Table 7 Multiple regression analysis of the relationship between the seriousness of the disposition imposed by the court for breaching offences and CCOs who undertook the initial training course, level of risk of clients and training education and experience of CCOs

Variable	B	Standard error	Significance
Trained gp	-.383720	.192168	.0234
Education	.002631	.037456	.9440
Riskscore	.068353	.017270	.0001
Training	.005289	.005991	.3781
Experience	-.010815	.047731	.8209
(Constant)	-.394054	.429614	.3598

Key
Dependent variable
1. No offence
2. Good behaviour bond/adjournment
3. Fine
4. Community-based order/corrections order
5. Suspended sentence/intensive corrections order
6. Prison/youth training centre

Trained Group
Clients of those CCOs who completed the initial training course compared to control group clients

clients, resulting from the implementation of this project. Further, the impact cannot be explained by the risk levels of the clients, or by the education, training or experience of the community corrections officers.

Use of the supervision model and recidivism

Further confirmation of the value of the supervision model is provided by considering the relationship between the extent to which CCOs used the model and client recidivism. The files of each of the clients in the study were given a rating out of ten in relation to the extent to which the file notes reflected the use of the supervision model. Table 8 shows that there was a statistically significant difference between the official breach rates of clients who were supervised by CCOs who were rated as making more use of the model, and clients of CCOs who were rated as making less use of the

Table 8 Use of the model by CCOs and client recidivism

	More use of model (Rated 5+) (n=93)	Less use of model (Rated 4-) (n=273)
Official breaches (p=.003)	23% (22)	38% (104)
Imprisonment (p=.190)	15% (14)	19% (52)

model. The imprisonment rate is outside the .10 level, although this can be explained by the fact that the model was more likely to be used with high-risk clients. Where CCOs in the experimental group were rated as making more use of the model (rated 5+), the recidivism rates were even lower (15 per cent, 7/46, official breaches; and 4 per cent, 2/46, imprisonment).

Which aspects of the model were related to recidivism?

It is clear that the use of the model was related to reduced recidivism rates. Which particular aspects of the model were related to reduced recidivism is more difficult to establish, particularly given the tendency for CCOs to use each of the aspects of the model at the same time. The different aspects of the model are also often interrelated. For example, one of the pro-social actions which was rewarded by CCOs was working through the problem solving process. An analysis of the impact of the various components of the model will be provided in a later publication.

Conclusions and implications

Conclusions

This study provides strong support for the view that supervision in Community Corrections, which is based on certain principles, can have an impact on client recidivism. When this study is considered in the context of the studies and reviews of studies referred to in the introduction, it seems reasonable to generalize that supervision in Community Based Corrections does have an impact on clients, and that supervision characterized by certain principles and approaches will reduce recidivism rates in a variety of community corrections settings. It also seems reasonable to conclude on the basis of this study that at least some, if not all CCOs, can be taught within a relatively short time, to implement the practices which are related to reduced recidivism rates.

Obstacles to the project

The results of this study have been achieved despite the pressure on CCOs who were involved in the project. This pressure included mounting workloads and endless competing demands. It was exacerbated by the fact that supervising and management staff in the regions, for the most part, were not familiar with the model and were not able, therefore, to support staff in its use. The difficulty of achieving a rigorous implementation of the model was made even more difficult by the fact that there were no direct benefits to participants in the project for using the model, other than the prospect of improved client progress. It is perhaps remarkable that the CCOs who participated in the project were able to achieve the results that they did.

Implications

This study has shown, like several previous North American studies, that recidivism in Community Based Corrections can be reduced by up to 50 per cent through the implementation of appropriate supervision practices and programmes. The implications of this, in both financial and human terms, are substantial. The Department of Community Based Corrections in Victoria, Australia is in the process of implementing the supervision programme described in this study on a statewide basis. It is anticipated that it will result in substantial benefits for the department and for the Victorian public.

Acknowledgements

The assistance of Community Based Corrections in Victoria and the Australian Criminology Research Council is gratefully acknowledged for their support in this project.

References

Andrews, D. A. (1982). *The Level Of Supervision Inventory* (Carlton University, Ottowa, Canada).

Andrews, D. A., Keissling, J. J., Russell, R. J. and Grant, B. A. (1979). *Volunteers and the One to One Supervision of Adult Probationers* (Ontario Ministry of Correctional Services, Toronto).

Andrews, D. A. and Robinson, D. (1984). *The Level of Supervision Inventory: Second Report* (Ontario Ministry of Correctional Services, Canada).

Andrews, D. A., Keissling, J. J., Robinson, D. and Mickus, S. (1986). 'The risk principle of case classification: an outcome evaluation with young adult probationers', *Canadian Journal of Criminology*, 28(4), 377–84.

Andrews, D. A., Zinger, I., Hoge, R. D., Bonta, J., Gendreau, P., Cullen, F. T. (1990). 'A clinically relevant and psychologically informed meta-analysis', *Criminology*, 28(3), 369–429.

Carkhuff, R. R. (1969). *Helping and Human Relations* (New York, Holt, Rhinehart and Winston Inc.).

Carkhuff, R. R. and Berenson, B. G. (1977). *Beyond Counselling and Therapy* (New York, Holt, Rhinehart and Winston Inc.).

Cochran, D., Brown, M. E. and Kazarian, R. (1981). *Executive Summary of Research Findings from the Pilot Court Risk/Need Classification System, Report 4* (Office of the Commissioner of Probation, Massachusetts, USA).

Compton, B. R. and Galaway, B. (1989). *Social Work Processes* 4th edn (California, Wadsworth Publishing).

Doel, M. and Marsh, P. (1992). *Task Centred Social Work* (Ashgate).

Egan, G. (1986). *The Skilled Helper* (Caifornia, Brooks/Cole Publishing Co.)

Ferguson, J. E. (1983). 'A Neo-Lewinian Approach to the Identification of Mechanisms of Change in Research with Offenders', unpublished PhD thesis, Carleton University, Canada.

Fo, Walter and O'Donnell, Clifford (1974). 'The buddy system: relationship and contingency conditions in a community prevention program for youth with non professionals as behaviour change agents,' *Journal of Counselling and Clinical Psychology,* (April 1974), 163–9.

Fo, Walter and O'Donnell, Clifford (1975). 'The buddy system, effect of community intervention on delinquent offences', *Behaviour Therapy*, 6, 522–4.

Gendreau, P. and Leipciger, M. (1978). 'The development of a recidivism measure and its application in Ontario', *Canadian Journal of Criminology*, 20, 3–17.

Gendreau, P. and Ross, B. (1979). 'Effective correctional treatment: bibliotherapy for cynics', *Crime and Delinquency*, (October 1979), 463–89.

Goldberg, E. M., Stanley, S. J. and Kenrick, J. (1984). 'Task centred casework in a probation setting', in Goldberg, E. M., Gibbons, G. and Sinclair, I. (eds.), *Problems Tasks and Outcomes: The Evaluation of Task Centred Casework in Three Settings* (Allen and Unwin, London).

Grinnell, R. and Stothers, M. (1988). 'Utilising research designs', in Grinnell, R. M., *Social Work Research and Evaluation* (F. E. Peacock, USA).

Keissling, J. J. (1982). *The Problem Solving Dimension in Correctional Counselling* (Ontario Ministry of Correctional Services, Ottowa, Canada).

Lipsey, Mark W. (1991). 'Juvenile delinquency treatment: a meta-analytic inquiry into the variability of effects', in *Meta-Analysis for Explanation* (Russell Sage Foundation, Spring 1991, California).

Lunden, R. (1989). 'Parole release and discharge from prison: a comparison study', Massachusetts, paper presented to the American Society of Criminology Conference, November 1989.

Martinson, R. (1974). 'What works? Questions and answers about prison reform', *The Public Interest*, 35, 22–34.

Martinson, R., Lipton, D., Wilks, J. (1975). *The Effectiveness of Correctional Treatment: A Survey of Treatment Evaluation Studies* (New York, Praeger Publishers).

Microsoft Corp, (1990). *Statistical Package for the Social Sciences* (SPSS Inc., 1984–90, USA).

Motuik, M. S., Motuik, L. L., Bonta, J. (1992). 'A comparison between self report and interview based inventories in offender classification', *Criminal Justice and Behaviour*, 19(2), 143–9.

O'Connor, I., Wilson, J. and Thomas, K. (1991). *Social Work and Welfare Practice* (Melbourne, Longman Cheshire).

Reid, W. J. and Epstein, Laura (1972). *Task Centred Casework* (New York, Columbia University Press).

Reid, W. J. (1978). *The Task Centred System* (New York, Columbia University Press).

Reid, William J. (1992). *Task Strategies, An Empirical Approach to Clinical Social Work* (New York, Columbia University Press).

Saunders, P., Ross, S., Trotter, C., Nelson, Z., Abamonte, P., and Toner, P. (1987). *Evaluation of Community Based Corrections Offender and Assessment Form* (Office of Corrections, Victoria).

Seaberg, J. R. (1981). 'Sampling procedures and techniques', in Grinnell, R. M. (ed.), *Social Work Research and Evaluation* (F. E. Peacock Publishers Inc., USA).

Trotter, C. J. (1990). 'Probation can work, a research study using volunteers', *Australian Journal of Social Work*, 43(2), 13–18.

Truax, C. B., Wargo, D. G. and Silber, D. (1966). 'The effects of group psychotherapy with high accurate empathy and non possessive warmth upon female institutionalised delinquents', *Journal of Abnormal Psychology*, 71(4), 267–74.

Weinbach, R. W. and Grinnell, R. M. (1987). *Statistics for Social Workers* (New York, Longman).

Whitehead, J. T., Lab, S. P. (1989). 'A meta-analysis of juvenile correctional treatment', *Journal of Research in Crime and Delinquency*, 26(3), 276–95.

15

Specialist activities in probation: 'confusion worse confounded'?

GEORGE MAIR

Introduction

Traditionally, probation officers have had a considerable degree of autonomy in how they go about their work. While there have been fashions in working which have come and gone, historically probation officers have been only marginally and loosely controlled within a non-bureacratic management structure; they have never been fully incorporated into a formal bureaucratic system. This situation has been progressively changing and some of the implications of this will be touched upon below, but it remains the case that probation officers still enjoy a considerable degree of independence and discretion in what they do and how they do it despite ten years of governmental initiatives which began with the *Statement of National Objectives and Priorities* (Home Office 1984).

One criticism which has been made often of probation work and which derives at least partially from the independence and discretion of probation officers, is its inconsistency; offenders are dealt with rather differently depending upon the probation area in which they are located. Community service has been particularly criticized in this respect, although straightforward probation supervision has not been immune. In this chapter I want to consider the case of specialist activities run by the probation service within the context of autonomy, independence and wide discretion. How do these impact upon specialist activities and what are the implications of this for effective, efficient, economic and equal service for offenders?

A fairly loose definition of specialist activities will be adopted which can include the obvious, such as work with sex offenders or drug misusers, employment schemes or help with accommodation, but which also covers probation centres (or day centres as they used to be), money payment supervision orders, bail information schemes and the like. Excluded are straight probation, community service and the combination order.

The remainder of the paper is divided into three sections. First, a brief assessment of the nature of the problem. Second, some possible explanations of why the situation is as it has been described. And third, a discussion of what the future might hold for specialist activities in the probation service.

The nature of the problem

In a research project carried out for the Home Office towards the end of the 1980s, Martin Davies and Andrew Wright found that half of the probation officers they surveyed (n=785) described themselves as employed in specialist duties (for example civil work, day centre, hostels, prison-based, etc.) and more than half claimed to have a specialist area of knowledge or expertise which either led to them being allocated special cases or being used in a consultative capacity by colleagues. Specialist knowledge covered such diverse subjects as drugs, welfare rights, sex offending, psychodynamic casework, adult literacy, debt counselling, outdoor pursuits and HIV/AIDS (Davies and Wright 1989). It was rather surprising to find such a large proportion of probation officers who defined themselves as specialists. In the context of the research, Martin Davies argued that this finding had implications for the training of probation officers, but it also raises profound questions about the effectiveness of probation work generally.

One of the consistent findings of research which has been carried out into specialist probation activities is that there is wide variation in the approaches taken. The research carried out into day centres in the second half of the 1980s (Mair 1988) found that: the centres were unevenly distributed around the country; they had varying numbers and types of staffing; they accepted different kinds of offenders (and non-offenders); they opened for different periods of time each week and for different numbers of days; an order could be for 30, 40, 45, 50 or 60 days (and some centres operated two levels of order); programmes of activities varied widely, as did the numbers attending centres and their offences. The report's major conclusion was 'to emphasise the great differences which exist amongst day centres. It is clear that such disparities do not lead to equitable treatment for offenders: and they also raise serious issues concerning the efficiency, effectiveness and economy of day centres'. A later study looking at the reconviction rates associated with day centres found some with rates of lower than 45 per cent while others had rates in excess of 80 per cent (Mair and Nee 1992).

A similar situation was found in a study of the policy and practice of money payment supervision orders (MPSOs) (Mair and Lloyd 1989). A few probation areas actively discouraged MPSOs, some viewed them positively, and the majority had no policy whatsoever in respect of them. Practice varied too with some areas using probation officers to supervise MPSOs, some relying on ancillaries, and some trying out volunteers. The actual supervision process could vary from the odd letter to many face-to-face meetings with offenders in order to try to impose some order upon messy financial situations. Almost 10 per cent of MPSOs ran for less than three months, while 25 per cent ran for two years or more. The conclusion of the report spoke of MPSOs as being in a state of 'considerable confusion. Any signs of coherent and uniform approaches to the use of MPSOs are difficult to discern'.

The same kind of picture is to be found again and again in reports on specialist activities. Paul Henderson, then of the National Institute for Social Work, in his study of community probation work found a situation characterized by uncertainty about what community probation work was and by diversity in the models being used by those who claimed to practice it (Henderson and del Tufo 1991). HM Probation Inspectorate in a thematic inspection on offender employment and the work of the probation service concluded that 'there is considerable room for those involved at an operational level to develop a more managed and co-ordinated response to the subject' (HMIP 1992). And David Downes too has noted a lack of coherent policy and practice with regard to employment schemes for offenders (Downes 1993). Another thematic inspection of the work of the probation service in serving the needs of children involved in separation or divorce noted the wide variations in 'the current provision and operation of the civil work service provided by the nine probation areas involved in this . . . inspection' (HMIP 1991). This finding has been echoed by work carried out by Adrian James and his colleagues on court welfare work. They found that:

differential practices reflect fundamental differences of opinion both

within and between areas about the nature of the task in preparing a
welfare report, in the amount of time that should be devoted to past cases
and voluntary referrals, the kind of conciliation service required and much
else besides. (James and Hay 1992)

Even in an area where there has been a good deal of centralized planning and development – bail information schemes – there remain
differences between schemes, although these are not considerable and
may diminish over time (Lloyd 1992; HMIP 1993). Finally, evidence
from three other recent research projects suggests that variation
remains a key characteristic of probation work with sex offenders
(Barker and Morgan 1993), with drug-related offenders (Nee and
Sibbitt 1993), and in the area of probation motor projects (Martin
1994).

Overall, then, the evidence shows that specialist activities in
probation are neither uniformly distributed nor consistently
organized and operated. They tend to be developed on an *ad hoc*
basis and, as a result, are fragmented and widely varying. An argument can be made that this demonstrates local flexibility and
innovation – and this is certainly not a point which should be
dismissed out of hand. But it can also be argued that it shows uncon-
trolled discretion, lack of accountability, reinvention of the wheel,
'flavour-of-the-monthism', and that it results in inefficiency and
ineffectiveness and provides a poor service to courts and offenders.

Explaining the situation

Why has this situation come about? One key factor, as has been
noted, is the autonomy and independence which have been granted –
possibly by default – to probation officers. Because of the nature of
their work and the traditional one-to-one casework approach, it is
difficult to keep a close watch on probation work and to insist that it
be carried out in certain ways. Unfortunately, this tends to lead
towards an extreme whereby there are as many approaches to dealing
with offenders as there are probation officers; a situation which is
viewed positively by officers and exemplified by such clichés as
'there's no such thing as a normal probation order'. The solution to
this extreme is pictured as closing down all of these options and
forcing probation officers to utilize only one approach; this, of
course, is anathema to officers. The fact that either of these two
extremes is ever likely to happen is irrelevant.

Specialist activities tend to be a 'bottom-up' development and as such lack rational planning and co-ordination. A frivolous example will illustrate what is meant. A probation officer wakes up one morning and decides that she is rather bored by mundane, straightforward probation work. She remembers that there have been a few cases of garden gnome theft recently in her area which seemed to rouse some interest and she decides to become an expert in dealing with garden gnome thieves. She sets up a little programme with the tacit consent of her senior probation officer, talks about it at various conferences, a few other probation officers in different parts of the country realize that this is an interesting area or notice a rash of such thefts and set up programmes of their own. Relatively quickly, there are more than a dozen specialist programmes for garden gnome thieves and numbers are growing. By the time the Home Office, the Association of Chief Officers of Probation, or the Central Probation Council has realized that there are such programmes, it is too late to attempt to co-ordinate them easily. Various approaches have been developed and are held as sacrosanct by their disciples, although there is no research evidence to suggest success. Imposing some form of order or guidelines by this stage is rather like closing the stable door after the horse (or perhaps the gnome) has bolted.

This caricature uncovers the essential elements which – to a greater or lesser extent – lie behind the way in which specialist probation activities are developed and organized. At best, probation officers perceive a new problem which demands a response, but it may be boredom or a desire to get on and be noticed. How often are trends in garden gnome theft monitored in order to assess whether there are enough offenders to keep a programme going for years? If there are not enough offenders then a programme will stumble along, changing its target group in order to justify its existence, watering down its original intentions, and then presumably wondering why it does not work.

There is, too, an element of competition amongst probation services, whereby if Upshire has a garden gnome programme then Downshire must have one. From a good number of years of personal experience of probation research it is clear to me that probation officers who wish to set up a specialist programme rarely know where to get information about previous efforts, or fail to consult widely with colleagues in other areas. Indeed, locally available resources may be ignored in the desire for probation services to provide their own programmes (it should be noted that in some cases, of course, there may be no locally available resources or they may be inappropriate). Thus, programmes are set up on an *ad hoc* basis, they are not fully contextualized within the local probation service, and they lack a clear rationale or theoretical foundation.

Local management must take some of the blame for all of this, and so too must the Home Office. There is no reliable mechanism whereby a new initiative can be brought to the attention either of the Home Office or the professional probation associations. In the late 1980s when risk of custody scales were spreading rapidly, the Home Office only found out about this development when many areas had already introduced scales. Far too often such scales were not well designed, had not been properly validated and were transferred to other areas without any revalidation. This kind of situation could have had serious consequences for prediction scales generally, for the reputation of the local probation service and for the sentencing of offenders.

When the day centre study which was carried out in the mid-1980s was being planned, it came as a considerable surprise to find that there was no list of day centres held in the Home Office. There is still no list of specialist activities held by the Home Office, and this lack of knowledge is at least partly responsible for the uncoordinated development of specialist activities. It also makes life a little harder for research as in at least four recent cases a census of all probation areas has had to be conducted prior to the research proper.

The future

There are already underway several developments which should help to impose some order upon this confused situation. The introduction of national standards, although not directly related to specialist activities, should have a general – though perhaps not immediate – impact in terms of encouraging more consistent approaches (a review of the standards is underway). Similarly, the new 'partnership' policy should encourage probation services to take a closer look at the specialist activities they offer and decide whether these can be more effectively and appropriately delivered by other agencies. It is unfortunate that neither of these developments is being accompanied by research to determine the nature and level of their impact. There is also the example of the model followed for the development of bail information schemes where a National Steering Group has tried – fairly successfully – to control such schemes by providing official endorsement. On the subject of employment there is now a National Offender Employment Forum and work is underway to develop guidance on employment issues for the probation service. And a paper setting out guidance for the service on addressing problems of drug and alcohol misuse among offenders is due to be issued in 1995. While these latter two developments are positive responses, they are entering the game late in the day when trying to impose a coherent structure will be much more difficult.

The Home Office Research and Planning Unit (RPU) has put forward plans for an annual register of specialist activities, which would be made available to the probation policy division and HMIP as well as all probation services. This would help the Home Office keep abreast of specialist developments, and help probation services see what other areas are doing. It is hoped that we might be able to begin collaborative work on this in the near future.

Ideally, one might envisage a system whereby any novel specialist programmes could be identified at a very early stage – preferably before they had begun operating, at the planning/design stage. Monitoring should have been carried out to ensure that there would be an adequate throughput of appropriate offenders, and the proposed programme should be based upon some coherent theory. The programme could be brought to the attention of HMIP who, perhaps with the RPU, could ensure that some form of basic 'natural history' of it all was prepared. After a minimum of twelve months, decisions could be made as to whether or not such a programme was necessary or desirable in other areas. At this point a number of programmes utilizing different models of organization and operation could be set up and a research/evaluation exercise designed. On completion of the research, good practice guidelines for such a programme would be issued and a uniform monitoring system for all specialist programmes of the specific type put in place. A system such as this would not eliminate the flexibility of local probation services or inhibit the desire or need to be innovative; it would control and channel discretion and lead to greater consistency.

The approach to specialist activities up to now has been almost one of 'let a thousand flowers bloom' and then benign neglect. Individual specialist activities may only account for a small proportion of probation work but taken together they probably now take up more than half of such work. A more co-ordinated and structured approach can only be to the advantage of all concerned, and particularly offenders.

References

Barker, M. and Morgan, R. (1993). *Sex Offenders: a framework for the evaluation of community-based treatment* (London, Home Office).

Davies, M. and Wright, A. (1989).*The Changing Face of Probation* (Norwich, University of East Anglia).

Downes, D. (1993). *Employment Schemes for Ex-Offenders* (London, Home Office).

Henderson, P. and del Tufo, S. (1991). *Community Work and the Probation Service* (London, HMSO).

HMIP. (1991). *The Work of the Probation Service in Serving the Needs of Children Involved in Separation or Divorce* (London, Home Office).

HMIP. (1992). *Offenders into Work: report of a thematic inspection* (London, Home Office).

HMIP. (1993). *Bail Information: report of a thematic inspection* (London, Home Office).

Home Office. (1984). *Probation Service in England and Wales: Statement of National Objectives and Priorities* (London, Home Office).

James, A. and Hay, W. (1992). *Court Welfare Work: research, practice and development* (University of Hull, Centre for Criminology and Criminal Justice).

Lloyd, C. (1992). *Bail Information Schemes: practice and effect*, RPU Paper 69 (London, Home Office).

Mair, G. (1988). *Probation Day Centres*, HORS 100 (London, HMSO).

Mair, G. and Lloyd, C. (1989). *Money Payment Supervision Orders: probation policy and practice*, HORS 114 (London, HMSO).

Mair, G. and Nee, C. (1992). 'Day centre reconviction rates', *British Journal of Criminology*, 32(3).

Martin, J. (1994). *Probation Motor Projects in England and Wales*.

Nee, C. and Sibbitt, R. (1993). *The Probation Response to Drug Misuse*, RPU Paper 78 (London, Home Office).

16

Criminal justice cultures: negotiating bail and remand

FIONA PATERSON AND CLAIRE WHITTAKER

Introduction

In this chapter we are going to use some findings from an observational study of how bail decisions are made within the Scottish criminal justice system in order to explore the notion of criminal justice culture and its usefulness as an explanation for bail practices. The study was carried out between 1991 and 1993.[1] It focused on sheriff court cases[2] and its purpose was to provide both a *description of bail practice* and practitioner accounts and to develop an *explanation of that practice* in order to consider its significance for future policy on bail. To collect the information we asked police and prosecutors (procurators fiscal) about their Bail Act decisions over a twelve-week period in each of three areas (Doon, Tweed and Braid).[3] We observed court practices in the areas and we interviewed sheriffs and those defence agents who appealed a bail decision during the study. Cases were followed through to final disposal, and crown counsel and bail appeal judges were also interviewed. In addition, we conducted a census of court use of bail in the study areas over a nine-month period. In this chapter we are going to focus on the prosecution and court stages of bail. We shall start off by explaining how bail is operated in Scotland, look at some of the patterns of bail decisions which we identified in the study courts and then consider alternative models of decision-making (traditional model and cultural model) and discuss some of their implications.

Bail in Scotland

The 1980 Bail . . . (Scotland) Act has been created and operates within a different legislative framework to the Bail Act of 1976 in England and Wales and a different range of options are available to criminal justice decision-makers. The police in Scotland cannot release people on bail, but they have the options of: reporting an incident to the procurator fiscal who may have an accused summonsed to court; releasing the accused on undertaking to appear at court on a specified date (which must be within one week of arrest); and detaining someone in custody to appear at court on the next lawful day.

There are three options that the court can take if the case does not reach final disposal at the first diet. The least restrictive outcome of court is that the accused may be ordained to appear at court on a certain day. If they fail to appear they may be charged with contempt of court, but there are no other restrictions on the accused. This is similar to a remand on unconditional bail in England and Wales. Secondly, the accused may be granted bail with standard conditions. These are: to appear at court on a certain day; not to commit an offence on bail; and not to interfere with witnesses. The court can attach any other condition to the bail order in order to secure the protection of the public and the administration of justice. These are known as special conditions and are similar to a remand on conditional bail in England and Wales. Thirdly, the accused can be remanded in custody. Case law has established that if the accused enters a plea of not guilty, the sheriff can only refuse bail if the procurator fiscal opposes bail in court. If the accused enters a guilty plea, the remand decision is totally at the discretion of the sheriff. In England and Wales there is a statutory presumption in favour of bail and the defendant does not apply for bail unless the prosecutor objects to bail in court. In Scotland the presumption in favour of bail has been established by case law and it is necessary for the accused to make a bail application to the court, regardless of whether or not the prosecution objects to bail.

There are three types of offence which are recorded under the Scottish Bail Act. The charges most frequently libelled are those of failing to appear at court (Bail . . . (Scotland) Act 1980 S(3)(1)(a)) and of breaching a condition by offending while on bail (Bail . . . (Scotland) Act 1980 S(3)(1)(b)), although this section of the Act also covers breach of other conditions, including special conditions. In England and Wales there is no comparable offence to the charge of offending on bail although there is now legislation to enable the courts there to treat the committing of an offence while on bail as an aggravation.

Patterns of bail

From the court census, which recorded bail decisions for first appearances in the study courts over nine months, we identified wide variations in practice. Figure 1 shows that of the three courts, Doon had the highest use of bail, and Braid had the highest use of remands in custody.

Figure 1 Sheriff court bail census: outcome of first court (%ages).*

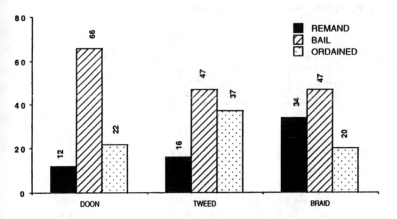

*Includes solemn and summary cases. Doon n = 814; Tweed n = 1620, Braid n = 1073.

A high use of bail was accompanied by a high use of police custody, with police in Doon detaining people in custody at twice the rate of police at Braid. Braid and Tweed sheriff courts liberated just under 50 per cent of accused on bail, but Braid remanded in custody twice the proportion that were remanded in custody in Tweed and nearly three times the proportion that were remanded at Doon. In Tweed 37 per cent of accused were ordained to appear again, whereas at Doon and Braid only 20 per cent were ordained to appear at the next hearing.

One response to this is simply to say that these differences can be explained by differences in the seriousness of case being processed in each area. However, as important as seriousness is for understanding what happens with particular cases in the criminal justice system, we found that of *at least as much importance* is the relationship between different parts of the criminal justice system and the ways in which they approach the processing of cases. This is why it is to practice which we must look to understand the way in which the Act is being operated. We examined this in some detail by looking at a sample of accused whose cases were recorded in the census (main sample). These are the accused who were the focus of our observation field-work. Over twelve weeks in each area we observed all cases where accused were detained in custody by police or released on under-taking (Figure 2).

Figure 2 Percentage of main sample* accused for whom procurator fiscal opposed bail (custody and undertaking).

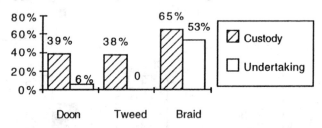

*Custody: Doon n = 115; Tweed n = 167; Braid n = 151; Undertaking: Doon n = 32; Tweed n = 20; Braid n = 19

The higher use of remand at Braid is partially explained by the fact that the fiscal there was much more likely to oppose bail than the fiscal in other areas. The difference in responding to accused on undertaking in each area was stark, with bail not being opposed for any of those accused in Tweed but being opposed in over half in Braid. It is worth noting that, in Doon, when fieldwork started some prosecutors expressed surprise at the inclusion of undertakings in the study since they rarely opposed bail in such cases; in Tweed prosecutors were mystified at their inclusion in the study; but in Braid their inclusion went unremarked.

In the present discussion we focus on accused in custody cases. The distinctiveness of prosecution response to accused at Braid held when we distinguished those involved in solemn and those involved in summary cases (that is serious cases where trial would be by jury or which could go to the High Court; and less serious cases where trial would be before a single sheriff who could impose a maximum custodial sentence of three years). Bail was opposed for accused in around one-third of summary cases where the accused appeared from custody and just over a half of accused in solemn cases in Doon and

Tweed. In contrast, in Braid, bail was opposed in just over half of accused in summary cases and nine out of ten accused in solemn cases. Prosecutors in Braid therefore opposed bail much more frequently for accused in all case types than did prosecutors in other areas. Indeed the proportion of accused in solemn cases for whom bail was opposed in Doon is similar to that for accused in summary cases in Braid. The more frequent opposition to bail by prosecutors in Braid was consistent across the four main categories of case which we examined (Figure 3).

Figure 3 Percentage of main sample accused (police custodies) for whom procurator fiscal opposed bail by case type.

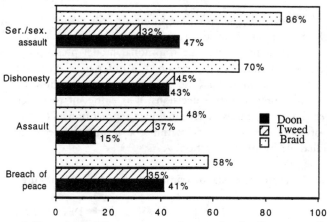

Figure 4 Outcome of first court: main sample pleading not guilty in summary cases: percentage where procurator fiscal opposed bail.

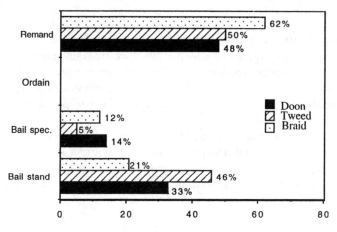

As could be expected, given the census results, for accused in main sample cases not only were the prosecutors in Braid more likely to oppose bail in court, but there was an increased chance that the court in Braid would refuse bail once it had been opposed, even for accused pleading not guilty in summary cases (Figure 4).

Figure 4 shows that while bail was refused for around half of accused in the summary cases in Doon and Tweed where the fiscal opposed bail, in Braid bail was refused for over 60 per cent of such accused and only 21 per cent were granted bail with standard conditions compared to one third in Doon and almost half in Tweed.

Models of decision-making

What this implies is that what we would describe as the 'traditional model' of criminal justice decision-making cannot help us to understand these bail practices. The traditional model presupposes that differences in pattern can be explained by differences in cases and in the practices of *individual* decision-makers. It assumes that to understand criminal justice decisions, it is sufficient to understand that legitimate responses of criminal justice practitioners to pre-given facts of cases can only vary within the legally defined limits of individual practitioner discretion.

Figure 5 Traditional model of criminal justice decision-making.

FACTS	+ INDIVIDUAL	+ LAW	⟶ DECISIONS
OF	DISCRETION		
CASE			

The inadequacies of atomized models of explanation are, of course, not surprising to any social scientist. What we are arguing here is that a more satisfactory explanatory model of the way in which the law on bail is being applied – that is one which can account for the type of systematic variation which we have identified – needs to take account of

— the *form* of criminal justice relationships – which are established by the institutional structure of the criminal justice system and its integral relationships of power and authority
— the *content* of the relationships – how that structure is negotiated

by those working within it (that means recognizing the localized context of decisions)
— the *focus* of the relationships – the level and type of local criminal activity and the constituent features of the cases (incident/accused/victim/evidence) which are being dealt with in the criminal justice system.

The interaction between these elements produces not simply a series of individual decisions, but generates a *culture* which operates to encourage some types of decision and to discourage others. Such a model can help us consider the dynamics of the relationships between structure, knowledge and social interaction and enable us to make sense of the systematic differences which we have identified in bail decision making in the study areas. Figure 6 shows the elements which interact in the construction of a criminal case in response to an incident.

Figure 6 Cultural model of criminal justice decision-making.

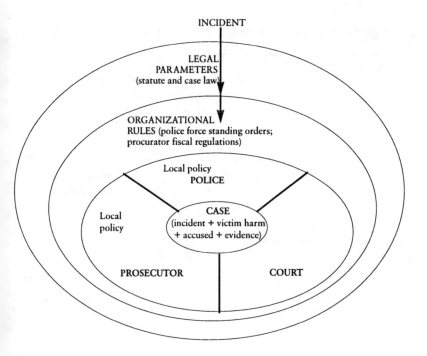

The culture is produced by the interaction of all parts of the system, it is not simply the result of the wishes of one part, such as the court, although the impact of pressure from one part of the system on another will be affected by authority relations within the system. For this reason courts are of particular significance. In addition, there tends to be a heightened awareness of court views since they are more visible to the public and criminal justice practitioners. This is because, unlike police and prosecution bail decision-making – which are not public and, if they are discussed at all, are only discussed in the privacy of the police or prosecutor's office – court deliberations on bail and commentary on police and prosecution action tend to be pronounced in public in the courtroom. Those elements of criminal justice culture which are less visible are nevertheless important since, as we have argued, local criminal justice culture is produced and reproduced by the interaction and experience of all criminal justice agencies within different localities. The patterns we have described are therefore the results of these interactions. We have developed a typology of the criminal justice cultures which we studied (Figure 7).

Figure 7 Typology of criminal justice cultures.

Culture type	Police	Prosecution	Court
Bail (Doon)	high use of custody	*presumption of bail* for police custodies and undertakings	*high use of bail* low use of remand and ordain *low use of custodial sentences*
Liberation (Tweed)	low use of custody medium use of undertaking	*presumption of ordain* unless police custody	*high use of ordain* medium use of bail low use of remand *low use of custodial sentences*
Remand (Braid)	low use of custody	*regular opposition to bail* for cases released by police	*high use of remand* medium use of bail low use of ordain *high use of custodial sentences*

Negotiating bail and remand

The two examples of ways in which these cultures were manifest at the point of negotiating bail and remand and which we will discuss here are: prosecutor interpretations of record and courtroom interaction around bail applications. Both fiscal decisions about their attitude to bail and courtroom discussions of bail tend to be very brief – usually taking no more than two or three minutes. The volume of cases and the short time available for processing them together promote the routinization of practice and help to foster the development of the shared assumptions necessary for practitioners to get through prosecution and court business. These shared assumptions are the localized norms or parameters within which practitioners work to interpret the law and they serve to reduce the number of cases over which the appropriate course of court action is disputed. These norms are a product not only of past criminal justice decisions, but also of present practice. For the most part practitioners' awareness of norms tends to take the form of the anticipation of likely court response to cases and a recognition that 'the way things are done' in one court may differ from the way in which they are done in another. This is often understood as being about the preferences and idiosyncrasies of particular sheriffs although, as we have suggested above, a broader perspective on criminal justice relations is more appropriate.

Record is usually the focus of court interaction on bail, and prosecutors at Braid were more likely to interpret the record of main sample accused as 'serious' than were prosecutors in the other areas. This was a major explanation of why they were more likely to oppose bail. It should be said that although accused at Braid were no more likely than accused in other areas to have previous convictions, they were more likely to have served custodial sentences (49 per cent of police custodies at Braid had served a custodial sentence in the previous three years compared with 41 per cent at Tweed and 31 per cent at Doon). However, the key distinction between the interpretations of record by prosecutors at Braid and those at Doon and Tweed related to their views on bail history. Bail history refers both to the existence of current bail orders and to an accused's record of bail convictions. In all areas, records showing convictions for an accused failing to appear at court were likely to result in fiscals opposing bail. However, prosecutors at Braid were more likely to consider that the existence of a current bail order or of any Bail Act conviction, whether for failure to appear or for offending on bail, as being a contra-indicator for bail. In contrast, prosecutors in Doon and Tweed were more likely to temper their view of the significance of bail history by taking greater account of the age of offending on bail convictions, the length of time a bail order had been in existence or the extent to which the bail associated case was similar to the present case. Disputes in court about whether or not bail was appropriate for particular accused tended to turn on interpretations of criminal record. A defence agent who could successfully bring the court to accept *their* interpretation of an accused's record rather than that of the procurator fiscal would be likely to have their client released on bail.

Courtroom discussions, being for the most part brief, were to a significant extent reliant on the shared assumptions of those involved. Shared assumptions are, as we have indicated, usually tacit as it is only necessary for them to be referred to directly, to the extent that any understanding is not shared by all participants. This is most likely to happen when encounters involve strangers, such as prosecutors, defence agents and temporary sheriffs who do not normally appear in a particular court. We want to stress that the existence of shared assumptions did not mean that prosecutors always agreed with court outcomes or that sheriffs necessarily refused bail when it was opposed. Nor did it mean an absence of defence or prosecution argument on bail applications. Rather, it meant that most courtroom exchanges focused on the charges outlined on the complaint (though not the detail of the incidents), details of individual criminal records and sometimes some information about the social circumstances of accused, rather than on how the cases should be approached or on the position on bail adopted by prosecutors or defence agents.

During the study we observed instances where understandings were not shared and which threw localized norms into relief. In Doon and Tweed such incidents took the form of sheriffs questioning the appropriateness of opposition to bail, defence agents being questioned about their failure to make an application or being advised about the timing of a bail application. In Braid they were always about the prosecution's *failure to oppose bail* and therefore about the court's inability to remand such accused. For example, in Doon, when a prosecutor who normally worked elsewhere opposed bail in a case where the sheriff indicated that there should have been no question of a remand, the sheriff on granting bail, turned to the fiscal and said that it would be 'draconian' to remand in a case which would not receive a custodial sentence. However, in Braid, where there was little shared understanding of the relative role of the fiscal and the sheriff in relation to bail, prosecutors would often be reproached in court for not opposing bail.

> Sheriff (sarcastically and incredulously):
> Bail is not opposed, Mr Procurator Fiscal. Well, well – there's something – disqualified driving and drunk driving and bail is not opposed.

Such statements were not restricted to particular cases and would sometimes be made between cases. For example, as one accused left the dock and another was brought in, the sheriff addressed the prosecutor directly.

> I thought that the public interest was a consideration in deciding on bail.

In interview, a sheriff at Braid referred directly to this type of courtroom incident.

> I really do resent in some cases having to grant bail on the directions of the high court because the Crown does not oppose it in a case where I think it should be refused . . . I have adopted a formula in a case such as that, of saying that bail is granted solely on the ground that the prosecutor does not object and I insist that appears in the bail interlocutor, because the newspapers who are the people who are always bleating about this that and the other, don't consider the niceties of things and always blame the court.

In the context of this pressure by the court for remand, it is unsurprising that a higher proportion of those accused for whom the fiscal opposed bail were remanded in that area. Sheriffs in the other study areas expressed a reluctance to remand people pre-trial, especially if they were young, and argued that in summary cases there should rarely be any question of a pre-trial remand

> I remain to be convinced that the public will be any better protected by such containment for a limited period before conviction rather than after it. (sheriff at Tweed)

> If it's a young person, by that I mean someone under 25, I'd be very, very reluctant. If it is someone with a bit of a criminal record brought to my attention by the procurator fiscal I might have to think about it . . . I prefer on summary criminal matters to allow them bail. Especially young people. (sheriff at Tweed)

This contrasted directly with the views expressed at Braid about pre-trial remand.

> There are lots of problems caused by young people. If they are left out then they will simply commit more offences . . . Regular housebreakers are a worry to the public and they should be remanded. (sheriff at Braid)

Conclusions: implications of criminal justice cultures

Although many implications arise from the existence of different criminal justice cultures we can explore only two here. In order to do this we shall first briefly look at the outcomes for accused in the main sample summary cases referred to earlier.

As would be expected, Figure 8 shows that Braid had a higher use of imprisonment for summary cases than Doon and Tweed. Both Doon and Braid had a high proportion of accused whose cases were marked as no further proceedings or who were not convicted. This high level is particularly important if it is considered in the context of local propensities to remand or release on bail. At Doon 80 per cent (24) of those who were not convicted had either been bailed or ordained during the case. In Tweed the proportion was 82 per cent (14). However, in Braid 48 per cent (14) had been remanded. An important implication of the culture of remand is therefore that more people who were not ultimately convicted of the crimes of which they were accused had spent time in prison.

A further, and longer-term implication of an increased readiness to resort to custody can be considered by looking at the impact of local criminal justice cultures on individual cases. Cases of one accused in each area and who had similar characteristics will be discussed. All were sixteen, each had appeared more than once in the sample and each was involved in a mixture of dishonesty, breach of the peace and minor assault. In Doon and Tweed these accused were released on bail and ultimately given non-custodial sentences, in Braid the accused was remanded at the second court appearance and then given a custodial sentence.

The accused in Doon came into the sample five times during the twelve-week period of the study, mainly in connection with dishonesty offences. There was no loss and no victim in an incident involving a breach of the peace and the loss to the victims in the other cases was, respectively, £10–£50 recovered; £101–£250 not recovered;

Figure 8 Final disposal: main sample accused in summary cases (police custodies) (percentage).

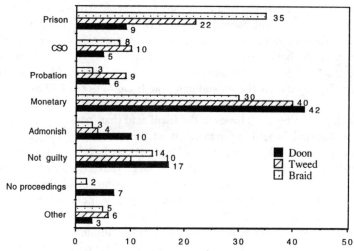

'Other' = sentence deferred, hospital order, case incomplete. The number of cases categorized as 'other' is higher at Tweed and Braid. A cut-off point for data collection had to be set which was September 1992 for Doon and Tweed and March 1993 for Braid. These dates were 15 months after the end of fieldwork in Doon, 9 months in Tweed and 11 months in Braid. Cases remaining incomplete after this date were recorded as 'other'.

£51–£100 (damage); £10-£50 (damage). On his first appearance the fiscal agreed bail at marking and in court as, although he had a record of having appeared before the children's panel, he had no previous convictions. During the study this accused was released on bail three times by the court. However, at the fourth case the fiscal marked the case as bail to be opposed because of the three bail orders for analogous charges and the fact that thirteen other charges were expected. On this occasion the accused pled guilty and was granted bail. On the fifth appearance the fiscal agreed bail because of his 'relatively short record' and also they believed that the evidence in this case was not strong. Bail was granted by the court. For none of these cases did the offender receive a custodial sentence: probation, two fines of £40 each and two community service orders.

The offender in Tweed came into the sample three times in connection with dishonesty, breach of the peace and minor assault.

There was slight injury to the victim in one case and the loss to the victims in the other cases was, respectively, £51–£100 recovered; no loss or damage. In the first case, the fiscal agreed bail – knowing that the accused had substantial previous involvement with the panel and a pending case. However, the fiscal stated that this accused would seem to the court as if he had no previous convictions. At court the accused entered a guilty plea and sentence was deferred for a social enquiry report. At the second case, the fiscal opposed bail as it was only one week since the accused had been released on bail for analogous offences. However, the fiscal said that it was unlikely that the accused would be remanded as he had only one previous conviction on which sentence had been deferred, 'but it's my duty to try and get him locked up if these [charges] are true'. In court the depute opposed bail on the grounds that the accused had already been put on bail the previous week and that the present charges related to two incidents, saying 'offences of this nature and escalating in this way indicate that there is no evidence that this young man is prepared to behave himself'. The defence agent emphasized the age of the accused saying that he was very young to be remanded and reminding the court of the presumption of innocence. The defence agent also stated that the accused lived with his mother and required medical treatment regularly. The sheriff granted bail saying that they were 'reluctant to lock someone up at such a young age and with such a short record'. In the third case, the fiscal agreed bail saying that they were reluctant to have someone of that age kept in custody. There was no discussion of bail in court. The offender received a community service order for all the charges.

The loss to the victims in the two cases involving the offender at Braid was respectively, £20 unrecovered; and £101–£250 unrecovered. The offender in Braid did not have any adult convictions although he was currently on a children's panel supervision order. During the period of the study the supervision order ceased as the panel felt it was having no effect. In the first case the fiscal agreed bail saying that the accused had been under supervision since 1988 but had repeatedly offended and this was increasing. The depute said that this incident would under other circumstances have gone to the district court but that he had put it to the sheriff court since the local district court rarely used custodial sentences: 'I'm not being vindictive, it's not in the public interest for him to think that he can go on behaving in this way. He has to understand what's involved if he is going to embark on an adult life of crime.' In court the depute agreed bail, asked for a special condition and this was granted. The offender turned up for his next court appearance. However, in his second sample case he was kept in custody by police and in this instance the fiscal opposed bail, saying that the accused had 'numerous outstanding charges' with a history of dishonesty dating back to 1988 (when he had been on supervision); he was on a recent bail order and had since been arrested again for another matter for which police had released him for summons (details of this case were therefore not recorded in the sample). The depute at marking said they would oppose bail 'to let him see what would happen to him', and in court the fiscal opposed bail saying that although this offender had no previous convictions he had numerous appearances before the panel and was currently on a supervision order which was about to be terminated. They stated that he was on recent bail and yet was again attracting the attention of the police three days later, 'it is obvious that he intends to continue offending'. The defence agent emphasized the age of the offender, describing him as 'very young and impressionable if remanded'. Bail was refused and an appeal on the grounds of age was also refused. The offender subsequently pled guilty to the charges in this second case and was remanded for social enquiry reports. However, later the defence agent requested a bail review and bail was granted. After release from this initial remand this offender did subsequently fail to appear for the sentence deferred and the trial diet for the earlier charge, and he was later remanded when he appeared from police custody having been arrested on warrant. He eventually received a three-month custodial sentence concurrent on both charges with one-month imprisonment to run consecutively on bail act charge.

In this case, although the prosecutor was initially not prepared to oppose bail, at the second case bail was opposed on the grounds of pending cases and the accused's history of dishonesty which had been dealt with by the children's hearing. This offender had appeared at court after his initial release on bail but he failed to appear after he had experienced remand. Letting him see what could happen to him in the criminal justice system did not secure this offender's compliance with the wishes of the court.

These examples illustrate some of the issues raised by the operation of particular criminal justice responses to accused. All these offenders were under twenty-one and had been involved in minor dishonesties. They fall within the group which we already know is highly likely to be involved in recidivism. Whereas the offenders at Doon and Tweed were repeatedly being detained in custody by the police and this resulted in repeat use of court bail for offences which ultimately attracted non-custodial sentences, the response of the criminal justice system at Braid was to bring the offender quickly into custody.

In Doon and Tweed the offenders were involved in a series of minor dishonesties, and their release would therefore involve some cost to the local community as well as making a contribution to levels of recorded offending on bail. Nevertheless, at the end of their cases they were going to be serving non-custodial sentences and this implies that, whatever problems these offenders may have caused prior to their conviction, remanding them would not have been a solution consistent with the court's sentencing response to their offences. In Braid, the criminal justice response would, in the short term, minimize the impact of the offender's behaviour on the community. However, it is not clear that an early remand for the accused at Braid was securing the administration of justice. In the longer term, should this offender have further contact with the criminal justice system, then the readiness of the system to bring him so quickly into custody and to retain him there at sentence would contribute to the creation for this sixteen year-old of a record which is more quickly going to be defined as 'serious', since a history of custodial sentences was in all areas taken as indicating this and therefore as a contra-indicator for bail.

This chapter has provided a preliminary exploration of criminal justice cultures and their implications for bail and remand. Levels of recorded bail abuse and levels of custodial remand are an ongoing concern. However, the public anxieties expressed about the recorded levels of each are an expression of anxiety about the effectiveness of the criminal justice system in both protecting the public and securing the administration of justice. What we have identified in our research is that different interpretations of the most appropriate means of securing these have consequences which must be considered both in their short-term and long-term implications. A failure to consider the extent to which individual decisions contribute to and are produced by local cultures generated within the criminal justice system, will inevitably limit our capacity for understanding bail.

Acknowledgements

This study was funded by the Scottish Office Home and Health Department. The research would not have been possible without the co-operation of sheriff court staff, police, procurator fiscal staff and members of the judiciary in the study areas who helped us by participating in the research. We are grateful to all who gave of their time to talk to us about their work. Finally, we would like to acknowledge the forbearance of our families who tolerated our long absences on fieldwork.

Notes

[1] Fiona Paterson and Claire Whittaker, *Operating Bail* (London, HMSO, 1994).

[2] Sheriff courts are presided over by a sheriff and jury (for cases being dealt with under solemn procedure) or a sheriff alone (for cases being dealt with under summary procedure). Any common law crime or statutory offence can be prosecuted summarily in the sheriff court except for those for which the high court has exclusive jurisdiction or unless statute specifies that they may only be tried under solemn procedure. Maximum powers of a sheriff court are fine not exceeding £2,000 or imprisonment of not more than three months. Maximum period of imprisonment is extended to six months for a second or subsequent dishonesty or offence involving personal violence. For full description of Scottish courts see A. L. Stewart, *The Scottish Criminal Courts in Action* (Edinburgh, Butterworth, 1990).

[3] To anonymize the study areas names of Scottish rivers have been used. The locations of the rivers do not reflect the locations of the areas studied.

17

Politics and prison management: the Northern Ireland experience

BRIAN GORMALLY AND KIERAN MCEVOY[1]

Introduction

Prison management must be one of the most difficult and complex areas of practice within the overall discipline of management. The prison manager has all the usual problems associated with getting things done through other people.[2] In addition, however, the main thing to be done is to keep a lot of other human beings in an unnatural and inherently stressful condition of captivity. With so many human factors involved, the currents of different interests, perceptions and emotions can easily develop into a destructive whirlpool. Furthermore, prison managers often perceive their area of practice as being frequently and comprehensively overrun by ideological and explicitly political demands which may have nothing to do with the immediate concerns of good management.

Recent experience in Britain would appear to support that view. The call for more 'austere' regimes is not, we may surmise, disinterested advice to prison managers, but rather an example of an ideological foray into territory long claimed as a political battleground. Similarly, the announcement by the home secretary of the building of six new prisons – to be placed under private management – is not simply a statement about the penological contention that 'prison works'. Leaving aside the arguments on that dubious view, few would dispute that it represents the importation into the prison service of an explicitly party political ideology – privatization – which has been developed in an intellectual arena quite separate from prison management (Ryan and Ward 1989).

On the other hand, many would claim that the way society administers its harshest sanction against the individual is an inherently political question (Garland and Young 1983). Indeed, the very concept of 'prison management' is at times impugned (Boyle 1984). Some elements of right and left may actually meet in denouncing the idea. It is seen, on the one hand, as devaluing the sacred duty of chastizing evildoers or, on the other, as masking the repressive conspiracies of an authoritarian state (Scraton *et al.* 1991). A broader consensus of opinion would accept that the demands of accountability require some political engagement with the prison system (Fitzgerald 1986). Certainly, it would be naive to suggest that the equally ideological concept of a value-free, politically disengaged but omniscient super management is an adequate riposte to the dynamics thrown up by the interaction between prison management and politics. Rather, what is needed is an acknowledgement that the relationship is fundamental and a systematic analysis of how it works.

The relevance of the Northern Ireland experience

We believe that Northern Ireland experience may give particular insight into the relationship between prison politics and management, precisely because the prison system has operated in an atmosphere of sharp and violent political confrontation.

In Northern Ireland, the standing of successive ministerial administrations has been largely defined, not by progress towards political settlement, but by progress in terms of security policy. In effect, that means the number of 'terrorists'[3] who can be locked up in prison. The vast majority of those thereby locked up will define themselves as political prisoners.

Perhaps the key political battle of the past fifteen years – the hunger strikes of 1980/81 – was focused explicitly on the prisons. During that time ten prisoners starved themselves to death over the symbols of criminal rather than political imprisonment, there was widespread violence, and the British government was widely criticized in the international community for its perceived intransigence (Beresford 1987: 132).

Prison matters are still of immediate political significance. Organized violence, either against rival paramilitary groupings or against prison staff, persists (Colville 1992). In terms of local party politics, practically the only issue to unite Unionist and Nationalist politicians on Belfast City Council in the early 1990s was the call for segregation of Republican and Loyalist remand prisoners in HMP

Belfast. In short, nowhere is the interaction between politics and prison management more acute.

It could, of course, be argued that the very singularity of the Northern Ireland experience makes it irrelevant for any other system. Certainly, the Northern Ireland prison population is an unusual one after twenty-five years of political violence. The IRA prosecuted its campaign of violence against what it regards as the British occupation of the North of Ireland (Bishop and Mallie 1989; Bowyer Bell 1979; Coogan 1985). Loyalist paramilitaries, who wish to maintain the link between Northern Ireland and Britain, continued their own campaign against the Catholic community, whom they perceive as sympathetic to the IRA and its objectives. The result, as we have indicated above, is a prison population consisting of at least two-thirds of prisoners whose original motivation was political, many of them serving long sentences.

We would argue, however, that every system has its unique features and problems, but that many issues of prison management – and its relationship to politics – remain the same. The principal focus of prison management must be the interaction with prisoners. How to exercise authority without violent confrontation; defining an irreducible bedrock of principle; delineating the limits of pragmatism; refining attitudes to prisoner organization; how to practice genuine negotiation without collaboration or collusion – these issues exist in any prison system and have been particularly illuminated in the Northern Ireland system over the past two decades. The interaction between politics and prison management is not a simple relationship here, any more than in more 'peaceful' jurisdictions. It is our perception, however, that the urgency and seriousness of prison politics in Northern Ireland shines a brighter light on the dynamics which exist in all prison systems.

The structure of our analysis

Our analysis of the Northern Ireland experience of the relationship between politics and prison management is structured as follows:

1. An exploration of terminological difficulty and the consequent construction of a four-point analytical framework within which many of the salient issues may be compared.
2. The application of this analytical framework to three models of

prison management which we believe have applied over the past two decades.
3. A discussion of some of the methodological and theoretical issues raised by the study, together with some tentative conclusions.

An analytical framework

The above discussion makes clear that there is not a simple relationship between politics and prison management. Indeed, a fundamental problem in this analysis is the definition of the elements at work. We must therefore attempt to define our terms. Politics is not an easy concept to define. None the less it is important that we outline what we are talking about. For if we see politics simply as the way relations between people are organized,[4] or if, indeed, 'the personal is political', then prison management is simply a subdivision of politics. On the other hand, if we only define politics as something done by politicians, we will miss the complexity of the actual interaction between managers and their ministerial overlords.

A slightly more sophisticated view is to restrict the term politics to the processes by which governmental decisions are influenced and made.[5] That definition has some analytical utility, but it does tend to separate off 'political' activity from similar processes, indistinguishable by way of the modes of thinking and forms of interaction involved, which lead to decisions in forums other than government. For our current purpose, the main problem with this is that all activity within a state system, except that explicitly designed to influence a ministerial decision, is designated as 'non-political'. To erect a *cordon sanitaire* between a narrow definition of politics and other forms of human interaction is not only to misrepresent reality but also to risk serious misunderstanding of the respective roles of politicians and managers.

Political scientists who favour the so-called 'policy approach' to the relationship between politics and administration, stress the interaction between politicians and senior managers. The implementation of policy is seen as a process of compromise and pluralist bargaining (Ham and Hill 1984). 'Administrators are as much involved in decision-making as elected politicians' (Loughlin 1992). However, it is not enough simply to stress the fact of interaction between managers and politicians; we have to investigate its character and extent.

Our view is that it is possible to construct an analytical model that can do some sort of justice to the complexity involved. Our approach to this problem is to begin by examining the concrete roles of the political leadership of the state (the government) and those who manage the various executive systems of the state. These latter may be civil servants, court officials, army officers, health service managers, police officers or prison governors. In general, the first role of the government is to determine policy in a particular sphere. Irrespective of how democratic a political system is or is not, a government will be reacting to some kind of constituency – or more usually, constituencies – within 'civil society';[6] its job is to translate the wishes of those constituencies into action by the state. The government has at least three fundamental ways of translating policy into practice. First, the passage of legislation (including any associated regulations). Second, the exercise of its monetary and fiscal powers and the allocation of the state funds thus raised. Third, executive action, which means, in practice, an instruction to one or more servants of the state to do or cease to do something.

In general terms, the role of state managers is to implement the will of the government as expressed in legislation, financial allocation or ministerial instruction. It is therefore possible to distinguish between the normal spheres of action of government politicians and state managers without denying a continuity of both modes of thinking and forms of human interaction between these spheres. In other words, both politicians and managers take 'political' decisions, but in different concrete circumstances and, hence, with different levels of significance on a general/particular continuum.

We may therefore divide issues (matters about which decisions must be taken) into strategic and tactical or (for convenience of engaging with the debate we have introduced, and risking giving the impression of a strict dichotomy we reject) political and managerial. On the whole, but by no means exclusively, politicians make decisions about the former and managers about the latter. When it comes to a particular executive system of the state, in our case the prison system, it is possible to visualize two 'blocks' of issues which roughly correspond to the spheres of operation respectively of politicians and managers. It is further possible to construct a typology of issues which groups them in ways which may help to illuminate the nature of the relationship between particular political stances and particular managerial styles. The following are examples of how this might be done.

'Political' issues
— Ideological debate about the function of prisons (for example rehabilitation or humane containment).
— Shifting emphases on particular elements of the prison regime (for example security, conditions for prisoners).
— The use of prisons for 'external' purposes, practically and/or symbolically (for example changing regimes to emphasize an overall 'tough' approach to law and order, using regimes as part of a war against terrorism).
— The 'invasion' of ideologically determined policies from other sectors of society (for example privatization).

'Management' issues
— Security levels and practices.
— Discipline and punishment methods and policy; nature of rules and adjudicatory mechanisms on a due process/ discretionary continuum.
— Level and forms of inmate organization and interaction with the authorities; extent of recognition of prisoner leaders; extent of freedom of association.
— Practical existence of, and regime emphasis on, work, training, sport, education.
— Regime symbolism – prison clothing, enforcement of prison work, prison officer uniforms, logos and emblems.
— Family/community contact – forms of, and facilities for, visiting; mail procedures; access to telephones etc.
— Nature of release, parole and home leave procedures and nature of control over them.

Our view is that it is possible to take a selection of these management issues and examine them against an analysis of the contemporary political status of the prison system as defined by the current interplay of the political issues identified above.

Clearly, the above are only some of the more significant issues to arise out of prison management. We ought to note also that, for the purposes of this model, we have ignored the relationship between management and staff, and the latter's role, morale and forms of union organization. Our current concern is the relationship between management and prisoners, though we understand that it is mediated through the ranks of prison officers. Neither have we listed the range of issues around the organization of management itself, though we understand the importance of matters such as the relationship between central administrators and governors. Another aspect of the equation is the changing policies of resistance, struggle and co-operation which have been employed by politically motivated prisoners.[7] To an extent, account is taken of these in our description of the management regimes, but a balanced account would give them more weight.

All of these issues can affect, and be affected by, the relationship between politics and management, but to include them would make this sketch of the Northern Ireland prison system unduly cumbersome.

An analytical model must also take into account the fact that the nature of the relationship between government and state managers will vary, both between different executive systems and in one system over time. So, the relationship between the government and the police is different from that between it and the armed forces. The home secretary and the Metropolitan police commissioner have a different relationship to that between the lord chancellor and the lord chief justice. Furthermore, a different relationship existed between the home secretary and the Prison Department of the Home Office and the same minister and the new Prisons Agency.

There are, therefore, different possible modes of articulation between government and state managers. If we are to construct an analytical model which will help us to understand the relationship between politics and prison management, we must identify the elements which will vary with each mode.

The first is clearly the structural element. This may be defined by legislation, regulation or constitutional convention (the last may sometimes be enforceable at common law). So, an agency or other variety of quango will usually be established in statute or ministerial regulation which will lay down the structural relationship between the relevant minister and the body itself. Again, with regards to the police, for example, the office of constable is held to embody a certain constitutional discretion in the upholding of law which can translate into the concept of operational autonomy for the head of a police force (Walsh 1983). The extent and nature of the lines of accountability so established are an obvious starting-point in analysing the mode of articulation between government politicians and managers.

Second, but perhaps as important, is the actual use made of the structural relationship at a given time or within a given framework. 'What matters here is not the formal structure of the organisation as defined on paper but the "real" relationships of power and influence that may not exactly coincide with such paper definitions' (Loughlin 1992: 62). This can only be discovered by empirical observation, but the crucial measure is the actual scope of executive action/instruction. For example, in the case of prisons, to what extent do ministers actually take decisions in individual cases. The empirical enquiry needs to establish, on the one hand, how far into the 'tactical' range of decision-making ministerial action extends and, on the other, what level of 'strategic' decision-making is, in practice, in the hands of managers.

So far we have attempted to elucidate the relationship between politics and prison management by reference to the interaction between government and managers. We have noted, however, that government itself has to be responsive to a variety of constituencies within civil society. A government, in our system, is, of course, answerable to the voters every five years or so. In practice, however, a government will also take account of the views, known or imputed, of a range of interest groups which might include the party conference, sections of the media, various pressure-groups, staff unions, academics and so on. It may be possible for the managers of a state system to engage, to a greater or lesser extent, with these same interest groups. Some political scientists call these 'policy communities' which 'cluster around policy arenas such as agriculture, education and health' (Loughlin 1992: 63). In other words, there is a politics centring around every major state system, assuredly including the prison system, which can be influenced by those working in that system.

Another focus of analysis should be, therefore, the modes of interaction between a state system and elements of civil society. This should take account of the extent of 'transparency' or openness of the system, the extent and nature of any formal and informal accountability for managerial action and the extent to which managers consciously attempt to influence political debate.

This framework gives us, then, a set of comparative indicators with which to draw pictures of given prison systems at given times, highlighting the nature of the interaction between politics and management. To recapitulate, the elements of the framework are:

1. The political status of the prison system as defined by the current interplay of the groupings of political issues we have identified.
2. The nature of the management style of the prison system, analysed by reference to the list of management issues identified above.
3. The particular mode of articulation between government and prison management as defined by reference to both structural and actual arrangements.
4. The nature and extent of modes of interaction between the prison system and elements of civil society, encompassing issues of transparency of the system, accountability for management decisions and engagement in political debate.

Comparisons between jurisdictions, or within one jurisdiction in time, may allow causal inferences to be drawn about the interaction between politics, management and structure. Moreover, it should be possible to develop models, or ideal types, which have some wider application, out of empirical studies across time or location.

The Northern Ireland experience

It is this analytical framework which we have tried to apply to the history of the Northern Ireland prison system since 1969. It is our contention that there have been three models of prison management deployed in Northern Ireland during this period. We developed these as models for the management of politically motivated prisoners and suggested that they might have relevance for the management of other divided prison populations and perhaps wider significance for the management of political violence in general (Gormally *et al.* 1993) We argue that these relate to actual historical events but they also serve as distinct theoretical constructs or 'ideal types', which explain how prison systems can operate in situations of social and political conflict. Each model, however, also implies a specific relationship between politics and prison management and should be amenable to analysis using the framework we have outlined above.

The three models we have termed:

1. Reactive containment, 1969–76.
2. Criminalization, 1976–81.
3. Normalization, 1981 onwards.

Reactive containment

This model covers the period from the first active committal of British troops to the conflict in Northern Ireland until the middle 1970s. At first, the soldiers were interposed between Catholics and Loyalists, the latter supported by some elements of the police. Quite quickly, however, the army took on a counter-insurgency role, identifying as the enemy the recently revived IRA. In August 1971, internment without trial was introduced and lasted until close to the end of this period in 1975. These were by far the worst years of violence in the period at which we are looking.

As a general description of security policy, reactive containment can be seen as a relatively crude response to an actual, or potential, armed insurrection. It is fundamentally a military model though it can be implemented by police forces and other security bodies. Its mind-set is of a 'war' against a distinct 'enemy.' It finds difficulty in engaging with the complexities of a divided society. It incorporates the military horror of a war on two fronts and, where there is more than one source of political violence, identifies one as the only, or main, enemy.

The essential characteristics of reactive containment are the suppression and containment of the insurrectionary enemy; a willingness to use conventional military force; the prorogation of aspects of civil liberties; contemporaneous negotiation with the 'enemy' and with other political forces in the search for a political settlement. The model implies an acceptance that the violence is political in origin, however 'wrong,' and therefore confers some kind of legitimacy on its perpetrators.

If we attempt to apply our analytical framework, we can see the following patterns:

The political status of the prison system – 'political issues'
The prison system was completely subordinated to the overall security policy; there was no debate at all about the suitability of the system for the job it was asked to do. There were only two prisons in Northern Ireland, the Victorian Crumlin Road in Belfast and the Georgian Armagh women's prison. When internment was introduced, army camps at Long Kesh and Magilligan were added to the 'prison stock' and, even, for a while, a prison ship, the Maidstone.

During this period, there were convicted politically motivated prisoners as well as internees, but it appears that little distinction was made between their respective statuses at governmental level. The prison system, both internment camps and the old, traditional gaols, was designed to contain an insurrectionary enemy while the emergency was dealt with by military and/or political means.

Nature of the management style – 'management issues'

During this period, the prison system ran three basic regimes: for internees, for 'special category' status prisoners and for 'ordinary' (that is non-political) prisoners.

Internees were held in physical conditions and under a regime that approximated in almost every way to the classic notion of a prisoner of war camp. Surprisingly enough, so were convicted prisoners who had been granted 'special category' status. Until early 1972 these prisoners were held in Crumlin Road gaol in non-segregated accommodation, with no free association and forced to wear prison uniforms. Then, Billy McKee, formerly head of the Belfast Brigade of the IRA, led forty Republican prisoners on hunger strike for prisoner of war status. William Whitelaw, then secretary of state for Northern Ireland, conceded the concept of special category status as McKee neared death.

What this actually entailed was that convicted prisoners also had *de facto* prisoner of war status. They were segregated from 'ordinary' prisoners and prisoners of opposing paramilitary groups. Most sentenced prisoners were held in Nissen huts at Long Kesh, with usually three huts within each compound or 'cage'. Prisoners were allowed to associate freely, to wear their own clothes, to drill and hold lectures and, in practice, to run their compounds along military lines. Each cage had its own officer in command (OC) and all negotiating with the prison authorities was done through him (Adams 1990: 11). Apart from organized searches, neither prison officers nor soldiers entered the cages. The Army provided armed guards for the watch-towers, gates and perimeter and extra muscle for riot control, searches and so on. The prison governors were in nominal control of the prisons but, since the Army was the final arbiter on security, there is no doubt where effective power over management lay.

During this period we see the overall political priorities of govern-ment reflected with stark clarity in the management of the prison system. What was going on within the prisons was a microcosm of what was happening outside the walls. Inside the prisons, negotiation between prison authorities and prisoners was achieved through the paramilitary command structures; similarly the government was involved in clandestine dialogue with IRA officers on the outside.

Mode of articulation between government and prison management

Common to all our models, with the exception of the first two and a half years of reactive containment, is the structural relationship between politicians and prison management. In March 1972, the Stormont regional parliament, unique in the UK, was prorogued and the Northern Ireland government dismissed. Direct rule from Westminster was instituted. A team of British ministers, led by a secretary of state of Cabinet rank, was installed to run the region. With them they brought British civil servants to fill all the senior, sensitive posts of government and to 'seed' some of the middle ranks of the local civil service.

The old Stormont ministries were reorganized as departments of the Northern Ireland government. All were eventually responsible to the Northern Ireland Office, which is a department of state of the United Kingdom, or an 'imperial' department, as the internal jargon has it. However, all security functions were kept within this senior, and, above assistant secretary level, wholly British-staffed, department. So, the old Stormont Ministry of Home Affairs was subsumed under the Northern Ireland Office, together with its responsibility for prisons.

In general, this system of government has been regarded as temporary, filling in until agreement on a new form of government for Northern Ireland has been reached (Hadfield 1992: 7). As one initiative after another has failed, however, the system has achieved effective permanence. In any event, not even in the heady days of the power-sharing executive (January to May 1974) did anyone suggest handing back control of security to local politicians. So, after more than two decades, the current structural relationship between politicians and prison management has a certain historical stability.

The main points of this structure are as follows. The secretary of state has three or four ministers under him. A fairly senior one, though not necessarily the secretary of state's deputy, will be responsible for security matters, including prisons. However, in this area at any rate, the secretary of state appears to feel free to dabble in any issues arising without going through his junior. It would not be unusual for the secretary of state's office to make direct contact with a middle-ranking civil servant in the prisons section to ask about a particular incident.

In civil service terms, the prison department of the Northern Ireland Office is headed by the controller of prisons. Under him are four directors of, respectively, regimes, operations, personnel and services. Governors are line managed by the director of operations, but all the directorates have routes into the day-to-day management of the prisons.

The structural relationship between politicians and prison managers in Northern Ireland is therefore clear. A Cabinet minister runs a department of government, together with several junior ministers, and the prisons are managed by civil servants directly responsible to the ministers. The actual use made of this formal structural framework has, however, varied between our different models.

In the first years of reactive containment, the prisons were nominally under the control of the local minister of home affairs. However, the British Army, which in practice dominated the prisons after August 1971, was under direct British political control, so it can be assumed that the Stormont minister's influence was less than decisive. From March 1972, British ministers had direct, formal control.

It is clear that they were ready to use it. The granting of special category status was, of course, an act of huge significance for prison management. Similarly, the temporary release of Gerry Adams from prison in 1972, in order to be part of an IRA delegation flown to London for peace talks, could hardly be a more graphic example of ministerial 'interference' in prison management.

Having said that, the small group of governors and administrators that existed in 1969, regarded the new expansion of their system as a challenge. In spite of Army supremacy, and the tensions it caused, prison managers were determined that the system become as civilian (or at least, non-military) as possible, as soon as possible. Hence, ministerial approval was sought for a massive recruitment drive for prison officers with large wages offered. In the mean time, large numbers of secondees from the English and Scottish prison systems were enticed to work in Northern Ireland.

So, in this early period, we see direct, intrusive engagement by politicians with prison management, but also the beginning of a prison management with an identity to win, both in terms of coming out of the shadow of the Army and arguing its sectional concerns with ministers.

Modes of interaction between prisons and civil society

In this period, there is little enough to say about this element. It is very difficult to discern any independent interaction between prison management and elements of civil society outside. In so far as there was a fierce debate about the prisons, it was part of a larger argument about security policy and civil rights. In this period, where the dominant political ethos was confrontation with an insurrectionary enemy, it would have been virtually inconceivable for management to engage in a separate politics around prison issues.

None the less, whether at political direction or not, prison management did engage in some activities which could be seen as modifying the counter-insurgency thrust. In 1970, the Northern Ireland Association for the Care and Resettlement of Offenders was established with Ministry of Home Affairs, and then Northern Ireland Office, support. The prison service actually, and for the one and only time, ran an open prison at Castlecoole in 1970–71. In 1975, a public planning inquiry was held into the proposal to build a new prison at Maghaberry (which finally opened in 1986). This inquiry, which would not have been necessary had emergency powers been invoked, cut down the size of the proposed prison and, in general, acted as though the prison system was 'normal'.

Attempts were made to 'normalize' internment by getting voluntary organizations involved in the 'resettlement' of ex-internees. When NIACRO refused to do this, a short-lived Resettlement Association was set up by government. Within the prisons, an attempt was made to legitimate internment by the establishment of tribunals which heard anonymous accusations from behind screens and then purported to decide whether detention was justified.

None of these engagements amounted to a great deal at the time. However, they are interesting in pointing up how, even in a chaotic time of confrontational crisis, some kind of 'normal' relationship with civil society is possible.

Criminalization

This covers the period from the time of the decision to end special category status (early 1976) to the end of the major hunger strikes (1981). It coincides with a period of vigorous anti-terrorist activity when the policy of the government was, as the then (Labour) secretary of state, Roy Mason put it, 'to squeeze the Provisional IRA like toothpaste out of a tube'.[8] It was a time of extensive covert activity by the SAS and other Army units, though the 'primacy of the police' was being expressed as the dominant security theory. The special Diplock courts[9] were busy, as were the police interrogation centres. Between 1976 and 1979, 3,000 people were charged with 'terrorist' offences, most of them on evidence obtained by confessions (Bishop and Mallie 1989: 321) The RUC were under intense pressure to secure convictions and they responded by resorting frequently to physical beatings, threats, verbal abuse, intimidation and generally oppressive treatment in an effort to extract confessions in the interrogation centres (Taylor 1980; Walsh 1983: 94; Hogan and Walker 1989: 116).

The fundamental principle emerging in this period is the attempt to delegitimize and criminalize what had hitherto been regarded as explicitly political violence. It is an attempt to remove any legitimacy from the 'terrorists'. Negotiations are rejected and the total defeat of violence is held out as a real possibility.

We can analyse what all this meant for the prison system by applying our analytical framework.

The political status of the prison system – 'political issues'
If there is a clear example of the political use of prisons, for reasons not directly connected to their prime function of containment, this period is it. The prisons were put in the front line of a political/ military campaign which was initiated without reference to the particular interests of the system.

In terms of our typology of 'political' issues as given above, the positions held by government at this time represented both the use of prisons for 'external' purposes and the 'invasion' of ideologically determined policies from other sectors.

To take the latter aspect first, the policy of criminalization was one aspect of a fundamental shift in British security policy. This shift was to make a move, real or apparent, from a classic counter-insurgency stance to that of a neutral referee, 'holding the ring', while forces fundamentally domestic to Northern Ireland fought out the bit. So-called 'Ulsterization', was part of this shift, moving the security emphasis from the British Army to the Royal Ulster Constabulary and the locally recruited Ulster Defence Regiment.

Perceived as necessary to this strategy was the denial of any kind of insurgent status to those who would claim it.[10] In Northern Ireland circumstances, where no paramilitary organization effectively controlled territory or administered a population, the main area where insurgent or 'political status' could be claimed was in prison. Special category status was seen as an effective acceptance of that claim. It had to be reversed.

Criminalization proceeded in the belief that those convicted by the system could be coerced and cajoled into acceptance of their role as criminals. Such an outcome would have a major delegitimizing effect on violence outside the prisons and cast fundamental doubt on the motivation of those involved. So, every symbol of difference between 'terrorists' and ordinary criminals, any notion of the political character of some inmates, had to be removed. The policy involved the end of 'special category status', the rigid enforcement of the wearing of prison uniforms and the doing of prison work and a refusal to recognize the existence of paramilitary organizational structures. Here, then, the 'external' purpose of delegitimizing groups of 'terrorists' was to be achieved by the deliberate use of the prison system.

Nature of the management style – 'management issues'

As we have noted, in this period political decisions related directly to the way in which groups of prisoners were managed. The effect on the prison system, especially at the Maze, makes a grim chronicle.

Any person convicted of a scheduled offence after March 1976 was treated as an ordinary criminal. Men were sent to newly constructed prison buildings (quickly dubbed the H-blocks, since they were built in the shape of the letter H) erected alongside the compounds in Long Kesh. Women were accommodated in the old prison at Armagh. As a symbol of the new policy direction, Long Kesh was renamed the Maze Prison.

On 14 September Ciaran Nugent, an IRA prisoner, was the first prisoner sentenced under the new policy. When asked for his clothes size for a uniform he reportedly replied, 'They will have to nail a prison uniform on my back first'. (Republican Fact File: 1991) Nugent was put in a cell without clothes, covering himself with the blanket for his bed. Several hundred Republican prisoners – up to one-half of the men arriving at the Maze/Long Kesh – followed Nugent 'on the blanket'.

It was an offence under the prison rules to leave one's cell improperly dressed so, in practice, prisoners were confined to their cells for twenty-four hours per day. Access to television, books and newspapers was refused. Refusal to wear prison clothes was a breach of prison discipline and the prisoners lost entitlement to the 50 per cent remission scheme operating in Northern Ireland at that time.

Normally, prisoners are entitled to three 'privileged visits' and one statutory visit per month, but breach of rules meant the cancellation of the three privileged visits and their refusal to wear the uniform to the visiting area cost prisoners the fourth visit. Contact with the outside world was thus limited to one censored letter per week (Beresford 1987: 27). After some fights with prison officers where furniture was smashed, beds and footlockers were removed leaving prisoners two men to a cell, with a mattress, three blankets and a bible each. After several months the prisoners compromised and wore the uniform for their statutory visit. A pattern which was to become familiar, of confrontation and brinkmanship, began to take shape.

In 1978 a dispute arose over washing and using the toilet. The prisoners began to refuse to leave their cells and thus the 'no wash' or 'dirty' protest began. After several confrontations between prison officers and prisoners in the Maze over the emptying of their chamber pots, prisoners began to throw the contents out through the windows of their cells and the spy holes in the doors. Prison officers retaliated by throwing it back in the cells and the prisoners began to smear the excrement on the walls, floor and ceiling of their cells.

The conditions in which the prisoners were living, and the failure of efforts outside prison to resolve the dispute, led to the prisoners seeking redress in the tactic of hunger striking, by which Billy McKee and others had secured special category status in the first place. They had for some time been trying to persuade the leadership of the IRA outside the prison to give permission for a hunger strike to begin (Beresford 1989: 360).

Finally, on 10 October 1980, the IRA Army Council having given its consent, it was announced that a hunger strike would be called in ten days. This was temporarily settled after fifty-two days, but the apparent agreement between prisoners and the British government soon broke down. Another hunger strike began on 1 March 1981, the fifth anniversary of the end of political status.

The strikers formulated five demands: the right to wear their own clothes; to refrain from prison work; to associate freely with one another; to organize recreational facilities and to have one letter, visit and parcel a week; and to have lost remission time restored. Bobby

Sands, the leader of this second hunger strike, issued the following statement as it began:

> We are still able to declare that the criminalisation policy which we have resisted and suffered, has failed . . . If a British government experienced such a long and persistent resistance to a domestic policy in England, then that policy would almost certainly be changed . . . We have asserted that we are political prisoners and everything about our country, our arrests, interrogations, trials and prison conditions, show that we are politically motivated. (Iris 1991: 17)

Later, Margaret Thatcher, the prime minister, declared: 'A crime is a crime is a crime . . . It is not political, it is a crime' (O'Malley 1990: 60). On 17 April the death of Bobby Sands produced a world-wide response. Three other hungerstrikers had joined Sands two weeks into his fast and the process continued until ultimately ten hungerstrikers were to starve themselves to death.

Mode of articulation between government and prison management

As we noted in the previous section, the formal structural relationship between government and prison management in Northern Ireland has remained constant since 1972. In terms of actual arrangements, the whole character of criminalization makes clear that ministerial action extended deep into the tactical range of decision-making. What is more, the extensive literature on the hunger-strike period makes it clear that the British Cabinet and the prime minister herself took many decisions at that time.

'Executive action' by ministers took some curious forms during this period. There were secret negotiations between IRA representatives and code-named government agents, reputed rivalry between the Foreign Office and MI5 and deals apparently offered then withdrawn (Beresford 1987). This is murky territory and not directly relevant to this chapter. What appears fairly clear, however, is that politicians were in a situation of hands-on control. The precise ways in which their control was exercised, and the exact form of interaction with managers at this time, are not matters now within the public domain and are unlikely to be so for many years.

Modes of interaction between prisons and civil society

To say that there was a politics generated around the Northern Ireland prison system during this period would be an understatement.

As we have noted, the prisons were at the very centre of political debate about Northern Ireland, locally, in a UK context and internationally. However, that was very largely a consequence of the overall political stance of government which had made the prisons a focus of security policy. This aspect of the analytical framework is designed to illuminate the extent to which the prison system itself was engaging in a dialogue with civil society.

In one sense, the interaction was quite extensive. Areas of the prison system, especially Magilligan Prison, were becoming more 'normal', compared with their internment camp origins. Boards of Visitors were operating and voluntary organizations concerned with offenders were growing.

Having said that, there was no independent initiative by prison management to engage in any kind of a politics which would modify, much less contradict, the overwhelming political thrust coming from above. Any contact with the media, which was extensive, or the production of 'factual' material about the prisons, can only be seen in the context of an overall, government-led propaganda offensive. In this period, there was no political room for moderating, mediating influences.

Normalization

In many ways, the hunger strikes were a Pyrrhic victory for the British government. Not only had ten prisoners died, in circumstances that led to international obloquy, but eighteen prison officers had also been murdered and forty-six other people killed during the hunger-strike period (Bishop and Mallie 1989).

After the end of the hunger strike the majority of the prisoners' demands were quickly implemented. Secretary of State Prior announced that prisoners could wear their own clothes; remission was restored on condition of good behaviour; the demands relating to mail and visits had already been met. Prison work at the Maze was later ended as a security risk after thirty-eight prisoners escaped in 1983 (Hennessey 1983–4; Dunne 1989). The rethink that produced a policy which we term 'normalization', was underway.

This covers the period from the hunger strikes to the present day (1993). Normalization[11] represents a realization and acceptance that political violence and division are a 'normality ' of a given criminal justice system and society – part of a broader range of other 'normalities' which should receive equal emphasis such as ordinary crime, ordinary policing, unemployment etc. – and an acceptance of the anomalies that this entails. The application of our analytical framework gives us a more detailed picture.

The political status of the prison system – 'political issues'

The main principles of normalization derive from a number of political decisions, clearly taken at governmental level.

The first is an acceptance that the prison system is not a mechanism that can 'defeat' political violence; rather it is a mechanism for managing some of its human consequences. This involves an explicit abandonment of the policy of criminalization, in so far as that is designed to coerce prisoners into a practical and symbolic acceptance of the status of common criminals.

The second major political decision amounts to an estimation that political conflict and division are likely to exist for the foreseeable future and hence must be seen as 'normal'. This is the watershed decision which leads to the change from attempting to solve a problem to trying to manage it. Those responsible for normalization believe that, if they can, they should manage the situation without too many obvious derogations from international norms of civil liberties and in a way which minimizes unnecessary trouble.

The third major political decision underpinning normalization is a recognition of the effective 'permanence' of 'temporary' legislative and administrative structures which have been adapted to contain political violence. This decision is the operational consequence of the acceptance of the normality of division and violence. It means that the 'special' methods for dealing with politically motivated offenders will be an essential element of the criminal justice system for the foreseeable future.

These political decisions have particular relevance for the prisons and, we think, arose directly out of the prison experience of the late 1970s and early 1980s. It is, however, a matter for debate and empirical study, whether these principles apply to other aspects of the security apparatus or criminal justice system.

The extent to which the above decisions were taken clearly and consciously by ministers is also a matter for debate. It appears to us, that the decision to abandon criminalization had to be taken by ministers. Beyond that, however, we feel that there has been a certain withdrawal by politicians from an arena in which they got their fingers badly burned. To an extent, managers have used that space to develop strategic directions which may go beyond original political expectations. We will return to this issue in the section on the mode of articulation between politicians and managers in the era of normalization.

Nature of the management style – 'management issues'

The key element of normalization, from a management point of view, is the change in relations with politically motivated prisoners. They are recognized as forming groups who are distinct from 'ordinary' prisoners and from each other. In no sense is this simply a collapse in front of the organized power of paramilitary groupings. Nor is it simply a grudging acceptance of reality. It is a clear-sighted attempt to manage the consequences of imprisoning quantities of disciplined, politically motivated people, divided into two or more mutually hostile factions. It is proactive and designed to implement the political decisions of normalization.

The practical policy of the prison service includes elements of flexibility and negotiation but also an attempt to limit, quarantine and marginalize the paramilitary groupings. Furthermore, there are elements of a carrot and stick approach, which is designed to wean paramilitary adherents from their allegiance. It could be argued that there are contradictory elements in the practical management of the service, and there is certainly tension around how far recognition of, and co-operation with, paramilitaries should go. None the less, the elements of a distinct management style can be discerned.

The first element in this style consists of a practice of flexibility and negotiation. Flexibility must be an essential part of any prison regime. The potential for disruption and violence is always there when quantities of people are detained against their will. Rigidity and strict adherence to rules which may have limited perceived legitimacy are likely to provoke dissent and occasional violent outbursts. That is particularly the case when there are organized groups of inmates with a coherent ideology which will lead them to seize on grievances, injustices and rigidities within the regime as points of mobilization for organized protest.

The fundamental issue at stake between prison authorities and politically motivated prisoners is their political status. Formal political status (that is recognition of non-criminality and acceptance that they were imprisoned only for political opposition) has never been on the practical agenda since the beginning of the troubles. However, conflict has revolved around symbols that can be seen to point either in the direction of political recognition or towards criminalization.

One of the most important of these symbols has been 'segregation'. In essence, this means the holding together, in one part of a prison, of those of a similar political allegiance. An interpretation of normalization as a passive process would see a simple recognition of reality in the segregation of politicals from 'ordinaries' and each other. The prison managers have carried out segregation to an extent, but only reluctantly and with a lively appreciation of the practical consequences.

Segregation means the straightforward establishment of para-military command structures, the disciplining of waiverers, the possible intimidation or corruption of prison officers and easier planning for escape. So there has been a reluctance to adopt segregation by the prison authorities and a consistent campaign to resist its extension and to increase the number of 'integrated' areas of prisons (Colville: 1992).

Interestingly, the recent report of the chief inspector of prisons on the Maze, whose recommendations have been published for the first time, suggested greater freedom of association on the H-Block wings (Tumim 1994). This implies more paramilitary organization and less direct control by prison staff. In fact the bulk of Tumim's recom-mendations lend themselves to a fairly radical interpretation of the thrust of normalization. However, the prison system now contains segregated and non-segregated areas and a range of regimes with differing levels of security.

Negotiation and consultation with prisoners might be seen as an inevitable and indispensable part of prison management. After all, it is a truism that prisons require the consent of prisoners to operate at all. Indeed, it is part of the policy of normalization that a wide range of negotiation should take place. However, when one is dealing with politically motivated prisoners, there are decisions on matters of principle to be taken.

Negotiation with politically motivated prisoners means negotiation with a paramilitary line of command. That is obviously granting a certain level of recognition to the paramilitary organization and, it might be argued, to go some way towards recognizing them as prisoners of war.

Normalization rejects the symbolism which might be imputed to such negotiation. It is pragmatic and does not waste time and effort wilfully ignoring the reality that paramilitary prisoners do elect spokesmen and that they are the only route of communication with the authorities that the prisoners will use.

The limits and content of negotiation will always be issues, of course. From management's point of view, the narrower the range, the more discussions centre on the practical details of prison life, the more prisoners are accepting the legitimacy of the prison system. From the prisoners' point of view, the fact of negotiations themselves gives some credibility to their own command structure. It seems a reasonable quid pro quo.

In relation to politically motivated prisoners, the second element of normalization's strategy is to attempt to restrict, isolate and marginalize paramilitary groupings. The leadership of the Prison Service is prepared to acknowledge explicitly that it is engaged in a struggle with the paramilitaries. Their existence and the politics that brought them into being are recognized, but they are regarded as enemies of the state and of democracy whose influence must be limited and challenged.

Thus the Prison Service Strategic Plan drew a line at the *status quo* in late 1991.

We shall create conditions which will offer all prisoners . . . the opportunity to serve their sentences free from the influence of paramilitary organisations: By continuing to resist further segregation which acts against the best interest of prisoners, the efficiency of the Service and the long term stability of the wider community. (Serving the Community 1991: 12)[12]

The third major element that the policy of normalization suggests in terms of relations with politically motivated prisoners is a practice of what we have described as 'constructive engagement' with individual prisoners. A less kind description would be a campaign of psychological warfare designed, in the first place, to break prisoners away from their paramilitary allegiances. A secondary purpose is to reduce the level of military or associated political activism amongst those who insist on maintaining their attachment to paramilitary organizations. This involves a carrot and stick approach, as, perhaps, do all such campaigns.

In this case, the carrot, or, at least, policies which have both a carrot and stick element, are predominant. 'Reformed' paramilitaries, serving indeterminate sentences, can expect to serve a little less time than their obdurate colleagues. In terms of regimes, there is supposed to be somewhat stricter security imposed on segregated areas of the system and a more relaxed and open lifestyle for conforming prisoners.

It is Maghaberry Prison, the new, purpose-built establishment, completed on a green field site in the mid 1980s, which was designed as the main site of the system's engagement with ex-paramilitary prisoners. In good physical conditions, with enhanced access to education and work opportunities, conforming prisoners are encouraged to prepare for life outside (Northern Ireland Prison Service 1989–90). Judge Tumim, however, criticized the concept of improving the regime at Maghaberry at the expense of the Maze, implicitly, therefore, rejecting the idea of regime-based inducements to paramilitaries to give up their allegiance (Tumim 1994). The disingenuous response of the Prison Service was to deny that they had ever tried to do any such thing (NIO press release 1 February 1994).

This, now authoritatively criticized policy, is one side of the Prison Service's declared commitment to individuality of treatment, that is, treating prisoners as individuals regardless of religious or political beliefs. This is a policy which is presented as based on humanitarian principles and honouring the commitments to equality of treatment that all Northern Ireland institutions are now encouraged to make. It is also, however, specifically seen as anti-paramilitary in the sense of declaring against the legitimacy of their organization within the prisons. The Prison Service line is that individual needs cannot be properly met when a prisoner is shielded from view and contact with the authorities by a paramilitary command structure. In fact, however, none of the paramilitary organizations have policies preventing their members taking advantage of welfare or other facilities.

The negative side of 'individualization of treatment' is being a lone prisoner faced with the power and authority of the whole system. It is an example of the paternalism which permeates many prison managements that individuality of treatment is assumed to be an unalloyed good thing. Leaving aside any qualms about the concept of human beings as atomized individuals, if the system were totally benevolent, that might well be the case. Needless to say, individual prisoners sometimes find it hard to discern that benevolence.

In contrast to the theory of individualization of treatement is the reality of productive co-operation between authorities and groupings of prisoners. Yet such co-operation should not be seen as a 'soft' approach by the authorities, for it is part of the policy of normalization to extend the areas where paramilitaries are forced to choose between uncomfortable rejectionism and the practical benefits of co-operation.

An unusual example of this process is the system of home leave which operates in Northern Ireland. In the last few months of their sentence, all prisoners are entitled to periods of home leave in order to get used to outside society. These are usually a couple of days every month or so. However, more interesting is the availability of Christmas and summer home leave. These periods of leave are offered to almost all prisoners who have served more than twelve years. Over the Christmas holiday, and for two weeks in the summer, hundreds of still committed paramilitary prisoners, amounting to almost one third of the prison population, are allowed out to stay with their families or friends. So far, no paramilitary prisoner has failed to return in the years of the scheme's operation. This is a privilege also extended to ordinary prisoners, although a small number of them either fail to return or return late.

Many paramilitary prisoners define themselves as prisoners of war with the duty of escape, yet they voluntarily walk out of their prison and walk back, twice a year. It is equally paradoxical that the authorities are happy to release 'terrorists' for a summer holiday but maintain that they are too dangerous to be released finally. It is hard to find strict logic in practices like this. It is easy, however, to find good sense and a pragmatic collaboration between supposed enemies.

In general, normalization implies a policy of minimizing causes and occasions of conflict with prisoners and their families. This involves the development of a culture of realism and a readiness to spend money to avoid trouble. Until recently, money had not been a problem for the Northern Ireland Prison Service. Nowadays, however, the stringent controls on public expenditure are biting here as well. It will be interesting to see when 'lack of money' becomes a more popular excuse for not doing something to benefit prisoners and their families than 'security'.

The fundamental purpose here is not simply to avoid conflict for its own sake, but also to avoid occasions and issues around which politically motivated prisoners and their supporters outside might mobilize. We have argued that prisons in Northern Ireland have been a political battleground. Under normalization, however, the actual terrain of conflict is limited as much as possible. Over large tracts of the system, the supposed combatants actually coexist and collaborate. Only a few pieces of territory are actually contested by authorities and prisoners.

To use a slightly different analogy – conflict in the prisons is a long way from total war. It is more like some of the semi-ritual battles of the Middle Ages, where rules of chivalry and codes of war restricted actual fighting to a controlled and limited passage of arms. It is the policy of the Prison Service to extend the areas of no hostility and remove, as far as possible and without compromising on principle, each and every *casus belli*. This is management taking the decision to keep overtly political conflict out of its area of responsibility.

There are many more management issues that could be described. However, the selection presented should give an indication that the management of Northern Ireland prisons has taken a different direction in the past decade or so. The management consequences of a political stance of realism, and perhaps a certain disengagement, also seem clear. The extent to which these factors are connected with the practical interactions between politicians and managers and between the latter and civil society will be explored in the next two sections.

Mode of articulation between politicians and prison managers

We have described the formal structural relationship between politicians and the managers of the prison system in the section on reactive containment above. The point requiring stress here is that none of the senior posts within management have any constitutional existence or statutory recognition. Neither the Prison Act (Northern Ireland) 1952, nor the latest edition of the Prison Rules (1982)[13] contain any reference, for example, to the controller of prisons. The only 'management' post mentioned is the governor, who is described as being 'in command' of a prison. There is no doubt that there is dissatisfaction about this position within the senior ranks of management. It is our perception, though of course these debates go on largely in private, that there is significant support for the 'agentization' of the Northern Ireland prison service along English lines. However, our purpose in this section is to describe the current position.

In spite of the lack of structural autonomy, it is our view that the management of the Northern Ireland service has achieved a certain level of operational autonomy. One reality is that ministers in charge of prisons in Northern Ireland tend to be subject to not only the whims of the electorate but also to the fact that Northern Ireland is often seen as the 'Outer Siberia' of British political appointments. Consequently those civil servants in charge of the prison service have actually been a much less transient population.

In conversation, one of the current authors commented to a senior manager that it was not clear to him whether the policies, which we here describe as normalization, were generated at ministerial or civil service level. The reply was, 'It is not clear to you because it is not clear!' However, the respondent went on to say that in his period in post there had been five prisons ministers, 'so draw your own conclusions'.

In fact, much of the generation of ideas seems to take place within formal and informal groupings of senior civil servants. Of course, their relative autonomy and their ability to take decisions breaking with past policy relies on acquiescence by politicians, at the least. Moreover, they are working in a grey area and 'outside' political intervention can always take place.

In these circumstances, and without access to empirical observation of the actual process of decision-making, conclusions about the extent of the practical autonomy of prison service management can only be tentative. It does appear, however, that the influence of managers has extended into the 'strategic' area. While ministerial approval was no doubt sought, the content of both the Prison Service Strategic Plan, *Serving the Community* (NIO 1991) and the *Code of Conduct for Prison Officers* (NIO 1991), seems to have been worked out largely by civil servants. Indeed, a series of internal meetings and some involving 'stakeholders' of the service, facilitated by outside consultants, led to the generation of the strategic plan.

This kind of deeply influential work demonstrates that there is a corps of managers with sufficient self-confidence and practical autonomy to engage in strategic decision-making.

Modes of interaction between the prisons and civil society

There is no doubt that the management of the prison service has, during this period, attempted to influence constituencies within civil society. Again, we must raise the caveat that their structural relationship with politicians requires the latter's acquiescence, at least, in this kind of activity, but it is our perception that the initiative has come from management.

The principle is that progress made in terms of prison management is accessed and presented in the most positive light possible for the managers. We believe that this is achieved by carefully targeting both the general public and key agencies who have an interest in the operation of the prisons here. We believe that, since 1981, the prison authorities have been quite successful in establishing the terms of reference for the debate on prisons.

The importance of the media in terms of defining the parameters and images of the conflict in Northern Ireland has always been in the forefront of government strategy. The techniques employed by the government have ranged from informal censorship of television and press by pressurizing journalists and their controllers (Chibnall 1977; Madden 1979; Curtis 1984) to black propaganda (Foot 1989) or 'psychological operations' (Hooper 1983) and, since 1989, a ban on the spoken words of members of Sinn Fein and the Ulster Defence Association.[14] However, the techniques employed by the prison service over the past decade or so, whilst including at least some of the above elements, have arguably been somewhat more sophisticated.

It is clear that the impetus for this change in public relations direction came from the failures of the hunger strike era. During that time, particularly by the international press, the British government was widely perceived and portrayed as being unsubtle, recalcitrant and unfeeling (Beresford 1987; O'Malley 1990). Senior civil servants are privately quite frank that these were dark days for the Service when the IRA without doubt 'won the propaganda war'. Since that time a dedicated public relations branch for the Prison Service has been established and now ranks amongst the best organized and most efficient of the Northern Ireland government.

The Service now routinely employs 'off the record' briefings, adopts a policy of 'glasnost', allowed BBC television cameras to make a detailed documentary inside the Maze in 1990 and much access since, engages in long-term strategic planning in public relations to pre-empt emotive prison-based anniversaries such as internment and the hunger strikes, encouraged a royal visit by Princess Anne to Maghaberry in May 1992. These are all examples of a management which has learnt the important lesson of an era of violent confrontation when international sympathy went to the underdog.

The central text of the public relations agenda of normalization is to demonstrate how 'normal', 'well run' and 'forward looking' are our prisons.

The television documentary, where the programme-makers were given virtually unlimited access to interview all prisoners and use whatever film footage they wished, was particularly interesting. The public were allowed to see quite openly the operation of the paramilitary command structure within the prison. Although this had its risks, in terms of familiar charges that, 'the terrorists run the prisons', it was obviously felt that these would be counterbalanced by the visible exposition of a peaceful prison. In the documentary, a commanding officer of Republican prisoners, many of whom had been on the dirty protest and hunger strikes, was filmed in formal negotiation with prison officers about the substandard size of the sausage rolls. In public relations terms the parameters of the debate had changed dramatically.

Paramilitary organizations and their respective political parties tend to be ostracized and marginalized by the media because of their espousal of the use of violence, except at times of particular conflict or drama. In general, the only real challenge that can be presented to the government's view of things in the media comes from those who have become authoritative sources because of their 'technical expertise' in prison policy or service provision.

In addition to the odd academic specializing in prisons, agencies such as NIACRO with a policy comment and/or service delivery brief to prisoners and their families are the obvious port of call for any journalist who wishes to look beyond the official line. It is here, in the active local print and broadcast media, that we can see the public profile of what is becoming a 'policy community' around the prison system. As might be expected, prison managers have a somewhat ambiguous attitude towards this 'community', which can often be quite critical. However, in general, it has been welcomed and used. For example, as we have noted, in preparing their long-term strategic document *Serving the Community*, the Prison Service set up a series of meetings where 'stakeholders' in the criminal justice system were allowed to present their views in an interchange with government.

The 'stakeholder' concept is quite interesting. For example, one would have thought that those with the biggest 'stake' in a prison system would be prisoners and their families, followed closely by staff. However, the term has been interpreted to mean voluntary organizations, Boards of Visitors and representatives from other bits of government and the criminal justice system. The major civil liberties lobby group in Northern Ireland, the Committee on the Administration of Justice, has usually been excluded from these kind of meetings. However, this group has had several bilateral meetings with the Prison Service and the latter seems to be getting used to hearing, at least, a civil rights perspective. In addition, there is currently a culture of amenability where major figures within the prison establishment are willing to leave themselves open to meetings and discussion. Debates both in public and private are often frankly and strongly argued but rarely acrimonious.

Even paramilitary organizations themselves have to a degree been indirectly involved in policy debate. Of course, there is regular contact with paramilitary representatives inside the prisons and any documents they draw up are read avidly. There is also acknowledged, though indirect, contact through organizations like NIACRO, which on occasion act as conduits for communication. The authors accept that all this dialogue must, by definition, be within the limited parameters of the operation of the prison system. However, such a dialogue between the managers of a system and quasi-independent expert 'outsiders' is central to the development of normalization. Questioning of official policy, which, during the periods of reactive containment and criminalization would have been 'giving succour to terrorism', have been transformed into 'constructive criticism' by normalization.

There has therefore been created a real 'policy community', which can reflect back, both to managers and politicians, views held by some elements in civil society. Under pressure from politicians, whether those in government or others, managers can now point to constituencies which may either support their position or, indeed, wish to go beyond it. There is now a politics around the Northern Ireland prison system which is distinct from the general ideological battles which make up the political/military war which has disfigured our polity.

Discussion and conclusion

At the beginning of this chapter, we said that prison management was a difficult thing to do and suggested that some managers may feel it is made harder because of the involvement of politics and politicians.

We noted that simplistic views of the relationship between management and politics were unhelpful and, to try and understand the complexity of the issue, developed a tentative analytical framework. This is designed to allow a view of the politics/management relationship through an analytical grid of comparative indicators. Comparisons between prison systems across time and space should help understanding of the dynamics involved. They might even help us predict the possible result of various input changes into a given system, such as a new government policy or agentization. We took this framework and applied it to the Northern Ireland prison system as it has changed over the past twenty-five years. What issues has that exercise raised, and what conclusions can we draw?

First, let us look at some possible critiques of our methodology. The analytical framework is open to the criticism that it is, first, too simplistic, second too static and third, does not take account of the concrete ideological, class and power relations which may determine the social configuration of a given prison system in a given society at a given time.

In answer to these charges, we may argue as follows. The analytical framework is selective, and we have pointed out some of the many important elements which it omits. However, any analysis, if it is to avoid stultifying complexity, must single out what appear to be the most significant dynamics in a social situation. It is open to anyone to add or subtract from the elements we have chosen to discuss in order to present what seems to them a more helpful picture.

Again, any extraction of selected elements from a real social situation 'freeze frames' the picture and hence loses some feel for the process of change and interaction. Given the particular elements we have chosen, however, we feel there is room within this 'static' framework for a sufficient discussion of the way relationships between them change over time.

The third charge is more serious. For if, by ignoring the greater forces in society which determine the nature of a social institution, we imply that its internal dynamics are all that matter, we are guilty of misrepresentation and a narrow view of social relations which we do not happen to hold. So, if we imply that, for example, the extent of autonomy of prison management can determine, on its own, the political and social significance of a prison system, we are wrong.

We believe, however, that that would be an incorrect interpretation of our methodology, for the following reasons. First, our framework begins with the political stance of the state leadership towards the prison system. Clearly, that will often be determined by factors extraneous to the operation of the prison system itself and we have highlighted that fact in the course of our analysis of Northern Ireland. It is beyond the remit of this article to debate the possible economic, social and ideological origins of any particular such political stance. However, nothing in our methodology prevents that from being done in any given case.

Second, we have deliberately not included some of the theoretical insights into the role of prisons in society which have been developed over the years, but neither does our methodology exclude them. In this article we are directly interested in the dynamics involved in the relationships between prison managers and politics and politicians. We understand that they take place within a context which can only be fully comprehended by the application of an overarching theoretical framework dealing, in a more sophisticated manner than we have, with such categories as the state, civil society and the role of punishment in a hegemonic ideology.

We believe that our analysis would be enriched by, for example, a study of how the theories of Foucault on the role of prisons in society could improve our understanding of the interaction between prison management and civil society (Foucault 1977). Similarly, if we accept Garland's views of prison as a central social institution,[15] what does that say about the role in society of those who actually manage that institution? We think that this kind of application of theory to practice remains to be done. Our attempt at a simple framework, designed to make the debate about prison management and politics easier to handle, does not prevent, and may arguably facilitate, such future studies.

Let us now look at whether we can draw any conclusions from our case studies. An obvious, if extreme, one is that if prisons are conscripted into some central, overriding campaign by the state, then their particular concerns are ignored. Reactive containment demonstrated a complete dominance of political will and a virtual lack of identity of the prison system. Such situations may rarely arise in such an extreme form, yet prison managers may recognize milder versions from their own experience and may beware the potential consequences.

Criminalization demonstrated the dangers of making prisons themselves a political battleground. Here, prison managers and staff found themselves fighting on a front line for which, arguably, they were ill-prepared and ill-equipped. In such situations, politicians, like Great War generals sitting far behind the lines, will take decisions which might mean life or death for those at the front. A general point might well be that thinking prisons can actually win a war, or solve a social problem, is the most dangerous of illusions. As we put it, prisons are there to manage the consequences of social conflict, not to end it. Or as Garland puts it, '[prison is] a back-up which is often able to do nothing more than manage those who slip through . . . networks of normal control and integration' (Garland 1990: 289).

Normalization could be read as a success story in which the managers are the heroes, politicians the (absent) villains and prisoners bit players. That is not how we see it. It is true that ministers seem to have withdrawn somewhat from the prison arena after the hunger strikes. Yet we have noted that ministerial acquiescence, at least, is required in any policy change when managers are straight civil servants, and the politicians cannot be excluded from any credit that is around. Again, for any sensible and humane action by a prison manager there has to be an equivalent reaction from prisoners. Without changing patterns of policy by prisoners, which is a story in itself, managers would find great difficulty in changing anything.

We have pointed to a real degree of autonomy of prison managers under normalization. From a general point of view, the interesting thing is that that has been achieved within a formal structure of a government department. That may go to point out that the formal relationship between managers and politicians is not the main thing; the point is what actual autonomy is held by managers. Though we do not have prison examples, Northern Ireland is rich in examples of quangos set up as formally autonomous executive arms of government. In practice, this has sometimes meant that an unfortunate board of government appointees is forced, both by budgetary restraints and policy directives, to implement deeply unpopular government policy over which they have no real say. The government washes its hands, pointing to the autonomy of the board, the board claims it has no choice and the view of the people affected falls down the 'democratic deficit' left between.

None the less, one of the lessons of normalization has to be that, if ideological prejudice is abandoned, the business of running a prison effectively will necessarily generate a culture of good sense and compromise. That implies, of course, 'good' management, not sloppy, confused or prejudiced management. And good management can never, in our view, be apolitical. It requires a lively sense of history and more than a passing acquaintance with sometimes arcane political ideology to understand the views of prisoner groupings in Northern Ireland. Furthermore, good management must know its own limitations and the consequences of the irresponsible exercise of power.

A more detailed examination of management under normalization than we have had space for would reveal many weaknesses. We have not drawn attention to what we regard as 'failures' of normalization, which include the refusal to segregate remand prisoners and a mass strip search of the women's prison two years ago. Indeed, a more radical reading of normalization than we have given here might reveal contradictions which cast doubt on the quality of management.

Let us take space to draw out that point a little. It might be argued that, if the main point of your management was to contain, in humane conditions, a large group of people, then some kind of collective bargaining with them would be at the centre of your policy. Indeed, the increasing acceptance of prisoners' councils and even unions in comparable jurisdictions would seem to point in that direction. It would be wrong to say that our prison managers accepted the need to deal with paramilitary groupings reluctantly, for normalization represents an active and confident engagement. Yet there is a fundamental contradiction within the system, given the loud proclamation of a policy of individual treatment. That harks back to a largely discredited rehabilitative ideal on the one hand and, on the other, actually denies the humanity of prisoners by denying their social nature. There is still a view within prison management that part of the job is to change the politics of its charges. In our view, that is a mistaken objective and hinders the main thrust of good sense represented by normalization in general.

Our final criticism of management under normalization is the failure to grasp the civil liberties perspective. It might be felt that that is asking too much in a region which has had laws which derogate profoundly from international standards of human rights since its creation. However, once in prison, there is no particular reason why extraordinarily oppressive rules and practices are necessary. There is no doubt that things have changed for the better under normalization. But commitments are made only to 'fairness', never to 'justice'. In fact, due process in the prison setting is increasing. More than 50 per cent of all judicial reviews in Northern Ireland relate to the prisons. No doubt our prisoners are a particularly litigious lot, but the number of judicial reviews points both to the number of things that are arguably wrong with the system and the extent to which practices that will stand up in court are having to be introduced. How much better if prison management was proactive in this regard and agreed to be bound by rules and practices which reflected basic standards of civil liberties and due process.

If there is one conclusion which we wish to draw more than any other, it is about the importance of developing a productive interaction between prison managers and outside society. We have described the way in which this has happened in Northern Ireland and, we believe, it makes a return to the criminalization days almost inconceivable. There is a policy community around the prison system which has much strength. No doubt it would win few votes if it stood for election, but it has real influence none the less.

In curbing the excesses of ideological waves that sometimes threaten to swamp the prison system, a sensible, informed policy community can be a useful breakwater. At the end of the day, it must be right that well-managed prisons make better politics than prisoners on roofs. The task is, not just to convince politicians of that, but also to create a constituency in society with sufficient strength to make it an incontestable fact.

Notes

[1] The authors are deputy director and information officer of the Northern Ireland Association for the Care and Resettlement of Offenders (NIACRO). The views expressed are not necessarily those of the Association.

[2] Perhaps prison managers more than most will empathize with this definition of management: 'Figuring out what to do despite uncertainty, great diversity, and an enormous amount of potentially relevant information; getting things done through a large and diverse set of people, despite having little control over most of them' (Kotter 1982).

[3] In this chapter we use the phrase 'terrorists' only in inverted commas, because it is an ideologically loaded term. But the legal definition is: 'Terrorism means the use of violence for political ends . . .', Section 66 of the Emergency Provisions Act (Northern Ireland) 1191. We therefore follow the logic of this definition and use the terms 'politically motivated violence' and 'politically motivated prisoners (or offenders)'.

[4] 'The activity of attending to the general arrangements of a set of people

whom chance or choice has brought together' (M. Oakeshott in P. Laslett (ed.), *Philosophy, Politics and Society* (Oxford, 1956)).

5   See the discussion in M. Finley, *Politics in the Ancient World* (Cambridge, 1983).

6   In this text we mean to infer a fairly simple definition of civil society such as that given by McIntosh in G. McClelland *et al.* (eds.), *State and Society in Contemporary Britain* (Cambridge, 1984). 'Civil society refers to all those social institutions and relationships which arise, through voluntary association, outside the sphere of direct state control, and which belong to the domain of "society" rather than the state' (p. 20).

7   For an analysis of these, see McEvoy (1994).

8   Quoted in *Sunday Tribune* (Dublin), 27 February 1994.

9   No-jury courts, with somewhat amended rules of evidence, introduced as a result of the Diplock Report in 1972 (Diplock 1972).

10 See Protocol 1 and 2 and Common Article 3 of the Geneva Convention 1948.

11 We need to distinguish our use of the term 'normalization' from other usages which would see it as a propagandist attempt to minimize the effect of violence. We use it in a technical sense to describe the current policies of the prison service.

12 *Serving the Community* is probably the basic text of normalization in Northern Ireland's prisons, as will become clear in our numerous references to it.

13 A new edition was planned for publication in 1994.

14 Following the IRA and Loyalist ceasefires of autumn 1994 this ban was rescinded.

15 For example: 'What appears on its surface to be merely a means of dealing with offenders so that the rest of us can lead our lives untroubled by them, is in fact a social institution which helps define the nature of our society, the kinds of relationships which compose it, and the kinds of lives that it is possible and desirable to lead there' (Garland 1990: 287).

References

Adams, G. (1990). In Hadfield, B. (ed.), *Northern Ireland: Politics and the Constitution*.

Beresford, D. (1987). *Ten Men Dead* (London, Grafton).

Bishop, T. (1989). *The Provisional IRA* (London, Corgi).

Bishop, P. and Mallie, E. (1989). *The Provisional IRA* (London, Corgi).

Bowyer Bell, J. (1979). *The Secret Army* (Dublin, Academy Press).

Boyle, J. (1984). *The Pain of Confinement: Prison Diaries by Jimmy Boyle* (London, Pan).

Chibnall, S. (1977). *Law and Order News* (London, Tavistock).

Colville, M. (1992). *The Colville Report: a Report on the Operational Policy*

in Belfast Prison for the Management of Paramilitary Prisoners from
Opposing Factions Cmmd. 1860. (London, Her Majesty's Stationery
Office).

Coogan, T. P. (1985). *The IRA* (London, Fontana).

Curtis, L. (1984). *Ireland: the Propaganda War* (London, Pluto).

Diplock. Lord. (1972). *The Diplock Report: The Report of the Commission
to Consider Legal Procedure to Deal with Terrorist Activities in Northern
Ireland*. Cmmd. File 186. (Belfast, HMSO).

Dunne, D. (1989). *Out of the Maze: The True Story of the Biggest Jail Escape
since the War* (Dublin, Gill and MacMillan).

Finley, M. (1983). *Politics in the Ancient World* (Cambridge, Cambridge
University Press).

Fitzgerald, M. 'The telephone rings: long term imprisonment,' paper
presented at the 18th Cropwood Conference, University of Cambridge,
March 1986, quoted in Scraton *et al.*, *Prisons under Protest*.

Foot, P. (1989). *Who Framed Colin Wallace?* (London, Macmillan).

Foucault, M. (1977). *Discipline and Punish: The Birth of the Prison* (New
York, Pantheon).

Garland, D. (1990). *Punishment and Modern Society* (Oxford, Clarendon
Press).

Garland, D. and Young, P. (1983). *The Power to Punish: Contemporary
Penalty and Social Analysis* (London, Heinemann).

Gormally, B., McEvoy, K. and Wall, D. (1993). 'Criminal justice in a divided
society: Northern Ireland prisons.' in Tonry, M. (ed.), *Crime and Justice: A
Review of Research* (Chicago, University of Chicago).

Gowan, D. and Young, T. (1983). *The Power to Punish: Contemporary Penalty
and Social Analysis* (Edinburgh, Canongate).

Hadfield, B. (ed). (1992). *Northern Ireland: Politics and the Constitution*
(Buckingham, Open University Press).

Ham, C. and Hill, M. (1984). *The Policy Process in the Modern Capital
Estate* (Brighton, Rechie).

Hennessey, James. (1983–4). *The Hennessey Report: Report of an Enquiry by
HM Chief Inspector of Prisons into the Security Arrangements at HMP
Maze*. Cmmd. 203. (London, HMSO).

Hogan, G. and C. Walker. (1989). *Political Violence and the Law in Ireland*
(Manchester, Manchester University Press).

Hooper, A. (1983). *The Military and the Media* (Aldershot, Gower).

Iris. (1991). 'The H Block Hunger Strike,' 16 (May), 2–64.

Kotter, J. P. (1982). 'What effective general managers really do', *Harvard
Business Review*, November/December 1982.

Loughlin, G. (1992). 'Administrative policy in Northern Ireland,' in Hadfield,
B. (ed.), *Northern Ireland: Politics and the Constitution*.

Madden, P. (1979). 'Banned, censored and delayed', in *Campaign for Free
Speech in Ireland. The British Media and Ireland: Truth the First Casualty*
(pamphlet) (London, Information on Ireland).

McEvoy, K. (1994). 'Politically Motivated Prisoners in Northern Ireland: Strategies of Resistance, Cooperation and Cooption'. Unpublished PhD chapter Queen's University Belfast).

McIntosh, M. (1984). In McClelland, G. *et al.* (eds.). *State and Society in Contemporary Britain* (Cambridge, Polity Press).

Northern Ireland Prison Service. (1991). *Serving the Community: The Northern Ireland Prison Service in the 1990's* (Belfast, HMSO).

Northern Ireland Prison Service. (1990). *Annual Report on the Administration of the Northern Ireland Prison Service* (Belfast, HMSO).

Northern Ireland Prison Service (1990). *The Code of Conduct of the Northern Ireland Prison Service* (Belfast, HMSO).

Oakeshoot, M. (1956). In Laslett, P. (ed.), *Philosophy, Politics and Society* (Oxford, Oxford University Press).

O'Malley, P. (1990). *Biting at the Grave: The Irish Hunger Strikes and the Politics of Despair* (Belfast, Blackstaff).

Republican Fact File. (1991). 'Republican prisoners and the prison struggle in Ireland – criminalisation: defeated by prison resistance' (Belfast, Sinn Fein Foreign Affairs Bureau).

Ryan, M. and Ward, T. (1989). *Privatisation and the Penal System: The American Experience and the Debate in Britain* (Milton Keynes, Open University Press).

Scraton, P., Sim, J. and Skidmore, P. (1991). *Prisons Under Protest* (Milton Keynes, Open University Press).

Taylor, P. (1980). *Beating the Terrorists: Interrogation in Omagh, Goth and Castlereagh* (Harmondsworth, Penguin).

Tumim, S. (1994). *Recommendations of HM Chief Inspector of Prisons on HM Prison Maze* (Belfast, Northern Ireland Information Service).

Walsh, D. (1983). *The Use and Abuse of Emergency Regulation in Northern Ireland* (Nottingham, Russell).

18

Pre-court diversion and youth justice

MAGGY LEE

Police cautioning is now arguably the predominant means of dealing with young offenders outside the formal court system in England and Wales.[1] In 1992, 90,100 young people under the age of seventeen were cautioned by the police for indictable offences, but only 20,400 were found guilty in court of such offences (Home Office 1993). In a welfarist rhetoric, young people are given a police caution – a second chance – rather than being sucked into the formal court system. Within official circles, it has been argued that the court experience is a potentially negative and stigmatizing one: delay in the entry of young people to the criminal justice system may prevent their entry altogether (Home Office 1980; 1990b).

Whilst the emphasis and conclusion of different commentators on pre-court diversion may vary, one of their common assumptions is a 'benevolent' analysis (Sampson *et al.* 1988) of the means and ends of youth justice reform. In so far as inconsistent decision-making, 'unintended' consequences (for instance 'net widening') and variations in cautioning rates are identified as the main operational malfunctions, all that is needed is a clearly defined focus (for instance, to define what constitutes 'true' diversion), more rigorous application of the national cautioning standards by the police (Wilkinson and Evans 1990; Evans 1991), better recording procedures and tighter control of multiple cautioning (Home Office 1994), or some form of fine-tuning in service delivery (Allen 1991a; King 1991; NACRO 1988). Indeed, 'quality control' of service delivery in youth justice is arguably facilitated by greater co-ordination of the work of the police and other agencies, better management and monitoring, more sharing of information and expertise, more unified strategies and the like (Giller and Tutt 1987; Home Affairs Committee 1993; Mair 1990; Moxon 1985).

There is perhaps a second way of looking at pre-court diversion, which challenges the notion that more means better. In what Sampson and others (1988) have identified as a 'conspiratorial model' of multi-agency practice, the drive towards the bureaucratization of pre-court decision-making is part of a general process of ever-increasing coercion by the state. The main argument seems to be that alternatives to court are but an extension of formal regulation, its mere mask or agent (Pratt 1986). Phil Scraton (1985) has described multi-agency work involving the police as a 'police-led' strategy designed to 'take over' other agencies and use them for its own ends of 'total policing'. Similarly, Paul Gordon (1987) argues that whilst community policing (with its different strands of juvenile liaison, community involvement, corporate approach to policing, and so on) appears to offer an alternative to repressive police practices and strategies, it is but one aspect of a disciplinary regime aimed at reinforcing social discipline along a continuum of coerciveness and engineering consent and support for the police.

What is missing in both these approaches, however, is what pre-court justice actually means to young people. To date there has been no systematic research on the experience of pre-court diversion from the viewpoint of those at the receiving end of police cautioning. Police cautioning is said to be an alternative to the adversarial arrangements, legal formality and the criminalizing ethos of the youth court (formerly known as the juvenile court) system. Furthermore, there is an implicit assumption that the informal handling of delinquents (as in the Scottish Children Hearings System) may promote a sense of partnership between the state and parents of the offenders. In reality, to what extent does the normative agenda of pre-court diversion indicate an alternative discourse in youth justice? Do the young people and their parents regard diversion as 'in their best interests'? Do they accept the moral authority of the police? Does the organization of police cautioning provide a fair and progressive alternative to the punishment paradigm of the court system? Or has it simply altered the place and meaning of punishment in youth justice?

This chapter is based on a three-year research study on pre-court diversion and multi-agency liaison in four police force divisions in England.[2] The research project is based on case studies, observations of multi-agency forum (also known as Juvenile Liaison Panel or Bureau) meetings and police cautioning sessions, and a series of interviews with practitioners and professionals within the justice system – for instance, probation officers, social workers, education welfare officers, crown prosecutors, juvenile magistrates, police officers – as well as young people and their parents who received a caution at the police station.

Entering the system

The Police and Criminal Evidence Act 1984 (PACE) has been hailed as an important piece of legislation, which seeks to balance the rights of the individual against the need of the police to investigate offences diligently and expeditiously. Together with the accompanying codes of practice (paras. 3.6, 3.7 and 13.1) it lays out specific requirements to be placed upon the police and the rights of the alleged juvenile offender. Where an arrested juvenile is to be interviewed by the police, an 'appropriate adult' must be present. The appropriate adult is usually the juvenile's parent or, if the child or young person is in the care of the local authority, an officer of the local authority. In theory, the principal task of the appropriate adult is to ensure that the interview is conducted fairly, to ensure that the young person's rights are complied with and, where necessary, to facilitate communication.

It is, however, meaningless to refer to these rules as 'rights' in the abstract (Association for Juvenile Justice 1990). Whilst the Codes of Practice insist that the role of the appropriate adult is not a passive one and that the appropriate adult is not expected to act simply as an observer, the police themselves might expect just that, according to some researchers and commentators. Based on their research into police interrogations of alleged offenders (both adults and juveniles) in ten police stations, Sanders and Bridges (1990) found considerable 'rule breaking' in the oral provision of legal rights, 'informal' interrogations in the absence of an appropriate adult to secure information about other unsolved crimes, 'rule bending' by playing on the fears of the parents and juveniles or through the use of 'ploys'. All this led them to conclude that rather than eliminating police malpractice, the Police and Criminal Evidence Act seems to have changed it, made it less overt and hence more difficult to detect and control.

Their findings have particular relevance to our discussion here. Many parents and social workers may be drawn into their first contact with the police as an 'appropriate' person present during interview. Although one of the stated intentions of requiring the presence of an 'appropriate adult' where a juvenile is interviewed is to ensure that the interview is conducted fairly, parents may be unsure of their exact role: do they counsel and advise the young person, or simply observe the proceedings? There is some evidence in this study to suggest that parents who took an active stance and interrupted the police interview could attract considerable police hostility. In the following case study of arson (setting fire to an athletics equipment store), the parent was denounced as 'uncooperative' in the police file. Such assessment was passed on to the Juvenile Liaison Panel as part of the background information. The police interview notes, however, shed light on the basis for the police assessment:

Police officer: Everyone else is saying that you are responsible. They have detailed exactly how you are responsible, so would you care to take this opportunity without me badgering it out of you, to say exactly what your involvement was?

R made no reply and looked over to his father.

Father: I wish the tape to be stopped and I advise (my son) to say no more until we consult our solicitor. Thank you.

Police officer: You need not make any comment at this stage, if you require a duty solicitor present this could be arranged.

Father: No, we will listen to the statement, as I say, we will make no comment unless my son is charged with this. I will consult a solicitor, I'll wait until then. (Excerpt from police file.)

The above example highlights the problematic issue that an insistence on the exercise of legal rights can be interpreted by the police as being 'obstructive'. At a more general level, the active presence of parents and social workers may be seen as a challenge on police territory (Holdaway 1983) as it threatens the smooth functioning of the system. The result is that instead of opening up the closed world of the police station, the 'appropriate adult' may merely act as an adjunct to the authority of the police, a compliant condoner of poor police practice, or a 'stimulant for a whole range of threats and hostilities from the police' (Thomas 1988).

Parental responsibility and control

At another level, the role of the 'appropriate adult' ties in with police perceptions of parental responsibilities. Whilst police inspectors who were interviewed unanimously stressed that it was important for parents to be present at interviewing and cautioning sessions, the importance seemed to be related not so much to legal considerations as to their search for control indicators. In other words, the presence of the parents at police stations served a function quite different from those stated under PACE:

> The parents' attitude is as important as the juvenile's attitude. You do get a feeling whether parents are supportive or anti-authority. (Interview with police inspector)

> You want to know what the parents think of the offence, and what they are going to do about it. (Interview with police inspector)

Police officers who were interviewed seemed to have a certain image of the 'irresponsible poor' parent – getting drunk; smoking and going to the bingo three times a week; spending money on luxury items such as the video; not knowing the whereabouts of their children; inability to get their children to school. This emphasis on the perceived home background – especially the moral character of parents, parental responsibility, and the level of parental control over their children – seemed to stem from a general principle that, when young people offend, the law has a part to play in reminding parents of their responsibilities. This is clearly one of the main arguments behind the Conservative government's White Paper *Crime, Justice and Protecting the Public* (Home Office 1990a) (with its unpopular and unsuccessful proposal to hold parents responsible for actions committed by children under ten) and the Criminal Justice Act 1991. The emphasis is on compulsory parental attendance at court, greater use of the power of the youth court to bind over parents, and on parental payment of fines, compensation and costs. On the surface, these legislative proposals to enhance parental responsibility seem to echo the welfare philosophy behind the early juvenile court movement as well as the Fabian reformers of the 1960s – that is, delinquency is indicative of a lack of proper parental care, guidance and control. But as Rob Allen (1991b: 113) has pointed out, the emphasis of the new right of the 1980s is not on providing voluntary help and treatment in the form of family intervention by social workers but on tough, punitive sanctions to bring into line 'those parents who could cope, but simply chose not to'.

This emphasis on tough, punitive sanctions is not only relevant for the minority of violent, dangerous and persistent young offenders – witness the recent proposal for new secure training centres for the 'hard core' delinquents – and their recalcitrant parents. Instead, the punitive ethos of youth justice (together with its firm belief in individual and parental culpability) permeates the organization of pre-court justice and assessment even of those cautionable young people at the 'soft end'. Police inspectors who were interviewed suggested that reaction of parents at the cautioning session constituted a reliable gauge of the chances of reoffending – 'If they showed a couldn't care less attitude, then you can almost put your money on that juvenile would reoffend.' Questions of discipline and punishment were routinely put to the parents. But since the issues were often reduced to token gestures – such as cutting off the child's pocket money, grounding the child for a few nights, or even removing the television set from his/her room – the emphasis was less on the child's future offending than on the parents' apparent willingness to co-operate in the punishment and control enterprise.

Some parents admitted they felt very uneasy about those questions on home background; some clearly felt the home situation had nothing to do with the specific offence. A significant minority of these parents, however, went on to suggest that they felt it was part of a police strategy to punish them for their children's offences. They talked about feeling degraded and belittled before the police, an impression that the police were 'trying to bring you down'.

> I think they tried to embarrass you, or make you feel ashamed of your son's behaviour, as if you are the one who committed the crime. (Interview with parent)

> The way he said to my son, 'It is disgraceful on your part to have your dad dragged down to the police station, he has done nothing wrong', I mean, that would only make you feel worse, wouldn't it? (Interview with parent)

The rhetorical notion that pre-court diversion would promote and encourage parental participation or a sense of partnership between the state and the parents of offending children did not hold true in practice. On the contrary, both the normative agenda and the routine administration of police cautioning were inextricably tied up with the punishment paradigm of youth justice and divorced from any diversionary notion of gate-keeping.

As we shall see in the next section, cautioning sessions served a function akin to that of a 'degradation ceremony' (Garfinkel 1956), and the degrading tactics were directed towards the parents as much as the young people. Furthermore, the police who were interviewed were clearly interested in the parents' own ability to comply with regulations and values of respect for property and authority figures. The image of wilfully negligent and criminogenic parents colluding with or even commanding their children's delinquent behaviour were alluded to. In particular, parents who objected to a caution (none in the research study) could be criticized not only as uncooperative but also as having an 'attitude problem':

> Sometimes they come in here and sit there, look around or read a leaflet, and they just don't care. Some parents don't accept a caution. They think their son or daughter is not guilty of any offence. (Interview with police inspector)

> Many parents have an attitude problem. They think it is no big deal, and they walk out saying that to the kid. So what kind of an impact would a caution have? (Interview with police inspector)

> Some parents want their children to be brought to court to teach them a lesson; they do not care what is going to happen to their children. (Interview with police inspector)

A narrow escape?

Not all police inspectors explained the caution decision, its implications (for instance, that it is citable in court) at the beginning of the session. In some cases, the consent of the young person and parent(s) was sought only towards the end of the session, almost as an afterthought. Whilst the majority of young people and parents claimed they could follow the gist of what was being said to them, they tended to lack full comprehension. In particular, younger children found long words and legal terms alien. Some were at a loss when asked to sign the relevant form ('What is this for?'), and parents were confused ('What is its difference from a criminal record?'). Not all young people were able to understand the cautioning process, let alone any deterrent messages. On two occasions, the children brought before the police were obviously too young to understand what was going on. This did not escape the attention of the police inspector, who nevertheless insisted that a 'no further action' decision would not have been more appropriate because the 'evidence was there'. The following example illustrates the absurd or even bemusing result of this 'push-in' tendency on the part of the police. In this case, A (male, aged ten) was involved in what the police described as a 'shoplifting spree' with three other friends and cousins. A's case was not discussed in the multi-agency liaison forum and hence was solely a police decision. A's parents were both present at the cautioning session. A stood next to his mother, sucking his thumb and looking bewildered:

Inspector:	Why are you here?
A:	Handling stolen goods.
Inspector:	Yes, but what does handling mean?
A:	Don't know.
Inspector:	So you don't know why you are here?
Mother (aside):	Say you have been naughty.

Finding himself unable to get a satisfactory response from the child, the inspector then shifted towards other control indicators.

Inspector:	Is this the start of a criminal career, or just bad luck?
A:	Bad luck. (Still sucking his thumb and was told off by his mother).
Inspector:	Do you have trouble with him at home?
Father:	No.

Realizing the futility of delivering his standard moral lecture, the inspector simply went through the motion of telling A not to get into trouble again and then made him sign the form. The mother asked A if he could spell his name correctly and added, 'Sometimes he forgets!' (Excerpt from research notes.)

What seemed ironic in the cautioning process is that the actual production of pre-court justice relied heavily upon the punitive image of the formal court system itself. For one thing, the young person was invariably led to believe that prosecution had been in prospect – that he/she had had a narrow escape. Letters were sent out informing the young people and parent(s) to come to the police station, but they were left in suspense (sometimes deliberately) regarding the cautioning decision. This was calculated to maximize the impact of a caution.

The presentation of the prosecution decision as being balanced on a knife-edge could backfire, however, as the following example illustrates. In this case, P (male, aged fourteen) was accompanied by his local authority care worker. P seemed very nervous throughout the cautioning session and could not even remember his date of birth. He was only allowed to sit down after the inspector had explained the cautioning decision and made them sign the relevant papers.

Inspector:	What do you think would have happened to you if you hadn't been brought here to see me?
P:	Don't know.
Social worker:	To court.
P:	Yes, to court.
Inspector:	What do you think the judge would do to you then?
P:	They would punish me.
Inspector:	Yes, you would be fined, you could be put on probation. What is the last thing they could do to you?
P:	Send me to prison.
Inspector:	Your case has been considered carefully and we think you are worth another chance. So this is what it is – your second chance. Nothing will happen to you after this if you behave yourself, alright? But the minute you do something wrong and you get caught, you would be brought to court. Have you done something wrong before?
P:	Once before.
Inspector:	What was that about? (surprised)

The inspector did not know anything about P's first caution in relation to a case of shoplifting and was visibly embarrassed.

Inspector:	So this is your second cautioning then. You seem to have cracked the system. Two second chances! You won't come here again if you offend next time, I can promise you that. You'll go to court for this and the last offence as well, you'll get sent away then. (Excerpt from research notes.)

Although the presentation of the caution as the young person's *only* second chance could sometimes backfire, it seemed to have a strong immediate impact on most young people. Many young people who were interviewed said this was the single clearest message they received – that they would be sent to court or locked up next time.

Researcher:	How did you feel just now?

L: I felt like crying just now. That's what the inspector said –
                I will be taken to court and sent away if I get into trouble
                again next time.

In pre-court diversion, the key concepts for the police were intentionality, remorse, responsiveness and commitment to a moral order – for instance respect for private property or authority. The question of motive continually recurred as problematic at cautioning sessions, but the emphasis was not so much on establishing individual culpability as on assessing the young person's attitude to authority ('So why did you break the window? Is it some sort of a strike at authority?' or 'Is this the sign of something big?'). The question of motive was almost inevitably the first or second question which the inspector asked and the one which a young person was least able to answer in an appropriate manner, if at all. Whatever answer could be given would almost certainly be unacceptable ('Because it looked fun!' or 'Just something to do!'), and most young people either stayed silent or replied that they did not know.

What was regarded as an 'appropriate' response seemed to be tied up with particular assumptions about female and male delinquency. Some police officers felt that despite the small number of girls processed into the justice system, the 'hard core' who were on par with the serious male offenders (or what one inspector called the 'hard bitch') could be more devious ('they cry and use that as a disguise') and more difficult to manage than their male counterparts ('they are more self-assured, more mature than boys, but also very surly'). Police inspectors who were interviewed pointed out they could only be sure a caution was appropriate when they could discern that the process of receiving it had made some immediate impact upon the young people (and perhaps the parents). This practical emphasis on visible impact – for instance, making a delinquent sweat – and its problematic implications for the management of girls echo the findings of Loraine Gelsthorpe's research study (1989: 105–6). Whilst girls who failed to visibly express their emotions or respect for authority could be labelled as 'surly' or 'cocky' (and perhaps less likely to be given a second caution by the same officer), those who did comply were also more likely than boys to be denounced as 'devious'.

Police as moral condemners

The majority of social workers, probation officers and education welfare officers interviewed in the research study had never attended a cautioning session. Whilst inter-agency consultation could be beset by tensions and contradictions in the decision-making stage,[3] there seemed to be a consensus among non-police agencies that a caution should be administered sternly and strongly – 'as a screw is turned very tightly on them', as one social worker put it metaphorically. Once a cautioning decision was made, its value as a lesson for young offenders seemed to be a mere replication of the court-based punishment paradigm but in a swift (ideally no more than eight weeks after the commission of the offence), economical and direct manner (face-to-face with the police and without legal representation).

Apart from their rank, police officers (all male in the research study) who administered the caution were not chosen on the basis of any special qualifications or training. In practice, the mere fact that an inspector had children of his own could be seen as a good enough reason to put him in charge of cautioning. Although police inspectors who were interviewed argued that every officer had his own style of administering a caution, they were keen to elaborate on their stock-in-trade strategies of how to achieve the greatest impact on the young people and parents. They were typically concerned with manipulating the ritualistic aspects of pre-court justice through spacing arrangements or communicative techniques, such as forcing eye contact ('Would you look at me when I'm talking to you?'). Others include:

> I use my body language, make the youngsters look at me, standing in front, and the parents sitting. If they're crying you know you're through. You need to shake them up, but you don't need to shout at everyone.

> I don't caution co-offenders together; kids tend to listen more attentively when they are on their own.

> If it is a first-time offender, I'll sit on a chair, make him or her stand in front of me, parents behind so the child won't be distracted.

> I used to talk to the parents first and make the youngster stand outside, like a headmaster.

This dramatic staging of cautioning and enforcement of ritualistic boundaries of face-to-face communication set the tone of pre-court justice. Although questions of 'who did what, when and why?' were typically directed towards the young people, cautioning sessions were, in the main, occasions for the delivery of moral lectures. From the police point of view, a caution could include two main facets: a stern 'dressing down' and a 'heart-to-heart talk' (unless, of course, the young person was seen as too delinquent to benefit from some friendly advice).

The 'heart-to-heart talk' covered almost invariably the adverse consequences of having a criminal record, such as difficulties in settling down, having a family, earning other people's trust and, most importantly, finding a job. As the following inspector demonstrated, the main purpose was to point out to the young person 'the road he is heading down':

Inspector: You want to get a job in a few years' time, don't you? You will not get a job if you have a criminal record. If two people are applying for the job at the same time and one has a criminal record and the other doesn't, who do you think they will employ? You?

J: No. (Excerpt from research notes).

That the vision of employment prospects for young people who stayed out of trouble was blatantly inapplicable to the realities of contemporary economic development was rarely questioned by the police inspectors. As far as their structural position in the job market is concerned, young people have arguably constituted one of the most vulnerable and marginal sections of the work-force – the 'reserve army of labour'. Seen in this context, the elaborate lecture on the moral value of work ethic, respectability and stability (sometimes directed to children as young as thirteen years of age), the importance of being integrated into the next generation of disciplined adult workers – all this seemed to bear little meaning on the survival strategies and limited possibilities of many of the young people appearing before the police.

Another facet of the moral lecture was a 'dressing down' of the young person, focusing on the issue of individual culpability, remorse, the disgrace to the parents, the school or even the whole community. Questions such as 'What do you feel about your responsibility?', 'What do you think you have learnt from this incident?', 'Do you know you have let down your parents?' were frequently directed at the young people. More importantly, the moral lecture highlighted and condemned the young person's status as a criminal. This was despite the triviality of some of the offences involved and the rhetoric of diversion, that is to reduce the potentially damaging effects of stigmatization and labelling.

Inspector:	Why are you here in the first place?
P:	I don't know.
Inspector:	So why did you do it? (staring into P's eyes)
P:	Don't know.
Inspector:	What makes you think of getting into the locker and taking the watch?
P:	Don't know (very soft spoken).
Inspector:	Speak up a bit. What were you going to do with the watch?
P:	I haven't thought about it really.
Inspector:	You stole something and you don't know what to do with it!
P:	I will probably throw it away.
Inspector:	Other people would ask you questions about the watch, wouldn't they? So that makes you what?
P:	A thief (almost in tears).
Inspector:	A thief, uh! (Excerpt from research notes).

This ceremonial 'stripping of a man of his dignity' as a prelude to judicial punishment in court has been thoroughly explicated and analysed by Garfinkel (1956). What the cautioning system seems to have done is to reproduce and institutionalize the degradation ceremony in the pre-court arena and to reinforce the role of the police (rather than the magistrates in court) as moral condemners. The police effort to bring down the young person could be both a means and an end in itself. Not only was the visible impact (if any) regarded as an indicator of the appropriateness and effectiveness of a caution, but it was the *only* immediate 'punishment' within the police powers:

> I can use the tone of my voice, shuffle papers around, but at the end of the day there's not much I can do with the kid really. (Interview with police inspector)

Justice, fairness, and punishment

The majority of juveniles who were interviewed thought they were given a caution mainly because they had never been in trouble before and/or because the offence was not too serious. This seemed to be in line with 'just deserts' principles arguably embodied by the Criminal Justice Act 1991 (cf. Section 1.6 of the White Paper *Crime, Justice and Protecting the Public*: Home Office 1990a). But as Parker and others

(1981: 118) have argued, such a neat conclusion negates 'the full complexity of the views of those subject to the juvenile justice process and the often bitter and problematic nature of their own experiences'. For instance, although young people in their study voiced a broad agreement in ranking the court's range of disposals, their negative personal experience in court, perceptions of authority figures, inappropriateness and severity of the sentence, and an awareness of police power to define and 'bump up' charges, all served to erode the notion of justice as fairness.

There is, however, another aspect of the 'full complexity of the views' of the young people that merits some attention. Juvenile offending, especially offences of assault, often occur as but one step in a protracted series of encounters or conflicts. Harry Blagg (1985) has made a similar point in relation to the difficulties involved in developing personal reparation as part of a diversionary strategy. This is particularly so in cases of fights between peers or bullying among school-children, which may take place for a confused set of reasons; victims, offenders and bystanders all may carry some responsibility. Some of the cases in this research study involved a degree of physical violence between school-children, peers at a youth club or in the local neighbourhood. Some young people who were interviewed mentioned either a long-standing dispute with the 'victim', having been 'set up', or a feeling that the 'victim' also shared part of the blame. In so far as the caution was presented by the police as an alternative to criminal proceedings, they felt relieved at not having to go to court. Nevertheless, they also showed signs of resentment for being held solely responsible for the offence ('It's not just all me. Why should I be the only one told off by the police? But I'm not saying it's all him.'). The general point is that the moral authority of the police is ultimately mediated by the complexity of such feelings and perceptions of the young people, all of which may serve to erode the notion of pre-court justice as fairness.

The majority of young people in the research study had never been cautioned before and, therefore, did not really know what to expect. Some had picked up impressions from friends or from relatives. When asked to describe what they made of the cautioning session, and specifically how they felt and to what extent they thought the police were harsh or sympathetic towards them, the response was mixed. The majority of the young people regarded the purpose of a caution and the role of the police inspector in punitive terms, that is punishing them for what they had done. Although the majority of them perceived the cautioning process in a routine and matter-of-fact manner ('It's basically a telling-off'; 'The officer is alright, just doing his job'), others who were previously interviewed at the police station or who had been cautioned before responded in more emotive terms:

> It was awful. I feel I'm in such a mess. I will not get into trouble again. I don't want to come back to the police station (still in tears).

> I thought it would be more frightening . . . Not actually shouting at me, but raising his voice.

> I think I have got off lightly. I thought it would be a lot stricter, a lot more yelling at me this time. I could not sleep last night, I was so worried. Really lucky of me.

> I was frightened . . . it was not what I had expected . . . Well, yes, a telling-off, but not like this. (Like what?) The way he just stared at me, like he was angry.

It seemed what the young people thought of the caution, what they had expected, and whether they felt they were treated sympathetically or too harshly by the police, were all tied up with the experience of their previous encounters with the forces of law and order. Hence they spoke not only of the cautioning inspectors who 'stared' or 'looked down at me', but also the interviewing officers who 'kept me in the cell' or said 'something terrible would happen to me', the officers who had stopped and searched them on the streets – these were all authority figures who had more power over them and over the definitions of the situation. None of the young people who were interviewed expected or considered the pre-court caution to be a 'heart-to-heart talk'. This is broadly in line with other court-based research findings which indicate that young offenders regard the judicial system's prime task in terms of punishment and control rather than care and treatment (Morris and Giller 1977; Parker *et al.* 1981).

In one case, the female juvenile cynically rejected the 'helping' role of the police. Without further comparative information, it is difficult to tell whether the 'heart-to-heart talk' with girls in general takes on a paternalistic dimension. But in this particular case, M (female, aged fifteen, setting fire to a waste paper basket) was cautioned in the presence of her social worker, and proved to be one of the 'unruly resources' (Brown 1991: 75) who challenged the smooth running of the session, the police's moral authority, and visibly embarrassed the inspector:

Inspector: I know you have been treated heavy-handedly in the past. If only you would let me help you. We don't want to keep hassling you.

M: How can you help me then?

Inspector: You tell me, love.

M: You can't help me. I can only help myself. Nobody can. I have got my own mates. Nobody can tell me not to do this, not to do that. I am in charge of my own life. (Excerpt from research notes.)

A soft option and an easy way out?

Similarly, the majority of parents did not look to the police to provide help and guidance for their children. Since no home visit reports had been prepared on these families, it was not possible to find out their experience of and views about social workers and probation officers. Nevertheless, most parents said they wanted the caution to be 'over and done with in one day'. In particular, the parents were sceptical of getting the social services involved, partly because of their perceptions of social workers as 'do-gooders' or 'child-snatchers' and partly because of the way they perceived the offence itself:

I can't see how bringing in the social services would help actually. Because in a case like this, it has nothing to do with the way we bring up our kids or anything like that. It was only a spur of a moment thing, my son did something stupid and that was it. (Interview with parent)

Only one parent suggested that some follow-up work by the youth and community services could keep his son 'in line'. The majority of them also described the purpose of a caution in terms of a 'telling-off' or 'teaching the child a lesson'; some even expected harsher words from the police:

Researcher: What do you think of the caution just now?

Father: I thought it would be harsher than that. No, not taking him to court, but a good telling off. Similar sort of, er . . . not atmosphere, but similar sort of situation if you went to court, but not actually in court *for this sort of thing*. (emphasis added)

Indeed, a significant minority of the parents specifically mentioned the triviality of the offending behaviour involved. And if we examine closely the nature of behaviour or damages or value of goods stolen in all cases, offences of 'criminal damage' could mean, in practice, breaking the window of a butcher, damaging three bags of grain in a farm, or demolishing two straw stacks in the field. The offence of 'arson' in one case involved setting fire to a waste paper basket. Similarly, the value of goods stolen in theft-related offences ranged from as little as £5.50 (a toy duck), a barrel of beer from an Indian restaurant to £185 (a camera). Partly because of this gap between the perceived triviality of the offending behaviour and the formal charges brought by the police, parents did not always feel a caution was the best way of dealing with the incident. In one case where N (male, aged twelve) demolished two straw stacks in the field, the parents complained that their son would have apologized to the farmer and they would have paid compensation – 'the police should never have processed the case formally in the first place'.

Nor did parents necessarily regard a caution as a 'let off'. Although we saw in earlier sections that parents' and young people's understanding of the implications of a caution was at best vague and partial, some parents were highly sceptical of the police's claim that a caution was simply a 'private matter':

Researcher: Do you think a caution is a let off?
Mother: No, I don't. Because that could still be used against him, that isn't totally wiped out. (Interview with parent)

Or as other parents suggested in the interviews:

It isn't really a private matter between the police and (my son). Oh no! He's still on bail; he has done a criminal act in the eyes of the police, you know, so they can use it again, like the inspector just said, if there's any more trouble, that can be used, that can sway what the next result would be because he's got a caution.

Not a let off . . . because he has to be very careful from now on. The school somehow has learnt about this, and he has been very worried.

It's not an easy way out. He has been told off by the officer, hasn't he? For this kind of offence which is very minor really, it's a bit over-reacting if you ask me.

It's not really a let off. You see, there would be a lot to do in the society if the police took everybody to court for the first offence, and probably the cost involved, and the end result of it won't be worth it.

Discussion

For most of the young people and parents who were interviewed, the police cautioning session was their first encounter with the forces of law and order. Bearing in mind that these young people (white and predominantly male) were almost by definition minor, first-time offenders and hence not seen as a serious threat to law and order, it is perhaps not surprising that the majority of them did not experience rough policing or express any strong sense of resentment, injustice or disillusionment with the way they were treated. But for many of them, one thing seemed clear: they saw the purpose and administration of police cautioning in punitive terms, not in terms of offering help, guidance or encouraging participation of the parents and young people.

Whilst pre-court diversion may have its roots in the radical 'destructuring' movements in the 1960s (Cohen 1985)[4] and may be something potentially challenging, it has increasingly been incorporated into a bureaucratic model of swift dispensation of justice in the 1990s. Police cautioning in its present form may be an alternative strategy of dealing with young people but only in an *administrative* sense. This limitation also characterizes the development of diversionary measures as part of a wider strategy to cope with increasing crime rates and to stabilize the case loads of youth justice administration in many other European countries (Dunkel 1991). With the rise of managerialism and social auditing in the public sector, efficiency devices such as reducing court overload, delays and guilty pleas, restrictions on cases coming into the appeal system, refusal of legal aid for frivolous cases, have been proposed to make the legal system more efficient, economic and effective. Seen in this light, the diversion of uncontested cases out of court, a truncated or even 'trial free' system of youth justice which by-passes the lengthy and costly processes of full investigation, prosecution, legal aid, and adjudication, may be more in tune with the principles of economic expediency (Jones 1991). Pleas of guilty are no longer good enough: they must come earlier (for instance, at the pre-court cautioning stage) rather than later.

Without any alternative means of measuring or monitoring the long-term success (or otherwise) of police cautioning, punishing the delinquents on the spot may well be regarded as the only direct indicator of efficiency and effectiveness. What is ironic is that in diversionary practices, the police ultimately have to evoke the punitive images and sanctioning power of the formal court system to make a strong impact on the young people. Given that the normative agenda in assessing and categorizing young people and their families in the pre-court arena seems inextricably tied up with the court-based delinquency control paradigm, diversion has arguably achieved a kind of symbiotic existence with the formal court system, the one sustaining and implying the existence of the other.

What we may be witnessing in the pre-court arena is a reaffirmation of the place and meaning of punishment within the traditional youth justice system. As McConville and others (1991: 130–1) have pointed out:

> In the rhetoric of criminal justice both prosecution and caution are seen as being positive means of dealing with crime. Both are geared towards achieving the objectives of the criminal justice process in deterring further offences, in protecting the public, in bringing home to the offender the wrongfulness of the relevant conduct and in educating the offender in the social values embodied in the criminal law . . . Any notion that caution is an appropriate means of mitigating the law's response is rejected as a usurpation of a function which properly belongs to the courts.

In so far as police cautioning represents a punitive strategy of dealing with juvenile offending, it is much less accessible to the public, much more behind the scene and socially invisible than other forms of punishment. But despite the delinquency control aspect of diversion, the police and other youth justice specialists in this study all tended to represent themselves in a positive, utilitarian way, as carrying out a useful social task. Given that most cautioning sessions lasted for no more than fifteen minutes, punishment could only be conducted in a routinized, matter-of-fact manner. Even the most visible form of punishment (for instance reducing someone to tears) was represented in utilitarian, rationalized terms of cost-effectiveness.

This necessitates a re-examination of the place and meaning of punishment in youth justice reform. As part of the general process which David Garland (1990: 187) has described as 'the civilization of punishment':

The social tasks involved in punishment have been delegated to specialized agencies on the margins of social life, with the effect that they have, to some extent become hidden . . . Our practices of punishment have ceased to be social in the full sense and have become increasingly technical and professional. To the extent that the role of the public – or even of those who claim to represent them – has been diminished, the role of the expert has been correspondingly increased and, in the same movement, technical knowledge and diagnoses have displaced (or else disguised) moral evaluation and condemnatory judgement.

For many young people, there may be a very real difference between being 'told off' by the police and being dealt with in court. But in so far as some young people and parents experience police cautioning as punitive and humiliating, there is a danger in glorifying police cautioning as being 'in the best interests' of these families.

Notes

[1] A police caution is a formal warning given to a person (juvenile or adult) who admits to having committed a criminal offence which could have led to prosecution (Home Office 1994).

[2] Lee, M. (1992). 'Pre-court Diversion and Multi-agency Liaison in Juvenile Justice: in whose best interests'. Unpublished PhD thesis, University of Cambridge.

[3] See also Blagg *et al.*; Davis *et al.* (1989) and Evans (1993) for a discussion of the competing ideologies and power differentials in inter-agency liaison.

[4] As Stan Cohen (1985: 30–6) has argued, the diversionary movement derives its initial appeal from wider ideologies (for instance decentralization, decriminalization, self-help deprofessionalization, delegalization, demedicalization) than is implied by the limited question of how many offenders should be sent to court or custody.

References

Allen, R. (1991a). 'Caution "plus" or prosecution "minus"', paper presented at a National Conference on Police Cautioning: Home Office Circular 59/1990. January 1991, Nottingham Polytechnic.

Allen , R. (1991b). 'Parental responsibility for juvenile offenders', in Booth, T. (ed.). *Juvenile Justice in New Europe* (Sheffield, Joint Unit for Social Services Research).

Association for Juvenile Justice (1990). *Guidance for Policy and Practice in Juvenile Justice* (London, AJJ).

Blagg, H. (1985). 'Reparation and justice for juveniles', *British Journal of Criminology*, 25(4), 267–79.

Blagg, H., Pearson, G., Sampson, A., Smith, D. and Stubbs, P. (1988). 'Inter-agency co-operation: rhetoric and reality', in Hope, T. and Shaw, M. (eds.), *Communities and Crime Reduction* (London, HMSO).

Brown, S. (1991). *Magistrates at Work* (Milton Keynes, Open University Press).

Cohen, S. (1985). *Visions of Social Control* (Cambridge, Polity Press).

Cutler, J. (1990). 'Children's crimes – should parents pay?', *Childright*, 65, 9–11 (London, Children's Legal Centre).

Davis, G., Boucherat, J., Watson, D. (1989). 'Pre-court decision-making in juvenile justice', *British Journal of Criminology*, 29(3), 219–35.

Dunkel, F. (1991). 'Legal differences in juvenile criminology in Europe', in Booth, T. (ed.), *Juvenile Justice in New Europe* (Sheffield, Joint Unit for Social Services Research).

Evans, R. (1991). 'Police cautioning and the young adult offender', *Criminal Law Review*, August 1991, 598–609.

Evans, R. (1993). 'Before the court – understanding inter-agency consultation with juveniles and young adults', paper presented at the British Criminology Conference, University of Wales, July 1993.

Garfinkel, H. (1956). 'Conditions of successful degradation ceremonies', *American Journal of Sociology*, 64, 420–4.

Garland, D. (1990). *Punishment and Society* (Oxford, Clarendon).

Gelsthorpe, L. (1989). *Sexism and the Female Offender* (Aldershot, Gower).

Giller, H. and Tutt, N. (1987). 'Police cautioning of juveniles: the continuing practice of diversity', *Criminal Law Review*, May 1987, 367–74.

Gordon, P. (1987). 'Community policing: towards the local police state?' in Scraton, P. (ed.), *Law, Order and the Authoritarian State* (Milton Keynes, Open University Press).

Holdaway, S. (1983). 'Police and social work relations: problems and possibilities', *British Journal of Social Work*, 16(2), 137–60.

Home Office (1980). *Young Offenders*. Cmnd. 8045 (London, HMSO).

Home Office (1984). *Cautioning by the Police: A Consultative Document* (London, HMSO).

Home Office (1990a). *Crime, Justice and Protecting the Public*. Cmnd. 965 (London, HMSO).

Home Office (1990b). *The Cautioning of Offenders* (Circular 59/1990. London, HMSO).

Home Office (1993). *Criminal Statistics, England and Wales 1992* (London, HMSO).

Home Office (1994). *The Cautioning of Offenders* (Circular 18/1994. London, HMSO).

Home Affairs Committee (1993). *Juvenile Offenders: Sixth Report of the Home Affairs Committee, Session 1992–93, Volume 1* (London, HMSO).

Jones, C. (1991). 'The auditing of criminal justice: economy, effectiveness and efficiency goals versus substantive justice ends', paper presented at the British Criminology Conference, University of York, July 1991.

King, R. (1991). 'Cautioning: panels or bureaux?', paper presented at a National Conference on Police Cautioning: Home Office Circular 59/1990. January 1991, Nottingham Polytechnic.

Lee, M. (1992). 'Pre-court Diversion and Multi-agency Liaison in Juvenile Justice: in whose best interests'. Unpublished PhD thesis, University of Cambridge.

Mair, G. (1990). 'Evaluating the effects of diversion strategies on the attitudes and practices of agents of the criminal justice system', paper presented at the Council of Europe 19th Criminological Research Conference, Strasbourg, 26–29 November 1990.

McConville, M., Sanders, A. and Leng, R. (1991). *The Case for the Prosecution* (London, Routledge).

Morris, A. and Giller, H. (1977). 'The juvenile court – the client's perspective', *Criminal Law Review*, March 1977, 198–205.

Moxon, D. (1985). *Managing Criminal Justice* (London, HMSO).

NACRO (1988). *Juvenile Cautioning: Co-ordination and Community* (London, NACRO).

Parker, H., Casburn, M. and Turnbull, D. (1981). *Receiving Juvenile Justice* (Oxford, Basil Blackwell).

Pratt, J. (1986). 'Diversion from the Juvenile Court', *British Journal of Criminology*, 26(3), 212–33.

Sampson, A., Stubbs, P., Smith, D., Pearson, G. and Blagg, H. (1988). 'Crime, localities and the multi-agency approach', *British Journal of Criminology*, 28(4), 478–93.

Sanders, A. and Bridges, L. (1990). 'Access to legal advice and police malpractice', *Criminal Law Review*, July 1990, 494–509.

Scraton, P. (1985). *The State of the Police* (London, Pluto).

Thomas, T. (1988). 'The Police and Criminal Evidence Act 1984: the social work role', *Howard Journal of Criminal Justice*, 27(4), 256–65.

Wilkinson, C. and Evans, R. (1990). 'Police cautioning of juveniles: the impact of Home Office Circular 14/1985', *Criminal Law Review*, March 1990, 165–76.

Crime, justice and the underclass

19

The politics of youth crime prevention: developments in Australia and England and Wales

JOHN MUNCIE, GARRY COVENTRY
AND REECE WALTERS

Introduction

Faced with dramatic increases in recorded crime, escalating costs of criminal justice agencies, and precious little evidence to support the continuance of policies of deterrence and control, governments across the western world have increasingly turned to notions of crime prevention as offering alternative means of responding to the problem of crime. Yet the term 'crime prevention' has no readily identifiable definition or uniform meaning. Indeed, the establishment of police forces and model prisons in the early nineteenth century was as much legitimated by their presumed potential to prevent crime, as was the development of neighbourhood watch and car watch schemes in the late twentieth century. This chapter disentangles the multiplicity of meanings that are attached to 'prevention' and provides a critical assessment of the diverse ways in which the term has come to find practical expression. In the main it draws on current policy initiatives in Australia and England and Wales. It is not intended to offer a thorough comparative analysis of these countries, or to identify instances of 'good' practice, but rather to highlight the significant limitations of, and omissions in, contemporary crime prevention discourse. For example, in contrast to the dominant policies and practices found in contemporary Australian and English and Welsh jurisdictions, it argues for a radical reconceptualization of the terms 'crime' and 'prevention' in order to break out of the inherently debilitating, myopic and narrow focus of current debate. Put at its simplest, if we are seriously interested in formulating and promoting policies which are likely to impact on anti-social and offending behaviour, we need to move beyond a discourse of crime, law and order and towards a discourse of social justice, empowerment and the enhancement of human and social development.

Throughout we concentrate on youth and young people as our key empirical referent: not because we share the view that it is these sections of the population which are repeatedly the most troublesome, but rather because, quite clearly, the future of any society depends on how far we are prepared to invest in the social development of all young people in the present.

The social construction of youth crime

The most obvious and compelling picture of crime that can be gleaned from official crime statistics in both England and Wales and Australia is that those under twenty-one years of age commit about a half of all offences recorded by the police. For this reason the 'young offender' holds the potential to repeatedly occupy the dubiously privileged position of society's premier 'folk devil'. This remains the case even when the same official statistics record dramatic decreases in young offending as occurred in both countries in the late 1980s and early 1990s. At such times the official statistics are either simply deemed to be 'wrong', unreflective of social reality, or 'manufactured' because of demographic changes (reductions for example, in the numbers of 15–17 year olds in the population) and increases in informal cautioning by the police. As marked increases in burglaries and auto theft were reported in the past decade (1983–93), it was widely *assumed* that this was almost exclusively the work of young people. As a result, the term 'crime' remains closely associated with, and frequently used as a shorthand expression for, 'youth crime' (White 1990: 105). The term 'youth crime' similarly deserves deconstruction. It implies a criminal propensity in all sections of this population, whilst official records and policies characteristically single out male and working-class young people as the key object of concern and target for intervention.

Police records and court statistics suggest that in England and Wales the peak age of offending is between fifteen and seventeen, whilst in Australia it stands at late teens and early twenties. Rarely is the critical attention given to apparent decreases in crime, applied to these figures. Given that recorded figures at best only cover a third of all crime committed, it is probably more accurate to answer the questions 'Is youth crime so prevalent?' and 'Is it increasing or decreasing?' by admitting that we do not know (Muncie 1984: 61). What official statistics can more reliably tell us is that the offences for which young people are cautioned or convicted cluster around minor property crimes, such as transit offences, shoplifting and other theft. Young people in both countries do not appear significantly, for example, in offences against the person, fraud, firearm related, drug, and sexual offences (Potas *et al.* 1990; Home Office 1991a). Local crime surveys and self-report studies in England and Wales, however, have suggested that offending by young people is both widespread and ubiquitous, but also that much of this is of a trivial nature and likely to be 'grown out of'. Some form of deviant, anti-social or criminal behaviour thus appears as an essential element in the normality of the lives of the vast majority of young people, and particularly young males. Over 80 per cent of known offenders are males: a factor which is frequently noted, but its broader significance rarely subjected to serious comment. It also seems safe to assume that when young males do figure highly in official statistics, it is not usually because of the seriousness of their offences, but because of their high visibility. Their tendency to occupy and use public space (the street, the shopping mall, the football terrace) and to be in the company of peers are significant factors in their behaviour being reported and known to the police. Opportunities for crime at work and in the hidden economy are not only out of the reach of young people but are also generally excluded from the official statistics and the media/political gaze.

Despite these statistical uncertainties and competing realities, the issue of youth crime does, however, continually resurface as a key political issue. However, the way in which political parties, the media and law enforcement agencies depict young offending probably tells us more about the behaviour of these institutions, than it does of young people themselves. In contemporary conservative rhetoric (for example the Conservative party in the United Kingdom; the Liberal-National coalition in Australia), young offending is depicted as symptomatic of recent breakdowns in moral authority, parental discipline and nuclear family structures (usually viewed as a result of 1960s permissiveness). In turn, this is assumed to have created a 'new barbarism' to which the current labels of 'nasty persistent juvenile offenders' and 'bail bandits' (United Kingdom) and 'larrikins, thugs, animals, druggies and dole bludgers' (Australia) are readily applied.

The application of labels, though, lends itself to stereotyping and confusion. In England and Wales the spectre of a distinct group of 'persistent young offenders' – beyond control, beyond redemption – has failed to materialize in empirical research (Hagell and Newburn 1994). Such labels tend not only to encourage an unreflective condemnation of youthful behaviour, but also place it in the context of warning of an accelerating process of demoralization within society at large. Within such an ideology the three themes of individual responsibility, self-control and deterrence predominate. The social causes and context of crime are sidestepped by the insistence that people break the law through personal choice, self-volition and lack of adequate means of control. It makes no sense then to search for ways of alleviating causes or to reform. Rather, the logic of such ideology contends that criminality can only be contained (or managed) by issuing 'credible threats' based on the certainty and severity of punishment and increases in legislative powers. Translated into crime prevention policy, this means that developing the deterrent effect of law enforcement and criminal justice agencies and reducing opportunities for crime through situational strategies have, historically, achieved a dominance over other prevention initiatives which may aim to improve social conditions and enhance employment, educational, leisure and recreational opportunities. More recently, both in England and in several Australian jurisdictions, the need for alternative prevention policies has been emphasized, citing the failure of the criminal justice system to reduce and/or control crime. The degree to which such 'alternatives' are capable of challenging, or are simply co-opted by, a law and order ideology is discussed below.

What the conservative discourse tends to omit is that (a) concern about youth crime is not unprecedented, but is an historically recurrent feature of western societies; (b) youth crime is relatively insignificant compared to the hidden and diverse practices of white-collar and corporate crime; and (c) young people do not exist in some social vacuum, but are affected by, and respond to, the life chances with which they are faced. Our conceptualization of young people in general, and young offending in particular, is diametrically at odds with the images conveyed in dominant political and media discourse. Where the dominant discourse talks of youth, we argue that analysis should be grounded in a critical awareness of the race, gender, class and regional differences which comprise this section of the population. In particular, we recognize that the development of an effective youth policy will be seriously flawed if it continues to focus predominantly on male, working-class and urban young people – the current and recurring folk devil of political attention. Whereas 'new right' authors, such as Charles Murray (1990), are happy to account for youth crime through notions of the 'barbaric male' for whom marriage is the 'indispensable civilising force', we contend that there is a more complex set of relations at work which may connect the censured status of criminality and the socially revered status of masculinity. Just what are we condoning in the phrase 'boys will be boys'? Where the dominant discourse talks of new and unprecedented levels of youth crime and thus the argued urgent need to instigate new mechanisms of control, we view the issue as historically recurring, as symptomatic of politically expedient attempts to raise contemporary levels of anxiety and to enable forces of reaction to remain in ascendancy. In England and Wales this is typically achieved by glorifying a mythical trouble-free past (Pearson 1983). Finally where the dominant discourse talks of moral breakdown and lack of self-control, we maintain that the issue of youth crime is centred upon a complex set of social and economic processes that not only profoundly shapes the life experiences of young people, but also the willingness of the state to criminalize. Most significant of these in the past two decades has been the restructuring of western economies in which the size of unproductive (marginalized) populations has rapidly grown. A by-product of this situation is the assumed rise in crime and disorder amongst young people. But such restructuring has also created growing numbers of unemployed, homeless, powerless, disaffected and 'abandoned' young men and women (Williamson 1993; Presdee 1990). It is our contention that the 'youth problem' is constructed predominantly in terms of criminality because this acts to divert attention away from the recurrent failures of government and social institutions to recognize and respond to the needs and difficulties faced by young people in general. The issue has been granted a political significance, not only out of all proportion to the seriousness of young offending, but to the detriment of developing mechanisms to aid social integration.

It follows, then, that any effective youth crime prevention strategy first needs to move towards a depoliticization of the issue, to recognize that offending behaviour is largely of a transient and trivial nature and then to seek the inclusion of young people through educational, employment and community involvement, rather than exclusion through criminalization. In order to break out of the myopic and restrictive discourse so firmly established by conservative and new right ideology, it is necessary also to move towards a reconceptualization of notions of youth crime and offending in terms of young peoples *disaffection* and *social dislocation*. This is not to deny the existence of young offending and its impact on victims, but to promote a more informed and measured analysis of its extent, seriousness and social context.

The re-emergence of 'crime prevention': political rhetoric and policy developments

As Laycock and Heal (1989) and South (1987) suggest, the idea of crime prevention has long been used as a justifying rationale for the work of criminal justice agencies. The instigation of a professional police force in the early nineteenth century was sustained on these grounds, although its subsequent development did focus more on investigation, detection and prosecution. Similarly, the development of reformatories in the mid nineteenth century and their subsequent evolution into approved schools and community homes in England and Wales and Youth Training Centres in Australia was legitimated through a belief in their rehabilitative effect and ability to prevent reoffending. Indeed, the perspective which maintains that crime can best be prevented through increasing police resources, strengthening court powers and imprisoning more people for longer – a law enforcement perspective – still exerts a primary and powerful influence. The assumed deterrent effect of tough legal sanction remains a characteristic immediate political response to young offending, as witnessed by the imposition of maximum 25-year custodial sentences in Western Australia and 5-year sentences in England and Wales, in reaction to the life-threatening aspects of the 'joy-riding' phenomena of the early 1990s. Similarly, in England and Wales plans are in place to build a new generation of secure training centres for 12- to 15-year-old 'persistent offenders'; to lower the serious offending tariff from the age of thirteen to ten; and to end the system of repeat cautioning, whilst in Victoria, Australia moves are afoot to hear juvenile cases in the adult magistrate courts and to replace concurrent sentences for multiple offences with automatic consecutive sentences; and in Western Australia to make imprisonment mandatory for repeat offenders. However, there is precious little evidence to suggest that such displays of 'getting tough on crime' have anything more than a politico-populist rationale. Despite substantial increases in criminal justice expenditure and resources – particularly police powers and staffing – overall recorded crime continues to rise in both countries (despite some annual blips). An increased commitment to youth custodial sentencing, particularly in England and Wales in the 1970s, and again in the mid-1990s, continues to do little to overcome a reoffending rate of 75 per cent within two years of release. Similar negative and counterproductive results of custodial sentencing are reported in Australia (although an accurate picture of reoffending rates is confounded by the rather *ad hoc* basis of data collection in that country). However, in contrast to England and Wales, some Australian states, such as Victoria, witnessed no burgeoning juvenile custodial population in the 1970–85 period. Rather a number of youth training centres for 14- to 17-year-olds were closed and, under the auspices of the Department of Community Services, the range of community disposals enhanced. Whilst the precise reasons for this diversity remain unclear, a key factor lies in the Australian Labour party's avoidance of the forms of authoritarian and centralized control, characteristic of Thatcherism. In Australia political strategies in criminal justice (and other) matters have tended to be rather more 'corporatist' than 'confrontational' (Muncie 1991). A resurgence of the forces of reaction in the late 1980s, particularly in Liberal-controlled States, such as New South Wales, may, however, come to place the continuing relevance of such an analysis in question (McNamara 1992). But writing in the mid-1990s, Corns can still report that in states such as Victoria there remains 'one of the most reliable, efficient and credible criminal justice systems in Australia and indeed in the western world'. He goes on to claim that whilst major problems exist, *'relative to other jurisdictions* [it is] well regarded nationally and internationally as a model to follow' (Corns 1994: 27).

An alternative conception of 'prevention', which has gathered strength since the 1960s, has been that of *situational crime prevention*. Here it is argued that most crime is opportunistic and that crime rates can be effectively reduced through environmental design, target hardening and situation management. The origins of this approach in England and Wales lie in the report of the Cornish Committee of 1965. Particular attention was given to the role of the police and the need to establish new posts of police crime prevention officers and a centralized crime prevention advisory and training unit. However, its impact was limited at the time because of the prevailing political commitment to develop policies of law enforcement and reactive policing. It was not until the early 1980s that the concept of situational prevention was revitalized and at this time was also seriously taken up in Australia. The reasons for its re-emergence were myriad – the most significant being the clear failure of law enforcement policies in both countries to have any effect on crime rates. In England and Wales, recorded crime had continued to increase at the rate of about 6 per cent per annum. The rhetoric of 'getting tough' came to look increasingly thin. In tandem, rapidly escalating costs to administer expanded criminal justice systems appeared to deliver a poor cost-effective return. Such 'failure' was a particularly severe embarrassment to a government in England and Wales which was elected in 1979 on a law and order ticket (an embarrassment which has continued to grow through three successive re-elections). The response from the right has been to broaden its intervention by arguing that criminal justice policy and practice can only have a limited impact on crime control. Rather the sources of crime and also the means for its control were deemed to lie in the actions of individual citizens and their local communities. Thus public responsibility came to be pivotal in such schemes as the target hardening of homes, businesses and personal possessions and through an assumed greater security offered by membership of neighbourhood watch. It was this ideological shift which opened the door to strategies of prevention, and to the incorporation of a whole number of central government departments, local authorities and voluntary agencies into the business of crime control. In Australia, a number of situational crime prevention strategies have been implemented with consistent support from the police, both Liberal and Labour governments and significantly from major insurance companies. At their centre has been the establishment of various 'watch' programmes, notably neighbourhood watch and car watch, which operate in close association with local police departments. Indeed the strategy of mobilizing residents to discourage or deflect potential offenders from their local communities has, for McNamara (1992: 105), been the only 'explicit community crime control strategy that has emerged to the present date' in some Australian states.

Whilst this logic of crime prevention is primarily 'watch' based, it has also characteristically addressed environmental issues, such as the redesign of public transport facilities in order to improve surveillance of passengers, the redesign of coin-operated telephones and fuel meters to discourage theft and vandalism and dramatic increases in video surveillance of roads and public places. More recently in England, the success of the Conservatives' attempt to persuade the 'community' to take such responsibility for crime control has resulted in the paradoxical development of private (or local council) security patrols in residential areas where householders are able and prepared to meet such costs and a rise in vigilantism in areas where they are not. Both can be viewed as symptomatic of a radical redefining of the limits of the state's core responsibilities towards law enforcement.

Bright (1991) concludes that a situational strategy clearly carries advantages in its ability to reduce the incidence of some crimes. If most crime is opportunistic (as the Cornish Report assumed) then improved household and car security, greater surveillance, better lighting, and architectural design can be expected to have some effect. However, situational responses, and the theory of rational choice on which they are based, are limited in their applicability. They do not, for example, address a whole range of crime including corporate crime, domestic violence and racially motivated crime. Despite successes in some areas (see Clarke 1993; Heal and Laycock 1987), the dangers of hardening specific crime targets remain those of: the development of a fortress mentality in which homeowners become obsessed with physical security, and fear of crime increases, rather than reduces; the displacement of offences to other areas or to other targets; and increased criminal sophistication in methods of theft, burglary and robbery. The extent of such 'displacement' is difficult to measure and remains unknown, but clearly the reduction of opportunity in some areas can lead to escalation in others. For example, the payment of wages by cheque extends opportunities for computer fraud; whilst the fitting of steering wheel locks to modern cars increases the potential theft of older models (see Trasler 1986). As well as encouraging an overly defensive perspective on crime prevention, such measures are also clearly unrealistic for a majority who do not have the economic means to choose to implement these strategies or the political power to compel planning authorities to take their concerns into consideration. In short, they tend to benefit the 'middle and upper classes at the expense of the poor' (Weiss 1987).

Above all the situational approach does not necessitate any radical rethinking of policy on the part of governments. Rather it allows evasion of responsibility for the failure of law and order measures, prolongs the disavowal of the social causes of crime and, in particular, helps to deny any acknowledgement that social and economic policies which have helped to generate unemployment, poor housing, reduced state welfare or urban decay might in any way be related to the increase in recorded rates of crime. Crime, again, can simply be defined in the neo-classical terms of low self-control and individual responsibility and attention to addressing its social context sidestepped in favour of an unproven administrative pragmatism. As Iadicola (1986) observed, a conservative bias is also maintained because individuals and communities continue to receive a limited and particular definition of crime which only addresses crimes of the powerless.

Nevertheless, the impetus given to 'prevention' in the early 1980s gathered strength through the decade. In particular, the recognition that situational measures needed the compliance and participation of a wide range of public and private institutions, central and local decision-making bodies and could be carried out through a variety of voluntary agencies and individual action, opened another door for notions of *community crime prevention* to enter the political arena. In England and Wales an interdepartmental circular of 1984 was issued by central government and sent to all chief constables and local authority chief executives encouraging them to co-ordinate their resources in the prevention of crime. Through this initiative the concept of interagency co-operation was realized. Once more, central government was attempting to distance itself from its traditional role as the natural provider of public services. Now responsibility was firmly placed on the shoulders of 'communities'. Whilst the precise constitution of 'communities' remained unclear, the involvement of non-criminal-justice agencies did significantly hold the potential to broaden the concept of prevention to include such elements as housing allocation, welfare rights, employment opportunities, informal social control mechanisms and the provision of diversionary activities for young people. To date, community crime prevention in England and Wales has materialized in the 1986 five towns initiative, the 1987 Safer Cities programme and in 1988 the establishment of Crime Concern to act as a consultant and disseminator of 'good practice' in local crime prevention work. In Australia, community crime prevention remains largely wedded to notions of neighbour-hood watch, community policing and police/community consultation.

It remains unclear though to what extent the wider social contexts of crime have been (or can be) addressed at this level. Whilst community crime prevention signals a shift in emphasis, in practice, it appears to act predominantly as a means through which local collaboration can be gained in devising and implementing strategic situational measures. For example, the primary activities sponsored by Safer Cities included home security schemes, design modifications, improvements to lighting, estate security improvements and manage-ment measures to address city centre nuisance (Bright 1991). Community crime prevention thus appears to herald more of a shift in organizational and managerial matters, than a reappraisal of how crime can be understood and responded to.

Its main initiatives, those of collaboration and partnership, remain key elements of government policy in England and Wales (Home Office 1991b). A similar strategy is being adopted by Labour administrations in Australia, particularly South Australia and Queensland. For example, South Australia's 1989 five-year Crime Prevention Strategy invoked ideas of developing a *coalition against crime* in which local businesses, the media, community leaders as well as the police would play a pivotal role. To date this has materialized in the establishment of 'exemplary projects' (though mainly of the situational variety), the earmarking of special funds to encourage self-determination in Aboriginal communities and the establishment of local crime prevention committees to meet particular localized needs.

In these developments we witness one part of a profound restructuring of criminal justice systems and a radical redefining of what constitutes the core function of government. Inter-agency approaches effectively devolve frontline responsibility for the management of crime away from central or state government and on to other social agencies. As such, governments appear to be absolving themselves of direct responsibility for breakdowns in law, order and justice. Rather 'fault' is now located *inter alia* in lack of individual/family/community networks of control; poor management systems and lack of market competition. In tandem, questions of crime and punishment are being removed from a political and moral arena and relocated in a 'depoliticised and hence uncontentious scientific/technical realm' (Pitts 1992). The management of crime via community participation is thus best viewed as one element within a broader strategy to create a cost-effective, efficient and economically viable criminal justice system without challenging its fundamental purpose and rationale (McLaughlin and Muncie 1993).

Whilst the status of crime prevention has come to occupy a higher public profile in the past decade, the particular forms in which it has been realized have done little to overcome the idiosyncratic ideology of 'law and order' that continues to characterize – albeit to different degrees – both an Australian Labour and a British Conservative administration. Rather, law enforcement and preventive techniques of crime control have been rendered compatible and mutually reinforcing (O'Malley 1992: 267). The discourse of individual responsibility and rational choice – in the committal of crime and also in the establishment of private measures of self-protection – neatly dovetails with notions of both a strong state and individual self-interest in a free-market economy that are at the centre of the new right's vision of a post-socialist and post-oppositional society.

Social crime prevention for young people: an enlightened step forward?

In response to the shortcomings of the 'defensive' strategies which predominated in the 1980s, the most recent initiatives in the field have attempted to supplement these with programmes of *social crime prevention*. These have to date almost exclusively been developed as responses to youth crime. They can be distinguished from other approaches by the extent to which they recognize that socio-economic structures and the institutions of socialization (family, school, employment) can promote dispositions towards offending and likelihood of detection. The targets of intervention thus *potentially* include not only urban planning, but employment opportunities, education policy, family policy, health policy and policies related to recreation, leisure and culture (Graham 1990: 18–19). At first sight, such an approach may seem to offer an oppositional discourse to that underlying conservative political ideology in that it appears to support a causal analysis which suggests that crime is generated by relative deprivation, unemployment, failure of the education system, financial insecurity and so on, rather than individual pathology. However, the way in which social crime prevention has tended to be realized in practice is through a series of programmes which seek either to remove young people from the street by providing supervised leisure activities or to provide special skills training and opportunities to improve self-respect and competency (Rosenbaum 1988: 351). Some programmes may explicitly recognize structural constraints and determinants, but their targets invariably become individualized and behavioural. Primary attention is given to responding to the symptoms, rather than the causes of young people's disaffection and dislocation. Thus King (1989: 299), commenting on developments in England and Wales, is able to argue that social crime prevention is largely presented by government bodies, not as 'tackling the causes of young people's anti-social behaviour, but as taking steps to guard against these personal misfortunes'. Similarly Stanko and Hobdell (1993) note that given the high rate of men as perpetrators and victims of violence, the Home Office is peculiarly silent on advice to men on violence avoidance. To do otherwise would be tantamount to acknowledging a connection between social conditions, masculinity and criminality. In England and Wales, then at least, the main bodies responsible for publicizing and implementing forms of social crime prevention have been the voluntary sector, local authorities and such independent bodies as Crime Concern, rather than central government. In Australia, by contrast, such work was initially promoted by the Australian Institute of Criminology and developed through the Youth Bureau section of the Commonwealth government. Subsequently several state governments have attempted to provide explicit statements on the ideology and philosophy of prevention, taking the French *bonne maison* model as a yardstick, but also concerned to integrate practice with broader theoretical principles. In itself this reveals a willingness on the part of Australia's Labour administrations (federal and state) to broaden some aspects of the issue.

In England and Wales, what should be done to prevent young offending has never been precisely spelt out in any official crime prevention discourse. The 1991 Home Office report *Safer Communities*, for example, devotes only five paragraphs to the issue. Whilst acknowledging that the vast majority of criminal activity by this age group involves less serious offences and constitutes behaviour which is anti-social and troublesome, rather than strictly criminal, the report is most concerned to encourage young people to participate in the work of existing multi-agency prevention partnerships to gain their co-operation and compliance. In characteristically vague terms, it argues that some of the steps that 'might be taken' in consideration of the issue of young people and crime include 'specific initiatives to engage "hard to reach" young people', initiatives to promote individual and social responsibility, access to educational training and employment opportunities, improving recreational opportunities and initiatives to tackle specific problems faced by young people such as homelessness and drugs misuse. A more recent announcement of policy from the Home Office (7/1/93) contained no specific reference to youth crime at all. It has been left to the voluntary sector and local authorities to establish specific programmes often on a piecemeal, *ad hoc*, short-term and low-financed level, in the absence of any firm commitment from central government. Probably the most ambitious strategy of social crime prevention in England and Wales was the housing estate projects established by NACRO in the 1980s. These, however, were designed more to develop general mechanisms of 'community safety' than respond directly to the problems facing young people in particular. Nevertheless, their attempt to reduce crime problems on housing estates did broaden the range of issues involved to include the safety of vulnerable groups, support for victims, as well as enhancing opportunities for young people. However, this usually involved a combination of situational and social measures as determined through local consultation, rather than the development of a fully social youth policy. A 1992 policy statement from NACRO's young offenders committee has attempted to move in this direction by arguing that attention should be directed more at the disadvantages faced by young people (for example lack of income support, accommodation and leisure facilities) rather than a narrow focus on crime and troublesome behaviour.

The 1990 document issued by Crime Concern – *Youth Crime Prevention* (Findlay *et al.* 1990) – provides a number of examples of existing youth crime prevention practice in England and Wales. These are sponsored and organized by a mix of voluntary agencies, local authorities, charitable trusts, social services, local businesses, police authorities and education authorities. They include neighbourhood-based strategies such as developing after-school projects, holiday activity schemes, youth clubs and motor projects; issue-based strategies such as establishing advice agencies to provide counselling on drug prevention, welfare rights and anti-racist support groups; and police/school-led initiatives to encourage the involvement of young people in local prevention work. Most stress the need to work *with* young people, to respond to *their* needs and to facilitate ownership and control of projects *by* young people rather than for them.

A similar wide variety and diversity of practice characterizes the eleven projects established by the Australian Youth Bureau and the Bicentennial Youth Foundation in 1991–2. These were funded by central government to provide a broad range of services to young people, resident in very diverse Australian communities: inner city, metropolitan cities, provincial cities, rural towns and outback Australia. The specific project goals varied from preventing recidivism of petrol sniffers, to improving communication skills and providing employment and leisure opportunities. Similarly, they involved a combination of inputs from youth groups, housing and welfare organizations, to the police and offices of correction. The types of young people identified and targeted for intervention were similarly diverse, from offenders to the 'at risk' and Aboriginal and non-English speaking populations. This first national initiative was largely exploratory. Its remit stipulated no set agenda, or central directive, other than a desire to encourage, and subsequently evaluate, the 'innovative'. Each of the projects though clearly reflected the political preference of the federal Labour government to develop a social-justice-oriented approach to crime prevention.

The potential of such a strategy is that (in theory) it should at least facilitate the following short-term 'benefits' to selected young people and/or their communities:

1. Temporary access to low-skilled industrial work
2. The development of literacy and communication skills
3. The enhancement of self-awareness, self-autonomy and decision-making (individual competence)
4. Temporary access to otherwise denied leisure activities
5. Access to individualized counselling, casework and advocacy
6. The granting of youth sector resources to otherwise neglected local communities

Evaluation of these Australian projects has however found that a 'social justice' rationale is readily subverted in the day-to-day problems of project management and by political environments which are unsympathetic to this approach (Coventry and Walters 1993: 11). Despite the wide range of strategies employed, from industrial training schemes, wilderness camps, mentor programmes, auto mechanics and theatre productions to encounter groups, none were able to deliver any long-term or sustainable outcomes. Frequently, the project workers were swamped by the need to provide crisis intervention services, in which broader, medium- or long-term issues inevitably became lost (ibid. 65). No evidence emerged that any initiative held the promise to prevent youth crime to any large extent. Indeed 34 per cent of the young people reoffended whilst on a programme. However, from a social justice position such a 'result' is meaningless in a broader context of providing social and employment skills and dealing with problems of homelessness and low self-esteem. But long-term outcomes are clearly not amenable to immediate statistical measurement or to the current clamour for cost-benefit analysis (ibid. 101).

In essence, the rationale of such projects, both in Australia and England and Wales, rests with their ability to divert young people away from potentially troublesome and damaging situations, by offering a range of direct services specifically designed to meet some of their needs. However, whilst such activities may provide a temporary palliative to some of the pressing social problems faced by young people it is clear that they alone do not constitute a comprehensive social policy approach to crime prevention. It is fair to argue that a fully social crime prevention strategy is far from being realized in either country. As currently conceived social crime prevention for young people is a limited and limiting discourse because of the following factors. Firstly, any project which ostensibly aims to meets the needs of young people under the aegis of crime prevention, runs the risk of stigmatizing and eventually criminalizing its participants. There is clearly a danger when the provision of financial and other resources depends on the prior identification of delinquent or 'at risk' bodies. The tendency is for all aspects of social policy to become increasingly governed by an overriding concern for crime and crime control. Social policy becomes crime-led and ultimately incorporated as another element of criminal justice policy. Secondly, the history of juvenile diversion schemes is replete with practices which in effect increase the numbers coming into contact with the official justice system (Cohen 1985). Many young people targeted by prevention projects are considered by staff to be 'at risk' of offending behaviour, either for the first time or for a repeated occurrence: a status which is likely to bring them further to the notice of formal agencies of control. The danger exists that participants who 'fail to respond' to a particular preventive setting become all the more vulnerable to an escalation in penalties. A problem for some projects, therefore, is that their operations are simply grafted on to the operations of the criminal justice system, rather than remaining independent with no formalized connections to the police, courts and corrections. It is internationally recognized that the most effective way of achieving long-term deterrence and community safety is by preventing young people from entering the criminal justice system in the first place. The principles of diversion from prosecution/court and custody as a last resort indeed underpin recent legislation enacted in both England and Wales and Australia. Yet such legislation remains driven by, and always susceptible to, an overriding ideology of punitive control in which, in the mid-1990s, the principles of cost-reduction and cost-effectiveness sit uneasily against those of unlimited crime control expansion. However, within both the managerial and authoritarian strategies of the state the more fundamental principles of social integration, social justice and social development remain tangential. Moreover, the consistent danger of developing quasi-welfare and community-based initiatives lies in the long-recognized contradiction that if a young person is eventually sentenced to an institution, then that person will be seen as having already 'failed' elsewhere (Krisberg and Austin 1993). It is in such circumstances that the labels of 'persistent offender', 'hard core' and 'intractable' can be readily applied and exclusion encouraged. The concept of 'social crime prevention' – because of its ill-defined and vague nature – is readily co-opted and incorporated into existing criminal justice discourse. Thirdly, current projects are structured largely to focus on the immediate problems of individual young people. Whilst this may be a praiseworthy goal and can deliver some successes, an overemphasis on activity-based interventions encourages the dissolution of any long-term objectives, and is reflective of a failure to impact on the broader social contexts of disadvantage and disaffection. The problems facing young people cannot be eliminated with quick-fix approaches. The benefits of a preventive approach based on principles of social development ultimately requires a commitment to long-term change which cannot simply be measured in reducing the costs of crime and crime control, but by improving the quality of life for all young people.

Towards a reconceptualization of youth crime prevention

It is generally agreed that there are three major models of crime prevention, although various observers have used different terms to describe them. Weiss (1987), for example, identifies: situational crime prevention; the 'stake in conformity' approach, and; informal control and community. These approximate to the general scheme described by Iadicola (1986): the 'victimization deterrence' model; the 'social disorganization and social control' model, and the 'community control and social change' model.

As we have noted situational crime prevention aims to deter potential offenders largely by surveillance, security devices, and architectural design. It is based on a conservative ideology which views criminality as evidence of lack of social and self control. Such programmes have been generally criticized for their tendency to displace the commission of offences to other community sites and/or commodities; and their tendency to increase community dependency on the police (either in its public or private forms), rather than 'promote the development of important informal social controls' (McNamara, 1992: 106).

The 'social disorganization and social control' model is in part reflective of the social reformism of the Chicago School and of the strain theory of the 1950s. The thesis advanced is that a lack of adequate resources or measures for integration which characterize socially disorganized communities needs to be addressed, particularly if young people are to develop a legitimate identity and a stake in conformity. A recent reworking of such themes is encapsulated in Braithwaite's (1989) notion of reintegrative shaming. This calls for a reduced reliance on deterrent measures and their replacement by participatory forms of community moralizing through which offenders may be persuaded to view their criminal acts as socially and morally unacceptable. However, as Braithwaite acknowledges, to avoid shaming simply degenerating into moral outrage also requires the development of social conditions in which the values of mutual interdependency and communalism can be recognized. And, of course, it is precisely these values which are negated in the competitive individualism of free-market economies.

A third model – that of community control and social change – is thus based not only on notions of informalism and non-coercion but also on power sharing, social justice and economic equality. Such measures are essential elements in the development of an alternative to both 'law and order' and 'social reformist' responses. This approach in turn requires processes for social development and social change.

It is important to note that such 'pure' models of crime prevention are rarely implemented. In reality a 'pot-pourri' of programmes operate under the rhetoric of community and social crime prevention. Examination of these programmes reveals a set of organizational tensions, requiring a variety of agencies to make choices about matters such as key theoretical assumptions about what is crime, targets of intervention, sites of intervention, duration/intensity of intervention and, so on. Resultant prevention strategies, therefore, are often riddled by contradiction with little likelihood of achieving intended outcomes (Coventry 1993).

Nevertheless, our reading of current international literature and evaluation of youth crime prevention practice in Australia notes the beginnings of some acknowledgement that if social justice, in general, and prevention, in particular, are to be taken seriously then questions of social development and social change must be addressed (cf. Currie 1988; Graham 1990; Oughton 1991; NACRO 1992; Krisberg and Austin 1993). However, such awareness to date remains wedded to 'crime' as the key signifier and target for intervention. Whilst many are engaged in the struggle to define 'crime prevention' and indeed highlight its potential to open a window of opportunity to challenge traditional law enforcement approaches (Tuck 1987; McNamara 1992), few attempts have yet been made to go beyond its intrinsically limited boundaries. Indeed, we would argue that the continuing emphasis on *crime* prevention acts to systematically exclude any alternative readings of the relationship between social problems and social order. The absence of any integrated, and potentially challenging, set of policies focusing on young people and their social, economic and political conditions has led to a range of fragmentary initiatives, of which concern with youth crime prevention is but one example. Current emphasis on this issue carries the danger of it leading the agenda, of absorbing all other potentially progressive interventions into its terms of reference. 'Crime prevention' by current definition is about reducing or rectifying troublesome behaviour. By default it has a disturbing tendency to establish the boundaries of policy for all young people. In the process, notions of positive and creative citizenship are de-emphasized through a myopic focus on troublesome behaviour.

Thus we would argue that young offending needs to be placed in the context of the life experiences and chances facing young people. Crime should be seen as one element in processes of disaffection and dislocation. In short, if prevention is to be taken seriously it needs to be taken out of the discourse of crime and requires a rethinking of priorities in which governments and the wider community are aware of the structural disadvantages facing young people and recognize they have a responsibility for enhancing their personal and social development. At the very least an agenda needs to be established whereby concern over crime is linked to other issues of community significance, such as the damaging consequences of corporate crime, racial and sexual discrimination and youth powerlessness in general. Current notions of 'prevention' are thus too narrowly conceived. Whatever 'prevention' means as a short- or medium-term strategy, it remains wedded to a continuum of responses in which the major rationale remains that of the formal social control of the marginalized. The dangers inherent in only involving people in system advocacy/social development schemes as a result of their potential or actual criminal behaviours are evident if crime remains the focus of intervention, rather than questions of young people's powerlessness and lack of access to political decision-making and meaningful work opportunities (Coventry, Muncie and Walters 1992). For this reason, the evaluation of the youth crime prevention projects in Australia eventually recommended to the Canberra government, not the refining of project aims, but the decriminalization of certain offences, the redefinition of some crimes (for example drug and substance abuse) as a matter of health policy, the depoliticization of the youth crime issue, the shifting of resources from crime control to other public service agencies, (for example to ensure adequate income support and accommodation), the control of media reporting and a reappraisal of the whole terrain of 'prevention' (Coventry and Walters 1993: 115–18).

When the concept of youth crime is reconceptualized in terms of disaffection, dislocation, marginalization and structural disadvantage and the concept of prevention reconceptualized in terms of social development and social change, the potential for intervention is broadened from a negative focus on young people as a problem and towards a positive evaluation of their role as future citizens. From such a formulation the rationale of any intervention lies not in the potential to provide regulatory control, but in the ability to reduce self and social harm. If, and when, formal state intervention is involved it is entertained only as a last resort and based on principles of reintegration, rather than exclusion. We would argue that the only defensible rationale for the existence of a criminal justice system lies in its ability to be a part of an integrative system. This can be further expressed as the necessity not to criminalize social policy but to socialize criminal justice and crime prevention policy; or more broadly, to subordinate questions of crime control to those of a wider social justice agenda. An enlightened approach to youth crime reduction is ultimately bound up, not with the identification and management of delinquent bodies, but with the pursual and adequate resourcing of mechanisms for social justice. Without such an agenda we are left with a series of *ad hoc*, short-term and low-financed initiatives which may provide some temporary relief for a few but which will leave the majority of marginalized youth untouched, unsupported and vulnerable to further criminalization.

References

Blagg, H. (1987). 'Social crime prevention and policies for youth in England', *Home Office Research and Planning Unit Research Bulletin* No. 24 (London, Home Office).

Blagg, H., Pearson, G., Sampson, A., Smith, D. and Stubbs, P. (1988). 'Interagency cooperation; rhetoric and reality' in Hope and Shaw (eds.), *Communities and Crime Reduction*.

Bottoms, A. E. (1990). 'Crime prevention: facing the 1990s', *Policing and Society*, 1.

Braithwaite, J. (1989). *Crime, Shame and Reintegration* (Cambridge, Cambridge University Press).

Bright, J. (1991). 'Crime prevention: the British experience', in Stenson, K. and Cowell, D. *The Politics of Crime Control* (London, Sage).

Clarke, R. (1980). 'Situational crime prevention', *British Journal of Criminology*, 20(2).

Clarke, R. (ed.) (1992). *Situational Crime Prevention: successful case studies* (New York, Albany, Harrow and Heston).

Cohen, S. (1985). *Visions of Social Control*, (Cambridge, Polity Press).

Colvin, M. (1991). 'Crime and social reproduction', *Crime and Delinquency*, 37(4).

Cooper, B. (1989). *The Management and Prevention of Juvenile Crime Problems*, Crime Prevention Unit. Paper No. 20 (London, Home Office).

Corns, C. (1994). 'Politics, discretion and prosecutions', *Socio-Legal Bulletin* No. 11 (La Trobe University, Australia).

Coventry, G. (1993). 'Dangerous liaisons: shaping youth policy by crime prevention programming', Conference Paper, Melbourne, unpublished.

Coventry, G., Muncie, J. and Walters, R. (1992). *Rethinking Social Policy for Young People and Crime Prevention* (NCSLS La Trobe University, Australia).

Coventry, G. and Walters, R. (1993). *National Evaluation of Youth Crime Prevention Projects Final Report: Prospects and Problems in Australian Youth Crime Prevention Programs* (NCSLS La Trobe University, Australia).

Crawford, A., Jones, T., Woodhouse, T. and Young, J. (1990). *Second Islington Crime Survey* (London, Middlesex Polytechnic).

Currie, E. (1988). 'Two visions of community crime prevention' in Hope and Shaw (eds.), *Communities and Crime Reduction*.

Findlay, J., Bright, J. and Gill, K. (1990). *Youth Crime Prevention: A Handbook of Good Practice* (London, Crime Concern).

Graham, J. (ed.) (1990). *Crime Prevention Strategies in Europe and America* (Helsinki Institute for Crime Prevention and Control).

Hagel, A. and Newburn, T. (1994). *Persistent Young Offenders* (London, Policy Studies Institute).

Heal, K. and Laycock, G. (eds.) (1986). *Situational Crime Prevention: from theory into practice* (London, HMSO).

Heal, K and Laycock, G. (1987). *Preventing Juvenile Crime: The Staffordshire Experience*, Crime Prevention Unit. Paper No. 8 (London, Home Office).

Heal, K and Laycock, G. (1988). 'The development of crime prevention: issues and limitations' in Hope and Shaw (eds), *Communities and Crime Reduction*.

Hogan, M. (1991). 'Youth crime prevention and the new federalism: the role of governments' in Halstead, B. (ed.) *Youth Crime Prevention* (Canberra, Australian Institute of Criminology).

Hogg, R. (1989). 'Criminal justice and social control: contemporary developments in Australia', *Journal of Studies in Justice*, 2.

Home Office, DES, DE, DHSS and Welsh Office (1984). *Crime Prevention, Circular 8/1984* (London, Home Office).

Home Office (1989). *Tackling Crime* (London, HMSO).

Home Office (1990). *Partnership in Crime Prevention* (London, HMSO).

Home Office (1991a). *A Digest of Information on the Criminal Justice System* (London, HMSO).

Home Office (1991b). *Safer Communities: the local delivery of crime prevention through the partnership approach* (The Morgan Report) (London, HMSO).

Hope, T. and Shaw, M. (eds.) (1988). *Communities and Crime Reduction*, (London, HMSO).

Hope, T. and Shaw, M. (1988). 'Community approaches to reducing crime' in Hope and Shaw (eds.), *Communities and Crime Reduction*.

Iadicola, P. (1986). 'Community crime control strategies', *Crime and Social Justice*, 25.

King, M. (1988). *How to make social crime prevention work: The French Experience* (London, NACRO).

King, M. (1989). 'Social crime prevention à la Thatcher' *Howard Journal*, 28(4).

Krisberg, B. and Austin, J. (1993). *Reinventing Juvenile Justice* (London, Sage).

Laycock, G. and Heal, K. (1989). 'Crime prevention: the British experience' in Evans, D. and Herbert, D. (eds.), *The Geography of Crime* (London, Routledge).

McNamara, L. (1992). 'Retrieving the law and order issue from the right: alternative strategies and community crime prevention', *Law in Context* 10(1).

McLaughlin, E. and Muncie, J. (1993). 'The silent revolution: market-based criminal justice in England', *Legal Studies Bulletin*, 9 (La Trobe University, Australia).

Muncie, J. (1984). *The Trouble with Kids Today: Youth and Crime in Post-War Britain* (London, Hutchinson).

Muncie, J. (1991). 'The deinstitutionalisation of juvenile and young offenders in Victoria, Australia', *International Journal of Social Work*, 34(3).

Murray, C. (1990). *The Emerging British Underclass* (London, Institute of Economic Affairs).

NACRO Young Offenders Committee (1992). 'Stopping youth crime' *Childright*, 83.

O'Malley, P. (1992). 'Risk, power and crime prevention', *Economy and Society*, 2(3).

Oughton, D. (1991). 'Developments in crime prevention in New Zealand: an overview' (Australian Institute of Criminology Conference Paper, Adelaide, unpublished).

Parliamentary All Party Penal Affairs Group (1983). *The Prevention of Crime among Young People* (London, Barry Rose).

Pearson, E. (1983). *Hooligan: A History of Respectable Fears* (London, Macmillan).

Pitts, J. (1992). 'The end of an era', *Howard Journal*, 31(2).

Potas, I., Vining. A. and Wilson, P. (1990). *Young People and Crime: Costs and Prevention* (Canberra, Australian Institute of Criminology).

Presdee, M. (1990). 'Creating poverty and creating crime: Australian youth policy in the eighties', in Wallace, C. and Cross, M., *Youth in Transition* (Brighton, Falmer).

Rosenbaum, D. (1988). 'Community crime prevention: a review and synthesis of the literature', *Justice Quarterly*, 5(3).

South, N. (1987). 'The security and surveillance of the environment' in Lowman, J., Menzies, R. and Palys, T. (eds.), *Transcarceration: Essays in the Sociology of Social Control* (Aldershot, Gower).

Stanko, E. A. and Hobdell, K. (1993). 'Assault of men: masculinity and male victimisation', *British Journal of Criminology*, 33(3).

Trasler, G. (1986). 'Situational crime control and rational choice: a critique' in Heal and Laycock (eds.), *Situational Crime Prevention: from theory into practice*.

Tuck, M. (1987). 'Crime prevention: a shift in concept', *Home Office Research and Planning Unit Research Bulletin* No. 24 (London, Home Office).

Weiss, R. P. (1987). 'The community and prevention' in Johnson, E. H. (ed.), *Handbook on Crime and Delinquency Prevention* (New York, Greenwood Press).

White, R. (1990). *No Space of their Own: young people and social control in Australia* (Cambridge, Cambridge University Press).

Williamson, H. (1993). 'Youth policy in the United Kingdom and the marginalisation of young people', *Youth and Policy,* 40.

20

Criminal Justice Act 1991 – management of the underclass and the potentiality of community

SIMON GARDINER

The aim of this article is to evaluate competing explanations of the rationale behind the Criminal Justice Act 1991, with its emphasis on a 'dual track' approach to sentencing policy or 'punitive bifurcation' as it has become known – punishment in the institution and in the community. One major contention is that in some sense it can be explained as having facilitated the extension of the state's operations or 'social control' into the community. I will consider various issues concerning the concept of social control in the context of what seems to be an attempt of movement in post-industrial society from punishment based on incarceration and institutions to decarceration and a movement (expansion) outwards into the community. This has been termed the 'dispersal of discipline' thesis.[1] However, I will argue that rather than focusing on the individual there is a development to the control of groups.

I would like to suggest that we are in a period of social change or at least a period of uncertainty. The phrase 'new times' has been coined (Hall and Jacques 1989), and there are a number of post-scenario terms competing with each other including post-structuralism, post-modernism, post-Fordism and post-industrialism. The latter has been used since the 1960s and is, I believe, appropriate because it indicates graphically a change in social order and social relations that cannot necessarily be explained using orthodox analysis. The sociological meaning of post-industrial society is of one moving away from an industrial base to a service-oriented economy and development of bodies of knowledge as the means of policy formation for society – a new form of social management.[2] It does not deny the continued existence of 'modernity' in the same way that post-modernism clearly implies. As Habermas (1981) argues, modernity has not yet run its course and perhaps one of the most valuable roles that post-modern scenarios can play is to inform and supplement contemporary modernist ideas.

The Criminal Justice Act 1991 (CJA) has been an attempt to absorb the diversity of different penal methods into one rational order: punishment. The message is clear: there is a continuum of punishment from the institution into the community. The negative reaction to some of the provisions in the Act indicates that attempts to create such a unitary approach are doomed to failure in an ever increasingly diverse and fragmented society. I will argue that the reality of the CJA is that it is largely a response in terms of management (see Feely and Simon 1992) of an aggregate group of people rather than individuals. I will also argue that it is the 'underclass' which is the target group which contemporary penal policy is developing strategies to control. However, even though the grand narratives of modernity are under attack and seen as unable to provide us with truisms of human and social existence, one characteristic of the CJA is immutable – the community. Even the underclass needs community! Adopting a 'left realist' perspective, I will show that the community is the forum for the attainment of social justice, and I will assert that it is the most effective context for the operation of penal measures. The underclass and community are easily portrayed as being in opposition. Both these concepts need to be examined. I will argue that we must see the underclass as an ideological construction which obfuscates the reality of contemporary life, and that we should see community as a context which we need to reconstruct and whose potentiality we need to exploit.

CJA 1991: background and rationale

The CJA came into force in England and Wales on 1 October 1992 and has led to some controversy. Some thirty magistrates resigned in protest against the act.[3] Two elements of the act have been highlighted as the most contentious – Section 29 which limits the power of the court when sentencing for the immediate offence to take into account previous convictions and, secondly, income-related unit fines. The lord chief justice, Lord Taylor, said that the act has put judges into an 'ill fitting straight jacket', restricting the sentences they could impose and he argued that there needed to be an urgent review so that 'sanity could be restored'. He went on to say: 'However forward thinking the penologists, criminologists and bureaucrats in Government departments, their views should not be allowed to prevail so as to impose a sentencing regime so incomprehensible to right-thinking people generally.'[4]

The home secretary, Kenneth Clarke, had stated his intention to 'revisit the act' during the spring of 1993. In Parliament on 13 May he announced that there were going to be legislative changes in the near future to abolish unit fines and to reinstate the court's right to consider fully an offender's previous convictions when sentencing for the instant offence(s). The Criminal Justice Act 1993 has amended both of these provisions.[5]

A brief note needs to be made on the background of the CJA. The aims of this piece of legislation were first articulated in 1987, soon after the Conservative government had won its third election in a row. The act was to fit in with the general developments in sentencing policy and practice over the previous twenty years which had provided a wider range of sentences available to the courts and conditions for their use. It was also to be radical in limiting to some extent the autonomy of discretion that the sentencers had previously exercised. Britain has maximum discretionary sentences for the vast majority of crimes, and sentencers have historically had almost absolute freedom in fixing the sentence they thought appropriate. The Court of Appeal had issued a number of guideline judgments on sentences for some of the most serious offences,[6] and other matters such as the account to be taken of previous convictions or related offences. The aims of this new act were seen at this early stage as the reduction of crime, keeping less serious offenders out of prison, satisfying public demand for a crackdown on sexual and violent crimes, achieving greater stability and the hope of a small reduction in the prison population. There had been a feeling that although most courts were involved in good sentencing practice, there was a lack of consistency. There was a concern that custody was sometimes being used unnecessarily, especially when Britain was compared with other European countries with significantly lower rates of incarceration. There was a growing belief that custodial sentences should be avoided unless justified by the seriousness of the offence, or by the need to protect the public. There was official awareness of research which supported the argument of the criminalizing effects of prisons. As the White Paper (1990: para. 2.7) indicated, 'For most offenders, imprisonment has to be justified in terms of public protection, denunciation and retribution. Otherwise it can be an expensive way of making bad people worse'.

The government was also aware of the increasing problem of prison overcrowding that was subsequently to become so visible in the prison riots of 1990, and of the increasing costs of keeping offenders in custodial institutions. It was regarded that an offender should not receive a disproportionately severe sentence simply because of his or her previous record, although a good record could count in mitigation. The court should be sentencing the offender for the instant offence and not resentencing for previous offences already dealt with. This was merely restating existing Court of Appeal guidelines.[7]

The Home Office was starting to have more faith in community correctives as the way ahead. Well-managed and demanding programmes in the community could be equally effective as a punishment. A change of emphasis was needed in the status of community measures. The term 'alternative to custody' was used for such sentences as community service orders. Probation was an alternative to a sentence and not a sentence in itself. Fines were seen as being increasingly ineffective. This was due to the inability of people on low incomes to pay fines at what was considered a realistic level, and also the limited amounts that could be levied against wealthy offenders. What followed was five years of extensive consultation, with the government putting forward its proposals in a green paper in 1988 and a white paper in 1990. The result was the CJA, which in general terms, was consolidating previous legislative and Court of Appeal sentencing guidelines.

However, there clearly have been some problems with the application of the legislation. The statutory rules concerning the unit fines produced big differences in the amounts paid according to the calculation of the offender's income.[8] Each offence was given units according to its seriousness. These units were multiplied by the defendant's weekly disposable income to produce the fine. However, the statutory provision set the figures for assessment of income at much higher levels than those used in the pilot study. The trial of unit fines in a small number of courts around the country had been highly successful, but the result was that in practice some individual cases led to fines clearly out of proportion to the crime's seriousness[9]. The other controversial provision, Section 29, has been seen as too restrictive by the courts who felt that it had limited their discretion to take full consideration of circumstances surrounding the crime.[10] This indicates the traditional tension between the executive and judiciary on the issue of autonomy of discretion in sentencing.[11]

The CJA can be officially seen as an attempt to de-centre the prison in penal policy and to divert less serious offenders into community correctives. Historically, such measures have almost inevitably led not to any meaningful decarceration but to an extension of the penal web to an ever increasing number of individuals. Christie (1993) meticulously shows the great expansion of the rates of imprisonment in western countries in recent history. This has occurred at a time of increasing availability and use of community alternatives. The community still, however, has a great attraction as a meaningful form of punishment, and for a large number of offenders it is the mechanism by which punishment can have a positive role. There are social control implications in extending the penal web outside of the institution, but I will argue that this can be a mechanism that can help achieve greater social justice in a period when crime is seen as such an irreducible social problem.

Crisis: what crisis?

The official rhetorical explanation of the CJA is that it is a progressive liberal bureaucratic reformist response to the perception that prison has failed to alleviate the increasing rates of crime on the basis of the much-used indicator, the rate of recidivism. 'Nothing works' is the cry, but there is a belief that maybe by increasing the punitive nature of community correctives, more success might be achieved. In addition, these measures will have greater public acceptance and especially with those involved in sentencing. The CJA can be seen as a continuum in the developing emphasis of measures for convicted offenders in the community, and in fact can be seen as reinforcing the dual track penal policy of reliance on institutional and non-institutional forms of punishment. This examination of the effect of community measures should not only be carried out on a theoretical level, and the interstices between theory and practice need to be acknowledged. There is a widespread belief that the penal system has a 'crisis of legitimacy', in terms of lacking moral authority. This is a claim with which we have become familiar, but it is one that we need to be able to put into context by being able to construct an idea of what we expect of a penal system in post-industrial society. How can it be made to work? Claims that the whole system or parts of it are in crisis have been a familiar cry for many decades.

I contend that the prison is the most visible component of a system that lacks a general legitimacy in the eyes of the public, the clients and workers within the institutions who have no clear working ideology.[12] The Woolf and Tumim Report (1990) proposed reinforcing the standards of justice for prisoners with a clear expectation of the rights each individual prisoner could expect from the prison authorities in the form of a 'contract or compact'. Their consent to the system was seen as crucial for it ever to have a chance of working. More critical accounts tend to focus on the system's lack of transparency, a perception of decreasing authority to control on behalf of the prison officers, and the legitimacy of the system itself (see Fitzgerald and Sim 1979). However, once again the focus is on the prison as the microcosm of the system, even if writers such as Bottoms (1980) have widened out the discussion to argue that the crisis is one of the whole system. There is a general crisis of legitimacy and a corresponding crisis in financial resources. This has been underpinned largely by the 'collapse of the rehabilitative ideal' and the official response which sees the way ahead as a return to the 'absolutist retributionism' of an earlier age. The official rhetoric has become permeated with the principle of 'just deserts' (although it was spelt with two s's in the White Paper) and commensurable sentences both in institutions and in the community.

There is a need to abstract the analysis to a higher level, to see it as more complex and to move away from rational accounts of the 'crisis of legitimacy'. It needs to be acknowledged that the penal system is a collective of many elements and competing interests and needs to be positioned within the socio-economic context.[13] The current 'crisis' has been a developing one. The 1980s experienced an ever increasing crime rate as identified through official statistics and victim surveys, and increasing rates of incarceration. The crisis is an accelerating problem. In one sense, the CJA can be seen as the latest official response to a dissatisfaction with prison originating in the 1960s. Since then in Britain there has been a growth in the already existing alternatives to custody so that Britain now provides the largest number of non-custodial sentences available anywhere in Europe. However, the collapse of the 'rehabilitative ideal', both in custodial and non-custodial institutions, has fuelled the development of a justice model and the emphasis on 'just deserts'. The CJA sees that sentences can be constructed in terms of punishment and control. It is very much a response to individual criminal acts. As was said in the Green Paper (1988), 'People have a choice whether or not to commit a criminal offence'.

The CJA indicates the latest official acknowledgment of the failure of rehabilitation. There is essentially a clearer choice for sentences between custody and community punishment. Whether it can help cure the perceived lack of legitimacy of community correctives awaits to be seen. There may be continued official support for punishment as a mechanism of crime control,[14] but perhaps the reality is that we all expect too much of punishment. As a mechanism and social practice within the continuum of the criminal justice system, the effect of a punishment can only ever be a reactive one. Garland (1985: 80) emphasizes its inherent limitations owing to 'the tragic quality of punishment . . . at once politically necessary . . . and penologically limited in (their) capacity to control crime'.

Social control and management

The alternative view is that which can be seen from a critical (new deviancy/radical criminology) paradigm. This emphasizes the CJA as the latest support for community punishment and a response by the state to crisis and a breakdown in consent to the existing social order. The approach of the British government during the 1980s and 1990s has continued what was identified by Hall (1978) as 'authoritarian populism' – an official emphasis on 'law and order ideology'. Within this paradigm, the CJA and similar measures are devised to achieve hegemonic consent. The prison has not been a success but has the role of dealing with serious offenders. Community measures are more likely to achieve consent and should be looked at more favourably, but they can only work if they are not seen as soft options: they should be punitive rather than rehabilitative in nature. The act seems to extend the operation of the state through various agencies into the community. This is the latest statutory provision to provide alternatives to incarceration. The difference with the CJA is that there is an increasing emphasis on punishment in the sense of restricting liberty in the community. As the White Paper (1990: para.4.5) indicates: 'Restrictions on liberty . . . become the connecting thread in a range of community penalties as well as custody.'

This would superficially seem to have the effect of extending the control over the individual. Where the seriousness of the offence does not warrant a custodial sentence, this is going to help determine the restrictive nature of the community punishment. Applying Foucault's (1975) contentions that the prison developed primarily as a mechanism of surveillance and discipline or training, and the fact that community penal developments lead to dispersal of discipline, the result is that control of the state has become wider. Additionally, of course, the empirical evidence suggests that non-custodial measures have developed as 'supplements' rather than alternatives to prison and have not, in fact, led to meaningful decarceration but to an extension of the scope of the criminal justice system over offenders. The reality is that this extension of the system has occurred with a corresponding increase in the use of custodial sentences and prison population. It is not individuals who are the primary target of this increased social control. We are increasingly witnessing the development of control techniques over specific groups in society.

Talk of decarceration and social control is problematic. I do not intend to re-examine the debate concerning decarceration and the implications for social control that has developed over the past fifteen years between such writers as Scull (1977; 1983), Cohen (1979; 1983; 1985; 1987), Matthews (1987) and Bottoms (1983). However within this debate and most noticeably from Mathiesen (1983), there is the view that community penal measures not only enable increased control on an individual level but also the control of groups in what is increasingly a fragmented society. Mathiesen (1983: 140) sees these developments as moving away from traditional individualistic control to:

> focus on control of whole groups and categories through planned manipulation (with good intentions of establishing brakes on crime) of the everyday life conditions of these groups and categories. TV cameras on subway stations and in supermarkets, the development of advanced computer techniques in intelligence and surveillance, a general strengthening of the police, a general strengthening of the large privately run security companies, as well as a whole range of other types of surveillance of whole categories of people – all of this is something we have got to get, and have begun to get use to.

He argues (1983: 41) that this will not lead to the death of the prison. The prison continues to be widely used, but he sees it increasingly being used as 'a last resort' for the 'utterly uncontrollable'. They will have this role as a back drop as the 'external or societal-control system will gradually expand and become continually more extensive and important'. This Orwellian view of developments in penal policy is not always obvious. In Britain the public generally is certainly under surveillance more than ever before.[15] These techniques are being applied increasingly to offenders.[16] Bloomberg (1987) identifies the development of techniques of supervision based on surveillance of offenders in some states in the United States. A number of terms are used – home confinement, community control, house arrest. He says (1987: 63), 'These trends should lead us to question whether we are indeed approaching Orwell's 1984 or . . . as the coming of a minimum security state in which ever-increasing state intervention and control can be anticipated'.

This view of a minimum security society has been echoed by other writers. Marx (1988) seems more alarmed than Bloomberg when he talks about the 'maximum security society', where the link between public and private is blurred and citizens become subject to constant observation and a totality of society is created. The state of Florida is currently testing a satellite community surveillance system for targeted offender groups that monitors their movements twenty-four hours a day (see Bloomberg *et al.* 1993). The development of total surveillance technologies and the construction of social groups of offenders and other problem populations such as a perceived 'underclass', extends social control in the form of management. Under the CJA, the availability of curfew orders as a sentence on its own or in combination with others, limits the actions and movements of offenders. The act allows this to be backed up with the use of electronic monitoring.[17] The trials in four areas in 1989 were not seen as being obviously successful (see Mair and Nee 1990). However the government sees it as having a strategic role in the future.[18]

I agree with this analysis. Legislative provision such as the CJA significantly increases the potentiality for expansion of social control into the community, facilitated by the emphasis of a clear commitment to punishment. The modifications to community service orders, the changing of the nature of probation and the more punitive effect of fines, are examples of a greater disciplinary disposition to their juridical base. This advancement is matched by other technical developments, a movement to a new form of social control. Not only is there greater social control of the individual, technology is promoting the managing of social groups and problem populations: the spectre of the underclass is raised. The emphasis is on management and containment, regulating deviancy at a minimum cost.[19] This approach has been termed the 'new penology', and this new discourse of penality has its origins in the United States. As Feely and Simon (1992: 470) argue:

> The new penology is neither about punishing nor about rehabilitating individuals. It is about identifying and managing unruly groups. It is concerned with the rationality not of individual behaviour or even community organisations, but of managerial processes. Its goal is not to eliminate crime but to make it tolerable through systematic coordination.

The origins of this approach can be seen in the right realism/ administrative criminology movement with individuals such as J. Q. Wilson prominent. Prison will continue to be used for those perceived as dangerous and serious offenders and the community used for the rest of this criminogenic underclass. The community will be used increasingly because of some perceptions of the dysfunctional effects of the prison, but primarily as it is seen as cheaper. I will argue at the end of the chapter that, from a left realist paradigm, community correctives have the potentiality to achieve greater social justice, but only after we have begun to reconceptualize community. However, I first of all need to discuss further the notion of an underclass and consider what its implications are for criminology and as a target of the criminal justice system.

The underclass: reality and myths

The term 'underclass' emerged during the 1980s as a common expression describing a collection of different subgroupings forming one group or classification of society at the bottom of the social hierarchy, whose members are disempowered and excluded from mainstream economic activity and social citizenship. Individuals in this group are then linked with particular types of crimes and as a group are seen as criminogenic. It does not have a clear or exact sociological definition,[20] and is increasingly being used in a popular and political sense. As Bagguley and Mann (1992: 113) say: 'It's rare for sociological terms to enter journalism, popular fiction and political debate, but the "underclass" succeeds where others fail.' In Britain, it tends to have been used by contemporary sociologists as indicating those who have been excluded from mainstream society. This includes a diversity of people: the long-term unemployed, the homeless, those who have become disenfranchised from the political system, the elderly poor, disadvantaged minority groups, habitual recidivists? These constituents of the underclass are represented as basically criminogenic as they are drawn out of social participation. The argument proceeds that the growing underclass is a major contributor to why we are experiencing a commensurable rise in crime. This growth of an underclass rationalizes greater social control, but by cost-effective means of management. I believe great care needs to be taken in examining this social concept. As Macnicol (1990: 23) says: 'The concept of the "underclass" is a recurrent political and social science myth, or, at best a statistical artefact.'

It can be a very useful phenomenon to use in examining state control of the bottom groupings in the social hierarchy, but when the use has become widespread and diverse without foundation in rigorous empirical evidence, the use of such a term beyond a popular metaphor is limited. Underclass simplifies a complex range of social relations and processes and runs the danger of leading to ideological obfuscation of the social processes which cause poverty and deprivation. Also the development of the term in recent years almost denies the existence of an equivalent social strata at the base of the working class within the social hierarchy. The popularizing of the term in Britain in the 1980s and 1990s conceals that other terms have been used in the past to describe the same social concept. There is nothing new about an underclass in that sense.[21] In the United States where the term was first used in the 1960s, it has almost exclusively been applied to blacks living in poverty in urban ghettoized areas.[22] In the 1830s, social researchers noted a group of blacks who were seen as being in a mire of poverty and the term 'rabble' (see Lawson 1992) was given to them. They continued to be seen as wedded to poverty, and the 'culture of poverty' thesis was developed to explain its existence. In Britain and other western countries its use has not been so closely associated with a particular ethnic group. In 1981, the term entered popular culture and middle-class America's vocabulary, when Ken Auletta published three articles in the *New Yorker* magazine.[23] This popularization of the term, together with vagaries of a clear sociological meaning, has led to the discourse of underclass being much more influential than any real understanding of its importance for contemporary social policy. There are three main explanations of the underclass that can be isolated.

Culture of dependency theory

The first is that developed and popularized mainly by Murray (1984) in the early 1980s in the United States. He follows a tradition in the US on the neo-conservative right who firmly blame the welfare state for creating a 'culture of poverty'.[24] A welfare dependency that is intergenerational has been created leading to illegitimacy and single parents, drop-out from the labour market and increasing rates of crimes of violence. The welfare state has created the environment for the underclass to develop, a social group who are inherently crimino-genic. He argues that the unfettered market would not have allowed such patterns of social behaviour as single-parent families to develop and create a breeding ground for today's social problems. Not surprisingly, a comment on the back of his book calls it 'The Reagan Administration's New Bible'. His ideas, along with those such as Milton Friedman and Robert Nozick[25] arguing for the drawing back of the state and the free operation of the market, were influential on the social policy initiatives of the Reagan government and, predictably, Murray's rhetoric and ideas were shipped over to Britain. In 1989, he wrote an article for the Murdoch-owned *Sunday Times* indicating that Britain had its own underclass. After transferring many indices of measurement from the United States, Murray (1990: 3) concluded that 'Britain does have an underclass . . . out of sight. But it is growing rapidly'.

This view blames the poor and the criminal classes within the underclass as responsible for their position. They constitute a dependency culture which perpetuates its own misery by living off welfare payments, which finances a lifestyle of idleness and crime. The underclass is alienated from traditional decent values: two-parent families, the work ethic. In America this is synonymous with colour, in Britain it is more generally with the poor. This is individual responsibility 'writ large'. Not surprisingly, Murray along with his particular brand of social policy, has links with the criminological theory held by those such as J. Q. Wilson who support genetic theories suggesting that people are born to be poor and with a propensity to criminality. Crime is predominantly caused by nature and not nurture.

The Policy Studies Institute has developed the arguments of Murray to support social policy changes reducing the effect of the welfare state. They perpetuate the view that the welfare state has led to a dependency culture. Smith (1992) admits that there is a problem of definition but argues that for there to be meaningful political debate, there needs to be empirical research towards establishing its constituency and size. He does, however, see that a working definition is that of family units who are economically dependant on state benefits, excluding state pensioners. Willet (1992) subdivides this group into the long-term unemployed, unskilled workers in erratic employment and young single mothers – all dependent long-term on benefit, specifically income support. He goes on to make a distinction with this underclass and between those who are in low-paid employment who he calls the 'respectable poor'. Although he does not expressly say so, implicitly it is those on long-term benefits who are the 'undeserving poor'. He argues that those relying on benefit alienate the low-paid poor. He attempts to support this distinction by using, as an example, tip-offs to social security investigators concerning individuals involved in the so-called 'black economy' whilst they are still claiming as an indication of the moral value of sustaining oneself and family on low-paid work.[26] He further argues that there has been a decline in the work ethic and that benefits have sapped the independence of individuals and their self-reliance. The solution which the Institute sees is that the state should cease to be a provider and move towards being a facilitator. It supports measures such as lower taxation, help for the behavioural poor and making divorce harder to obtain. What this analysis does not provide is a rigorous explanation of the multifaceted causes of contemporary poverty. As Cornford (1992: 76), director of the left-of-centre Institute for Public Policy Research states:

> I am sceptical that the definition of an underclass will provide any useful clues about how to deal with poverty . . . we could greatly alleviate poverty and reduce the nightmare of an underclass, directly and immediately by reversing many of the policies adopted over the last decade . . . we have witnessed an onslaught on the poor and ought to make amends . . . what we lack is the political will. We shall not generate that by punishing the shortcomings of the poor.

The underclass again raised its head in the debate initiated by the government concerning possible changes in the amount and distribution of expenditure on social security. There is a popular view that there are those wedded to and reliant on welfare support, with particular focus on increasing rates of illegitimacy and single-parent families. Murray (1993) has been given the opportunity to repeat his views and reinforce his argument for urgent and radical governmental action.

> A political consensus for radical change will have to wait until the social costs of abandoning the 'principle of legitimacy' are palpable and disastrous. By that time, the opportunity to restore a liberal society will probably have been lost.

In comparison with the United States where colour has been used as the most obvious predictor of membership of the underclass, in Britain, Murray uses illegitimacy. Campbell (1993) points out the irony of illegitimacy rates rising from 10.6 per cent in 1980 to 25.6 per cent in 1988: one legacy of the Thatcher years. Murray argues that increasing illegitimacy will lead to fatherless families and communities without fathers, and that marriage is what constitutes families. As Campbell (1993: 308) argues:

> Murray's thesis is intensely gendered. He is the scourge of the mother-scrounger . . . What is remarkable about Murray's thesis is the invisibility of women, mothers, grandmothers, aunts, as the real, live, operational carers . . . Among the underclass theorists, woman's economic dependence is dignified as the condition of active fatherhood; her independence as the cause of absent fatherhood.

This view of the social danger of single-parent families and illegitimacy has been countered.[27] The break-up of the two-parent nuclear family may be mourned, but the reality is that allowing mothers to bring up children on their own and without reliance on men has been part of the increased empowerment of women in contemporary society.

So Murray clearly has his critics. As Bagguley and Mann (1992: 118) state:

> Murray is one of the lucky few who get the opportunity to air their prejudices in public . . . perhaps the really dangerous class is not the underclass but those who have propagated the underclass concept . . . because it is ill defined and sloppy the underclass can mean whatever the user intends it to mean. Vandalism, hooliganism, street crime, long-term unemployment, joyriders, drug abuse, urban riots, a decline in social values, single mothers and a host of other 'social problems' have been pinned on the underclass.

The underclass is popularly portrayed as being omnipotent in its influence and a cause of increasing levels of anti-social and violent crime. Murray relies heavily on criminal statistics to prove his contention that 'the habitual criminal is the classic member of the underclass'. He makes comparisons with crime statistics in America and shows that, although the rate of violent crime in Britain is not as high as America, it is increasing and in fact Britain has higher relative rates of property crime. But as Deakin (1990: 87) says, 'No-one who has had first-hand acquaintance with the collection of criminal statistics would dream of using them as the basis for a theory of social change'.

The causes of criminal activity by those at the bottom of the social hierarchy are not advanced by Murray's arguments. His ideas fall conveniently alongside those of Prime Minister John Major who has famously stated 'society needs to condemn a little more and understand a little less'. Murray's concentration on the underclass perpetuating habitual criminality, with the most likely 'underclass criminals' being male youths from single-parent families dependant on welfare, is also based on a weak premise.[28] Kinsey (1993) has carried out research in Scotland and concluded that such contentions are not sustainable. Campbell's remarkable account of the riots of 1991 as indicative of wider changes in British political and social life, argues that the key issue of the 1990s is not recognizing the underclass, but understanding the notion of 'lawless masculinity'.[29]

Murray's work fuels media speculation on contemporary social life and suggests easy answers. As Walker (1990: 53) succinctly states:

> There are two main deficiencies to Murray's thesis. In the first place he fails to provide any scientific proof that the underclass exists. Substituting for such evidence are innuendos, assertions and anecdotes. Secondly, as a guide to policy, his thesis is, at best, misleading and, at worst, a dangerous diversion from the major problems of poverty and deprivation facing Britain.

Underclass: discourse of poverty

The second view on the underclass has been from the centre-left of the political spectrum. The American, William Julius Wilson has developed the social democratic liberal response to Murray's assertions.[30] He sees the geographical isolation of the underclass and the emergence of the inner city ghettos as the product of the organization of the United States economy in conditions where the history of discrimination and deprivation has disadvantaged the black population. Wilson does not agree that the poor live in a 'culture of poverty', but he argues they do suffer the effects of social isolation and have developed a 'ghetto culture'. His work has focused on the 'frostbelt or rustbelt cities' of the North and Mid-West of the United States which have suffered widespread de-industrialization during the 1980s. Unlike other liberals who saw the use of the term underclass as having obvious cultural and racist connotations and blaming victims for their position, he recognized that black neighbourhoods in these cities had undergone considerable changes with subsequent increases in anti-social and violent behaviour. Wilson (1987: 8) talks of the underclass as, 'Individuals who lack training and skills . . . individuals who are engaged in street criminal activity and other forms of aberrant behaviour, and families who experience long-term spells of poverty and/or welfare dependency'.

It is the decline in manual work that has led to the inability of black non-skilled or semi-skilled workers to support a family, and the subsequent demographic movements of successful upwardly mobile blacks moving out of ghetto areas. Those left behind are increasingly isolated from mainstream social life as community institutions collapse and informal social control dissipates. Wilson argues that this underclass is more likely to have illegitimate children, engage in crime and have an acceptance of joblessness. In clear opposition to Murray, however, he advocates increased state intervention as the way to alleviate these social conditions. Policies are advocated that guarantee a full-employment economy, provide more effective unemployment insurance and other social services, achieve greater race and class desegregation within metropolitan areas and revitalize community institutions in inner city areas.[31]

His work evidences good use of empirical evidence to support his arguments.[32] This analysis provides a positive way ahead to alleviate the underclass and the term's increasing use. However, as Jencks (1992: 16) says, agreeing partially with Wilson's analysis of the economic and demographic changes during the 1980s, the emergence of Wilson's ghetto culture is not so mono-causal.

At least two other factors probably played an important role. First the white middle class, whose cultural norms dominate the mass media, became more tolerant of 'deviant' behaviour. Secondly, the civil rights movement made young blacks less willing to accept subservient roles, especially in settings dominated by whites.

Studies in Britain have shown a similar correlation with ethnic minorities suffering as an underprivileged class,[33] although as Moore (1992: 6) says of this country, 'It would be hard nonetheless to sustain the argument that the black population is downtrodden into isolation, apathy and desire. I have seen no research which says that this is the case'.

Also in Britain a similar analysis has seen the underclass having a wider membership. Field (1989) sees the underclass as being defined mainly in terms of economic deprivation. It is comprised of those who have become separated from the working class generally: the long-term unemployed, single-parent families and the elderly poor. Many of these have given up the rights of citizenship and membership of social life. As Halsey (1989: 16) says,

> The class structure of industrial societies, including Britain, is developing an under-class of those who can not be placed in the stable workforce of the formerly employed . . . They suffer a cumulation of social pathologies – educational failure, illiteracy, broken families, high crime rates, poor housing and spatial concentration in the inner city. They are disproportionately recruited from the young and ethnic minorities, and they lead a ghetto existence outside of the normal social contract of citizenship and with little or no stake in official society.

For Field (1989: 2–4) there are four main causes of the underclass. There has been a move away from the economic objective of full employment and a belief in work bringing social benefits for workers and their families. Unemployment has the opposite effect and causes downward social mobility for those excluded from the labour market. Secondly, the Thatcher years have led to a breakdown in the notion of social citizenship and an emphasis on individual enterprise. Thirdly, even though during the 1980s living standards rose at a record rate, the poor have been excluded from an equitable share which has led to increasing disparities in ownership of wealth. Lastly, he argues, there has been a change in public attitudes to individuals' pasts and origins. Those from a working-class background who have been in work and benefited materially by the Thatcher years, have developed a 'drawbridge mentality', and are not concerned that their former peers have not benefited to the same degree as themselves.

A variation of this explanation comes from Dahrendorf (1985), from a similar central social democratic perspective, but with some doubts as to contemporary social development. He argues that the underclass is equated with an unemployed group surplus to the needs of post-industrial society. He projects that this group will grow to about one third of the working population of Europe and will be the victim of constant unemployment, with only minimal political and social participation and a more than average risk of being involved in criminal activities. These people will be found increasingly in the inner cities of major European urban areas. 'Anomie' will flourish in these no-go areas. This produces a worrying picture of post-unification Europe. This emerging underclass will over-represent ethnic minorities. Dahrendorf argues that European governments must face up to the reality of these structural changes. He argues that they continue to see issues such as long-term large-scale unemployment through a modernist paradigm as being simply a period of recession in the normal economic cycle.

Underclass: the actuality of capitalism

A third view is a classical Marxist perspective that sees this problem population or underclass as threatening the social relations of production in capitalist societies.[34] Their marginalization identifies and calls into question the social conditions and patterns of distribution in capitalist society. There is a crisis in legitimacy and this population presents an acute problem of social control. As Lord Scarman (1981: 107) said in his report on the Brixton riots, 'to ignore the existence of economic, social and political factors . . . without which the disturbances cannot be fully understood . . . is to put the nation in peril'.

Talking of the underclass, however, admits discussion of an 'overclass'. The disparity in ownership of wealth has grown since 1979: one result is that a disadvantaged underclass has become more visible. During the Thatcher years, there was a move from the less-well-off half of the population owning a third of wealth in 1979 to a quarter in 1991.[35] A total of 13.5 million are estimated to be living on under half of the average income, which is viewed as a realistic benchmark for the poverty line. This discussion of course also needs to be seen in the global context of the expanding north–south divide, with resources moving at an ever increasing rate from the underdeveloped to the developed world.

The vagaries of the use of the term underclass are crucial to understand. Its discourse is very powerful, its reality less convincing. The underclass needs to be seen for what it is, not an inevitable progression but as Ascherson (1993) describes it: 'the grandest engineering project of the 1990s, more ambitious than the Channel tunnel – the construction of the underclass'. The discourse of the underclass has been developed to deflect popular consciousness from one of the recurrent themes of modernity, the discourse of poverty. Unemployment has ceased to be a priority to tackle. The reality of official policy is management. Welfare payments have been reduced and inequality has been drastically increased. These are the natural consequences of a society that reifies individualism. The workings of the market produce winners and losers, and the losers are those who are marginalized too easily as the 'undeserving poor'.

Behind official rhetoric I believe that the state views the growth of a high-risk group that needs to be managed for the protection of the rest of society. The official response to this threat of the underclass has been to screw down the lid on social control. The specific bifurcation of the CJA provides the prison for controlling the most disruptive and dangerous members of the underclass within institutions, and community correctives against the persistent recidivist. The emphasis will increasingly be on management which, in terms of cost, is seen as more effective than the past heavy reliance on prison. It also needs to be seen as sufficiently punitive for the confidence of sentencers and the public. There is the danger of transition to a society with a permanent offender population, where Feeley and Simon (1993: 470) argue there will be an 'imperative of herding a specific population that cannot be disaggregated and transformed but only maintained – a kind of waste management function'.

Underclass and criminology

So what are the implications of the underclass for criminology and penal policy? This 'crime control model' emphasizes a 'get tough' policy with this 'enemy within'. The CJA reflects other changes during the 1980s and 1990s – massive investments in the infrastructure of law and order with, for example, increase in police numbers and an extensive prison building programme. Has crime increased in volume or seriousness to an extent which warrants this? Criminological literature is already very familiar with explanations of how dangerous populations that are inherently criminogenic need controlling. The argument that we are living in increasingly violent and perilous times is the rationale of increased control. Social constructivism is around every corner. Box (1987) posits the problem population – Mr Murray's underclass. He sees that the fiscal crisis of late twentieth-century Anglo-American society is the inevitability of 'capital accumulation'. A surplus labour force has grown that cannot be absorbed by capital. As Hall and Jacques (1989) argue, Marx may have been wrong with some of his predictions such as class being the motor of revolution, but he was right about capital: its global expansion continues and its by-products become more visible. It is the criminal justice system that is becoming the modern process for controlling this surplus population. Prison is one obvious mechanism: the removal from society (and the unemployment register), but community correctives are perceived as cheaper! A policy of attempted decarceration is seen as an appropriate response to fiscal crisis.

Christie (1993) argues that western advanced societies are becoming increasingly reliant on the prison as the state's primary mechanism of social control of the 'dangerous classes'. He uses the United States as the model to show how liberal society can start to move to an acceptance of large percentages of the population legitimately being incarcerated. His subtitle, 'Towards GULAGS, Western Style?', reinforces his prediction. Punitive bifurcation arguably has the same conclusion. Less reliance on the prison[36] will become more attractive as it is viewed as being potentially cheaper and more politically expedient.

The CJA can be seen as a response of post-industrial society to the emerging reality of a large collective, permanently marginalized grouping for whom 'relative deprivation' within the social structure is at its most chronic. The criminalizing of such a group is easily achieved; crime will be an everyday reality to it. As Lea and Young (1993: 88) say,

> It is clear that parts of the poor, particularly the lower working class and certain ethnic minorities who are marginalised from the 'glittering prizes' of the wider society, experience a push towards crime that is greater than elsewhere in the structure.

Criminal activity both in terms of offender and victim becomes normal. The government is able to criminalize more of the ways in which the members of this group might resist the deteriorating economic position and circumstances. 'Fear of crime' in inner city urban areas legitimizes greater surveillance and control.

Community – nostalgia and representation

I would like to speculate from a left realist perspective on the potentiality of community correction. Only through changes in the construction of social justice can the causes of marginalization of groups in society and the engendering of crime be rectified. A measure such as the CJA with its emphasis on community has potential as a progressive step to help facilitate this if stripped of its overt punitiveness and authoritarianism. The official rhetoric needs to be deconstructed to fulfil the capacity of these developments in penal policy, and practical strategies must be developed that make sense of trying to reintegrate offenders in the community. In clear opposition to the underclass with its consequence of 'exclusion', the community reinforces 'inclusion' within social life.

This shift in focus means that we need to question the nature of that community. The community is seen as the embodiment of our social relations with others and marks out bonds of solidarity and identity. It plays a powerful and important role in our political discourse, where it highlights our commitment to a common good that transcends individual interests. Its ideological role is immense: it promises to deliver so much, but is often used to mask hidden intentions, such as greater centralization and fiscal crisis. The community has increasingly been seen as being the appropriate forum for the implementation of social policy. The movement of caring for the mentally ill from closed institutions to open community occurred during the 1980s. In fact many parallels can and have been drawn between this occurrence and the process of decarceration in the criminal justice system (see Scull 1977). Community health care for the mentally ill would seem to be intuitively right, empowering those removed from society to live in the real world in a degree of non-intervention from the state. Decarceration has successfully taken place for many. But for others, the process has been one of 'transcarceration',[37] movement from one type of institutional control to another. Cohen (1985: 118) notes the nostalgia that the image of community conjures. He says, 'Not only is this a word rich in symbolic power, but it lacks any negative connotations . . . As in all forms of nostalgia, the past need not really have existed. But its mythical qualities are profound'. The community that modern society has to offer is far from the 'gemeinschaft' small-scale pre-industrial world. As Hunt (in Lowman 1987: 155) says,

> In any proposals for a community based justice system, it is essential to avoid romanticization of 'the community' as necessarily rational and compassionate; the community is just as capable of irrationality and vindictiveness as any official judicial institution.

The community and the opportunity for greater public participation has increasingly been moved into centre ground in developments in the criminal justice system. As there has been a move towards a 'justice model' of crime and punishment and a subsequent support for 'just deserts' in the absence of evidence to support other theories of why offenders should be punished, participatory justice and community involvement have been seen as one way to control the excesses of the mechanistic justice system.[38] There is, of course, a balance to be found between discretion and participation on the one hand and due process and natural justice on the other. The spectre of the vigilante and the lynch-mob are too easy to imagine.[39] This coercive action does not lack community involvement: it lacks participation of the parties most closely involved and denies the rights of the offenders.

Potentiality of community

In the last few years we have seen initiatives such as community policing (Scarman 1981), Neighbourhood Watch schemes (Husain 1988), mediation schemes between offenders and victims (Marshall and Merry 1990) and the Safer City programme (Tilley 1992) with its aim to reduce crime, to lessen the fear of crime and to create safer cities where economic enterprises and community life can flourish. We have to be careful in our understanding of community. As I have said it has an intuitive virtue and it is easy to accept it uncritically. It can too easily be utilized as a slogan, or mask other motivations for its use such as the almost inevitable reality of cost-cutting. However, it would be wrong to deny that there is not some real commitment by the state to developing more effective community measures for social problems. It is not all sloganizing. What is needed for these good intentions to be put into effect is to understand the true construction and dynamics of community in post-industrial society.[40]

In contemporary society, urban life continues. Domesticity is ordered and increasingly isolated and suburban. In inner city areas, corporate business dominates the scene. Squeezed between the dichotomy of these modern structures are the disadvantaged 'underclass', those denied access to social life. Society is seen as being increasingly fragmented.[41] Community, like social and political life, has become diffused. However, if social life based on strong communitarian responsibilities and beliefs allows individuals to assume power over their own lives with an increasing decentralization of power away from the 'state of modernity', community can increasingly be the forum for social justice. Even the underclass needs community. Its members are the victims of crimes; they too have a right to participate in civil society.

We need to start to see community as the context within which positive changes can be made in the issues of deviancy and general social reform. There needs to be a reconceptualizing of individual rights and increased wrestling of political power from the state. The critical legal studies movement with its attack on 'legal liberalism' and its support for a reconceptualizing of law on a communitarian basis is useful to consider (Hunt 1986; Kelman 1987; Bauman 1989). The work of Roberto Unger (1976; 1983) is particularly apposite. He advocates that social life be made more like political life and that what is required is a decentralization of the state to the individual so that individuals have power over their own lives in the community. Power is decentralized. This allows individuals to make the same reconciling political deals as those made by the state. This 'super-liberalism' reconstructs individual rights as supporting communal responsibility. These ideas are reflected within the sociology of law, where there is an increasing call to move away from the notion of 'law government'[42] towards the development of responsive law that facilitates reregulation of social life with an emphasis on community as the provider of social justice.[43]

Surprisingly, there are superficial similarities between the arguments of Unger and those of Murray. Murray's argument (1990: 34) for dealing with the underclass is to take the state out of people's lives by removing a great deal of the safety net of welfare provision by 'giving poor communities (and affluent communities too) a massive dose of self-government, with vastly greater responsibility for the operation of the institutions that affect their lives – including the criminal justice, educational, housing and benefit systems in their localities'. He believes communities or neighbourhoods will not tolerate bad social conditions or high crime rates, illegitimacy or idleness by the unemployed. They will run affairs so as to counter these tendencies. He supports the appropriateness of groups who have similar consensus beliefs to live in their own community and groups with different beliefs to live in separate communities. The development of autonomous small-scale community living sounds fine, but why will this, as he argues, be radical? Will it not only increase the existing divide between rich and poor, those in social life and those excluded? As Deakin (1990: 63) says,

> Murray calls for 'a massive dose of self-government'; fine, but where are the resources, human and financial to come from? He airily asserts that it is easy to combine sustaining current levels of expenditure for public systems with decentralised control over them.

This view of social organization without appropriate financial investment can only reinforce the *status quo* so obviously visible in post-industrial societies, where the overclass forgets about the underclass when the latter is out of sight and out of mind.[44] Deakin sees Murray's proposals as 'artificial homogeneity' and bringing with them 'a barely concealed authoritarianism'. Murray counters these claims by having to resort to the nostalgic view of community, the dangers of which I noted at the start of this discussion. He remembers his childhood in a mid-western town where children lived together without many concerns about their friends' positions in the social hierarchy. An almost absolute belief in social mobility shines through. As he says (1990: 82), 'The first lesson we were taught was that the only degrading kind of work was no work'. Murray would no doubt have this as a compulsory element of any national curriculum. The unreality of his thinking is exposed when he says (1990: 82), 'Perhaps I lived in an idyllic community and thereby am misled'.

Community and social responsibility

I agree! His arguments are fatally flawed and unfounded. The lack of empirical work to support the theorizing he so easily develops, makes his ideas limited in importance. It is crucial though that his ideas and those of his ilk are challenged when they are popularized and disseminated so easily within the current debate concerning today's perceived social problems. There are clear underlying tensions between the liberal consensual community of the neo-conservative right, where individualism and the market are dominant, and the development of social community where individuals feel true communitarian responsibilities. This incongruity needs to be engaged to provide strategies that will enable notions of community and regulation to be developed for the achievement of social justice. In the context of penal policy and community correctives, Lacey (1989: 175) asserts her rejection of the tradition of liberal thought as far as community:

> Here, I would argue, lies an important key to understanding the ideal of community . . . a commitment to, the adoption of responsibility for, the community of which one is a member. This commitment, realised ideally through participation in the process of government and administration, can be seen as the ultimate expression of humans as primarily social beings: community is a more 'natural' or appropriate assumption or ideal than is the liberal vision of persons as rational, calculating and self-interested.

As a society, we collectively need to develop this social conception of community and to recognize that, as Lacey asserts, we are primarily and essentially social beings. Liberal assumptions permeate the criminal law and criminal justice system to the extent that legal doctrine effortlessly divorces individuals and their actions from social relations and social institutions. The new right has been able to argue that in the battle between the naturalness of the market versus the intuitive or instinctive nature of community, there is no contest. They see community with its rules and restrictions as a brokered construct that creates a forum for the natural operations of the market. During the 1980s and 1990s, individualism in the sense of individual autonomy has become king. It is increasingly important to challenge this view and stress that individualism is the antithesis of politics and the desire of humans to live together. It is not the market that has provided us with the freedoms that we see as vital to modern society. Politics is the process by which these freedoms are achieved. As Crick (1964: 23) says, 'Politics is not just a necessary evil; it is a realistic good. Political activity is a type of moral activity; it is a free activity, and it is inventive, flexible, enjoyable and human'.

Individualism is an important part of human existence but not its essence. The individual can only achieve fulfilment in terms of community, and as members of communities we have a social responsibility to help others to be empowered. This counters the classical liberal view of individuals as rational, calculating and self-interested and reinforces the reality that commitment to society is more natural. Of course, this commitment materializes through participation in society and political mechanisms. Modern states have become increasingly centralized both in terms of public perception and political reality. But the local community can be reconstituted as a political forum. As Lea and Young (1993: 239) stress, there is a requirement for 'the institutions for local democracy . . . it is through participation in decision-making on matters that affect our lives that we learn political responsibility . . . that was the classic argument for democracy. It is as relevant today as it was two hundred years ago'.

Crucially, though, as far as the use of community correctives as a substitute for rather than a supplement to the prison are concerned, it is the sentencers' perception and understanding of community that needs to be examined and engaged (Ashworth 1992 and his view of the importance of judicial psychology). Some research has been carried out to examine the considerations of sentencers (Parker *et al.* 1989; Brown 1991). On magistrates' perception of community, Brown (1991: 112) agrees that the magistracy see themselves as the custodians of the community, but 'This kind of idealisation is only a possibility because the magistracy is not grounded in the community; its legitimacy as a representative is as mythical as the "normal family". The community which it represents is a notion . . . (an ideologically based one)'.

The future of community

This evolution to a greater social communitarian society allows people to develop new strategies to deal with offenders. Braithwaite (1989) argues that, in such a society, shaming of offenders can have a beneficial effect and be a just form of social control that is moralizing rather than punitive. Such an approach to community correctives can help to expose the myth of the underclass as inevitably criminogenic and thereby justifying an extension of oppressive social control as a construction. The community can be used as a forum for developing strategies for reforming social injustice, and the *spirit* of the CJA and its emphasis on movement to community correctives can be harnessed. If punishment is to reintegrate people into civil society, the community would clearly seem to be more appropriate than the prison. More fundamental is the need to engage in public debate to find what people's priorities are? Is it really a toughening approach to law and order because of the often repeated official claim of there being a 'fear of crime'? Or is it not invariably a desire for proper jobs and adequate social amenities? There needs to be a move towards the rejection of official constructions of problems. Left realism counters the way that the emerging administrative criminologists, many of them in the Home Office, have used surveys and statistics to facilitate the managing of crime. As Young and Matthews (1992: 21) argue,

> Left realism involves the repoliticization of crime . . . crime reduction requires . . . an appreciation of a wide range of political and structural processes which go beyond the boundaries of conventional criminology . . . crime control must become part of a comprehensive political programme.

Community-based correctives can be modified and harnessed to this end. Surveys such as the British Crime Survey show high levels of support for community-based measures for non-violent offenders. Rehabilitation and general deterrence are prioritized as appropriate objectives. This clashes clearly with the official rhetoric supporting the public desire for retribution. The development of community measures, in alliance with the use of prison for serious crimes of violence, can provide more appropriate alternatives that have public support, and whose effectiveness can be measured in ways other than recidivism. This needs to be part, of course, of other reforms such as a sentencing council (Ashworth 1992). As Matthews (1991: 151) says this would bring about,

> the deconstruction of the existing penal fortress and the setting up of more open and accountable institutions. These, with their differential levels of security, might encourage not so much the spread of the prison into the community but rather the expansion of the community into the prison.

The myth of the underclass needs to be exposed, and community reconceptualized so that community penal measures can be effective in securing greater social justice. There is a clear contradiction between the notion of a growing underclass and the aim of using the community as the forum for achieving social justice, especially in terms of the use of community correctives for larger numbers of offenders for whom prison is not justified. Left realism provides the basis for this reconstruction of community as a mechanism to defeat the creation and extension of the underclass. As Young and Matthews (1992: 6) say,

> Left realism then is the opposite of right realism. Whereas realists of the right prioritize order over justice, left realists prioritize social justice as a way of achieving a fair and orderly society, whereas right realists descend to genetic and individualistic theories to blame the 'underclass', left realists point to the social injustice which marginalizes considerable sections of the population and engenders crime.

The greater use of the community for the implementation of penal policy has its danger in terms of unprecedented invasion of privacy and state regimentation. Such measures are a part of a larger trend towards increased surveillance and control on the part of the state in post-industrial society. But the community has great potentiality. The social control consequences of community correctives need to be made more democratic and accountable. We need to make control more social. We need to reconstruct community in a way that will achieve social justice: we need to take community seriously.

Acknowledgements

I would like to thank the staff and students on the MA in criminology 1992–4 at Middlesex University for comments on this chapter and especially John Lea for his consideration of an earlier draft.

Notes

[1] Stan Cohen is most clearly identified with the 'dispersal of discipline' thesis developing the notion of discipline developed by Michel Foucault as the rationale of incarceration. Cohen's work is developed in a series of works (see later).

[2] For an account of the impact on criminology of post-modernism, see John Lea 'Criminology and postmodernism', unpublished conference paper presented at British Criminology Conference, University of Wales, Cardiff, July 1993.

[3] *The Times*, 14 May 1993.

[4] Lord Taylor, *New Law Journal*, 26 March 1993.

[5] A new Section 29 has been substituted by the Criminal Justice Act 1993, s.66(6). As Wasik and Taylor (1994) comment, it seems as though it gives the sentencer virtually complete discretion to take into account the

offender's previous record. Thomas (*Sentencing News*, 27 July 1993) believes that the old Section 29 has been 'replaced by a section with precisely the opposite effect'. The system of unit fines has been completely abolished by the Criminal Justice Act 1993, s.65(1), which has substituted a new Section 18 to the CJA. This provides two broad principles to be used in deciding on the amount of fine. Firstly, the court shall inquire into the financial circumstances. Secondly, the amount will be what the court considers 'reflects the seriousness of the fine'.

6 For example guidelines for rape offenders.

7 *R. v Queen* [1981].

8 See B. Gibson, *Unit Fines* (Waterside Press, 1990) for discussion on rationale and history of unit fines.

9 *The Independent*, 14 May 1993 – The problem was illustrated when a magistrate could only fine an out-of-work stockbroker £40 for helping to run a brothel whilst on the same day fining a £221-a-week catering assistant £400 for doing a U-turn in her car. Also if the defendant failed to fill out forms to assess means, the maximum penalty had to be imposed. In one notorious case a man was fined £1,200 for dropping a crisp packet, which was later cut to £48 once he had furnished the required information.

10 In *Bexley* [1993] 1 WLR 192 the lord chief justice said that it was 'little short of absurd' that the trial judge following Section 29 had failed to take into account previous drink-drive convictions when sentencing the defendant for three months and a driving ban of four years. This was increased to a sentence of eighteen months and the driving ban was doubled. This case officially recognized the criticisms made by Lord Taylor in public statements.

11 For some indications of the operation of the CJA in its early months, 'Monitoring of the Criminal Justice Act 1991 – data from a special data collection exercise', *Home Office Statistical Bulletin* 25/93. (1993). Also see Ian Crowe *et al.*, 'Evaluating the Criminal Justice Act 1991: some early indications of how agencies are responding'. Unpublished paper presented at the British Criminology Conference, University of Wales at Cardiff, July 1993.

12 Paul Cavadino and James Dignan (1992). They provide a good exposition of different accounts of the crisis, or as they call it the 'C' word – overused and imprecise. They argue that the 'orthodox liberal' account is on the basis of a number of specific developments such as bad conditions, overcrowding, industrial problems etc, within the prison. It provides a basically positivist account of the conditions of the prison, indicating causal relationships between these conditions and subsequent problems such as prison riots. If resources could be directed towards these conditions the problems within the prison will diminish or be cured. The rest of the penal system is largely ignored except in the sense that it is underused and anyway is not considered as more effective in terms of

recidivism. In fact, it is perceived on the whole by sentencers as being a 'soft option', a view perpetuated by other participants in the criminal justice system and also notably the media. Variations of this rational liberal account can be seen as broadening out the appropriate strategies that could be conducive to improvement.

13 Cavadino and Dignan (1992) use the term 'radical pluralism' for this position which they see capable of 'synthesizing' a number of competing accounts, and bringing together both material and ideological elements. They see that penal policy must be identified within the political and ideological context.

14 White Paper, (1990: para. 1.8), 'Punishment has a major role to play in reducing crime, but its role must not be over-stated. If crimes are not reported or detected, those who commit them cannot be brought to justice.'

15 The use of video cameras is increasingly common in urban areas as illustrated by their use in the disclosing of the boys who killed the 2-year-old Liverpudlian, James Bulger, when they were seen abducting him in a shopping centre (mall) and the IRA terrorists who left a bomb at Harrods store in London. Over recent months after such events, the interest shown by local authorities in video cameras for public areas in city centres has mushroomed (see 'Big Brother is here', *The Guardian*, 13 May 1993). Note too Terry Honess and Elizabeth Charman (1992). However, so far in Britain, the use of camcorders and videoing by private individuals and the use of such material to support legal proceedings is not as widespread as in the United States where it is becoming a common occurrence. Also see Phil Carney 'From Bentham to Beadle: the city of surveillance', (1994) Occasional Paper, Centre for Criminology, Middlesex University.

16 Diane Gordon (1990). She warns of the 'electronic Panopticon' of the future comprised of the totality of electronic surveillance.

17 The idea is said to have originated from a spiderman story in which the villain used an electronic bracelet attached to spiderman to track his movements. A New Mexico judge read the story and then approached a number of computer firms to establish the viability of such a practice.

18 There seem to be other interested parties as well. In 'Much profit in a prison' (*The Independent on Sunday*, 5 September 1993), Nick Cohen reports, 'Marconi and other defence companies are moving into the anti-crime and surveillance and hoping to revive the idea of electronic tagging of offenders, because they judge that the £3bn security market can help them survive the end of the Cold War.' Will electronic tagging go down in history as a part of the 'peace dividend'?

19 Also note the current debate in criminology concerning the change in status and regulation of public space with its privatization. See Ian Taylor, 'Critical criminology and the free market: theoretical and practical issues in everyday social life and everyday crime', published in this volume pp. 400–28.

20 J. Westergaard (1992). Westergaard indicates that there are a number of notions of the underclass: 'at least three different versions, never mind the variants within each of these'.

21 Bagguley and Mann (1992) indicate other sociological terms that have been used to indicate this social grouping – 'marginalized class', 'excluded groups', 'reserve army of labour', 'the pauper classes', 'the residuum'.

22 The history of the term can be found in Leslie Innis and Joe Feagin, '"The black underclass": ideology in race relations analysis', *Social Justice*, 16(4) (1989), and in Robert Aponte, 'Definitions of the underclass: a critical analysis', in Herbert Gans (ed.), *Sociology in America* (Sage Publications, 1990). For a discussion of the white underclass in the US see Ronald Mincy, *Is There a White Underclass?* (Washington DC, Urban Institute, 1988).

23 These are collected together in Ken Auletta (1982).

24 There are those who argue that Murray is not developing the classical 'culture of dependency' model, but an economic model that explains why groups of individuals have long-term dependency on state benefits. See Smith (1992).

25 The ideas of 'trickle-down' economics and a minimal 'night-watchman state' fit neatly with a 'culture of dependency' argument in the rhetoric of the new right.

26 This of course leads on to the argument of minimum wages that outlaw exploitation through low-paid work. The failure to ratify the social chapter of the Maastricht Treaty confirms the British government's position. Ralf Dahrendorf shows his support for such 'basic income guarantees' which he sees as one of the entitlements of citizenship, in 'Footnotes to the discussion' in Smith (ed.) (1992).

27 See Joan Brown (1990). She says, 'we have to be prepared to put effort and resources into programmes aimed at strengthening the two-parent family . . . . but we must also seek to strengthen the ability of one parent families to offer their children a sound family life, for as long as they hold that status . . . . we have to tackle the obstacles that prevent lone mothers from combining home responsibilities and the interests of the children with paid employment.'

28 In the United States there have been a number of recent works linking predominantly teenage delinquent gangs and the underclass. One notable book looking at Milwaukee is John Hagedorn (1988).

29 Campbell (1993: 319). She argues that underclass theorists have targeted single mothers and illegitimacy as the destroyers of order and community, but in fact their real concern is loss of moral respectability. Single mothers have been scapegoated for the breakdown of this order and not men in the council estates which were the theatre of the riots. As Campbell argues of the right-wing version of the underclass theory, 'its exponents are paralysed by the problem of marauding masculinities in the cities'. She argues that the reality is that, 'crime and coercion are sustained by men. Solidarity and self-help are sustained by women. It is as stark as that'.

[30] Most notably in William Julius Wilson (1987).

[31] See Howard McDougall, *Black Baltimore* (1992), where he shows how the poor black community has developed locally based self-help groups to further its grievances rather than using traditional political channels which he argues are much less effective.

[32] Some critics have argued that this has been at the expense of a lack of rigorous theoretical understanding of the underclass within the contemporary social structure. Bagguley and Mann have highlighted their concern at Wilson's evidence being used to support theories on the underclass from the conservative right. His findings of the reality of inner city life, mainly in the black ghettos, are similar to those of Murray. Without a clear theoretical position on the underclass, it is easy for others to extrapolate a 'culture of dependency' conclusion from his work. Perhaps it is not surprising that, in later work, Wilson has actively distanced himself from the terminology of underclass and substituted it with the notion of the 'ghetto poor'. See William Julius Wilson (1992).

[33] The work of John Rex and Sally Tomlinson in the late 1970s introduced the term of underclass in a second study of the approach of Birmingham City Council to immigrant housing policy. They describe minorities as, 'systematically at a disadvantage compared with working class whites . . . a separate underprivileged class'. A Panorama BBC TV programme 'Underclass in Purdah' (27 May 1993) indicated family breakdown in the once tightly knit Muslim community in Britain, leading to evidence of crime, drug abuse and the highest level of unemployment and poverty in Britain. Based on figures from the Institute of Policy Studies in 1992, when the unemployment rate for whites was 8 per cent, East-African Asians 9 per cent, Indians 11 per cent, Afro-Caribbeans 14 per cent, the figure for Pakistanis and Bangladeshis was 23 per cent.

[34] The notion of the 'lumpen-proletariat' or reserve army of labour has resemblance to the underclass. For Marx, the lumpen-proletariat had a function in relation to capital, as a reserve body of labour which helps the regulation of wage levels within the working class. The resemblance to Murray's view of the underclass can be seen with this extract from *The Communist Manifesto* (1848) which identifies the contradictory view that Marx had towards the very poor as an insignificant political group. As Marx and Engels say: 'The lumpen-proletariat, this passive purification of the lower strata of the old society, is here swept into the movement by a proletarian revolution, but in accordance with all its conditions of life is more apt to sell itself to reactionary intrigues.'

[35] Households below average income 1979–1990/91, (London, HMSO, 1993). Also see Townsend (1992). The Labour party's Commission on Social Justice states that extremes of income are wider than at any time since 1886 (*The Guardian*, 19 July 1993).

[36] The increasing policy of privatization of prisons can be another way that the government sees for cutting costs of punishment.

37 A number of studies can be found in Lowman, Menzies, Palys (eds.) (1987). In Britain, increasing numbers of the mentally ill are becoming involved with the criminal justice system with the police having to deal with consequences, for example, of their failing to take required medication. Homelessness and sleeping rough is another consequence. Here is the paradox of community action. It will only work if it is adequately resourced, and to reach its true potential it will probably cost more than institutional measures.

38 Roberts (1979) shows how so-called 'primitive' society operates systems of social control on the basis of decentralized discretionary local justice. Also see Christie (1977) where he argues his support for participation of parties in disputes which reflect and support community values and bonds.

39 Recent events including those in Liverpool after the killing of the four year old, Jamie Bulger, with the vigilante actions of local people who surrounded a house suspecting those inside of guilt, illustrate the other side of the idealized view of community.

40 It is useful to outline the historical development of community. In primitive society social life was close-knit, based on small kinship groups which lived and worked together, and personal relationships were fixed. In feudal society, a more developed sense of community grew with social relationships focusing on a central place such as the local manor. There were minimum levels of division of labour, but not to the extent that shared values were in great danger. The move to industrial society brought with it the feature of industrial cities where people began to be crowded together in a relatively limited amount of space, but with individuals being largely anonymous and socially detached from each other. The nuclear family has a paradoxical character – isolated from the productive aspects of life, but also concentrated in terms of kinship between spouses and children.

41 The notion of 'new times' has been raised. This can be seen with developments in political expression moving away from mass parties to pressure – and cause-groups. There has been the move from an emphasis on an industrial society based on large-scale mechanical technology to a society based on electronic and information technology. What are the implications of these changes for community? Is an increasing division between 'the haves' in mainstream social life and the 'have-nots' in the underclass inevitable?

42 Developed by the American legal realist, Karl Llewellyn in the 1920s.

43 This was stressed in Roger Cotterrell's keynote address to the Socio-Legal Studies Association Conference at the University of Exeter (March 1993). The use and meaning of community in legal discourse can be useful in trying to reconceptualize its meaning especially when using historical and anthropological investigations (see Roberts 1979) and comparative research (see Fitzpatrick 1992).

44 Mike Davis (1990) provides a factual account of the divided nature of

modern urban life with his inspection of Los Angeles. The work of Tom Wolfe (1988) perhaps better than any other contemporary fictional work represents the polarization of material conditions and social values between juxtaposed communities – in his book, the Manhattan and Bronx districts of New York.

References

Ascherson, N. (1993). *The Independent on Sunday*, 14 March.

Ashworth, Andrew (1992). *Sentencing and Criminal Justice*, 2nd edn. (Weidenfeld & Nicolson).

Auletta, Ken (1982). *The Underclass* (New York, Random House).

Bagguley, P. and Mann, K. (1992). 'Idle thieving bastards? Scholarly representations of the 'underclass', *Work, Employment & Society*, 1, 113–26.

Bauman, Richard (1989). 'The communitarian vision of critical legal studies', Hutchison, I. and Green, T. (eds.), *Law and Community: The End of Individualism* (Caswell, 1989).

Bloomberg, Thomas (1987). 'Criminal justice reform and social control: are we becoming a maximum control society', in Lowman, J. (ed.), *Trans-carceration: Essays in Sociology of Social Control* (Aldershot, Gower).

Bloomberg, T., Bales, K. and Reed, K. (1993). 'Intermediate punishment: redistributing or extending social control', *Crime, Law and Social Change*, 19.

Bottoms, Tony (1983). 'Neglected features of contemporary penal policy', in Garland, D. and Young, P. (eds.), *The Power to Punish* (London, Heinemann).

Box, Steven (1987). *Recession, Crime and Punishment* (London, Macmillan).

Braithwaite, John (1989). *Crime, Shame and Reintegration* (Cambridge, Cambridge University Press).

Brown, J. (1990). 'The focus on single mothers', in *The Emerging British Underclass* (London, Institute of Economic Affairs).

Brown, Sheila (1991). *The Magistrates at Work* (Milton Keynes, Open University Press).

Campbell, B. (1993). *Goliath: Britain's Dangerous Places* (London, Methuen 1993).

Cavadino, Micheal and Dignan, James (1992). *The Penal System: An Introduction* (London, Sage).

Christie, N. (1977). 'Conflicts as property', *British Journal of Criminology*, 1.

Christie, Nils. (1993). *Crime Control as Industry: Towards GULAGS Western Style?* (London, Routledge 1993).

Cohen, Stan (1979). 'The punitive city: notes on dispersal of social control', *Contemporary Crises*, 3.

Cohen, Stan (1983). *'Telling stories about correctional change'*, in Garland and Young (eds.), *The Power to Punish*.

Cohen, Stan (1985). *The Vision of Social Control* (Oxford, Polity Press).

Cohen, Stan (1987). 'Taking decentralisation seriously: values, visions and policies', in Lowman *et al.*, *Transcarceration: Essays in the Sociology of Social Control*.

Cornford, J. (1992). 'Policy issues and the underclass debate', in Smith (ed.), *Understanding the Underclass*.

Crick, Bernard (1964). *In Defence of Politics* (London, Penguin).

Crowe, I. *et al.* (1993). 'Evaluating the Criminal Justice Act 1991: some early indications of how agencies are responding'. Unpublished paper presented at British Criminology Conference, University of Wales, Cardiff July 1993.

Dahrendorf, Ralf (1985). *The Hamlyn Law and Order Lecture 1985* (London, Stevens).

Dahrendorf, R. (1987). 'The erosion of citizenship and its consequences for us all', *New Statesman*, 12 June.

Dahrendorf, R. (1992). 'Footnotes to the discussion', in Smith (ed.), *Understanding the Underclass*.

Davis, Mike (1990). *City of Quartz* (Vintage).

Deakin, N. (1990). 'Mr Murray's Ark', in *The Emerging British Underclass* (Institute of Economic Affairs 1990).

Feeley, M. and Simon, J. (1992). 'The new penology: notes on emerging strategy of corrections and its implications', *Criminology*, 4.

Field, Frank (1989). *Losing Out: The Emergence of Britain's Underclass* (Oxford, Blackwell).

Fitzgerald, Mike and Sim, Joe (1982). *British Prisons*, 2nd edn. (Oxford, Blackwell).

Fitzpatrick, Peter (1992). *The Mythology of Modern Law* (London, Routledge).

Foucault, Michel (1975). *Discipline and Punishment: The Birth of the Prison* (London, Penguin).

Garland, David and Young, Peter (eds.) (1983). *The Power to Punish* (London, Heinemann).

Garland, David (1985). *Punishment and Welfare: A History of Penal Strategies* (Aldershot, Gower).

Gordon, Diane (1990). *The Justice Juggernaut: Fighting Street crime, Controlling Citizens* (Newark, N.J., Rutgers University Press).

Habermas, Jurgen (1981). 'Modernity versus post-modernity', *New German Critique*, 22.

Hagedorn, John (1988). *People and Folks: Gangs, Crime and the Underclass in a Rust-belt City* (Lake View Press).

Hall, Stuart (ed.) (1978). *Policing the Crisis* (Basingstoke, Macmillan).

Hall, Stuart (1980). *Drifting into Law and Order Society* (London, Cobden Trust).

Hall, Stuart and Jacques, Martin (1989). *The Meaning of New Times: The Changing Face of Politics in the 1980s* (London, Lawrence and Wishart).

Halsey, A. (1989). 'Social trends since World War II', in McDowell, L., Sarre, P. and Hamnett, C. (eds.), *Divided Nation: Social and Cultural Change in Britain* (London, Hodder and Stoughton, 1989).

Home Office (1988). Green Paper. *Punishment, Custody and Community* Cm. 424 (London, HMSO).

Home Office (1990). White Paper. *Crime, Justice and Protecting the Public: The Govenment's Proposals for Legislation* Cm. 965 (London, HMSO).

Honess, Terry and Charman, Elizabeth (1992). *Closed Circuit Television in Public Places*, Home Office Research Group Paper 35 (London, HMSO).

Hunt, Alan (1986). 'The theory of critical legal studies' *Oxford Journal of Legal Studies*, 1.

Husain, Sohail (1988). *Neighbourhood Watch in England & Wales: A Locational Analysis* (Home Office Crime Prevention Paper 12), (London, HMSO).

Jencks, Christopher (1992). *Rethinking Social Policy: Race, Poverty and the Underclass* (Cambridge, Mass., Harvard University Press).

Kelman, Martin (1987). *A Guide to Critical Legal Studies*.

Kingdom, John (1992). *No Such Thing as Community? Individualism and Community* (Milton Keynes, Open University Press).

Kinsey, R. (1993). 'Innocent underclass', *New Statesman and Society*, 5 March.

Lacey, Nicola (1989). *State Punishment: Political Principle and Community Values* (London, Routledge).

Lawson, Bill (1992). *The Underclass Question* (Philadelphia, Temple University Press).

Lea, John and Young, Jock (1993). *What To Do About Law and Order?*, 2nd edn. (London, Pluto).

Lowman, J., Menzies, R. and Palys, T. (1987). *Transcarceration: Essays in the Sociology of Social Control* (Aldershot, Gower).

Macnicol, J. (1990). 'Nightmare on easy street', *The Times Higher Education Supplement*, 29 June.

Mair, G. and Nee, C. (1990). *Electronic Monitoring: The Trials and Their Results*, Home Office Research Study No. 120 (London, HMSO).

Mann, Kirk (1992). *The Making of an English Underclass? The Social Divisions of Welfare and Labour* (Milton Keynes, Open University Press).

Marshall, T. and Merry, S. (1990). *Crime and Accountability: Victim/ Offender Mediation Practice* (London, HMSO).

Marx, Gary (1988). *Undercover: Police Surveillance in America* (Berkeley, University of California Press).

Marx, Karl (1848). *Communist Manifesto*.

Matthews, R. (1989).'Alternatives to prison: a realist approach', in Carlen, P. and Cook, D. (eds.), *Paying for Crime* (Milton Keynes, Open University Press).

Mathiesen, Thomas (1983). 'The future of control systems – the case of Norway', in Garland and Young (eds.), *The Power to Punish*.

Moore, Robert (1992). 'Citizenship and the underclass'. Unpublished paper given at the British Sociological Conference 1992.

Murray, Charles (1984). *Losing Ground: American Social Policy 1950–1980* (New York, Basic Books).

Murray, C. (1989). 'Underclass', *The Sunday Times Magazine*, 26 November.

Murray, C. (1990). 'Underclass' in *The Emerging British Underclass* (London, Institute of Economic Affairs).

Murray, C. (1993). 'No point fiddling the welfare at the margin', *The Sunday Times*, 11 July.

Nozick, Ronald (1985). *Anarchy, State and Utopia* (Oxford, Blackwell).

Parker, Howard, Sumner, Maggie and Jarvis, Graham (1989). *Unmasking the Magistrates* (Milton Keynes, Open University Press).

Rex, John (1988). *The Ghetto and the Underclass: Essays on Race and Social Policy* (Avebury 1988).

Roberts, Simon (1979). *Order and Dispute: An Introduction to Legal Anthropology* (London, Penguin).

Sampson, R. and Laub, J. (1993). 'Structural variations in juvenile court processing: inequality, the underclass, and social control', *Law and Society Review*, 2.

Scarman, Lord (1981). *The Brixton Disorder: Report on the Inquiry by Lord Scarman* (London, HMSO).

Scull, Andrew (1977). *Decarceration: Community Treatment and the Deviant: A Radical View* (Prentice Hall).

Scull, Andrew (1983). 'Community correction: panacea, progress or pretence?' in Garland and Young (eds.), *The Power to Punish*.

Smith, David (ed.) (1992). *Understanding the Underclass* (London, Policy Studies Institute 1992).

Smith, D. (1992). 'Defining the Underclass', in Smith (ed.), *Understanding the Underclass*.

Taylor, I. (1993). 'Critical criminology and the free market: theoretical and practical issues in everyday life and everyday crime', paper presented at British Criminology Conference, University of Wales Cardiff, July 1993, also published in this volume, pp. 400–28.

Tilley, Nick (1992). *Safer City and Community Safety Strategies*, Home Office Police Research Group Crime Prevention Paper 38.

Townsend, P. (1993). 'Underclass and overclass: the widening gulf between social classes in Britain in the 1980s', in Payne, G. and Cross, M. (eds.), *Sociology in Action* (London, Macmillan).

Unger, Roberto (1976). *Law and Modern Society: Towards the Criticism of Social Theory*.

Unger, R. (1983). *The Critical Legal Studies Movement* (Harvard University Press).

Walker, A. (1990). 'Blaming the victim', in *The Emerging British Underclass* (London, Institute of Economic Affairs).

Wasik, Martin and Taylor, Richard (1994). *Blackstone's Guide to the Criminal Justice Act 1991*, 2nd edn. (Blackstone).

Westergaard, J. (1992). 'About and beyond the underclass: some notes on influences of social climate on British sociology today', *Sociology*, 4.

Willet, D. (1992). 'Theories and explanations of the underclass', in Smith (ed.), *Understanding the Underclass*.

Wilson, William Julius (1987). *The Truly Disadvantaged* (Chicago, Chicago University Press).

Woolf, H. and Tumim, S. (1990). *The Prison Disturbances* (London, HMSO).

Wolfe, Tom. (1988). *The Bonfire of the Vanities* (London, Jonathan Cape).

Young, Jock and Matthews, Roger (eds.) (1992). *Rethinking Criminology: The Realist Debate* (London, Sage).

21

Critical criminology and the free market: theoretical and practical issues in everyday social life and everyday crime

IAN TAYLOR

The 'utopianism' of *The New Criminology*

Written in a very different historical moment from that of the present, *The New Criminology* was a text in critical criminology, informed by a set of essentially 'utopian' concerns. Over the years, some commentators have seen this utopianism simply as a kind of misguided idealism, especially with respect to the 'fundamental facts of human nature' (Morgan 1978; Anderson 1992). These commentators point to the widespread crisis of the 'socialist idea' and to the continuing escalation of crime and social disorder — in Britain, but also in societies which describe themselves as socialist (China). It is important now to insist that these accusations mistake the idea of utopian critical analysis for the fallacies of merely idle utopian reflection. *The New Criminology* was certainly written from a position of political commitment exemplified in the call made towards the end of the concluding chapter for 'a criminology which is . . . normatively committed to the abolition of inequalities of wealth and power, and in particular of inequalities in property and life-chances' (Taylor, Walton and Young 1973: 281). That political commitment had the important effect of informing our attempt, as Habermas describes the critical-utopian project, at depicting 'alternative life possibilities . . . inherent in the historical process itself' (Habermas 1989b: 50): we did not want to accept the unequal and exploitative social formation with which we were presented, and we wanted to understand theoretically the ways in which crime, in so many empirically inescapable ways, was an expression of those inequalities and resoluble via an assault on those inequalities. The utopian critique which we tried to develop also involved an attempt to make plain what, from such a utopian-critical point of view, had to be true about hitherto-existing criminology: namely, that no matter how firm the commitment of any official criminology to a scientific neutrality or to a position of distance from 'politics', such avowedly neutral but actually uncritical claims must inevitably collapse into a political or moral prescriptiveness, usually of an individualistic kind and nearly always couched in terms of a conservative common sense, a practical philosophy of individual survival within existing competitive, unequal social arrangements. Towards the end of the concluding chapter of *The New Criminology*, indeed, we argued specifically that any criminology which was *not* 'normatively committed to the abolition of inequalities of wealth and power' was 'inevitably bound to fall into correctionalism' (Taylor, Walton and Young 1973: 281).

In one key respect, of course, that ringing pronouncement turned out to be incorrect. The kind of criminology which has emerged in Britain in the 1980s – which Jock Young elsewhere (1986) has characterized as 'administrative criminology' – has indeed betrayed an astonishing agnosticism in respect of the crushing (and now accelerating) inequalities of this society, but the result has *not* simply and only been a reinvention of the correctionalist project.[1] Correction implies the idea of crime reduction as well as individual and social reform – but it is quite clear in 1993 that the politicians and the administrators respons-ible for the crime problem in Britain have given up substantially on the idea of crime reduction, and that the official project is now one of containment and management of crime (which has in the process become, quite unambiguously, a technical field of administrative action, bound up, for example, with the selective introduction and evaluation of Safer Cities initiatives, target-hardening measures or new shift systems in individual police divisions). It was this narrow and technicist version of criminology, in an earlier incarnation – that is lacking both theoretical curiosity and political imagination – which was the target of what Alvin Gouldner, in his introduction to our text, described as our 'deliberate discourse', directed at the truth that:

> all studies of crime and deviance, however deeply entrenched in their own technical traditions, are inevitably grounded in larger, more general social theories which are always present (and consequential) even as unspoken silences. (Gouldner 1973: ix)

Gouldner was not able to anticipate the ways in which the language and practice of the 'technical traditions' of criminology could be so effortlessly transferred from the welfare state societies in which they were still embedded in the early 1970s to 'free-market societies' that emerged over the next few years. Analysing this same earlier post-war period of mildly social-democratic reconstruction, Habermas observed how:

> The *methodological* side of the project [was that] the welfare state compromise and the pacification of class antagonisms [were] to be achieved by using democratically legitimated state power to protect and restrain the quasi-natural process of capitalist growth. The *substantive* side of the project [was] nourished by the residues of a utopia of social labour: as the status of the employee is normalized through rights to political participation and social ownership, the general population gains the opportunity to live in freedom, social justice and increasing prosperity. (Habermas 1989: 55)

At that time:

> The presumption is . . . that peaceful coexistence between democracy and capitalism can be ensured through state intervention. (ibid.)

In contrast, by the late 1980s, the limited potential of the 'utopia of social labour' in stimulating progressive developments in the name of the citizenry *as a whole* became ever more clear. Some social democratic thinkers (whom Habermas dubs legitimists) responded to this crisis by trying to freeze and legitimize the existing balance of welfare state and the market economy, but, for Habermas, conservatives increasingly took the lead in tackling this crisis of the relationship of the state to the market via the promotion of alternative forms of *administration*, increasingly detached from what he refers to as 'public will-formation'. In such a conjuncture, he theorizes, there was:

> a transfer of normatively regulated parliamentary powers to systems that merely function, without normative regulation [turning] the state into one partner among many in the negotiation. This displacement of jurisdiction onto the neo-corporate grey areas withdraws more and more social matters from a decision-making process that is obligated by constitutional norms to give equal consideration to all who are concerned in any specific matter. (Habermas 1989b: 61)

From this perspective, any critical-utopian text (including *The New*

Criminology) written before the crisis of the 'the utopia of social labour', the attack on the state's monopoly ownership of responsibility for social organization, and the rise of what Habermas calls the neo-corporate administration of the relation between civil society and the market, will be dated and will need rethinking. But to recognize this is not to suggest that the newly dominant realms of administrative action (as exemplified, for example, in the multiagency policing of neighbourhood crime or the complex alliances responsible for the identification and surveillance of fraud) are in some sense now cleared of political or moral controversy, or free of the contradiction between merely private preoccupations and the larger issue of the public interest. It is to this issue – the relationship between critical criminology and the 'public interest' – that we will return at the end of this chapter.

The New Criminology and a theory of the social totality

The objective of *The New Criminology* in the early 1970s was not simply to indict existing official criminologies for their politics, whether explicitly or implicitly stated. It was also concerned with insisting on the incapacity of a criminology insulated from the realms of social theory ever to develop an adequate, 'fully social' theory of crime and deviance itself. The argument about the importance of such a fully social theory is present throughout the critical appraisal of hitherto existing criminology found in the body of the text, but it is most explicit in the model of a 'fully social theory of deviance' outlined in Chapter Nine. In our commentary on this model (which, to our knowledge, has only once ever been applied in an actual research publication (Lowman 1987), we argued:

> The formal requirements of a fully social theory . . . refer to the *scope* of the theoretical analysis. In the real world of social action, these analytical distinctions merge, connect and often appear to be indistinguishable. We have already indicated social reaction theory, which is in many ways the most sophisticated rejection of the simpler forms of positivism – as one-sidedly deterministic; in seeing the deviant's problems and consciousness simply as a response to apprehension and the application of social control. Positivistic explanations stand accused of being unable to approach an explanation not only of the *political economy of crime* (the background to criminal action) but also of what we have called the *political economy*, and *social psychology* and the *social dynamics* of social reaction to deviance.

And most of the classical and earlier biological and psychological positivists . . . are unable to offer out . . . a satisfactorily social explanation of the relationship between the individual and society: the individual appears by and large as an isolated atom unaffected by the ebb and flow of social arrangements, social change and contradictions in what is, after all, a society of social arrangements built around the capitalist mode of production. (Taylor, Walton and Young 1973: 276–7)

Summarizing the position from which we had launched our critique of hitherto existing criminologies, we concluded that

The central requirement of a fully social theory of deviance . . . is that these formal requirements must not be treated simply as essential factors all of which need to be present (in variant fashion) if the theory is to be social. (Taylor, Walton and Young 1973: 277)

Or, as we put it a few paragraphs later, in a slightly different way:

It is not just that the traditional focus of applied criminology on the socially-deprived adolescent is being thrown into doubt by the criminalisation of vast numbers of middle class youth (for offences of a hedonistic or specifically oppositional nature). Neither is it only that the crisis of our institutions has deepened to the point where the 'master institutions' of the state and of the political economy, are unable to adhere to their own rules and regulations . . . It is largely that the total *interconnectedness* of these problems and others are being revealed. (Taylor, Walton and Young 1973: 278. Italic type is my emphasis)

This is probably one of the points in the text in which the commitment to critical-utopian analysis of the social formation as a totality is most clear: elsewhere within the text, this specifically utopian critique of the social formation is submerged beneath the epistemological embrace of materialism, with its narrower visions and concerns. But, again:

A criminology which will be adequate to an understanding of these developments, and which will be able to bring politics back into the discussion of what were previously technical issues, will need to deal with society as a totality. (Taylor, Walton and Young 1973: 278)

So the task of a critical criminology was not simply to advance a critique of hitherto existing criminology: it was also to outline the analytical framework within which 'crime' could be located analytically in particular social formations at particular historical moments. In this sense, *The New Criminology* was not simply a piece of critique of the silences and the bad faith in hitherto existing criminology: it was also a text in social theory and, indeed, of a particular kind of social theory – arguing for the possibility of grasping, analytically, the idea of 'a social formation' and the possibility of linking such analysis to the explanation of particular instances of group action or even individual action in respect of rule-breaking, deviance or crime. It may be that this places *The New Criminology* firmly in the category, not only of utopian and critical texts but more generally in the category of modernist texts, which so many commentators of the 1990s might want now to consign to the rubbish-bin of history because of the self-evident collapse of the master narratives of progress and of rationality at the *fin de siècle*, but, for the moment, we have to leave that as it is.

The problem of social control

As a product of its time, *The New Criminology*'s analytic and political stance betrayed not only a concern to grasp the totality of the social formation (with a view to its transformation in the direction of 'freedom and democracy' and particularly of radically greater social and economic equality), but also a concern to make sense of crime as human action in terms of this larger understanding of what had been identified as an unfree, undemocratic and unequal social formation. Running through the text, therefore, there are the twin pulls, on the one hand, towards the realization of a 'just' set of social arrangements, and, on the other, to a notion of human liberty connected to the critique of social control in unequal societies. Coming out of the critique of Durkheim in Chapter Three is the outline of an account of a future, socialist and democratic society in which one could identify substantive as well as formal justice in respect of the organization of work and its rewards. Running through much of the rest of the text is a libertarian sentiment (a child of its time) to the effect that all existing instances of rule-breaking or deviant action were *ipso facto* instances of individual struggles against the 'normalized repression' that is characteristic of all unequal, and in particular capitalistically unequal, societies. In the much-discussed concluding refrain of the text:

For us, as for Marx and the other new criminologists, *deviance* is normal –

in the sense that men are now consciously involved (in the prisons that are contemporary society and the real prisons) in asserting their human diversity. The task is not merely to 'penetrate' those problems, not merely question the stereotypes, or to act as carriers of 'alternative phenomenological realities'. The task is to create a society in which the facts of human diversity, whether personal, organic or social are not subject to the power to criminalise. (Taylor, Walton and Young 1973: 282)

There is little doubt that this concluding flourish was ill-advised in appearing to call, with some versions of anarchist and libertarian social thought, for the removal of criminal law *per se* from civil society and perhaps also of any kind of authoritative or exemplary social control. It could be no part of a careful social-democratic utopian critique of the management of order, in a substantially unequal or a substantively just, but complex, mass-populated post-industrial society, to argue simply for collective self-regulation as a preferred or effective form of social control, or, indeed, to believe that the law and the system of social control have no importance in the general socialization or education of the citizenry (cf. Taylor 1981; Lea and Young 1984). Nor, we should affirm, could it be any part of a social-democratic justice programme to argue that individuals have an unlimited capacity for self-realization and or self-control. The point was well made by Elliott Currie (1974) in an extended review article on *The New Criminology* in his observation that *The New Criminology*'s idealist celebration of human diversity (most overtly expressed in the concluding chapter) was really at odds with the essentially materialist analysis in the body of the text, and how also the libertarian call for the removal of social control in the text amounted simply to an inversion of the correctionalism of orthodox criminology:

> where traditional criminology tended to see pathology everywhere, Taylor et al. see it *nowhere*; both positions seem to me to be essentially static, impoverished and divorced from close attention to the behaviour of real people in the real world. (Currie 1974: 112)

Currie went on to argue with an admirable directness – and also with great prescience in the light of the stress placed in later psycho-analytic literature, especially within feminism, on the material reality of personal disturbance and dysfunction – that:

> it's important to take into account the fact that people in the real world

often experience themselves as being simply fucked up – as being impelled towards behaviour that they themselves feel is destructive or self destructive or exploitative . . . this experience has to be a key aspect of any satisfactory theory of deviance. (ibid.)

Crime and 'diversity': the new poverty and widening inequality

In the aftermath of the fifteen years of free-market transformation in Britain, it is an inescapable observation that one of the most fundamental pressing sources of the feeling of personal disorder and hopelessness within the social formation as presently constructed, coupled in so many instances with feelings of destructiveness, is that of *continuing (and increasing) poverty and inequality*. In 1991, some 13.5 million people in Britain (24 per cent of the population) – including 3.9 million children under the age of sixteen – were living on less than half the average national household income (the nearest to a recognized measure of poverty in Britain): in 1979, only 5 million people were living below that line. The bottom 10 per cent of the population experienced a cut of 14 per cent in real income between 1979 and 1991, compared with a 36 per cent increase for the rest of the population in the same period (Department of Social Security, 1993). Much of this new poverty is concentrated amongst the unemployed: the official total of which in November 1992 was 2.9 million (or 9.6 per cent), but in unofficial estimates, there are several hundred thousand more. The value of the unemployment benefit for a married couple with two children has fallen by nearly 20 per cent in real terms since 1979;[2] and there are many more measures of poverty and inequality in what is now widely described, in rather cavalier a style, as a 'one thirds/two thirds society'. The emergence of this new poverty in Britain through the 1980s has a particular identifiable history, initially unleashed, as in the older industrial areas of the United States, by the generalized demise of mass manufacturing in the high-cost developed capitalist societies (Davis 1990; Currie 1990; Henry and Brown 1990), but then being constructed and institutionalized in the United Kingdom via a series of decisions on the part of free-market political leaders with respect to the rules governing entitlement to state and welfare benefit.[3] These changes have had their most severe effect on young people. In 1993, some half a million 18–24 year olds in Britain (including about 200,000 living independently of their parents) are entitled to state benefit of only £34.80 a week (or £4.87 per day).[4] Shelter, the charity for the homeless, estimates that 150,000 young people now become homeless every year.[5] The scale of the homelessness problem in Britain is a product of the state's final withdrawal from the provision of public housing and the entry into public housing of the selective disciplines of the free market, legislated by a free-market Conservative government during the early 1980s. It seems self evident that the simultaneous collapse of the labour market and the state's withdrawal from benefit provision for those under the age of eighteen have led to a sense of desperation amongst young people, and that at an age when, all criminologists agree, the 'onset of delinquency' is most likely to occur. Apart from the consequences of these developments for the social production of instrumental crime (burglary) and retreatism (drug abuse), we should also remind ourselves of the fundamental consequences which these changes are having on the character of what used to be called *the class structure of the industrial societies*. At one level, this results in the disappearance of the industrial working class in its familiar form (Gorz 1982) and, on another, it produces a much more complex social and economic configuration for which no agreed or simple sociological shorthand seems yet to be available. The changes induced by the crisis of mass-manufacturing in developed capitalist societies are now being amplified by the phenomenon of weak and uneven economic recoveries in the early 1990s that are having nothing like the beneficial consequences for employment that occurred in earlier post-war economic recoveries in the west: we are confronted with the phenomenon of 'jobless growth' (Currie 1993).

Diversity and gender inequality

What is absolutely clear about the new forms of social organization emerging out of the ruins of a manufacturing economy and the organized capital-labour relationship is the changing character of the *gender relationships*. In particular, we see lower rates of unemployment of women at many of the lower levels of the labour market, especially in the service industry: inasmuch as there is a breadwinner in many lower-class families in late industrial societies, it is very often the woman of the household. Other sea-changes in the relationships of men and women are occurring with enormous rapidity, though it is important to note that the changes in Britain are lagging far behind the changes that have occurred in North America, where confusion about gender roles and responsibilities is now the stuff of nearly all prime time television comedy (a sure sign of its popular importance). There is every good reason for giving a central place in any analysis of contemporary social strain, including crime and disorder, to the idea of 'masculine rage'.

The analysis of the inequalities built into gender relationships, in either their general or conjunctural form, was no more a feature of *The New Criminology* than it was of any other text in social theory of its time, and neither were the criminogenic aspects of this inequality identified and subjected to analytical critique. Ironically enough, of course, some of the offences committed by women and given headline treatment in the mass media (especially the murder of violent husbands, as in the case of Sara Thornton) are much more persuasive examples of individual struggles against 'normalized repression' than are, for example the ritualized tribal aggression of young men outside football grounds or many of the other delinquencies which were the implicit object of the analysis in *The New Criminology*. The ways in which the lives of young women are routinely tutored by parents (educating them in the fearfulness of public space and of interactions of men) are a rather more obvious example of 'normalized repression' within existing social arrange-ments than are the obstacles placed in the way of young men especially, but not simply, in their use of public space facilities. The idea that 'boys will be boys' and must be given the space to be so is an obvious example of such 'normalized' social expectation.

Any re-examination of the utopian-critical analysis in *The New Criminology* of what it conceptualized as 'the social formation' would clearly have to emphasize what Bob Connell called the *gender order* of late- or post-industrial market society, and also what Connell insists must be analysed as *a structure of subjectivities* of enormous power and significance for individuals, particularly in its familiar historically-transmitted, previously hegemonic form but also in its troubled and contradictory current expression (Connell 1987). It would obviously have to recognize, as a starting point, that:

> gender divisions are not an ideological addendum to a class-structured mode of production. They are a deep-seated feature of production itself. They are not confined to domestic work and paid work in industry. They are a central feature of industrial production too. They are not a hangover from pre-capitalist modes of production. As the cases of computing and world-markets factories show, they are being vigorously created in the most advanced sectors of the capitalist world economy. (Connell 1987: 103–4)

Barbara Ehrenreich and Ulrich Beck, amongst others, have begun to advance understanding of the way in which the transformations currently sweeping through established industrial societies are reorganizing the essentially feudal domains of the private household (where women are fatefully consigned to domestic labour, and men to a life of waged labour outside the household) (Ehrenreich 1984; Beck 1992: chap. 4). Much of the empirical literature which is specifically focused on the interpersonal and social effects of such domestic change deals with the travails of what used to be called 'the bourgeois family'; and it is on the basis of these studies of private households and the discussions of popular magazines and newspapers that Beck and Giddens have developed the thesis of 'reflexive modernization' in an attempt to capture a sense of the struggles taking place in this private sphere, especially over detraditionalized roles and role-performance. Other writers have approached some of the issues via their attempts to analyse the *structure of subjectivity*, specifically, *masculinity* in an essentialist fashion, that is independently of men's particular structural location and of any analysis of its uneven or contradictory expression in this particular historical moment (cf. for example, Cameron and Fraser 1987). In the early 1990s (and especially in 1993) we were offered accounts in the popular press and also in paperbacks which assign the blame for crime and disorder on inner-city or city-edge council estates to opposite ends of the *gender order* as it presents itself at the level of the underclass. Undoubtedly the greatest publicity and official support have been given to the extraordinarily misogynist and revanchist thesis of the 'single mothers' who are alleged to be getting pregnant in their hundreds and thousands with a view to obtaining advantage in the struggle for housing (Dennis and Erdos 1992). A polar opposite account has now been provided, with far less attention from the popular press and Westminster politicians, in the powerful indictment of the 'masculinist rage' of disenfranchised young men on public housing estates engaging in ram-raids, burglaries, riots and other more routine predations on communities in which the only really effective 'active citizenship' is provided by women (Campbell 1993)

In the aftermath of the demise of the social utopia of labour, the key issue for critical or utopian thinkers revolves around the issue of how to develop and ground a critique of the individualism and the market. Some feminist writers continue to argue an idea of a woman's interest (as for example in 'standpoint feminism' (Harding 1986, 1987; Smart 1990)), and so also do some black writers argue for an oppositional interest of oppressed people of colour (Gilroy 1982; Scraton (ed.) 1987). In other circles, there is energetic interest in recognizing a diversity of 'differences' in a kind of pluralistic critique of white, male, hegemonic power (cf. for example, Bock and James (eds.) 1992). *The New Criminology*'s 'modernism', by contrast, lay in its equation of the idea of a universal public interest (of a society organized as a set of shared public provisions with the maximum possible personal freedom, coupled with maximum social order underwritten by substantive social justice) with the metaphysic of labour – Habermas's 'utopia of social labour'. The issue, in the aftermath of the crisis of the utopia of social labour, is whether this modernist idea of an overwhelming co-operation of different publics in a shared set of social, legal and political arrangements remains either desirable or possible. I want to conclude these remarks in an examination of one key area in which such a sharing of 'the social', in a civil and moral fashion, is of vital everyday importance for all: the sharing of public space in everyday life in free-market society.

Inequalities in public space

Gender inequality

The relationship between 'hegemonic masculinity' (or, in Connell's terms, the *gender order*) and the fearfulness of public places for women in Britain has been graphically established in the feminist criminological literature (Hanmer and Saunders 1984; Hanmer, Radford and Stanko 1989; Stanko 1990) and also in feminist social geography (Valentine 1989; 1992). In many ways, it must be said, some of this British feminist endeavour is a reapplication of earlier feminist work in the United States, in which, for example, rape and sexual assault were seen as a given feature of hitherto-existing societies by virtue of the silent presence of the power of 'patriarchy' and a primary defining feature of fear and of social control for women (cf. Griffin 1969; Brownmiller 1973): there is sometimes a sense in such accounts of a gender order that is wrenched from its historical context and naturalized as an inevitable feature of 'masculinity'. So also in some black writing are expressions of white racism sometimes generalized outwards to all whites, in all historical moments and at all levels of the social formation.

Citizen consumers

One key problem, sociologically speaking, in these transhistorical generalizations about issues of gender and race and the oppressiveness of the social formation is that they do not generally attend to the unevenness of such oppression: the exceptions are of no real interest, perhaps, in the establishment of the rule. Elisabeth Wilson has recently challenged the idea that the urban environment is a kind of seamless web of fear and oppression for women, arguing, after Walter Benjamin, for the sense of freedom and possibility that are enshrined in some urban places, particularly, but not exclusively, in those devoted to shopping and the business of 'consumption' (Wilson 1991). Much of the critical literature on the North American-style indoor, covered, and air-conditioned shopping malls introduced into Britain in the last decade speaks of the sense of comfort and security which shoppers (still, in this country, primarily women) experience in these locales (Gardner and Sheppard 1989) (a finding which is very much confirmed in current research in which I am involved in Manchester and Sheffield on 'the public sense of well-being'). There is no question but that parts of the city centre in Britain, as well as some parts of the suburbs or the 'edge-cities' situated between major conurbations, are successfully being recreated as the kind of 'palaces of consumption' which are so celebrated by spokespeople for the 'enterprise culture'. One consequence, indeed, as Zygmunt Bauman has argued, may be the impoverishment of any developed sense of citizenship amongst 'the masses', who are now successfully reconstituted as 'consumers' ('happy robots' in no need of a politics of rights, other then consumer rights, and certainly no interest in a politics of responsibilities) (Bauman 1988). The construction of the happy consumer in the shopping mall must be recognized, too, of course, as an analogy with the process through which the mass media's representation of politics (as a consumer choice between mildly competing products) has undermined the idea of a public sphere of bourgeois rights and duties, as sketched out by Habermas (1989a).

The privatization of life and anxieties about life in public

Recognition of the successful construction of these pleasurable spheres of consumption, and analysis, without guarantees, of what from an earlier utopian perspective might be the undesirable political and social and personal consequences of the presence of these institutions within society, has tempted some critics into a despairing embrace of the 'nihilism' of mass consumer culture, focused on the immediacy of the sensory pleasures constructed within those spheres (cf. Kroner and Cook 1986). This kind of surrender to the private spheres of consumption, however, begs the issues that continue actively to occupy the masses themselves, in their necessary and regular use of vast stretches of public territories and public space that provide the predominant setting for the dramas, and the drudging routine, of everyday life. In the lived world that is the local neighbourhood, the main street, the estate, the downtown underpass, the railway station and bus station or the bus stop, the universally reported public mood is one of unease, dissatisfaction, fear or anxiety (cf. for example, the reports of the second Islington Crime Survey: Crawford *et al.* 1990) The patterns in that public fear, and the relation between those patterns of fear and the statistical distribution of crime, have become the topic of a minor industry of applied criminology in the United Kingdom as in the United States (the other free-market society to be reporting vast increases in crimes of violence). It is quite clear, for example, that whilst levels of fear and anxiety are very heavily concentrated amongst women, the *general* mood is one of anxiety and defensiveness, a kind of fortress privatism that is characteristic even of adult white men: the patriarch feels himself to be the potential victim of the intrusion of burglary, car theft and perhaps even of an unimaginable, shapeless assault (a 'mugging'). The existence of that level of fear across the country has fuelled the growth both of a private security industry specializing in the construction of fortress-like reconstruction of city centres at night (as in Milton Keynes) and also, more recently, in the provision of private police forces for affluent suburban areas. The level of fear reported in all the surveys is also closely associated with the now nearly universal recitation of catechism amongst nearly all professional groups (from the police to local councillors) as to there clearly having been a sudden and fundamental decline in standards of civility and of standards of behaviour 'amongst the British'. There is a widespread fear of 'the other' – specifically of other people(s) who may be encountered in the interactions of everyday life: so far from there being evidence, here, of a society acting in celebrating plurality and difference, there is evidence of a society acting in fear of difference, even now between an older adult and younger adolescent. Few grown men would now reprimand an unruly youngster on a bus for outlandish behaviour, even against a woman or a member of an ethnic minority group, for fear of violent retaliation. Chivalry is dead is the universal observation. There are few instances of young people even being apprehended by 'active citizens' for acts of litter or vandalism, even when such acts are committed against shared public provision. Police officers widely report the truth that they cannot any longer expect obedience to their writ in routine encounters with the young. The routine destruction by deprived and angry young men of public provisions (like telephones and bus shelters) continues unchecked, and uncheckable, by police, by the 'neo-corporate' administrative committees who manage free-market society or by the hypothetical active citizens of the locality: in Greater Manchester, for example, the level of bus shelter vandalism in and near public estates is now threatening the contract between the Passenger Transport Authority and the French construction company, J. C. Decaux, which supplies and maintains the shelters: the company had not taken the actual level of destruction into account in the original contract, because they did not believe the figures supplied them.

The good society

The issue here for the utopian-critic, still thinking in the transformative egalitarian and democratic tradition of *The New Criminology*, is how to respond to these reports, both analytically and also at the level of a moral engagement, specifically to the idea of a 'good society'?[6] It is self-evident that the idealist flourishes at the end of the final chapter of *The New Criminology*, and the criminology of the outlaw that surfaces elsewhere in the text, are of little help in this situation (specifically in the construction of a criminology of the good society), though it is diverting to note a reassertion of this kind of sympathetic phenomenology of criminal action in a recent American text (Katz 1988). Analysis that is still couched, as *The New Criminology* was, in terms of the critique of the 'total society' or of 'society as a whole' may also be unhelpful in the current moment, since, as Habermas has pointed out in his recent reflections on the idea of a public sphere:

> The presumption that society as a whole can be conceived as an association writ large, directing itself via the media of law and political power, has become entirely implausible in view of the high level of complexity of functionally differentiated societies. The holistic notion of a

societal totality in which the associated individuals participate like the members of an accompanying organization are particularly ill suited to provide access to the realities of an economic system regulated through markets and an administration regulated through power. (Habermas 1992: 443)

For Habermas, the 'abysmal collapse of state socialism' ushers in a new issue for utopians, or what he now calls 'radical democrats':[7]

> The goal is no longer to supercede an economic system having a capitalist life of its own and a system of domination having a bureaucratic life of its own but to erect a democratic dam against the colonizing *encroachment* of system imperatives on areas of the lifeworld. (Habermas 1992: 444)

His concept of the lifeworld obviously parallels Tony Giddens's idea of a life politics (Giddens 1991), but it differs from Giddens (who is now concentrating overwhelmingly on the spheres of intimacy) in its continuing emphasis on relations between individuals (in their own lifeworlds) and, following Claus Offe, their 'relations of association' which 'anchor people . . . in the social realm'. This is the problematic which is often identified in other social theoretical accounts as 'civil society'. It has to be said that this emphasis provides an important starting-point for addressing the kinds of issues addressed not only by conservative criminologists in their constant talk of the collapse of civility, conceived narrowly in terms of the failings of parents and teachers, but also the angry talk of 'people in the street' who actually appear most of all to be lamenting the character of their tearful everyday relations with 'other people' in a competitive, privatized market society, and who also appear to be striving for a sense of what Zygmunt Baumann, in a recent lecture, called 'moral space' (Baumann 1992) – space in which they can feel comfortable and at home, at one with their surroundings. In societies that are so constructed, subsequent to the collapse of class-based communities, the key organs of civil society – the anchors of human association – are few and far between: by and large, they remain, as they nearly always have been in many other moments of transformation and crisis both in western and eastern Europe, volunteer groups of the citizenry, in particular, community or neighbourhood associations, churches or other religious organizations, and small political groups (the ecologists) claiming to speak in the greater public interest, even if only on the dimension of community safety and fear.

The administered free market and everyday fear of crime

It is here that there is a massive contradiction at the heart of the *administered* free-market society: the neo-corporate groups and institutions which have emerged in the place of welfare state and local authority bureaucracies do not 'represent' either the larger public(s) that constitute this fractured post-industrial association of human beings living within marketized social relations. Generally speaking, whether from the private sector (like the infamous Group Four private security company) or from the public world itself (the community police officer re-established in many constabularies throughout the country in the 1980s), the neo-corporate groups have quite distant relationships with the citizens they claim to serve or defend (cf. McConville and Shepherd 1992). These relationships are characterized (very much like the local television news programme and its relationship with its audience) by a nervous and hyperactive *belief* in the existence of a close and responsive relationship, rather than by *demonstrable* relations of real solidarity. The problem is well illustrated at local level by the way in which local police subdivisions (have to) negotiate their relationship with local business groups, with politicians and with local residents in relation to local crime incidents and problematic symbolic locations. One of the striking features here is the mobilization by police of a low-level form of sociological-labelling theory in an attempt to minimize the nature of any local crime threat (for residents) whilst simultaneously urging awareness of its seriousness on local councils, and also presenting themselves as exemplary practitioners in the craft of high-tech prevention of crime to local business people.

The problem here, however, is not only that the police have to work within an undemocratic network of special interests, often responding in an *ad hoc* fashion to the interest (business group, residents association or councillor) with the loudest voice in the last liaison group meeting. In addition, one of the key problems, as Bea Campbell has brilliantly shown in her study of the policing of inner-city and council-estate young men, is also that the whole provision of police service is extraordinarily gendered: the male-dominated culture and military-style hierarchy of the police disables them from being able to work with local women's groups (like those described by Campbell on the Meadow Well Estate), whose lack of social power and assigned role in the public world of employment and careers constructs them as architects of their own vulnerability and victimization. As Bea Campbell then poignantly observes – by reference to a key dimension in what Bob Connell would identify as the *structure of cathexis* of the *gender order* – there is something about vulnerable women that renders them impossible allies for socially powerful, but personally insecure, men (for whom women must, above all, be strong) and the consequence is that the whole community, but particularly its women, is left to deal with the unchecked and uncorrected effects of *a mode of masculinity* that is evident both in the behaviour of local lawless young men (joy-riding, ram-raiding, burglarizing) and the local police (car chases, night raids, round-ups and street confrontations) (Campbell 1993: esp. ch.8). The problem is the generalized assumption that public spaces (from the playing fields in the parks to the streets outside the family homes) are for men.

I would also want to argue, however, that the problem in public space in the mid-1990s is not only that the prior claims to its ownership and use are exercised by men. It is also quite clear that the use of public space as such, in an increasingly privatized, consumer-dominated market society, has become problematic – not to say downright suspicious. The American criminologist Wesley Skogan inadvertently touches on this issue in his discussion, in *Disorder and Decline*, of the way in which a generalized sense of 'disorder' can evolve in previously stable neighbourhoods in a spiralling process of perceptions and incidents: he focuses, like much recent analytical writing on policing, on the perceived safety or otherwise of well-known symbolic locations in particular localities, like a local park in an area of Chicago (Skogan 1990: ch.2). He is able to show how incidents in such locations tend to be blown up in local gossip and the local press and so play an exaggerated role in the downward spiral of a neighbourhood's sense of its own security and well-being. A single observed drugs-sale, for example, can result in a park becoming defined as a major centre in the drug trade. Graffiti appearing in an area previously untouched by such 'sign-writers' may be read by residents as signifying the arrival of a new *set* of local problems or problematic people in a previously unproblematic area. What Skogan does not do, however, is to enquire theoretically into the possibility that *the idea of public space itself*, provided out of the public purse and allowing young people to gather away from parental supervision or out of sight together, has in itself become problematic in societies which place such normative emphasis on purely private consumption.

So also, it may be argued, is the very idea of young people 'hanging around' in a public place (engaged in the classic youthful behaviour of 'doing nothing') (Corrigan 1978) seen essentially to be strange in societies which have been placing pressure on young people to adopt an increasingly instrumental and competitive attitude to adolescence, as part of their preparation for the competitive search for accreditation and employment in competitive market societies.

The politics of public space in a free-market society

There is widespread evidence that the use of space has become a kind of street-level politics, echoing through the local newspaper press and the deliberations of local neo-corporate organizations, for example police-community liaison groups. The Comedia consultancy has been extremely active in pressing for the use of popular arts in the decoration of public facilities and spaces in Britain's urban centres (cf. Comedia 1991; Worpole 1991; and see also Fisher and Owen 1991). There is growing debate about the fears that are provoked by areas of derelict residual space, vandalized buildings, unattended public parks (especially in the aftermath of the dreadful murders of Rachel Tickell on Wimbledon Common in 1991, and of the 9-year-old Akhlaq Ahmed in a park in Slough in 1993) and also by the brutalized and 'anonymous' concrete 1960s shopping developments (like the Bootle shopping centre, the site of the abduction of 2-year-old murder victim Jamie Bulger in February 1993) and – what was previously the greatest of all symbolic locations for topophobia (or fear of place) (Tuan 1974; 1979) – the covered underground underpass. The danger is that this renewed interest in the aesthetics of urban architecture may develop without attention to the broader, political and social truth of the patterned inequality that obtains in the provision of space, both in quantitative and qualitative terms, across the pre-existing social formation, both *within* individual conurbations or regions and *across* them. Bea Campbell's powerful polemic reminds us not only of the terror of the lawless young men on the council estates of Britain, but also the sheer poverty of the buildings, spaces and outlooks that imprison the residents of the thousands of estates to which our urban poor are condemned (see also Parker 1983). This imprisonment of 'the underclass' in such a standard of housing (widely criticized a decade ago when observed to the east of the Berlin Wall) has apparently now become acceptable in free-market Britain: no public housing is now proceeding to provide replacement stock or an escape route for existing residents, and there can be no realistic expectation of many residents buying their way out. The result appears to be a kind of end-game on 'problem estates' to which there is no obvious social democratic (social worker) or free-market (local enterprise) solution (cf. Hope and Foster 1992). Contemporary talk of the 'one thirds/two thirds' society rarely extends to the sympathetic analysis of the extraordinary inequality in the provision of housing that is to be a taken-for-granted feature of free-market society in Britain – a fact of life, in a depoliticized environment, along with the abolition of manufacturing employment. But the disparate effects on those citizens of the free-market society – of a future in which there is no obvious escape from worklessness or desperately poor housing – are plain to see, and well known to those few helping professionals who are left, attempting to provide support for such people in their own localities. They are also sometimes visible to the mass of the population, in the form of the new class of beggars which has taken up residence in the city centres of the United Kingdom during the 1980s (Taylor 1990), although the full range of the problems of 'the underclass' tends not to intrude on the consciousness of the citizen-consumer most of the rest of the time. When they do intrude into the lives of the citizen-consumer, in the form of over-zealous street-tradespeople, beggars, drunks, vagrants, or simply 'unpleasant people', the result is usually a demand on the police to clear away the problem from public space used by 'others' (who are, in this way, claimed to represent public interest as a whole). In some parts of the United Kingdom, the political answer proposed to the problem of such contamination of public space by the underclass is, of course, the privatization of the city centres, and the creation of a fortress-like containment of the respectable citizenry, for example, by means of membership schemes run by private businesses. The privatization solution proposed by the Adam Smith Institute to the problem of crime control in English cities clearly envisages the wholesale exclusion of large classes of the citizenry both from privatized city centres and also from privatized local neighbourhoods (Elliott 1989). The way in which these inequalities in the city are neutralized, kept from the consciousness of the citizen-consumer, 'swept away' by the police on the demand of special interest groups or, in certain circumstances, activated as the ground for a policy of privatization is a study in itself. It is clear, however, that the elaboration of a kind of penal policy for policing existing public streets and public space is no solution to the pressing problem of how citizens of different backgrounds who also have massively unequal relations to the market can find a way of living with each other in our cities, and also a way of reducing the crime and incivility which characterizes this coexistence of unequals. The issue posed is whether forms of politics, oriented to the shared character and universal utility of all public space (from parks to shopping precincts) could potentially roll back the existing politics of *administration* that characterizes the approach to 'crime prevention' and urban safety in free-market Britain.

This is an issue of national significance, but I want to finish by insisting also on the importance of a utopian criminal-politics at the level of 'the regions'. Though I will mainly be discussing, for the moment, the significance of regional inequality in the United Kingdom, I do believe my remarks have pertinence for a 'Europe of the regions', especially in the open market of goods and labour which now exists (and which may, or may not, be further developed along the federal lines suggested in the Maastricht agreements).

One of the main expressions of the free-market government's concerns to audit performance, in particular, of public sector institutions (as a part of the *administration* of the infrastructure of market society) has been the production of a series of league tables regarding the performance and productivity of schools, health services and, most recently, of police. We have been asked to become aware, as citizen-consumers, of variations in the standards of service from different 'service-providers'. One of the most widely publicized of such differences in provision across the regions in 1993 was the differential success of regional constabularies with respect to the clear-up of reported crime: this was, indeed, one of the most widely publicized instances of administrative exposé of a service problem in the police in the months leading up to the release of the Sheehy Report, with its agenda for the introduction of market-forces accountability into the British police.

What is quite clear about the differential clear-up rates with respect to crime, and the performance and effectivness of police generally, is that they have to do with the overall workload in particular localities, particularly with respect to the level of crime and the resulting amount of calls upon the police for service and help; and what is also clear about the crime rate in the United Kingdom, though insufficiently discussed (except, perhaps, in terms of the overall comparison of England and Scotland) is the enormous variation of rates of crime by region. Late in 1992, the Labour party provided an enormous public service in releasing a report on the escalation of car crime in England and Wales, including within it a league table which details the enormous disparities in the number of car crimes (including car thefts) per 100,000 population across the forty-two police authority areas (Labour party 1992). The league table indicates, *inter alia*, that the highest rates of car crime in England and Wales in 1990 were in the Northumbria Constabulary area (4,360 per 100,000 population), Cleveland (4,271) and Greater Manchester (4,001): by comparison, the rate of car crime in Dyfed-Powys was only 776 per 100,000 and 1,173 in Suffolk. Even in Surrey, where the opportunities are presumably plentiful, there were only 1,433 per 100,000.

Similar league tables are now being produced in the literature for other categories of crime including, most notably, burglary. The production of these league tables brings to the attention of media and of the administrators of free-market society a truth which has always been well understood at the level of folklore in England and Wales – namely, that different places (towns, cities, 'parts of the country' etc.) have a markedly different propensity to crime. In 1991, for example, the rates of crime reported by the police in five force areas (all in 'the North of England' – so often spoken of at Westminster as a unitary area) were as noted in Table 1.

Table 1

Force	Rate per 100,000 population
Greater Manchester	1:6.8
West Yorkshire	1:7.0
Merseyside	1:9.4
South Yorkshire	1:10.6
Derbyshire	1:12.9

Source: Annual Reports of the chief constables for each of these forces, 1991.

It is clear that there are a host of technical issues involved in the interpretation of statistics reported by police force areas, and many an administrative criminologist would want to concentrate on these technical issues. But might it not also be the case, as certainly Emile

Durkheim would have us believe, that these statistics could be speaking to real differences about these regions and areas – 'social facts' that have to do with the particular configuration in these areas of human resources, labour markets, public housing provision, and other empirically identifiable features of these localities? In another cognate field of social enquiry, into which criminologists have only recently begun to trespass – namely, urban sociology – the variation in the life-chances of populations across different regions and areas is a domain assumption of the whole field. John Urry has been a pioneer of the attempt to understand the ways in which the 'spaces' in England and Wales that are empirically discussed as cities, towns or villages must also be understood as particular, localized distillations of the larger structure of class (Urry 1981). More recently, he has been concerned to enquire theoretically into the impact on particular localities of the transformations in manufacturing-industrial society – as well as the capacities of such regions to be proactive in the face of such changes – which he identifies with the end of organized capitalism and the coming of post-Fordism (Urry 1990).

Nearly all influential urban sociologists who are working on these transformations want to speak of a global change with particularly important effects at local level. It is vital for a critical-utopian criminal politics to start to think in these terms. Fully recognizing the dangers of extrapolating from one set of figures, we want simply to place on record in Table 2 the rate of increases in crime across the five police force areas identified earlier.

Table 2: Rates of increase in crimes known to the police (North of England), 1990–1

Merseyside	10 per cent
Greater Manchester	13 per cent
South Yorkshire	16 per cent
Derbyshire	27 per cent
West Yorkshire	27 per cent

Source: Annual Reports, as in Table 1.

These data, again, are very crude, as are so many other with which we have to deal – including those which speak to the overwhelming concentration of some of the most pressing problems of crime control in the 1990s in particular urban areas rather than others (the drug trade and, even more recently, the escalation in firearms possession and use). The simple point to make here is that the impact of free-market reorganization of work and production is on regions that are already unequal in identifiable ways, in terms of economic wealth and potential or *poverty* and social and political power or *powerlessness*. This unleashing of the free-market economy, coupled with the associated devolution of administrative power to neo-corporate organizations and away from local authorities and other welfare state organizations, is producing a new configuration of wealth and power, and poverty and powerlessness, in every particular region. A renewed form of inequality is emerging, of the kind which Harvey Molotch and John Logan have tried to conceptualize for the United States in terms of a typology of 'module production', 'headquarter' and other, residualized cities (Molotch and Logan 1987). Other commentators have written, in various moods of optimism or desperation, about the attempts being made not just in Britain but also across Europe, to rescue the future of declining industrial cities by the reinvention of those locations as heritage sites, tourist centres, or centres for sports and recreation. It seems idle to suggest that these processes of post-industrial reconfiguration of cities are unnconnected with the mushrooming problems of crime being reported in those locations, or that the variations of crime rates in different regions are unconnected with the character of the changes taking place in particular regional locations – though it is by no means the intention to suggest that there could be any simple one-dimensional relationship of cause and effect.

I began this chapter by recalling and elaborating the utopian-critical perspective which informed the writing of *The New Criminology*, and I also recounted our interest in a 'fully social theory' of deviance, located and lodged in a theory of society as a social totality or 'social formation'. Following Habermas's remarks on the collapse of nationally based utopias of social labour, and the widespread recognition of the globalization of post-industrial transformation, it may be that we need to rethink the ways in which such global social changes constitute what we called, in Chapter Nine, 'the wider origins of deviance', or what we might now want to discuss as the processes which seem set remorselessly to reproduce inequality, crime and social anxiety in Britain, only more intensively in some regions of it than others. This chapter is one attempt to think in such terms.

Acknowledgements

I would like to acknowledge the influence on this chapter of the many helpful discussions with Karen Evans and Penny Fraser, the research team of my ESRC project into 'Public Sense of Well-being'. More than anything, however, the paper has benefited from the gentle suggestions and overall wisdom of Ruth Jamieson. The chapter in its present form is entirely my responsibility.

Notes

1 A more recent characterization of official criminology as a 'jobbing criminology' has been offered by Loader and Sparks, in order to underline the moral abstentionism of a criminological project which is constantly caught up in applied pieces of consultancy research, and unable, or unwilling, to engage in popular public debate on issues of morality or the direction of 'society' or of official policies (Loader and Sparks 1993). I admire this formulation, but Jock Young's earlier description of an 'administrative criminology' is still better for our purposes here, since it actually anticipates, at least in its choice of terms, Habermas's strictures on the rise of a multiply-*administered* social formation in the wake of the crisis of welfare state-driven social reconstruction.

2 Melanie Phillips, 'The Road to Wigan Pier' *The Guardian*, 21 November 1993.

3 The impact of these changes in social welfare entitlement on crime rarely appear in the literature of official administrative criminology (and not much in any other kind of criminology either), though it is notable how the changes constitute the very stuff, the defining subject-matter, of the social-scientific discipline with an ostensibly close relationship, in terms of its line of vision, to criminology, namely 'social policy and administration'. One is driven to the observation that the insulation of disciplinary criminologists is not only from social theory, but from social science knowledge as a whole.

4 Alice Mahon MP, *MPs' Briefing Paper on Youth Poverty* (in support of motion for 6 July 1993).

5 This figure, and also the tendency to speak of one homogenous category of homeless young people, has been challenged in a study at the University of Surrey (Canter *et al.* 1993), which argues for a more differentiated appraisal of young people's motivations for leaving their parental homes and also for a more complex imagery of the young homeless, capable of recognizing a diversity of response to the fact of homelessness. This study may be an example of the ways in which some kinds of administrative social science – in this case, overlain by some sensitivity to youth cultural studies – rather miss the political point – in this instance, in respect of human needs and the entitlement of citizens to shelter.

6 The challenge of thinking about the future of urban life in terms of a vision of a good society can also, very powerfully, be posed from within a

perspective that embraces the consumerism and (post)-modernization of our cities, cf. for example, Hallsworth 1993 and Sennett 1990.

7   Habermas's analysis is very different from that of other scholars who have remained within the Marxist tradition in order to argue that the current reorganization of economic production taking place across the world constitutes, quite specifically, a new international *capitalist* division of labour, which should – and could in principle – eventually call forth some kind of anti-capitalist response. This kind of analysis also differs from Habermas in its continuing interest in the idea of *alienation* and *exploitation* being at the core of human relations, even in these new times (cf. Hall and Jacques 1990).

References

Anderson, Digby (ed.) (1992). *The Loss of Virtue* (London, Social Affairs Unit).

Baumann, Zygmunt (1988). 'Britain's exit from politics', *New Statesman*, 29 July, 34–8.

Baumann, Zygmunt (1992). 'Moral space', lecture to Department of Social Anthropology, University of Manchester, 5 December, also as Chapter 6 in *Post Modern Ethics* (Oxford, Basil Blackwell).

Beck, Ulrich (1992). 'I am I: gendered space and conflict: inside and outside the family', Chapter 4 in *The Risk Society* (London, Sage).

Bock, Gisela and James, Susan (eds.) (1992). *Beyond Equality and Difference: Citizenship, Feminist Politics and Feminist Subjectivity* (London, Routledge).

Brownmiller, Susan (1973). *Against our Will* (London, Penguin).

Cameron, Deborah and Fraser, Elizabeth (1987). *The Lust to Kill: A Feminist Investigation of Sexual Murder* (Cambridge, Polity Press).

Campbell, Beatrix (1993). *Goliath: Britain's Dangerous Places* (London, Methuen).

Canter, David *et al.* (1989). *The Faces of Homelessness in London* Interim Report to the Salvation Army, Guildford, University of Surrey (July).

Comedia (1991). *Out of Hours: a Summary Report* (London, Comedia/ Gulbenkian).

Connell, Robert W. (1987). *Gender and Power: Society, the Person and Sexual Politics* (Cambridge, Polity Press).

Corrigan, Paul (1978). 'Doing nothing' in Hall, S. and Jefferson, J. (eds.), *Resistance through Rituals* (London, Macmillan).

Crawford, Adam, Jones, Trevor, Lloyd, J. and Young, Jock (1990). *The Second Islington Crime Survey* (London, Middlesex Polytechnic).

Currie, Elliott (1974). Book review of *The New Criminology* in *Crime and Social Justice* (Fall–Winter), 109–14.

Currie, Elliott (1990). 'Heavy with human tears: free-market policy, inequality and social provision in the United States', in Ian Taylor (ed.), *The Social*

Effects of Free Market Policies (Hemel Hempstead, Harvester Wheatsheaf).

Currie, Elliott (1993). 'The private and public determinations of the structure and purposes of work in post-industrial societies', plenary lecture to the International Conference on the Public Sphere, University of Salford (January).

Davis, Mike (1990). *City of Quartz: Imagining the Future in Los Angeles* (London, Verso).

Dennis, Norman and Erdos, George (1992). *Families without Fatherhood* (London, Institute for Economic Affairs).

Department of Social Security (1993). *Households Below Average Income 1979–1990/1)* (London, HMSO).

Ehrenreich, Barbara (1984). *The Hearts of Men: American Dreams and the Flight from Commitment* (New York, Anchor Books).

Elliott, Nicholas (1989). *Streets Ahead* (London, Adam Smith Institute).

Fisher, Mark and Owen, Ursula (1991). *Whose City?* (London, Penguin).

Gardner, Carl and Sheppard, Julie (1989). *Consuming Passion: the Rise of Retail Culture* (London, Unwin Hyman).

Giddens, Anthony (1991). *Modernity and Self-Identity* (Cambridge, Polity Press).

Gilroy, Paul (1982). 'The myth of black criminality' in Miliband, R. and Savile, J. (eds.), *The Socialist Register* (London, Merlin Press).

Gorz, Andre (1982). *Farewell to the Working Class* (London, Pluto).

Gouldner, Alvin (1973). Introduction to Ian Taylor, Paul Walton and Jock Young, *The New Criminology* (London, Routledge and Kegan Paul).

Gouldner, Alvin (1979). *The Future of Intellectuals and the Rise of the New Class* (London, Macmillan).

Griffin, Susan (1971). 'Rape: the all-American crime', *Ramparts*, (September), 26–35.

Habermas, Jurgen (1989a). *The Structural Transformation of the Public Sphere* (Cambridge Mass, MIT Press).

Habermas, Jurgen (1989b). 'The new obscurity: the crisis of the welfare state and the exhaustion of Utopian energies' in Sherry Weber Nicholson (ed.), *The New Conservatism: Cultural Criticism and the Historian's Debate* (Cambridge, Polity Press).

Habermas, Jurgen (1992). 'Further reflections on the public sphere' in Calhoun, C. (ed.), *Habermas and the Public Sphere* (Cambridge, MIT Press).

Hall, Stuart and Jacques, Martin (1990). *New Times: the Changing Face of Politics in the 1990s* (London, Lawrence and Wishart).

Hallsworth, Simon (1993). 'From the radiant city to the safer city', paper presented to the International Conference on the Public Sphere, University of Salford (January).

Hanmer, Jalna and Saunders, S. (1984). *Well-Founded Fear: a Community Study of Violence to Women* (London, Hutchinson).

Hanmer, Jalna, Radford, Jill and Stanko, Elizabeth (1989). *Women, Policing and Male Violence* (London, Routledge).

Harding, Sandra (1986). *The Science Question in Feminism* (Milton Keynes, Open University Press).

Harding, Sandra (ed.) (1987). *Feminism and Methodology* (Milton Keynes, Open University Press).

Henry, Stuart and Brown, Jeffrey (1990). 'Something for nothing: the informal economy outcomes of free market policies' in Taylor, I., (ed.) *The Social Effects of Free Market Policies* (Hemel Hempstead, Harvester-Wheatsheaf).

Katz, Jack (1988). *Seductions of Crime* (New York, Basic Books).

Hope, Timothy and Foster, Janet (1992). 'Conflicting forces: changing the dynamics of crime and community on a "problem" estate', *British Journal of Criminology*, 32, 488–504.

Kroner, Arthur and Cook, Dave (1986). *The Post Modern Scene: Excremental Culture and Hyperaesthestics* (Montreal, New World Perspectives).

Labour Party (1992). *Putting the Brakes on Car Crime* (London, the Labour Party (December)).

Lea, John and Young, Jock (1984). *What is to be done about Law and Order?* (London, Penguin).

Loader, Ian and Sparks, Richard (1993). 'Ask the experts', *Times Higher Education Supplement*, 9 April, 16.

Lowman, John (1987). 'Taking young prostitutes seriously', *Canadian Review of Sociology and Anthropology*, 24(1), 99–116.

McConville, Mike and Shepherd, Dan (1992). *Watching Police, Watching Communities* (London, Routledge).

Molotch, Harvey and Logan, John (1987). *Urban Fortunes* (University of California Press).

Morgan, Patricia (1978). *Delinquent Fantasies* (London, Maurice Temple Smith).

Parker, Tony (1983). *The People of Providence: A Housing Estate and some of its Inhabitants* (London, Picador).

Scraton, Phil (ed.) (1987). *Law, Order and the Authoritarian State* (Milton Keynes, Open University Press).

Sennett, Richard (1990). *The Conscience of the Eye: the design and social life of cities* (London and Boston, Faber and Faber).

Skogan, Wesley (1990). *Disorder and Decline: Crime and the Spiral of Decay in American Neighbourhoods* (New York, the Free Press).

Smart, Carol (1990). 'Feminist approaches to criminology or postmodern woman meets atavistic man' in Gelsthorpe, L. and Morris, A. (eds.), *Feminist Perspectives in Criminology* (Milton Keynes, Open University Press).

Stanko, E. (1990). 'When precaution is normal: a feminist critique of crime prevention' in Gelsthorpe, L. and Morris, A. (eds.), *Feminist Perspectives in Criminology* (Milton Keynes, Open University Press).

Taylor, Ian (1981). *Law and Order: Arguments for Socialism* (London, Macmillan).

Taylor, Ian (1990). 'Sociology and the Condition of the English City: Thoughts from a Returnee' (inaugural lecture), *Salford Working Papers in Sociology No. 7*.

Taylor, Ian, Walton, Paul and Young, Jock (1973). *The New Criminology: for a social theory of deviance* (London, Routledge and Kegan Paul).

Tuan, Yi-Fu (1974). *Topophilia: a study of environmental perception, attitudes, and values* (Englewood Cliffs, Prentice Hall).

Tuan, Yi-Fu (1979). *Landscape of Fear* (Oxford, Basil Blackwell).

Urry, John (1981) 'Localities, regions and social class', *International Journal of Urban and Regional Research*, 5, 455–73.

Urry, John (1990). 'Places and policies' in Harloe, M., Pickvance, C. G. and Urry, J. (eds.), *Place, Policy and Politics: Do Localities Matter?* (London, Unwin Hyman).

Valentine, Gill (1989). 'The geography of woman's fear', *Arena*, 21, 385–90.

Valentine, Gill (1992). 'Images of danger: women's sources of information about the spatial distribution of male violence', *Arena*, 24(1).

Wilson, Elisabeth (1991). *The Sphinx in the City: Urban Life, the Control of Disorder and Women* (London, Virago).

Young, Jock (1986). 'The failure of criminology: the need for a radical realism' in Matthews, R. and Young, J. (eds.) *Confronting Crime* (London, Sage).

Worpole, Ken (1991). *Towns for people: transforming urban life* (Buckingham, Open University Press).

Index

Unless otherwise indicated, cases and Acts refer to British cases and Acts of Parliament for England and Wales